THE OLD TESTAMENT
FOR EVERYMAN

BOOKS BY FRANK DELL'ISOLA

Thomas Merton: A Biography
The God-Man Jesus
The Old Testament for Everyman

THE OLD TESTAMENT
FOR EVERYMAN

EDITED AND REARRANGED
IN A CONTINUOUS NARRATIVE

BY FRANK DELL'ISOLA

MEREDITH PRESS / NEW YORK

Library of Congress Catalog Card Number: 68–11333
Manufactured in the United States of America for Meredith Press

Dedicated to
the beloved memory of my uncle Carmelo,
who, when I was a child of six,
introduced me to the beauty and
inspiration of Holy Scriptures.

INTRODUCTORY NOTE

It was St. Jerome who sounded the warning note that "ignorance of the Scriptures is ignorance of Christ." And today this lack of knowledge of the God-Man is more pronounced because it is a plain fact that most people do not read the Bible. The measure and wealth of Holy Scriptures can best be summed up in the words of William Lyon Phelps who wrote: "Everyone who has a thorough knowledge of the Bible may truly be called educated; and no other learning or culture, no matter how extensive or elegant, can, among Europeans and Americans, form a proper substitute. Western civilization is founded upon the Bible; our ideas, our wisdom, our philosophy, our art, our ideals, come more from the Bible than from all other books put together."

The above words were the instruments which gave wings to the idea of writing *The God-Man Jesus,* a life of Christ as recorded by the four Evangelists and published by Bruce; and now these very same thoughts have brought me into the Old Testament, a work that is as rich in literary, historical, spiritual, and religious treasures as the New Testament. But so many of us, in attempting to find the inspiration and enlightenment of the Old Testament, lose our bearings by the sheer bulk of it. A great number of people are most anxious to read The Book of Books but the magnitude of the Bible frightens them away.

Some may be aware that the various passages have the answer to most of their spiritual and mundane problems, and they try to seek out the solution and the wisdom which is in the Word of God. But they soon grow weary of the task that confronts them: they must read and plow through hundreds and hundreds of pages of difficult material before they come upon a passage which may give them light and a fresh, new perspective.

But unfortunately very few of us possess the know-how to "strike that hidden, rich lode" of the Bible, and fewer still have the patience or the time to waste in a haphazard perusal of searching the Scriptures for

ix

the nourishment it contains. It was St. Jerome who wrote: "You cannot make your way into this inspiring and monumental work without having someone to go before you and show you the road."

With this thought in mind, I edited and arranged *The Old Testament for Everyman* in an abridged, continuous narrative, divesting it of some of the obscure writings of the major and minor prophets, the boring accounts of legislative tracts, the rituals, the genealogies, the proverbial philosophy of the old sages, and the repetitive histories of the rise and fall of the various kingdoms. Despite major editing, *The Old Testament for Everyman* has, I believe, an even balanced rhythm which gives it the impact of a novel that has a beginning, a middle, and an ending.

It was obvious from the start that a unified treatment of the Old Testament required the fusing of texts and events from different periods to better highlight the plight of those wonderful people, the Jews, and, at the same time, bring out the literary, the historical, and the religious point of view. I am aware that the "chronology" used here may not set well with certain biblical scholars, but I did not intend this work for the scholar. *The Old Testament for Everyman* was put together primarily for the common man who, in reading it, might derive from its pages the help and the sustenance to make his life fruitful, happier, and richer.

The stories of ancient Israel are the means of observing the unfolding drama of the coming of Christ; through them the reader can witness and relive the primitive history of the people of Israel. He is with them as they suffer persecutions, famine, disease, and wars; he travels with the Israelites from one wilderness to another, and he hears their complaints, witnesses their tribulations and despair. The reader is moved when he listens to their fervent pleas which beg for the mercy and bounty of God to descend upon them. Reading *The Old Testament for Everyman* gives one a clearer image of the events that led to the coming of the Messiah.

Besides highlighting the influence of God's Word upon ancient Israel, *The Old Testament for Everyman* starts its primitive story with the beginning of the world, the formation of plant and animal life, and the creation of our first parents, Adam and Eve. From here we enter the age of Abraham and go on to the election of the people of Israel; and from Moses to David we live the defeats and triumphs of these persecuted people, and we rejoice at their hard-won liberation and the wonderful education that eventually comes to them.

Slowly we witness the grandeur, the faith, and the courage of God's people: with King David we become active participants in the division of the kingdom under Roboam. This was a crucial time for the Israelites.

They suffer defeat after defeat; and we bear with them as they fall amid the ruins of their once mighty kingdom which was destroyed by the kings of Assyria. After much turmoil, bloodshed, and starvation, the people come into their own, and here the reader shares in the glory and victory of the kingdom of Judah which was the forerunner of the birth of Jesus.

It can be seen that *The Old Testament for Everyman,* from Genesis to Maccabees, becomes at once "the background of our Creator and Redeemer." One cannot appreciate a work of art without first acquiring some prior knowledge of it. And so it is with understanding and grasping and retaining the message and meaning of Christ; his words of wisdom and pre-Christian revelation come to us from the lips of the prophets, and through them we get an insight into his nature and wishes. The Son of God cannot be understood apart from the Old Testament story. Man must, in order to avoid a narrow and confused conception of God, recognize the steps taken by him which prepared mankind for the appearance of the Savior who in the fullness of time reunited all things in himself.

The truth of this is beautifully demonstrated when Christ spoke to the multitude: "Do not think that I have come to destroy the law or the prophets. I have not come to destroy, but to fulfill. For amen I say to you, till heaven and earth pass away, not one jot or one tittle shall be lost from the law till all things have been accomplished. Therefore whoever does away with one of these least commandments, and so teaches men, shall be called least in the kingdom of heaven; but whoever carries them out and teaches them, he shall be called great in the kingdom of heaven. For I say to you that unless your justice exceeds that of the Scribes and Pharisees, you shall not enter the kingdom of heaven" (Matt. 5:17–20).

The Old Testament for Everyman was born to convince a skeptical world that "Holy writ is set before the eye of the mind like a kind of mirror, that we may see our inward face in it; for therein we learn the deformities, therein we learn the beauties that we possess; there we are made sensible what progress we are making, there too how far we are from proficiency." *

But more than that, *The Old Testament for Everyman* may be called a ground plan of the story of ancient Israel. And it is my hope that it will be widely used as a first step to the perusal of the Old Testament in its entirety.

* Pope Saint Gregory I: Morals, 2, 1. (6th cent.)

CONTENTS

xiii

Contents

Thy Word is tested to the utmost,
 and thy servant loves it.
Defend thou my cause and redeem me;
 according to thy Word, grant me life.
For all flesh is as grass,
 and all its glory as the flower of grass;
the grass withered, and the flower has fallen,
 but the Word of the Lord endures forever.*

* Psalms 119:140, 149; Isaia 40:7–8.

THE OLD TESTAMENT
FOR EVERYMAN

CHAPTER ONE

The Fall of Man
and the
Beginning of Redemption

THE DIVINE ARTIST BEGINS HIS WORK

In the beginning God created the heavens and the earth; the earth was waste and void; darkness covered the abyss, and the spirit of God was stirring above the waters.

God said, "Let there be light," and there was light. God saw that the light was good. God separated the light from the darkness, calling the light Day and the darkness Night. And there was evening and morning, the first day.

Then God said, "Let there be a firmament in the midst of the waters to divide the waters." And so it was. God made the firmament, dividing the waters that were below the firmament from those that were above it. God called the firmament Heaven. And there was evening and morning, the second day.

Then God said, "Let the waters below the heavens be gathered into one place and let the dry land appear." And so it was. God called the dry land Earth and the assembled waters Seas. And God saw that it was good. Then God said, "Let the earth bring forth vegetation: seed-bearing plants and all kinds of fruit trees that bear fruit containing their seed." And so it was. The earth brought forth vegetation, every kind of seed-bearing plant and all kinds of trees that bear fruit containing their seed. God saw that it was good. And there was evening and morning, the third day.

And God said, "Let there be lights in the firmament of the heavens to separate day from night; let them serve as signs and for the fixing of seasons, days and years; let them serve as lights in the firmament of the heavens to shed light upon the earth." So it was. God made the two great lights, the greater light to rule the day and the smaller one to rule the night, and he made the stars. God set them in the firmament of the heavens to shed light upon the earth, to rule the day and the night and to separate the light from the darkness. God saw that it was good. And there was evening and morning, the fourth day.

Then God said, "Let the waters abound with life, and above the earth let winged creatures fly below the firmament of the heavens." And so it was. God created the great sea monsters, all kinds of living, swimming creatures with which the waters abound and all kinds of winged birds. God saw that it was good, and God blessed them, saying, "Be fruitful, multiply, and fill the waters of the seas; and let the birds multiply on the earth." And there was evening and morning, the fifth day.

God said, "Let the earth bring forth all kinds of living creatures: cattle, crawling creatures and wild animals." And so it was. God made all kinds of wild beasts, every kind of cattle, and every kind of creature crawling on the ground. And God saw that it was good.

This is the story of the heavens and the earth at their creation. When the Lord God made the earth and the heavens, there was not yet any field shrub on the earth nor had the plants of the field sprung up, for the Lord God had sent no rain on the earth and there was no man to till the soil; but a mist rose from the earth and watered all the surface of the ground. Then the Lord God formed man out of the dust of the ground and breathed into his nostrils the breath of life, and man became a living being. The Lord God planted a garden in Eden, to the east; the Lord God made to grow out of the ground all kinds of trees pleasant to the sight and good for food, the tree of life also in the midst of the garden, and the tree of the knowledge of good and evil, and he put there the man he had formed to till it and to keep it. And the Lord God commanded the man thus, "From every tree of the garden you may eat; but from the tree of the knowledge of good and evil you must not eat; for the day you eat of it, you must die."

Then the Lord God said, "It is not good that the man is alone; I will make him a helper like himself."

The Lord God cast the man into a deep sleep and, while he slept, took one of his ribs and closed up its place with flesh. And the rib which the Lord God took from the man, he made into a woman, and brought her to him. Then the man said,

4

"She now is bone of my bone,
   and flesh of my flesh;
She shall be called Woman,
   for from man she has been taken."

Both the man and his wife were naked, but they felt no shame.

Then God blessed them and said to them, "Be fruitful and multiply; fill the earth and subdue it. Have dominion over the fish of the sea, the birds of the air, the cattle and all the animals that crawl on the earth." God also said, "See, I give you every seed-bearing plant on the earth and every tree which has seed-bearing fruit to be your food. To every wild animal of the earth, to every bird of the air, and to every creature that crawls on the earth and has the breath of life, I give the green plants for food." And so it was. God saw that all he had made was very good. And there was evening and morning, the sixth day.

Thus the heavens and the earth were finished and all their array. On the sixth day God finished the work he had been doing. And he rested on the seventh day from all the work he had done. God blessed the seventh day and made it holy because on it he rested from all his work of creation.

THE TRIUMPH OF THE DEVIL

Now the serpent was more cunning than any beast of the field which the Lord God had made. He said to the woman, "Did God say, 'You shall not eat of any tree of the garden'?" The woman answered the serpent, "Of the fruit of all the trees in the garden we may eat; but 'Of the fruit of the tree in the middle of the garden,' God said, 'you shall not eat, neither shall you touch it, lest you die.'"

But the serpent said to the woman, "No, you shall not die; for God knows that when you eat of it, your eyes will be opened and you will be like God, knowing good and evil." Now the woman saw that the tree was good for food, pleasing to the eyes, and desirable for the knowledge it would give. She took of its fruit and ate it, and also gave some to her husband and he ate. Then the eyes of both were opened, and they realized that they were naked; so they sewed fig-leaves together and made themselves coverings. When they heard the sound of the Lord God walking in the garden in the cool of the day, the man and his wife hid themselves from the Lord God among the trees of the garden. But the Lord God called the man and said to him, "Where are you?" And he said, "I heard you in the garden, and I was afraid because I was naked; and I hid." Then he said, "Who told you that you were naked? You have eaten then of the tree of which I commanded you not to eat." The man said, "The woman you placed at my side gave me fruit from the tree and I ate." Then the Lord God said to the woman, "Why have you done this?" The woman said, "The serpent deceived me and I ate."

Then the Lord God said to the serpent:

> "Because you have done this,
>   cursed are you among all animals,
>   and among all beasts of the field;
> On your belly shall you crawl,
>   dust shall you eat,
>   all the days of your life.
> I will put enmity between you and the woman,
>   between your seed and her seed;
> He shall crush your head,
>   and you shall lie in wait for his heel."

To the woman he said:

> "I will make great your distress in childbearing;
>   in pain shall you bring forth children;
> For your husband shall be your longing,
>   though he have dominion over you."

And to Adam he said, "Because you have listened to your wife, and have eaten of the tree of which I commanded you not to eat:

> "Cursed be the ground because of you;
>   in toil shall you eat of it all the days of your life;
> Thorns and thistles shall it bring forth to you,
>   and you shall eat the plants of the field.
> In the sweat of your brow you shall eat bread,
>   till you return to the ground,
> Since out of it you were taken;
>   for dust you are and unto dust you shall return."

The Fall of Man and the Beginning of Redemption

The Lord God made garments of skin for Adam and his wife and clothed them. And he said, "Indeed! the man has become like one of us, knowing good and evil! And now perhaps he will put forth his hand and take also from the tree of life and eat, and live forever!" Therefore the Lord God put him out of the garden of Eden to till the ground from which he was taken. He drove out the man; and at the east of the garden of Eden he placed the Cherubim, and the flaming sword, which turned every way, to guard the way to the tree of life.

MAN REVOLTS AGAINST THE LORD GOD

The man knew Eve his wife, and she conceived and bore Cain, saying, "I have given birth to a man-child with the help of the Lord." Later, she bore his brother Abel. Now Abel was a keeper of flocks and Cain a tiller of the soil. In the course of time Cain brought to the Lord an offering of the fruit of the ground. Abel also brought some of the firstlings of his flock with their fat portions. The Lord was pleased with Abel and his offerings; but for Cain and his offering he had no regard. Cain was very angry and downcast. The Lord said to Cain, "Why are you angry and why are you downcast? If you do well, will you not be accepted; but if you do not do well, will not sin crouch at the door! Its desire is for you, but you must master it."

Cain said to his brother Abel, "Let us go out into the field." Now when they were in the field, Cain turned against his brother Abel and slew him. Then the Lord said to Cain, "Where is your brother Abel?" He answered, "I do not know. Am I my brother's keeper?" And the Lord said, "What have you done? The voice of your brother's blood cries to me from the ground. And now cursed are you in the soil which has opened its mouth to receive your brother's blood from your hand. When you till the soil, it shall not give its fruit to you; a fugitive and a wanderer shall you be on the earth." Cain said to the Lord, "My punishment is too great to bear. You are driving me today from the soil; and from your face I shall be hidden. And I shall be a fugitive and a wanderer on the earth, and whoever finds me will kill me." But the Lord said to him, "Not so! Whoever kills Cain shall be punished sevenfold." Then the Lord gave Cain a token so that no one finding him should kill him. And Cain went out from the presence of the Lord and dwelt in the land of Nod, to the east of Eden.

When the Lord saw that the wickedness of man on the earth was great, and that man's every thought and all the inclination of his heart were only evil, he regretted that he had made man on the earth and was grieved to the heart. Then the Lord said, "I will wipe from the earth man whom I have created—man and beast, crawling creature and bird of the air as well—for I regret that I made them." But Noe found favor with the Lord. Noe was a just man, blameless among the men of his day. He walked with God. And God said to Noe, "The end of all creatures of flesh is in my mind; the earth is full of violence because of them. I will destroy them with the earth. Make an ark of resin-wood; make it tight with fibre and cover it with pitch inside and out. This is how you shall make it: the length of the ark three hundred cubits, its width fifty cubits, and its height thirty cubits. Make an opening for the ark and finish it a cubit from the top. Set a door in the side of the ark; make it with a bottom, second and third level. For in truth I will bring the flood upon the earth to destroy from under heaven all flesh in which there is the breath of life. All that are on the earth shall die. But I will establish my covenant with you; you shall go into the ark, you, your sons, your wife and your sons' wives with you. Of every sort of living creature of all flesh you shall bring two into the ark, to keep them alive with you; they shall be male and female. Of birds according to their kind and of cattle according to their kind, of every kind of creature moving over the ground, two of each shall enter with you to be kept alive. Take with you also every kind of food that can be eaten and store it up with you, and it shall serve as food for you and for them."

Then the Lord said to Noe, "Go into the ark, you and all your household; for you, in this generation, I have found just in my sight. Of all clean animals take with you seven pairs, a male and its mate; and of the unclean animals two, a male and its mate; of the birds of the air also, seven pairs, male and female, that they may raise up offspring over all the earth. For after seven days I will send rain on the earth for forty days and forty nights, and I will wipe from the ground every living thing that I have made."

Noe did all that God commanded him. And after the seven days the waters of the flood came upon the earth. The flood continued forty days upon the earth. The waters increased and bore up the ark and it rose above the earth. The waters rose higher and increased greatly on the earth; but the ark floated on the surface of the waters. The waters rose higher and higher on the earth so that all the highest mountains everywhere under the heavens were covered.

All that were on the dry land in whose nostrils was the breath of life, died. And every living thing on the earth was wiped out, from man to beast, from reptile to bird of the air.

Then God remembered Noe, and all the wild animals and all the cattle that were with him in the ark. And God sent a wind over the earth and the waters subsided. The fountains of the deep and the floodgates of the heavens were closed. The rain from the heavens was withheld. The waters steadily receded from the earth; the ark rested on the mountains of Ararat. At the end of forty days, Noe opened the window which he had made in the ark, and released a raven. It flew to and fro until the waters had dried off the earth. Then he sent a dove to see if the waters had abated from the surface of the ground. But the dove found no place to alight, so she returned to him in the ark.

He waited another seven days, and again sent forth the dove from the ark. The dove came back to him in the evening, and there in her mouth was a green olive leaf! So Noe knew that the waters had abated from the earth. Then he waited another seven days, and sent forth the dove; but she did not return to him any more.

Noe removed the covering of the ark and saw that the surface of the ground had dried. Then God said to Noe, "Go out of the ark, you and your wife and your sons and your sons' wives with you. Bring out with you every living thing you have of all flesh: birds, cattle, and every creature crawling on the earth, that they may abound on the earth and be fruitful and multiply on the earth." Noe went forth with his sons and his wife and his sons' wives. All wild animals, all cattle, all birds and all creatures crawling on the earth: according to their kinds they went out of the ark.

Then Noe built an altar to the Lord; he took of every clean animal and of every clean bird, and offered holocausts on the altar. When the Lord smelled the sweet odor he said to himself, "I will never again curse the ground on account of man, for the inclination of man's heart is evil from his youth; I will never again destroy every living creature, as I have done. As long as the earth shall last, seedtime and harvest, cold and heat, summer and winter, day and night, shall not cease."

And God said, "This is the token of the covenant; I set it between me and you and every living creature that is with you, for all generations to come. I will set my bow in the clouds and it shall be a token of the covenant between me and the earth. When I bring clouds over the earth, and the bow appears in the clouds, I will remember my covenant which is between me and you and every living creature of

9

all flesh. Never again shall the waters become a flood to destroy all flesh."

The sons of Noe who went out of the ark were Sem, Ham and Japheth, and from these the whole earth was peopled.

THE MIXING OF TONGUES

The whole earth used the same language and the same speech. While men were migrating eastward, they discovered a valley in the land of Sennaar and settled there. They said to one another, "Come, let us make bricks and bake them." They used bricks for stone and bitumen for mortar. Then they said, "Let us build ourselves a city and a tower with its top in the heavens; let us make a name for ourselves lest we be scattered all over the earth." The Lord came down to see the city and the tower which men had built. And the Lord said, "Truly, they are one people and they all have the same language. This is the beginning of what they will do. Hereafter they will not be restrained from anything which they determine to do. Let us go down, and there confuse their language so that they will not understand one another's speech." So the Lord scattered them from that place all over the earth; and they stopped building the city. For this reason it was called Babel, because there the Lord confused the speech of all the earth.

THE STORY OF ABRAM

These are the descendants of Thare. Thare was the father of Abram, Nahor and Aran. Aran became the father of Lot. Aran died before his father Thare in the land of his birth, in Ur of the Chaldees. Abram and Nahor married. Abram's wife was Sarai and Nahor's wife was Melcha, the daughter of Aran, father of Melcha and Jescha. Now Sarai was barren; she had no children. Thare took his son Abram and his grandson Lot, the son of Aran, and his daughter-in-law Sarai, the wife of his son Abram, and led them from Ur of the Chaldees toward the land of Chanaan; but when they reached Haran, they settled there.

The Lord said to Abram:

"Leave your country, your kinsfolk and your father's house,
    for the land which I will show you;
I will make a great nation of you.
    I will bless you, and make your name great,

so that you shall be a blessing.
I will bless them that bless you,
    and curse them that curse you.
In you shall all the nations of the earth be blessed."

Abram went away as the Lord had commanded him, and Lot went with him. Abram was seventy-five years old when he left Haran. Abram took Sarai his wife, Lot his brother's son, all the property they had acquired and the persons they had got in Haran; and they departed for the land of Chanaan. When they came to the land of Chanaan, Abram passed through the land to the sacred place at Sichem, near the terebinth of More. At that time the Chanaanite was in the land.

The Lord appeared to Abram, and said, "To your descendants I will give this land." So Abram built an altar there to the Lord, who had appeared to him. He moved from there to the mountain region east of Bethel, and pitched his tent with Bethel to the west and Ai to the east. He built an altar there to the Lord and called on the name of the Lord.

Lot, who went with Abram, also had flocks, herds and tents, so that the land would not support them dwelling together; for their possessions were so great that they could not dwell together. And there was strife between the herdsmen of Abram's cattle and the herdsmen of Lot's cattle. At that time the Chanaanite and the Pherezite dwelt in the land. Then Abram said to Lot, "Let there be no strife between you and me, nor between my herdsmen and your herdsmen; for we are kinsmen. Does not the whole land lie before you? Withdraw from me. If you go to the left, I will go to the right; or if you take the right, then I will go to the left." Then Lot looked about and saw that the whole region of the Jordan toward Segor was well-watered—this was before the Lord destroyed Sodom and Gomorra—like the Lord's garden or like Egypt. So Lot chose for himself the whole region of the Jordan and journeyed eastward. Thus they separated from each other. Abram dwelt in the land of Chanaan, while Lot dwelt in the cities of the Jordan region, pitching his tent near Sodom. Now the men of Sodom were wicked, and sinned exceedingly against the Lord.

In the time of Amraphel king of Sennaar, Arioch king of Ellasar, Chodorlahomor king of Elam, and Thadal king of Goyyim, these kings waged war against Bara king of Sodom, Bersa king of Gomorra, Sennaab king of Adama, Semeber king of Seboim, and the king of Bala— that is, Segor.

The victors took all the goods of Sodom and Gomorra and all their provisions, and went their way; they also took Lot, Abram's nephew, and his goods, for he had been living in Sodom. Then came a fugitive and reported to Abram the Hebrew, who was living near the terebinths of Mamre the Amorrite, a kinsman of Eschol and Aner; these were allies of Abram.

When Abram heard that his kinsman had been taken prisoner, he called out three hundred and eighteen of his trained men, born in his house, and went in pursuit as far as Dan. He and his servants formed parties against them by night, defeated them and pursued them as far as Hoba, north of Damascus. He recovered all the goods; and his kinsman Lot and his goods he also recovered, besides the women and the people. When Abram returned from the defeat of Chodorlahomor and the kings with him, the king of Sodom went out to meet Abram in the valley Save, that is, in the king's valley.

Then Melchisedec, the king of Salem, brought out bread and wine; for he was a priest of the Most High God. He blessed Abram and said,

"Blessed be Abram by the Most High God,
　　creator of heaven and earth.
Blessed be the Most High God,
　　who has delivered your enemies into your hand."

Then Abram gave him a tenth of everything.

GOD'S PROMISE TO ABRAM

After these things the word of the Lord came to Abram in a vision,

"Fear not, Abram, I am your shield;
　　your reward shall be very great."

And Abram said, "O Lord God, what will you give me? I am childless, and the steward of my house, Eliezer, is my heir." Abram also said, "To me you have given no descendants; the slave born in my house will be my heir." But the word of the Lord came to him, "He shall not be your heir; your heir shall be one of your own flesh." Then the Lord led him outside and said, "Look at the heavens and, if you can, count the stars." And he said to him, "So shall your posterity be." Abram believed the Lord, who credited the act to him as justice. He said to him, "I am the Lord, who brought you from Ur in Chaldea, to give you this land to possess."

Sarai, Abram's wife, had borne him no children. She had an Egyptian maid named Agar. Sarai said to Abram, "The Lord has kept me from bearing; go in to my maid; perhaps I shall get children through her." Abram listened to Sarai. After Abram had lived ten years in the land of Chanaan, Sarai his wife took Agar, her Egyptian maid, and gave her to Abram, her husband, to be his wife. And he went in to Agar, and she conceived. When she was aware that she had conceived, she looked with disdain on her mistress. So Agar bore Abram a son; and Abram called his son Ismael.

When Abram was ninety-nine years old, the Lord appeared to him and said, "I am God the Almighty. Walk in my presence and be perfect. I will make my covenant between you and me, and will multiply you exceedingly." Abram fell prostrate, and God spoke to him thus, "This is my covenant with you: You shall be the father of a multitude of nations; you shall no longer be called Abram, but your name shall be Abraham. I will make you exceedingly fruitful; I will make nations of you, and kings shall descend from you. I will establish my covenant between you and me and your descendants after you throughout their generations, as a perpetual covenant, that I may be a God to you and to your descendants after you. I will give you and your descendants after you this land in which you are immigrants, all the land of Chanaan as a perpetual possession; and I will be their God."

God also said to Abraham, "You shall keep my covenant, you and your descendants after you throughout their generations. This is my covenant which you shall keep, between you and me and your descendants after you: Every male among you shall be circumcised. You shall circumcise the flesh of your foreskin; it shall be a token of the covenant between you and me. He that is eight days old among you shall be circumcised, every male throughout your generations, including the slave born in your house, or bought with money from any foreigner, not of your own race. Both he that is born in your house and he that is bought with your money must be circumcised. My covenant shall be in your flesh as a perpetual covenant. If any male have not the flesh of his foreskin circumcised, that person shall be cut off from his people; he has broken my covenant."

God said to Abraham, "Sarai your wife you shall not call Sarai but Sara. I will bless her, and will also give you a son by her; yes, I will bless her, and she shall be the mother of nations; kings of peoples shall descend from her." And as Abraham fell prostrate, he laughed and said to himself, "Shall a son be born to one who is a hundred years old? Shall Sara who is ninety bear a child?" Then Abraham said to God, "Oh, that Ismael may live in your favor!" God answered, "No, but Sara your wife shall bear you a son, and you shall call him Isaac. I will establish my covenant with him as a perpetual covenant for his descendants after him.

"As for Ismael, I have heard you. I will bless him and make him fruitful and multiply him exceedingly. He shall become the father of twelve princes, and I will make him a great nation. But my covenant I will establish with Isaac, whom Sara shall bear to you at this time next year." And when he had finished talking with him, God left Abraham.

Then Abraham took his son Ismael, and all who were born in his house, and all who had been bought with his money, every male in his household, and he circumcised the flesh of their foreskins on that very day, as God had commanded him.

THE SINS OF SODOM AND GOMORRA

Then the Lord said, "Because the outcry against Sodom and Gomorra is great, and their sin is very grave, I will go down to see whether they have done all that the outcry which has come to me indicates; if not, I will know."

Now the two angels came to Sodom in the evening, while Lot was sitting at the gate of Sodom. When Lot saw them, he rose to meet them, and falling prostrate to the earth, he said, "Come aside, my lords, into the house of your servant." Then they said to Lot, "Have you anyone else here? Sons-in-law, sons, daughters, or anyone you have in the city, take them out of the place; for we are about to destroy this place, because the outcry against them has become so great before the Lord that he sent us to destroy it." Lot went out therefore to speak to his intended sons-in-law, and said, "Come, leave this place; for the Lord shall destroy the city." But they thought he was jesting.

When morning came, the angels urged Lot on, saying, "Come, take your wife and your two daughters here, lest you perish in the punishment of the city." And as he lingered the visitors took him, his wife and his two daughters by the hand, through the mercy of the Lord toward him, and led him forth, and set him outside the city. When they had brought them forth, they said, "Flee for your life; do not look behind you nor stop anywhere in the valley; flee to the hills, lest you perish."

The Lord poured down on Sodom and Gomorra sulphur and fire from the Lord out of heaven. He overthrew those cities and the whole region, all the inhabitants of the cities and the plants of the soil. But his wife who was behind him looked back, and became a pillar of salt.

THE BIRTH OF ISAAC

The Lord looked after Sara as he had said; the Lord did to Sara as he had promised. Sara conceived and bore Abraham a son in his old age at the time which God had promised. And Abraham called the son whom Sara bore him, Isaac. When his son Isaac was eight days old, Abraham circumcised him as God had commanded him. Abraham was one hundred years old when his son Isaac was born to him. Sara said, "God has given me cause for laughter, and whoever hears of it will laugh with me." Again she said, "Who would have said to Abraham that Sara would nurse children? Yet I bore him a son in his old age."

The child grew and was weaned; and Abraham gave a great feast on the day of his weaning.

SARA'S ANGER

Sara saw the son of Agar the Egyptian, whom she bore to Abraham, playing with her son Isaac. She said to Abraham, "Cast out this slave-girl with her son; for the son of this slave-girl shall not be heir with my son Isaac." The matter was very distressing to Abraham on account of his son. But God said to Abraham, "Be not distressed on account of the boy and your slave-girl; heed all that Sara says to you; for through Isaac shall your descendants be called. But I will also make the son of the slave-girl a great nation because he is your offspring."

THE FAITH OF ABRAHAM

After these events God put Abraham to a test. He said to him, "Abraham." He answered, "Here I am." God said, "Take your only son Isaac whom you love and go into the district of Moria, and there offer him as a holocaust on the hill which I shall point out to you." Early in the morning Abraham harnessed his ass, took with him two of his servants and his son Isaac, and cut wood for the holocaust. Then he set out on his journey to the place which God had indicated to him. On the third day he looked up and saw the place at a distance. He said to his servants, "Stay here with the ass while the boy and I go there to

15

worship; then we shall come back to you." Abraham took the wood for the holocaust and put it upon his son Isaac while he himself carried the fire and the knife. As they walked together, Isaac said to his father Abraham, "Father." He answered, "Yes, son!" He said, "You have the fire and the wood, but where is the sheep for the holocaust?" Abraham replied, "God himself will provide the sheep for the holocaust, my son." And they went on together.

When they arrived at the place of which God had told him, Abraham built an altar there and arranged the wood on it. Then he bound his son Isaac and laid him on the wood upon the altar. Abraham stretched out his hand, and took the knife to kill his son. But an angel of the Lord called to him from heaven, "Abraham, Abraham!" He answered, "Here I am." He said, "Do not lay a hand on the boy; do nothing to him. I know now that you fear God, since you have not withheld your only son from me." Abraham looked about and saw a ram caught by its horns in the bush. He went and took it, and offered it as a holocaust in place of his son. Abraham named the place, "Yahweh-yireh." Hence even to this day people say, "On the mountain of the Lord provision will be made."

Again the angel of the Lord called from heaven to Abraham and said, "I swear by myself, says the Lord, since you have done this and have not withheld your only son, I will indeed bless you, and will surely multiply your descendants as the stars of the heavens, as the sands on the seashore. Your descendants shall possess the gates of their enemies. In your descendants all the nations of the earth shall be blessed, because you have obeyed me."

THE DEATH OF SARA AND ABRAHAM

Sara lived one hundred and twenty-seven years. She died in Cariatharbe, that is, Hebron, in the land of Chanaan. Abraham prepared to mourn for Sara and weep over her. Abraham's life span was one hundred and seventy-five years when he expired. He died at a good old age, an old man, after a full life. Abraham was buried with his wife Sara in the field which he had bought from the Hethites.

THE STORY OF ISAAC AND JACOB

This is the family history of Isaac, the son of Abraham. Abraham was the father of Isaac. Isaac was forty years old when he married Rebecca, daughter of Bathuel, an Aramean of Phaddan-Aram, and sister of Laban the Aramean. Isaac prayed to the Lord for his wife because she was barren. The Lord answered Isaac and his wife Rebecca conceived. The children jostled each other within her, and she said, "If this be so, why am I pregnant?" Then she went to consult the Lord. He said to her,

> "Two nations are in your womb;
> two peoples shall stem from your body.
> One people shall be stronger than the other,
> and the elder shall serve the younger."

When the time of her delivery came, there were indeed twins in her womb. The first to come forth was red. His whole body was like a hairy garment, so they named him Esau. Afterward his brother came forth, with his hand gripping Esau's heel; so he was called Jacob. Isaac was sixty years old when they were born.

When the boys grew up, Esau became a skillful hunter, a man of the open country, while Jacob was a settled man who stayed among the tents. Isaac preferred Esau because he was fond of game, but Rebecca preferred Jacob.

Once when Jacob was cooking some food, Esau came in from the field famished. Esau said to Jacob, "Let me have some of that red food, for I am famished." Hence he was called Edom. But Jacob replied, "Sell me first your birthright." Esau said, "I am dying; of what use to me is the birthright?" Jacob said, "Swear to me first." So he swore to Jacob, and sold him his birthright. Then Jacob gave Esau some bread and lentils. He ate and drank and went his way. Thus lightly did Esau value his birthright.

When Esau was forty years old he married Judith, daughter of Beeri the Hethite, and Basemath, daughter of Elon the Hethite. But they were a source of bitterness to Isaac and Rebecca.

When Isaac was old and his eyesight had failed, he called his elder son Esau, and said to him, "Son!" He replied, "Here I am!" He said, "You see I have grown old; I do not know when I may die. Take your weapons, quiver and bow; go out into the fields to hunt me some game. Prepare for me some savory food such as I like; bring it to me to eat, so that I may bless you before I die." Rebecca listened while Isaac was talking to his son Esau. When Esau had gone out into the field to hunt some game for his father, Rebecca said to her son Jacob, "I heard your father tell your brother Esau, 'Bring me some game; prepare some savory food for me to eat, and then I will bless you in the sight of the Lord before I die.' Now my son, do what I tell you. Go to the flock and bring me two choice kids that I may make of them savory food for your father, such as he likes. Then bring it to your father to eat, that he may bless you before he dies." Jacob said to his mother Rebecca, "But Esau my brother is a hairy man, while I am smooth. If my father touches me, it will seem to him that I am mocking him. Thus I shall bring a curse on myself instead of a blessing." His mother replied, "Let the curse fall on me, my son! Do but listen to me; go, get them for me."

He went, selected them, and brought them to his mother, who prepared savory food such as his father liked. Then Rebecca took the best clothes of her elder son Esau, which she had in the house, and put them on her younger son Jacob. She put the skins of the kids on his hands and over the smooth parts of his neck. Then she gave her son Jacob the savory food and bread she had prepared. He went to his father and said, "Father!" He answered, "Here I am. Who are you, my son?" And Jacob said to his father, "I am Esau, your first-born. I have done as you told me; sit up, please! Eat again of my game, that you may bless me." Isaac replied, "How did you find it so quickly, my son?" He answered, "The Lord your God let me come upon it." Then Isaac said to Jacob, "Come close that I may touch you, my son, to know whether you are really my son Esau or not." Jacob went close to his father; Isaac touched him and said, "The voice is the voice of Jacob, but the hands are the hands of Esau." (He did not recognize him because his hands were hairy like those of his brother Esau; so he blessed him.)

Isaac said, "Are you really my son Esau?" Jacob answered, "Yes, I am." Isaac continued, "Set your game near me, my son, that I may eat it, and bless you." He set it before him and he ate of it, and he brought him some wine, which he drank. Then his father Isaac said to him, "Come close and kiss me, my son." He came close and kissed him. When he smelled the fragrance of his garments, he blessed him and said:

> "The fragrance of my son
>   is like the fragrance of a field
>   which the Lord has blessed!
> God give you dew from heaven,
>   and fruitfulness of the earth,
>   abundance of grain and wine.
> Let nations serve you,
>   peoples bow down to you.

Be master of your brothers;
   may your mother's sons bow down to you.
Cursed be those who curse you,
   blessed be those who bless you."

Isaac had pronounced the blessing and Jacob had just left his father's presence, when his brother Esau returned from hunting. He also prepared savory food and brought it to his father, saying, "Sit up, father, and eat of your son's game, that you may bless me." His father Isaac said to him, "Who are you?" He answered, "I am Esau, your first-born son." Isaac was greatly disturbed, and asked, "Who was it, then, that hunted game and brought it to me? Before you came I ate heartily and then blessed him; and he shall be blessed." On hearing his father's words, Esau uttered a very loud and bitter cry, and said to him, "Father, bless me too." But he answered, "Your brother came deceitfully and received your blessing." Then he said, "Must he, true to his name Jacob, supplant me now a second time? He took my birthright and now he has taken my blessing." He added, "Have you not reserved a blessing for me?" Isaac answered Esau, "I have appointed him your lord, and have given him all his brothers as servants. I have enriched him with grain and wine; what then can I do for you, my son?" But Esau said to his father, "Have you only one blessing, father? Bless me also, my father." And Esau wept aloud.

His father Isaac answered him:

"Without the fruitfulness of the earth
   shall your dwelling be;
   without the dew of the heavens above.
By your sword shall you live;
   you shall serve your brother.
But when you become restive,
   you shall shake his yoke from your neck."

Esau bore Jacob a grudge because of the blessing his father had given him. He said to himself, "The time of mourning for my father is coming; then I will kill my brother Jacob." Rebecca was told of these words of her elder son, Esau. She summoned her younger son, Jacob, and said to him, "Your brother Esau intends to revenge himself on you by killing you. Listen to me therefore, my son; flee to my brother Laban in Haran. Stay with him awhile until your brother's fury subsides [until your brother's wrath against you relents], and he forgets what you have done to him. Then I will send for you and bring you back. Why should I be bereaved of you both on the same day?"

JACOB GOES INTO EXILE

Rebecca said to Isaac, "I am disgusted with life because of the Hethite women; if Jacob should marry a Hethite woman like these, a native of the land, what would life mean to me?" Isaac therefore called Jacob and having blessed him, charged him, "Do not marry any Chanaanite woman; go then to Phaddan-Aram, the home of Bathuel, your mother's father, and there choose your wife from the daughters of your uncle Laban. May God Almighty bless you, and make you fruitful; may he multiply you so that you may inherit this land in which you are immigrants, which God gave to Abraham."

Esau learned that Isaac had blessed Jacob and sent him away to marry; since he realized his father Isaac's displeasure with Chanaanite women, Esau went to Ismael, and in addition to the wives he had, married Maheleth, daughter of Abraham's son Ismael and sister of Nabaioth.

Meanwhile, Jacob left Bersabee and journeyed toward Haran. He came to a place where he spent the night because the sun had set. He took one of the stones of the place, put it under his head, and went to sleep there. He dreamed that a ladder was set up on the ground with its top reaching to heaven; angels of God were ascending and descending on it. The Lord stood beside him and said, "I am the Lord, the God of Abraham your father, and the God of Isaac. I will give you and your descendants the land on which you lie. They shall be as the dust of the earth. You shall spread abroad to the west, to the east, to the north, and to the south; in you and in your descendants, all the nations of the earth shall be blessed. I will be with you and protect you wherever you go. I will bring you back to this land; indeed I will not forsake you till I fulfill my promise."

When Jacob woke from his sleep he said, "Truly the Lord is in this place and I did not know it." Reverently he continued, "How awesome is this place! This is none other than the house of God; this is the gate of heaven." Jacob arose in the morning, took the stone which he had placed under his head, set it up as a memorial pillar and poured oil over it. He called the place Bethel; formerly the name of the city was Luza. Jacob also made a vow: "If the Lord is with me and protects me on my present journey, and gives me food to eat and clothing to wear, and a safe return to my father's house, the Lord shall be my God; and this stone which I have set up as a memorial pillar shall be the house of God. I will offer faithfully a tenth part of everything you give me."

Then Jacob continued his journey and came to the land of the people of the East. Looking about he saw a well in the open country, and three flocks of sheep lying nearby, for the flocks were watered from this well. But the stone over the mouth of the well was large. After all the shepherds were gathered there, the stone was rolled back from the mouth of the well and the flocks were watered. Then the stone was replaced over the mouth of the well.

Jacob said to them, "My brothers, where are you from?" And they answered, "We are from Haran." Then he inquired, "Do you know Laban the son of Nahor?" And they said, "We do." He asked further, "Is he well?" They replied, "He is, and here comes his daughter Rachel with his flock."

While he was still talking with them, Rachel arrived with her father's flock; for it was her custom to tend them. When Jacob saw Rachel, the daughter of his uncle Laban, with the flock, he drew near, rolled the stone from the mouth of the well, and watered his uncle's flock. Then Jacob kissed Rachel and wept aloud. Jacob told Rachel that he was her father's relative, a son of Rebecca, and she hastened to tell her father. When Laban heard about Jacob, his nephew, he hastened to meet him, received him with embraces and kisses, and brought him to his dwelling.

THE MARRIAGES OF JACOB

Laban had two daughters. The elder was called Lia, and the younger Rachel. Lia's eyes were weak, but Rachel was shapely and beautiful. Jacob loved Rachel. He said, therefore, "I will serve you seven years for your younger daughter Rachel." Laban answered, "It is better to give her to you than to another man; stay with me." So Jacob served seven years for Rachel, and they seemed to him but a few days because of his love for her. Then Jacob said to Laban, "Give me my wife; for the time has come for me to go in to her."

Laban gathered all the men of the place and gave a feast. That night he brought Lia, his daughter, to Jacob, who had relations with her. Laban gave his servant Zelpha to his daughter Lia to be her maid.

In the morning, to Jacob's amazement, it was Lia. Then he said to Laban, "What have you done to me? Did I not serve you for Rachel? Why then have you cheated me?" Laban replied, "It is not the custom in our country to give the younger daughter before the first-born; complete the week of this one's nuptials and I will give you the other in return for another seven years of service with me."

Jacob did so; he completed her week. Then Laban gave him his daughter Rachel in marriage. Laban gave his servant Bala to his daughter Rachel to be her maid. So Jacob went in to Rachel also; he loved her more than Lia, and served Laban another seven years.

When the Lord saw that Lia was disliked, he made her fruitful, while Rachel remained barren. Lia conceived and bore a son, naming him Ruben; "For," she said, "the Lord has had regard for my misery; now my husband will love me." Again she conceived and bore a son saying, "The Lord has heard that I am disliked; therefore he has given me this one also." She named him Simeon. She conceived again and bore a son, saying, "This time my husband will become attached to me, for I have borne him three sons." Therefore she named him Levi. Once more she conceived and bore a son, saying, "Now I will praise the Lord." Therefore she named him Juda. Then she ceased bearing.

CONFLICT BETWEEN RACHEL AND LIA

When Rachel saw that she was not bearing children to Jacob, she became jealous of her sister and said to Jacob, "Give me children or I shall die." Jacob became impatient with Rachel and answered her, "Can I take the place of God, who has made you barren?" She replied, "Here is my slave-girl, Bala; go in to her that she may bear on my knees, and I too may have children by her." She gave him Bala, her maid, in marriage, and Jacob had relations with her. Bala conceived and bore Jacob a son. Then Rachel said, "God has pronounced judgment in my favor, for he has heard my prayer and given me a son." Therefore she named him Dan. Bala, Rachel's maid, conceived again and bore a second son to Jacob. Then Rachel said, "I have used a clever device against my sister, and I have indeed prevailed." So she called him Nephthali. When Lia knew that she had ceased bearing, she gave Zelpha her maid to Jacob in marriage. Zelpha bore Jacob a son. Lia said, "What good fortune!" And she named him Gad. Zelpha bore Jacob another son. And Lia said, "What happiness! Women will call me happy." So she named him Aser.

During the wheat harvest, Ruben went into the field, found some mandrakes, and brought them to his mother Lia. Rachel said to Lia, "Give me some of your son's mandrakes." She answered her, "Is it a trivial matter to have taken my husband? Will you also take my son's mandrakes?" Rachel said, "Very well! In exchange for your son's mandrakes, Jacob shall lie with you tonight." As Jacob was returning from the field in the evening, Lia went to meet him and said, "You are to come to me; for I have bargained for you with my son's mandrakes." So he slept with her that night. God heard Lia's prayer, and she conceived and bore Jacob a fifth son. Then she said, "God has rewarded me because I gave my maid to my husband." She called him Issachar. Lia conceived again and bore a sixth son to Jacob. She said, "God has made me an excellent gift. Now my husband will honor me; for I have borne him six sons." Therefore she named him Zabulon. Afterward she bore a daughter whom she named Dina.

But God remembered Rachel; he heard her prayer and made her fruitful. She conceived and bore a son, and she said, "God has taken away my reproach." She named him Joseph, saying, "May the Lord give me another son."

JACOB'S STRUGGLES WITH LABAN

When Rachel had given birth to Joseph, Jacob said to Laban, "Let me return to my own home and country. Give me my wives for whom I served you, and my children; let me depart. You know well the service I have given you." Laban said to him, "If you please, I surmise that God blessed me because of you. Name your wages and I will pay." He answered, "But you know well how I have served you, how your stock fared under my care. Before I came you had little indeed, but now it has greatly increased. And now, when shall I provide for my own household?"

Jacob learned that Laban's sons were saying, "Jacob has taken all our father had, and he has acquired all these riches from what belonged to our father."

Jacob sent for Rachel and Lia, calling them to his flock in the field, and said to them, "I see that your father's attitude toward me is not what it was previously; but the God of my father has been with me. You yourselves know that I have served your father with all my strength, yet your father cheated me and changed my pay time after time; but God did not allow him to harm me. So God took away your father's stock and gave it to me. An angel of God said to me in a dream, 'Jacob!' and I answered, 'Here I am!' Then he said, 'Look and take note: I have seen all that Laban has been doing to you. I am the God who appeared to you at Bethel, where you anointed the memorial pillar and made a vow to me. Rise now, leave this land, and return to the land of your kin.' "

Rachel and Lia answered him, "Have we any share or heritage left in our father's house? Are we not regarded as strangers by him? For he has sold us, and entirely used up the money he received through us. Surely all the property God has taken away from our father belongs to us and our children. Do whatever God has told you."

When Laban had gone to shear his flock, Rachel stole her father's household idols; and Jacob outwitted Laban the Aramean by not mentioning to him his intended flight, and fled with all that belonged to him. Jacob set out, crossed the River and made for the highlands of Galaad.

Jacob had pitched his tent in the highlands when Laban overtook him. Laban said to Jacob, "Why have you acted so, deceiving me and carrying off my daughters like prisoners of war? Why did you flee secretly and steal away from me? You did not let me know, so that I could send you off with rejoicing and song, with tambourine and lyre. You did not allow me to kiss my sons and daughters; you have acted foolishly. It is in my power to do you harm; but last night the God of your father said to me, 'Take care not to say anything at all to Jacob.' "

Then Jacob became angry and remonstrated with Laban. "What is my offense or my crime," he said, "that you have pursued me, and have ransacked all my belongings? What household article of yours have you found? Put it out here in the presence of your kinsmen and mine that they may decide between us two. Twenty years now I have been with you; your ewes and your she-goats have never miscarried, nor have I eaten the rams of your flock. I have not brought to you any torn by wild beasts; I bore the loss myself. You held me responsible for anything stolen by day or night. The heat wasted me by day, the cold by night; sleep fled from my eyes. This has been my twenty years with you: I served you fourteen years for your two daughters, six years for your flocks; you changed my pay time after time. If the God of my father, the God of Abraham, and the God whom Isaac fears, had not favored me, even now you would have sent me away empty-handed. God saw my affliction and my toil."

Laban answered Jacob, "The daughters are mine, the grandchildren are mine, the flocks are mine, indeed all that you see is mine. What can I do today to these daughters of mine and to the children they have borne? Come, then, let us make a covenant, you and I; then the Lord shall be a witness between you and me."

Then Jacob took a stone and set it up as a memorial pillar. Jacob said to his kinsmen, "Gather some stones." And they gathered stones, made a heap, and ate there near the heap. Laban said, "This heap is a witness between you and me today, and [may the Lord watch between you and me when we are away from each other"].

Early in the morning, Laban kissed his grandchildren and daughters, bade them farewell, and returned to his home. Jacob also resumed his journey.

JACOB FEARS HIS BROTHER ESAU

Then Jacob sent messengers ahead to his brother Esau in the region of Seir in the country of Edom, commanding them, "Thus shall you say to my lord Esau: Your servant Jacob sends you this message: 'I have been dwelling with Laban and stayed till now, so I am sending word to my lord that I may find favor with you.'"

The messengers returned to Jacob and said, "We went to your brother Esau. He is coming to meet you with four hundred men." Filled with fear and anxiety, Jacob divided into two camps the people with him, as well as the flocks, the cattle, and the camels. He said, "Should Esau come on one camp and attack it, the other will be saved." Jacob prayed, "God of my father Abraham and God of my father Isaac, Lord who said to me, 'Return to your land and to your kin, and I will deal well with you': I am not worthy of all the kindnesses and the constant solicitude which you have shown your servant. With only my staff I crossed this Jordan; now I have grown into two camps.

"Save me from my brother Esau; for I fear that he is coming to kill me and all my family. You have promised, 'I will surely deal well with you. I will make your descendants as the sands of the sea, too numerous to count.'"

After sleeping there that night, he chose a present for his brother Esau from what he had with him: two hundred she-goats, twenty he-goats, two hundred ewes, twenty rams, thirty milch camels with their young, forty cows, ten bullocks, twenty she-asses and ten foals. He delivered these to his servants, in separate droves, instructing them, "Go ahead of me, but leave a space between one drove and the next." He charged the leaders, "If my brother Esau meets you and asks, 'To whom do you belong? where are you going? and whose animals are these before you?', you shall answer, 'They belong to your servant Jacob; they are a gift sent to my lord Esau, and Jacob is just behind us.'" He thought, "I will appease him with the gift that precedes me; then when I see him, perhaps he will be kind to me."

Jacob looked up and saw Esau approaching with four hundred men. So he divided the children among Lia, Rachel and the two maids, putting the maids and their children in front, then Lia and her children, with Rachel and Joseph in the rear. He himself went ahead of them, bowing to the ground seven times, until he reached his brother. Esau ran to meet him, embraced him, fell on his neck and kissed him. And they wept.

THE RETURN OF JACOB

That same day Esau started back on his way to Seir, while Jacob went to Socchoth, and built a home for himself and made sheds for his stock. During his journey from Phaddan-Aram Jacob came safely to the city of Sichem, in the land of Chanaan, and camped near the city. For the price of one hundred pieces of money he bought the plot of ground on which he had pitched his tent, from the sons of Hemor, the father of Sichem. There he erected a memorial pillar and named it "El, God of Israel."

They journeyed from Bethel, and when they were still a distance from Ephratha, Rachel gave birth to a child amid great pain. While she was in painful labor the midwife said to her, "Fear not; for this time also you have a son." As her soul was departing her—for she was at the point of death—she named him Benoni, but his father called him Benjamin. Rachel died and was buried on the way to Ephratha, that is, Bethlehem. Jacob erected a memorial over her grave; and this memorial marks Rachel's grave to this day.

THE DEATH OF ISAAC

Jacob went to his father Isaac at Mamre in Cariath-arbe, that is, Hebron, where Abraham and Isaac had sojourned. The lifetime of Isaac was one hundred and eighty years. Isaac breathed his last and died, and was gathered to his kin, an old man who had lived a full life. His sons Esau and Jacob buried him.

THE STORY OF JOSEPH

Jacob lived in the land of Chanaan, where his father had dwelt as a stranger. This is his family history. When Joseph was seventeen years old, still a mere youth, he was pasturing the flock with his brothers, the sons of Bala and Zelpha, his father's wives, and he brought a bad report to his father concerning them.

Israel loved Joseph best of all his sons because he was born in his old age. He made him a long tunic. When his brothers saw that their father loved him best of all his sons, they hated him and could not even greet him.

Now Joseph had a dream, and when he told it to his brothers, they hated him the more. He said to them, "Listen to this dream I had. We were binding sheaves in the field; my sheaf rose up and remained standing, while your sheaves gathered round and bowed down to my sheaf." His brothers answered, "Are you to be our king? Are you to rule over us?" And because of his dreams and words they hated him the more.

He had another dream which he also told to his brothers. "I had another dream," he said. "The sun, the moon and eleven stars were worshiping me." When he told that to his father and his brothers, his father reproved him. "What is this dream that you have had?" he said. "Can it be that I and your mother and your brothers will come to bow to the ground before you?" So his brothers envied him, while his father pondered the matter.

When his brothers had gone to pasture their father's flocks at Sichem, Israel said to Joseph, "Your brothers are pasturing the flocks at Sichem; get ready, I will send you to them." Joseph answered, "I am ready." "Go then," said Israel, "and see if all is well with your brothers and with the flocks; and bring back a report to me." So he sent him from the valley of Hebron, and he came to Sichem. A man found Joseph wandering about in the fields and asked him, "What are you looking for?" "I am looking for my brothers," he answered. "Tell me, please, where they are pasturing." The man said, "They have moved on from here because I heard them say, 'Let us go to Dothain.'" So Joseph went after his brothers and found them in Dothain. They saw him in the distance, and before he drew near them, they plotted to kill him. They said to one another, "Here comes that dreamer! Let us therefore kill him and throw him into a cistern; we can say that a wild beast devoured him. Let us see then what becomes of his dreams."

But when Ruben heard of it, he tried to rescue him from them saying, "We must not kill him." Then he continued, "Do not shed blood. Throw him into the cistern there in the desert, but do not lay a hand on him." His purpose was to rescue him from them and restore him to his father.

When Joseph came to his brothers, they stripped him of the long tunic he had on. They seized him and threw him into the cistern, which was empty and dry.

Then they sat down to eat. Looking up, they saw a caravan of Ismaelites coming from Galaad, their camels laden with gum, balm, and myrrh, with which they were on their way down to Egypt. Then Juda said to his brothers, "What is to be gained by killing our brother and concealing his blood? Let us sell him to the Ismaelites, and let us not lay hands on him; for he is our brother, our own flesh." His brothers agreed.

And when some Madianite traders passed by, they drew Joseph up out of the cistern; they sold him to the Ismaelites for twenty pieces of silver. And they took Joseph to Egypt.

When Ruben went back to the cistern and saw that Joseph was not in it, he rent his garments, returned to his brothers and said, "The boy is not there; and I, where shall I turn?"

Then they took Joseph's tunic and after killing a goat, dipped the tunic in the blood. They sent someone who brought the long tunic to their father with the message: "We have found this; see whether it is your son's tunic or not." He recognized it and said, "It is my son's tunic. A wild beast has devoured him; Joseph has been torn to pieces!" Then Jacob rent his garments, girded himself with sackcloth and mourned his son many days. Though all his sons and daughters tried to comfort him, he refused to be consoled, and said, "I will go down mourning, to my son in the nether world." So his father wept over him.

JOSEPH IS RESOLD; HE CONQUERS TEMPTATION; HIS IMPRISONMENT

When Joseph was taken down to Egypt, Phutiphar, an Egyptian, one of Pharao's officers, the captain of his bodyguard, bought him from the Ismaelites who had taken him down there. The Lord was with Joseph so that he was successful. He lived in the house of his master, the

Egyptian. When his master saw that the Lord was with him and prospered all his undertakings, Joseph found favor with him and became his attendant. He placed him in charge of his household, and entrusted all his property to him. From the time he placed him in charge of his household and over all his property, the Lord blessed the Egyptian's house on account of Joseph. The Lord's blessing rested on everything that was his, in house and field. He left everything he had in Joseph's charge, and having him, was concerned about nothing except the food he ate.

Now Joseph was well formed and handsome. Some time afterward, the wife of his master cast her eyes on Joseph and said, "Lie with me." But he refused, saying, "Because of me, my master is not concerned about anything in the house, but has put all that he owns in my care. He exercises no greater authority in this house than I, nor has he withheld a single thing from me, except yourself, because you are his wife. How then can I commit this great crime, and sin against God?" She urged Joseph day after day, but he would not consent to lie with her, or to be with her. On one such day, Joseph went into the house to do his work, while none of the household servants was at hand. She seized him by his garment and said, "Lie with me." But Joseph left his garment in her hand, and fled outdoors.

When she saw that he had left his cloak in her hand and had fled outside, she summoned the servants of her house and said to them, "Look! My husband has brought in a Hebrew to us to insult us. He came in to lie with me but I screamed. When he heard me raise my voice and call out, he left his garment beside me, and fled outdoors." She kept the garment beside her until his master came home; then she told him the same story. When the master heard his wife's story about how his slave had treated her, he became angry. Then Joseph's master took him and committed him to the prison where the king's prisoners were kept; so he remained there in prison.

But the Lord was with Joseph. He showed kindness to him and gave him favor with the warden, who put him in charge of all prisoners; and everything that was done there was done under his management. The warden did not concern himself with anything in Joseph's charge because the Lord was with him and prospered all that he did.

JOSEPH INTERPRETS PHARAO'S DREAM

Two full years afterward, Pharao had a dream. He was standing by the Nile. Seven cows, sleek and fat, came up out of the Nile and were browsing in the reed grass. After them, seven other cows, ugly and thin, came up out of the Nile, and stood beside those on the bank of the Nile. The ugly, thin cows devoured the seven sleek, fat ones. Then Pharao awoke. But he fell asleep again and had another dream. Seven ears of grain, fat and fine, were growing on a single stalk. After them sprouted seven other ears, thin and blasted by the east wind. The thin ears swallowed up the seven fat, full ears. Then Pharao awoke to find it was a dream.

When morning came he was troubled; so he summoned all the magicians and wise men of Egypt. Pharao related his dream to them, but there was no one who could interpret it for him. Then the chief butler said to Pharao, "Today I must recall my offenses. When Pharao was angry with his servants, and put me and the chief baker in custody in the house of the captain of the guard, on the one same night he and I each had a dream of peculiar significance to himself. A Hebrew youth was there with us, a slave of the captain of the guard. We told him our dreams and he interpreted them for us. He gave each the proper interpretation of his dream; and it turned out just as he had interpreted to us: I was reinstated in my office, but the other was hanged."

Then Pharao sent for Joseph, and they brought him quickly out of the dungeon. After he had shaved and changed his clothes, he came into Pharao's presence. Pharao said to Joseph, "I had a dream which no one can interpret; but I have heard it said of you that you know how to interpret a dream." Joseph answered Pharao, "Who but God shall give Pharao a favorable response!"

Joseph said to Pharao: "Pharao's dream is but one. God has revealed to Pharao what he is about to do. The seven fine cows are seven years, and the seven fine ears are seven years; it is but one dream. The seven thin, ugly cows which came up after them are seven years; and the seven empty ears blasted by the east wind are seven years. There will be seven years of famine. It is as I told Pharao: God has revealed to Pharao what he is about to do. Seven years of great plenty will come through the land of Egypt, but there will follow seven years of famine, and then all the plenty will be forgotten in the land of Egypt. The famine will devastate the land, and the plenty will not be discernible in the land, because of the famine which is to follow; for it will be very severe. The reason the dream was sent twice to Pharao is that the matter is determined by God, and God will soon bring it about. Let Pharao select an intelligent and prudent man, and give him charge of the land of Egypt. Let Pharao take action, appoint officials over the land, and prepare the land of Egypt through the seven years of plenty. And let them collect all the food of these good years to come, and store up under the authority of Pharao food in the cities, and preserve it. The food shall be a reserve for the land against the seven years of famine which shall be in the land of Egypt, so that the land will not perish by the famine."

The advice pleased Pharao and all his courtiers; so Pharao said to his court, "Can we find another like him in whom is the spirit of God?" Then Pharao said to Joseph, "Since God had made all this known to you, there is no one as intelligent and prudent as you; you shall be in charge of my palace and all my people shall obey your commands; only as regards the royal throne will I be greater than you." Pharao continued, "I give you charge of the whole land of Egypt." Taking the signet-ring from his own hand, he put it on Joseph's. He dressed him in linen robes, and put a chain of gold around his neck. He had him ride in his second chariot. And they cried out before him, "Bow down." In this way he put him in charge of the whole land of Egypt. Pharao said to Joseph, "I am Pharao; without your command, no one shall move hand or foot in the whole land of Egypt."

Then Pharao gave to him in marriage Aseneth, daughter of Phutiphare, the priest of On. He was thirty years old when he entered the service of Pharao. He left him and traversed the whole land of Egypt.

ABUNDANCY AND THE FAMINE

During the seven years of plenty the land produced abundant crops. So he collected all the food of the seven years of plenty in the land of Egypt, and stored it in the cities, placing in each city the food from the neighboring fields. Joseph heaped up grain in great quantities like the sands of the sea until he ceased measuring it, for it could not be measured.

Before the years of famine came, two sons were born to Joseph by Aseneth. Joseph named the first-born Manasse; "Because," he said, "God has made me forget entirely my sufferings and my family." He named the second one Ephraim and said, "God has made me fruitful in the land of my affliction."

When the seven years of plenty in the land of Egypt had passed, the seven years of famine began, as Joseph had foretold. There was famine in all other countries, while in all Egypt there was food. But when the whole land of Egypt also was famished, the people cried to Pharao for food. Pharao said to all the Egyptians, "Go to Joseph and do what he tells you." When the famine had spread throughout the land, Joseph opened all the store-houses and sold grain to the Egyptians; for the famine gripped the land of Egypt. And all peoples came to Egypt to buy grain from Joseph, for the famine was grievous everywhere.

Now Joseph was the governor of the land; it was he who sold to all the people of the land. Joseph's brothers also came and prostrated themselves before him. Joseph knew his brothers, but they did not recognize him. Remembering the dreams he had once had about them, he said, "You are spies; you have come to discover the weak spots of the land." But they said to him, "No, my lord; your servants have come to buy food. We are all sons of the same man. We are honest; your servants are not spies." But he said to them, "Not so, but you have come to discover the weak spots of the country." They replied, "We, your servants, were twelve brothers, the sons of the same man in the land of Chanaan. The youngest is at present with our father; another is no more." "As for my saying you are spies," Joseph rejoined, "this shall be your test: as Pharao lives, you shall not leave this place until your youngest brother comes here! Send one of your number to bring your brother while you others remain in bonds. Thus shall your statements be tested for their truth; if they are untrue, as Pharao lives, you are spies!" Then he consigned them to custody for three days.

On the third day Joseph said to them, "If you do this, you shall live. I am a God-fearing man. If you are honest, let one of your brothers remain confined in your prison, while the rest go and carry food for the needs of your families. You shall bring me your youngest brother. Thus your words will be verified, and you shall not die." And they agreed.

Now the famine in the land was severe, so when they had eaten all the grain they had brought from Egypt, their father said to them, "Go back and buy us some food." But Juda answered, "The man strictly warned us, 'You shall not appear in my presence unless your brother is with you.' If you will let our brother accompany us, we will go down to buy food for you. But if you do not let him, we will not go, because the man said to us, 'You shall not appear in my presence unless your brother is with you.'" Israel replied, "Why did you wrong me by telling the man you had another brother?" They answered, "The man questioned us in detail about ourselves and our family: 'Is your father still living? Have you another brother?' What we told him was in response to these questions. Could we possibly know that he would say, 'Bring your brother down'?"

Then Juda said to his father Israel, "Let the boy go with me, that we may begin our journey and save from death both you and ourselves, as well as our children. I will be surety for him. Hold me responsible for him. If I do not bring him back to you and place him before you, I shall be guilty of a crime against you all my life. Had we not delayed, we could by now have made the journey twice." Their father Israel said to them, "If it must be so, then do this: take some of the country's best products in your bags and bring them down to the man for a gift: some balsam, syrup, gum, laudanum, pistachio nuts and almonds. Also take double the money along; for you must return the money placed in the mouths of your sacks, in case a mistake was made. Take your brother too, and go back to the man. May Almighty God give you favor with the man so that he will release to you your other brother as well as Benjamin. As for me, if I must be bereft, let me be bereft."

So the men took their gift, and taking double the money with them, they went with Benjamin to Egypt and came before Joseph. When Joseph saw Benjamin with them, he said to his steward, "Bring the men into the house, and have an animal slaughtered and made ready, for the men are to dine with me at noon." He did as Joseph ordered, bringing the men to Joseph's house. They became frightened on being led to Joseph's house, and said, "It is on account of the money put back in our sacks the first time that we are brought in, so that he may seek an excuse to enslave us by treachery, and take our asses." So they went to Joseph's steward and spoke to him at the entrance of the house. "If you please, sir," they said, "once before we came down to buy food; but when we reached the stopping-place and opened our sacks, there in the mouth of his sack was each one's money in full. But we have brought it back with us, and also other money to buy food. We do not know who put the money in our sacks." "Be calm," he replied; "have no fear. Your God, the God of your fathers, put treasure in your sacks for you. I received your money." Then he brought Simeon out to them.

The man brought them into Joseph's house, gave them water to wash their feet, and fodder for their asses. Then they set out the present for Joseph's arrival at noon.

When Joseph came home, they presented him with the gift they had with them in the house, and prostrated themselves before him. He inquired about their health, and said, "Is your father, the old man of whom you spoke, in good health? Is he still living?" "Your servant, our father, is well; he is still living," they said, bowing low to him. Then Joseph looked up and saw his brother Benjamin, the son of his own mother, and said, "So this is your youngest brother of whom you spoke to me? God be gracious to you, my son," he continued. Thereupon Joseph broke off and was on the verge of tears, for his heart yearned for his brother. He retired to his room and wept.

Then he bathed his face and came out. Restraining himself, he said, "Serve the meal." It was served separately for him, for them, and for his Egyptian guests, because the Egyptians may not eat with the Hebrews; this is abhorrent to the Egyptians. They were seated in his presence in the order of age, from the oldest to the youngest; and at this they looked at one another in amazement. Joseph had portions brought to them from his own table, but Benjamin's portion was five times as much as any other's. They drank and became merry with him.

BENJAMIN AND THE SILVER CUP IN HIS SACK

Joseph gave orders to his steward, saying, "Fill the men's sacks with as much food as they will hold, and put each one's money in the mouth of his sack; but in that of the youngest put my cup, the silver cup, together with his money for the grain." The steward carried out Joseph's instructions. At daybreak the men were sent off together with their asses. They had not gone far out of the city when Joseph said to his steward, "Go, follow the men, and when you overtake them, say to them, 'Why have you returned evil for good? Why have you stolen the silver cup from me? It is the very one from which my master drinks. He will certainly guess where it is. This is an evil thing that you have done.'"

When he overtook them he repeated these words; but they replied, "Why does my lord speak this way? Far be it from your servants to do such a thing! We even brought back to you from the land of Chanaan the money we found in the mouths of our sacks. Would we then steal silver or gold from your master's house? If it is found with any one of us, he shall die, and we will be my lord's slaves." He replied, "Though it ought to be as you suggest, the one with whom it is found shall be my slave; and the rest of you shall go free."

Then each one of them quickly lowered his sack to the ground and opened it. A search was made beginning with the oldest and ending with the youngest, and the cup was found in Benjamin's sack. Then they tore their garments, and having reloaded the asses, returned to the city. Juda and his brothers arrived at Joseph's house while he was still there, so they fell to the ground before him. Joseph said to them, "What is this you have done? Did you not know that such a man as I would guess correctly?"

Juda replied, "What can we say to my lord? How can we explain matters so as to clear ourselves? God has discovered the guilt of your servants. We are indeed the slaves of my lord, both we and the one with whom the cup was found." "Far be it from me to act thus," said Joseph. "The one with whom the cup was found shall be my slave; as for the rest, go in peace to your father."

Then Juda approached him and said, "I beg you, my lord, let your servants speak to my lord, and let not your anger be aroused against your servant; you are as Pharao himself. My lord asked his servants, 'Have you a father or a brother?' And we answered my lord, 'We have an aged father, and a young brother, a child of his old age; his brother is dead, so that he is the only one left of his mother's children, and his father loves him.' Then you said to your servants, 'Bring him to me that I may look after him.' We told my lord, 'The boy cannot leave his father; his father would die if he were to leave him.' But you said to your servants, 'Unless your youngest brother comes with you, you shall not come into my presence again.' When we returned to your servant, my father, we reported to him the words of my lord. Later our father said, 'Go back and buy some food for us.' But we answered, 'We cannot go. If our youngest brother is with us, we will go down; for we may not see the man unless our youngest brother is with us.' Then your servant, my father, said to us, 'You know that my wife bore me two sons; one is gone from me, and I said: He has surely been torn to pieces; I have not seen him since. If you take this one also from me, and some harm befalls him, you will bring down my gray hairs in sorrow to the grave.' Now if I go to your servant, my father, and the boy is not with us—his life is so bound up with the life of the boy— he will die as soon as he sees that the boy is not with us; and your servants will bring down the gray hairs of your servant, our father, in sorrow to the grave. However, your servant became surety for the boy to my father, saying, 'If I do not bring him back to you, I will be guilty of a crime against you all my life.' Therefore, let your servant remain in place of the boy as a slave of my lord, but let the boy return with his brothers. How can I return to my father without the boy? Never could I witness the anguish that would come to my father!"

JOSEPH REVEALS HIS IDENTITY

Joseph could not control himself before all his attendants, so he exclaimed, "Let everyone withdraw from me." No one was with Joseph when he made himself known to his brothers. He wept aloud so that the Egyptians heard it. Joseph said to his brothers, "I am Joseph. Is my father still alive?" But his brothers could not answer him because they were terrified in his presence. Then he said to them, "Come closer to me." When they drew near, he continued, "I am your brother Joseph, whom you sold into Egypt. Do not be distressed nor angry with yourselves that you sold me here; for God sent me before you to save life. For two years now the famine has been in the land, and for five more years there will be neither plowing nor reaping. God sent me before you to preserve a remnant for you in the land, and to deliver you in a striking way. Not you but God sent me here, and made me a father to Pharao, lord of all his house, and ruler over all the land of Egypt.

"Go quickly to my father and say to him, 'Your son Joseph sends you this message: God has made me master of all Egypt; come down to me, and do not delay. You shall live in the land of Gesen and be near me, you, your sons, your grandsons, your flocks, your herds, and all that belongs to you. Five years of famine are still to come. I will provide for you there, that you, and your household, and all who belong to you may not be impoverished.' You yourselves see, and my brother Benjamin sees, that it is I who speak to you. Tell my father of my splendor in Egypt, and of all that you have seen. Hurry now and bring my father here." Then Joseph fell on the neck of his brother Benjamin and wept; and Benjamin wept on his neck. Joseph kissed all his brothers, weeping over each, and after that his brothers conversed with him.

When the news was received at Pharao's house that Joseph's brothers had arrived, Pharao and his court were pleased. Pharao said to Joseph, "Say to your brothers, 'Do this: load your animals, be off to the land of Chanaan; then come to me with your father and your families, and I will give you the best of the land of Egypt so that you shall eat the fat of the land.' Give them this command also: 'Take carts from the land of Egypt for your little ones and your wives. Bring your father and come. Do not be concerned about your goods, for the best of the whole land of Egypt is yours.'"

The sons of Israel did this. Joseph gave them carts as Pharao had commanded, and provisions for the journey. He gave each of them one festal garment, but to Benjamin he gave three hundred pieces of silver and five festal garments. Likewise to his father he sent ten asses loaded with the good things of Egypt, and ten she-asses loaded with grain, bread and provisions for his father on the journey. Then he sent his brothers on their way; and as they departed he said to them, "Do not quarrel on the way." So they went up from Egypt and came to their father Jacob in the land of Chanaan. They told him, "Joseph is still alive, and he is ruler over all the land of Egypt." But he was unmoved because he did not believe them. However, when they related to him all that Joseph had said to them, and when he saw the carts Joseph had sent to convey him, their father Jacob revived. "It is enough," said Israel. "My son Joseph is still alive; I will go and see him before I die."

Israel set out with all that belonged to him; and when he arrived at Bersabee he offered sacrifices to the God of his father Isaac. At night in a vision God said to Israel, "Jacob, Jacob." And he answered, "Here I am." Then he said, "I am God, the God of your father. Do not fear to go down to Egypt, for there I will make you a great people. I will go down to Egypt with you, and will surely bring you up again, after Joseph's hand has closed your eyes." Jacob departed from Bersabee. The sons of Israel conveyed their father Jacob, their little ones, and their wives in the carts Pharao had sent to transport him.

Israel sent Juda ahead of him to Joseph, so that he would meet him in Gesen. On their arrival in the land of Gesen, Joseph made ready his chariot and rode to meet his father Israel in Gesen. When he met him he fell on his neck, weeping long in his arms. Israel said to Joseph, "Now I can die, after seeing you still alive."

Joseph said to his brothers and to his father's household, "I shall go and inform Pharao, and say to him, 'My brothers and my father's household, who lived in the land of Chanaan, have come to me. The men are shepherds, for they breed livestock. They have brought their flocks and herds and all their possessions.' Accordingly, when he summons you and asks, 'What is your occupation?' you must answer, 'We your servants have bred livestock from our youth until now, both we and our ancestors,' in order that you may sojourn in the land of Gesen." For shepherds are all repugnant to the Egyptians.

Joseph came and told Pharao, "My father and brothers have come from the land of Chanaan with their flocks and herds and all their possessions, and they are now in the land of Gesen." He had selected five of his brothers, whom he presented to Pharao. When Pharao asked them, "What is your occupation?" they answered, "Your servants, both we and our ancestors, are shepherds. We have come to sojourn in your land, for there is no pasture for your servants' flocks, and the famine is severe in the land of Chanaan. Permit your servants to settle in the land of Gesen." Pharao said to Joseph, "Your father and your brothers have come to you. The land of Egypt is at your disposal. Settle your father and your brothers in the choicest section of the land. Let them live in the land of Gesen, and if you know of any able men among them, place them in charge of my own stock."

Then Joseph brought his father Jacob, and presented him to Pharao. Jacob greeted Pharao, who said to him, "How old are you?" Jacob answered Pharao, "The length of my pilgrimage has been one hundred and thirty years; short and wretched has been my life, nor does it compare with the years my fathers lived during their pilgrimage." Then Jacob bade Pharao good-by and left his presence.

Joseph settled his father and brothers in the land of Egypt, giving them property in the choicest section of the land, in the district of Rameses, as Pharao had ordered.

THE DEATH OF JACOB

Now Israel dwelt in Egypt, in the land of Gesen. They acquired property there, were fruitful, and became very numerous. Jacob lived seventeen years in the land of Egypt, and the length of his life was one hundred and forty-seven years. As the time approached for Israel to die, he summoned his son Joseph and said to him, "If I find favor with you, put your hand under my thigh, and act kindly and faithfully toward me. Do not bury me in Egypt, but let me rest with my fathers; carry me out of Egypt and bury me in their sepulchre." He answered, "I will do as you say." Then Jacob said, "Swear to me"; and Joseph swore to him. Then Israel bowed toward the head of the bed, and said to Joseph, "I am about to die. But God will be with you, and will lead you back to the land of your fathers." Then Jacob summoned his sons. He blessed them, and gave each his proper blessing. When Jacob had finished giving directions to his sons, he drew up his feet into the bed and expired. And he was gathered to his people.

Joseph fell on his father's face, weeping over him and kissing him. Then he ordered the physicians among his servants to embalm his father. They embalmed Israel, spending forty days at it, for it takes that much time to embalm. And the Egyptians mourned Israel for seventy days.

BURIAL IN CHANAAN

When the days of mourning him had passed, Joseph said to Pharao's household, "If I find favor with you, say to Pharao that my father at the point of death made me promise on oath to bury him in the sepulchre that he dug for himself in the land of Chanaan. Now therefore I beg to go up to bury my father, and I will return." Pharao replied, "Go up, and bury your father as he made you swear." So Joseph went to bury his father. Jacob's sons did for him what he had commanded them. They carried him into the land of Chanaan, and buried him.

After Joseph had buried his father, he returned to Egypt with his brothers and all who had gone up with him to bury his father. Joseph's brothers were fearful after their father's death, and said, "What if Joseph should hate us, and pay us back for all the harm we did him!" So they sent this message to Joseph, "Before he died, your father gave us this command, 'Thus shall you say to Joseph: Jacob begs you to forgive your brothers' crime, and the sin they committed in doing you harm.' Now we also pray that you forgive the crime of the servants of the God of your father." Joseph wept over their message to him. Then his brothers came to him in person and prostrated themselves before him, saying, "We are your slaves." But Joseph said to them, "Do not fear; can I take the place of God? You intended evil against me, but God intended it for good, to do as he has done today, namely, to save the lives of many people. Therefore do not fear. I will provide for you and your dependents." Thus he reassured them, speaking kindly to them.

THE DEATH OF JOSEPH

Joseph remained in Egypt with all his father's household. He lived one hundred and ten years. He saw Ephraim's children to the third generation. The sons of Machir too, the son of Manasse, were born on Joseph's knees.

Joseph said to his brothers, "I am about to die, but God will certainly come to you and lead you up from this land to the land which he promised on oath to Abraham, Isaac and Jacob." Joseph made the sons of Israel swear that, when God should come to them, they would carry his bones with them from that place.

Joseph died at the age of one hundred and ten years. He was embalmed and placed in a coffin in Egypt.

CHAPTER TWO

The Chosen People:
Their Struggle and Triumph

THE JEWS IN EGYPT

These are the names of the sons of Israel who, accompanied by their households, migrated with Jacob into Egypt: Ruben, Simeon, Levi and Juda; Issachar, Zabulon and Benjamin; Dan and Nephthali; Gad and Aser. The total number of the direct descendants of Jacob was seventy.

Now Joseph and all his brothers and that whole generation died. But the Israelites were fruitful and prolific. They became so numerous and strong that the land was filled with them.

Then a new king, who knew nothing of Joseph, came to power in Egypt. He said to his subjects, "Look how numerous and powerful the Israelite people are growing, more so than we ourselves! Come, let us deal shrewdly with them to stop their increase; otherwise, in time of war they too may join our enemies to fight against us, and so leave our country."

Accordingly, taskmasters were set over the Israelites to oppress them with forced labor. Thus they had to build for Pharao the supply cities of Phithom and Rameses. Yet the more they were oppressed, the more they multiplied and spread. The Egyptians, then, dreaded the Israelites and reduced them to cruel slavery, making life bitter for them with hard work in mortar and brick and all kinds of field work —the whole cruel fate of slaves.

The king of Egypt told the Hebrew midwives, one of whom was called Sephra and the other Phua, "When you act as midwives for the Hebrew women and see them giving birth, if it is a boy, kill him; but if it is a girl, she may live." The midwives, however, feared God; they did not do as the king of Egypt had ordered them, but let the boys live. So the king summoned the midwives and asked them, "Why have you acted thus, allowing the boys to live?" The midwives answered Pharao, "The Hebrew women are not like the Egyptian women. They are robust and give birth before the midwife arrives." Therefore God dealt well with the midwives. The people, too, increased and grew strong. And because the midwives feared God, he built up families for them. Pharao then commanded all his subjects, "Throw into the river every boy that is born to the Hebrews, but you may let all the girls live."

THE BIRTH OF MOSES

Now a certain man of the house of Levi married a Levite woman, who conceived and bore a son. Seeing that he was a goodly child, she hid him for three months. When she could hide him no longer, she took a papyrus basket, daubed it with bitumen and pitch, and putting the child in it, placed it among the reeds on the river bank. His sister stationed herself at a distance to find out what would happen to him.

Pharao's daughter came down to the river to bathe, while her maids walked along the river bank. Noticing the basket among the reeds, she sent her handmaid to fetch it. On opening it, she looked, and lo, there was a baby boy, crying! She was moved with pity for him and said, "It is one of the Hebrews' children." Then his sister asked Pharao's daughter, "Shall I go and call one of the Hebrew women to nurse the child for you?" "Yes, do so," she answered. So the maiden went and called the child's own mother. Pharao's daughter said to her, "Take this child and nurse it for me, and I will repay you." The woman therefore took the child and nursed it. When the child grew, she brought him to Pharao's daughter, who adopted him as her son and called him Moses; for she said, "I drew him out of the water."

MURDER AND FLIGHT

On one occasion, after Moses had grown up, when he visited his kinsmen and witnessed their forced labor, he saw an Egyptian striking a Hebrew, one of his own kinsmen. Looking about and seeing no one, he slew the Egyptian and hid him in the sand. The next day he went out again, and now two Hebrews were fighting! So he asked the culprit, "Why are you striking your fellow Hebrew?" But he replied, "Who has appointed you ruler and judge over us? Are you thinking of killing me as you killed the Egyptian?" Then Moses became afraid and thought, "The affair must certainly be known."

Pharao, too, heard of the affair and sought to put him to death. But Moses fled from him and stayed in the land of Madian. As he was seated there by a well, seven daughters of a priest of Madian came to draw water and fill the troughs to water their father's flock. But some shepherds came and drove them away. Then Moses got up and defended them and watered their flock. When they returned to their father Raguel, he said to them, "How is it you have returned so soon today?" They answered, "An Egyptian saved us from the interference of the shepherds. He even drew water for us and watered the flock!" "Where is the man?" he asked his daughters. "Why did you leave him there? Invite him to have something to eat."

Moses agreed to live with him, and the man gave him his daughter Sepphora in marriage. She bore him a son, whom he named Gersam; for he said, "I am a stranger in a foreign land."

GOD REMEMBERS HIS COVENANT

A long time passed, during which the king of Egypt died. Still the Israelites groaned and cried out because of their slavery. As their cry for release went up to God, he heard their groaning and was mindful of his covenant with Abraham, Isaac and Jacob. He saw the Israelites and knew. . . .

Meanwhile Moses was tending the flock of his father-in-law Jethro, the priest of Madian. Leading the flock across the desert, he came to Horeb, the mountain of God. There an angel of the Lord appeared to him in fire flaming out of a bush. As he looked on, he was surprised to see that the bush, though on fire, was not consumed. So Moses decided, "I must go over to look at this remarkable sight, and see why the bush is not burned."

When the Lord saw him coming over to look at it more closely, God called out to him from the bush, "Moses! Moses!" He answered, "Here I am." God said, "Come no nearer! Remove the sandals from your feet, for the place where you stand is holy ground. I am the God of your father," he continued, "the God of Abraham, the God of Isaac, the God of Jacob." Moses hid his face, for he was afraid to look at God. But the Lord said, "I have witnessed the affliction of my people in Egypt and have heard their cry of complaint against their slave drivers, so I know well what they are suffering. Therefore I have come down to rescue them from the hands of the Egyptians and lead them out of that land into a good and spacious land, a land flowing with milk and honey. So indeed the cry of the Israelites has reached me, and I have truly noted that the Egyptians are oppressing them. Come, now! I will send you to Pharao to lead my people, the Israelites, out of Egypt."

But Moses said to God, "Who am I that I should go to Pharao and lead the Israelites out of Egypt?" He answered, "I will be with you; and this shall be your proof that it is I who have sent you: when you bring my people out of Egypt, you will worship God on this very mountain." "But," said Moses to God, "when I go to the Israelites and say to them, 'The God of your fathers has sent me to you,' if they ask me, 'What is his name?' what am I to tell them?" God replied, "I am who am." Then he added, "This is what you shall tell the Israelites: I Am sent me to you."

God spoke further to Moses, "Thus shall you say to the Israelites: The Lord, the God of your fathers, has sent me to you.

> "This is my name forever;
> this is my title for all generations.

"Go and assemble the elders of all the Israelites, and tell them: the Lord, the God of your fathers, has appeared to me and said: I am concerned about you and about the way you are being treated in Egypt; so I have decided to lead you up out of the misery of Egypt into a land flowing with milk and honey.

"Thus they will heed your message. Then you and the elders of Israel shall go to the king of Egypt and say to him: The Lord, the God of the Hebrews, has sent us word. Permit us, then, to go a three days' journey in the desert, that we may offer sacrifice to the Lord, our God.

"Yet I know that the king of Egypt will not allow you to go unless he is forced. I will stretch out my hand, therefore, and smite Egypt by doing all kinds of wondrous deeds there. After that he will send you away. I will even make the Egyptians so well-disposed toward this people that, when you leave, you will not go empty-handed. Every woman shall ask her neighbor and her house guest for silver and gold articles and for clothing to put on your sons and daughters. Thus you will despoil the Egyptians."

"But," objected Moses, "suppose they will not believe me, nor listen to my plea? For they may say, 'The Lord did not appear to you.'" The Lord therefore asked him, "What is that in your hand?" "A staff," he answered. The Lord then said, "Throw it on the ground." When he threw it on the ground it was changed into a serpent, and Moses shied away from it. "Now, put out your hand," the Lord said to him, "and take hold of its tail." So he put out his hand and laid hold of it, and it became a staff in his hand. "This will take place so that they may believe," he continued, "that the Lord, the God of their fathers, did appear to you."

Again the Lord said to him, "Put your hand in your bosom." He put it in his bosom, and when he withdrew it, to his surprise his hand was leprous, like snow. The Lord then said, "Now, put your hand back in your bosom." Moses put his hand back in his bosom, and when he withdrew it, to his surprise it was again like the rest of his body. "If they will not believe you, nor heed the message of the first sign, they should believe the message of the second. And if they will not believe even these two signs, nor heed your plea, take some water from the river and pour it on the dry land. The water you take from the river will become blood on the dry land."

Moses, however, said to the Lord, "If you please, Lord, I have never been eloquent, neither in the past, nor recently, nor now that you have spoken to your servant; but I am slow of speech and tongue." The Lord said to him, "Who gives one man speech and makes another deaf and dumb? Or who gives sight to one and makes another blind? Is it not I, the Lord? Go, then! It is I who will assist you in speaking and will teach you what you are to say." Yet he insisted, "If you please, Lord, send someone else!" Then the Lord became angry with Moses and said, "Have you not your brother, Aaron the Levite? I know that he is an eloquent speaker. Besides, he is now on his way to meet you. You are to speak to him, then, and put the words in his mouth. I will assist both you and him in speaking and will teach the two of you what you are to do. He shall speak to the people for you: he shall be your spokesman, and you shall be as God to him. Take this staff in your hand; with it you are to perform signs."

MOSES JOURNEYS TO EGYPT

After this Moses returned to his father-in-law Jethro and said to him, "Let me go back, please, to my kinsmen in Egypt, to see whether they are still living." Jethro replied, "Go in peace." In Madian the Lord said to Moses, "Go back to Egypt, for all the men who sought your life are dead." So Moses took his wife and his sons, and started back to the land of Egypt, with them riding the ass. The staff of God he carried with him. The Lord said to him, "On your return to Egypt, see that you perform before Pharao all the wonders I have put in your power. I will make him obstinate, however, so that he will not let the people go. So you shall say to Pharao: Thus says the Lord: Israel is my son, my first-born. Hence I tell you: Let my son go, that he may serve me. If you refuse to let him go, I warn you, I will kill your son, your first-born."

GOD SPEAKS TO AARON

The Lord said to Aaron, "Go into the desert to meet Moses." So he went, and when they met at the mountain of God, Aaron kissed him. Moses informed him of all the Lord had said in sending him, and of the various signs he had enjoined upon him. Then Moses and Aaron went and assembled all the elders of the Israelites. Aaron told them everything the Lord had said to Moses, and he performed the signs before the people. The people believed, and when they heard that the Lord was concerned about them and had seen their affliction, they bowed down in worship.

PHARAO PUNISHES THE JEWS

After that, Moses and Aaron went to Pharao and said, "Thus says the Lord, the God of Israel: Let my people go, that they may celebrate a feast to me in the desert." Pharao answered, "Who is the Lord, that I should heed his plea to let Israel go? I do not know the Lord; even if I did, I would not let Israel go." They replied, "The God of the Hebrews has sent us word. Let us go a three days' journey in the desert, that we may offer sacrifice to the Lord, our God; otherwise he will punish us with pestilence or the sword."

The king of Egypt answered them, "What do you mean, Moses and Aaron, by taking the people away from their work? Off to your labor! Look how numerous the people of the land are already," continued Pharao, "and yet you would give them rest from their labor!"

That very day Pharao gave the taskmasters and foremen of the people this order: "You shall no longer supply the people with straw for their brickmaking as you have previously done. Let them go and gather straw themselves! Yet you shall levy upon them the same quota of bricks as they have previously made. Do not reduce it. They are lazy; that is why they are crying, 'Let us go to offer sacrifice to our God.' Increase the work for the men, so that they keep their mind on it and pay no attention to lying words."

So the taskmasters and foremen of the people went out and told them, "Thus says Pharao: I will not provide you with straw. Go and gather the straw yourselves, wherever you can find it. Yet there must not be the slightest reduction in your work." The people, then, scattered throughout the land of Egypt to gather stubble for straw, while the taskmasters kept driving them on, saying, "Finish your work, the same daily amount as when your straw was supplied."

The foremen of the Israelites, whom the taskmasters of Pharao had placed over them, were beaten, and were asked, "Why have you not completed your prescribed amount of bricks yesterday and today, as before?"

Then the Israelite foremen came and made this appeal to Pharao: "Why do you treat your servants in this manner? No straw is supplied to your servants, and still we are told to make bricks. Look how your servants are beaten! It is you who are at fault." Pharao answered, "It is just because you are lazy that you keep saying, 'Let us go and offer sacrifice to the Lord.' Off to work, then! Straw shall not be provided for you, but you must still deliver your quota of bricks."

The Israelite foremen knew they were in a sorry plight, having been told not to reduce the daily amount of bricks. When, therefore, they left Pharao and came upon Moses and Aaron, who were waiting to meet them, they said to them, "The Lord look upon you and judge! You have brought us into bad odor with Pharao and his servants and have put a sword in their hands to slay us."

MOSES PLEADS WITH GOD

Moses again had recourse to the Lord and said, "Lord, why do you treat this people so badly? And why did you send me on such a mission? Ever since I went to Pharao to speak in your name, he has maltreated this people of yours, and you have done nothing to rescue them." Then the Lord answered Moses, "Now you shall see what I will do to Pharao. Forced by my mighty hand, he will send them away; compelled by my outstretched arm, he will drive them from his land."

God also said to Moses, "I am the Lord. As God the Almighty

I appeared to Abraham, Isaac and Jacob, but my name, Lord, I did not make known to them. I also established my covenant with them, to give them the land of Chanaan, the land in which they were living as aliens. And now that I have heard the groaning of the Israelites, whom the Egyptians are treating as slaves, I am mindful of my covenant. Therefore, say to the Israelites: I am the Lord. I will free you from the forced labor of the Egyptians and will deliver you from their slavery. I will rescue you by my outstretched arm and with mighty acts of judgment. I will take you as my own people, and you shall have me as your God. You will know that I, the Lord, am your God when I free you from the labor of the Egyptians and bring you into the land which I swore to give to Abraham, Isaac and Jacob. I will give it to you as your own possession—I, the Lord!" But when Moses told this to the Israelites, they would not listen to him because of their dejection and hard slavery.

On the day the Lord spoke to Moses, he said, "I am the Lord. Repeat to Pharao all that I tell you." But Moses protested to the Lord, "If the Israelites would not listen to me, how can it be that Pharao will listen to me, poor speaker that I am!" The Lord answered him, "See! I have made you as God to Pharao, and Aaron your brother shall act as your prophet. You shall tell him all that I command you. In turn, Aaron shall tell Pharao to let the Israelites leave his land."

Yet he insisted, "If you please, Lord, send someone else!" Then the Lord became angry with Moses; still, the Lord, to bring the Israelites out of Egypt, spoke to Moses and Aaron and gave them his orders regarding both the Israelites and Pharao.

GOD MANIFESTS HIS POWER THROUGH MOSES

The Lord told Moses and Aaron, "If Pharao demands that you work a sign or wonder, you shall say to Aaron: Take your staff and throw it down before Pharao, and it will be changed into a snake." Then Moses and Aaron went to Pharao and did as the Lord had commanded. Aaron threw his staff down before Pharao and his servants, and it was changed into a snake. Pharao, in turn, summoned wise men and sorcerers, and they also, the magicians of Egypt, did likewise by their magic arts. Each one threw down his staff, and it was changed into a snake. But Aaron's staff swallowed their staffs. Pharao, however, was obstinate and would not listen to them, just as the Lord had foretold.

THE TEN PLAGUES OF EGYPT

Then the Lord said to Moses, "Pharao is obdurate in refusing to let the people go. Tomorrow morning, when he sets out for the water, go and present yourself by the river bank, holding in your hand the staff that turned into a serpent. Say to him: The Lord, the God of the Hebrews, sent me to you with the message: Let my people go to worship me in the desert. But as yet you have not listened. The Lord now says: This is how you shall know that I am the Lord. I will strike the water of the river with the staff I hold, and it shall be changed into blood. The fish in the river shall die, and the river itself shall become so polluted that the Egyptians will be unable to drink its water."

The Lord then said to Moses, "Say to Aaron: Take your staff and stretch out your hand over the waters of Egypt—their streams and canals and pools, all their supplies of water—that they may become blood. Throughout the land of Egypt there shall be blood, even in the wooden pails and stone jars."

Moses and Aaron did as the Lord had commanded. Aaron raised his staff and struck the water of the river in full view of Pharao and his servants, and all the water of the river was changed into blood. The fish in the river died, and the river itself became so polluted that the Egyptians could not drink its water. There was blood throughout the land of Egypt. But the Egyptian magicians did the same by their magic arts. So Pharao remained obstinate and would not listen to Moses and Aaron, just as the Lord had foretold. He turned away and went into his house, with no concern even for this. All the Egyptians had to dig in the neighborhood of the river for drinking water, since they could not drink the river water.

Seven days passed after the Lord had struck the river. Then the Lord said to Moses, "Go to Pharao and tell him: Thus says the Lord: Let my people go to worship me. If you refuse to let them go, I warn you, I will send a plague of frogs over all your territory. The river will teem with frogs. They will come up into your palace and into your bedroom and onto your bed, into the houses of your servants, too, and your subjects, even into your ovens and your kneading bowls."

The Lord then told Moses, "Say to Aaron: Stretch out your hand and your staff over the streams and canals and pools, to make frogs overrun the land of Egypt." Aaron stretched out his hand over the

49

waters of Egypt, and the frogs came up and covered the land of Egypt. But the magicians did the same by their magic arts.

Then Pharao summoned Moses and Aaron and said, "Pray the Lord to remove the frogs from me and my subjects, and I will let the people go to offer sacrifice to the Lord." Moses answered Pharao, "Do me the favor of appointing the time when I am to pray for you and your servants and your subjects, that the frogs may be taken away from you and your houses and be left only in the river." "Tomorrow," said Pharao. Then Moses replied, "It shall be as you have said, so that you may learn that there is none like the Lord, our God."

After Moses and Aaron left Pharao's presence, Moses implored the Lord to fulfill the promise he had made to Pharao about the frogs; and the Lord did as Moses had asked. The frogs in the houses and courtyards and fields died off. Heaps and heaps of them were gathered up, and there was a stench in the land. But when Pharao saw that there was a respite, he became obdurate and would not listen to them, just as the Lord had foretold.

Thereupon the Lord said to Moses, "Tell Aaron to stretch out his staff and strike the dust of the earth, that it may be turned into gnats throughout the land of Egypt." They did so. Aaron stretched out his hand, and with his staff he struck the dust of the earth, and gnats came upon man and beast. The dust of the earth was turned into gnats throughout the land of Egypt. Though the magicians tried to bring forth gnats by their magic arts, they could not do so. As the gnats infested man and beast, the magicians said to Pharao, "This is the finger of God." Yet Pharao remained obstinate and would not listen to them, just as the Lord had foretold.

Again the Lord told Moses, "Early tomorrow morning present yourself to Pharao when he goes forth to the water, and say to him: Thus says the Lord: Let my people go to worship me. If you will not let my people go, I warn you, I will loose swarms of flies upon you and your servants and your subjects and your houses. The houses of the Egyptians and the very ground on which they stand shall be filled with swarms of flies. But on that day I will make an exception of the land of Gesen: there shall be no flies where my people dwell, that you may distinction between my people and your people. This sign shall take place tomorrow." This the Lord did. Thick swarms of flies entered the house of Pharao and the houses of his servants; throughout Egypt the land was infested with flies.

Then Pharao summoned Moses and Aaron and said to them, "Go

and offer sacrifice to your God in this land." But Moses replied, "It is not right to do so, for the sacrifices we offer to the Lord, our God, are an abomination to the Egyptians. If before their very eyes we offer sacrifices which are an abomination to them, will not the Egyptians stone us? We must go a three days' journey in the desert to offer sacrifice to the Lord, our God, as he commands us." "Well, then," said Pharao, "I will let you go to offer sacrifice to the Lord, your God, in the desert, provided that you do not go too far away and that you pray for me." Moses answered, "As soon as I leave your presence I will pray to the Lord that the flies may depart tomorrow from Pharao and his servants and his subjects. Pharao, however, must not play false again by refusing to let the people go to offer sacrifice to the Lord." When Moses left Pharao's presence, he prayed to the Lord; and the Lord did as Moses had asked. He removed the flies from Pharao and his servants and subjects. Not one remained. But once more Pharao became obdurate and would not let the people go.

Then the Lord said to Moses, "Go to Pharao and tell him: Thus says the Lord, the God of the Hebrews: Let my people go to worship me. If you refuse to let them go and persist in holding them, I warn you, the Lord will afflict all your livestock in the field—your horses, asses, camels, herds and flocks—with a very severe pestilence. But the Lord will distinguish between the livestock of Israel and that of Egypt, so that none belonging to the Israelites will die." And setting a definite time, the Lord added, "Tomorrow the Lord shall do this in the land." And on the next day the Lord did so. All the livestock of the Egyptians died, but not one beast belonging to the Israelites. But though Pharao's messengers informed him that not even one beast belonging to the Israelites had died, he still remained obdurate and would not let the people go.

Then the Lord said to Moses and Aaron, "Take a double handful of soot from a furnace, and in the presence of Pharao let Moses scatter it toward the sky. It will then turn into fine dust over the whole land of Egypt and cause festering boils on man and beast throughout the land."

So they took soot from a furnace and stood in the presence of Pharao. Moses scattered it toward the sky, and it caused festering boils on man and beast. The magicians could not stand in Moses' presence, for there were boils on the magicians no less than on the rest of the Egyptians. But the Lord made Pharao obstinate, and he would not listen to them, just as the Lord had foretold to Moses.

Then the Lord said to Moses, "Early tomorrow morning present yourself to Pharao and say to him: Thus says the Lord, the God of the Hebrews: Let my people go to worship me, or this time I will hurl all my blows upon you and your servants and your subjects, that you may know that there is none like me anywhere on earth. For by now I would have stretched out my hand and struck you and your subjects with such pestilence as would wipe you from the earth. But this is why I have spared you: to show you my power and to make my name resound throughout the earth! Will you still block the way for my people by refusing to let them go? I warn you, then, tomorrow at this hour I will rain down such fierce hail as there has never been in Egypt from the day the nation was founded up to the present. Therefore, order all your livestock and whatever else you have in the open fields to be brought to a place of safety. Whatever man or beast remains in the fields and is not brought to shelter shall die when the hail comes upon them." Some of Pharao's servants feared the warning of the Lord and hurried their servants and livestock off to shelter. Others, however, did not take the warning of the Lord to heart and left their servants and livestock in the fields.

The Lord then said to Moses, "Stretch out your hand toward the sky, that hail may fall upon the entire land of Egypt, on man and beast and every growing thing in the land of Egypt." When Moses stretched out his staff toward the sky, the Lord sent forth hail and peals of thunder. Lightning flashed toward the earth, and the Lord rained down hail upon the land of Egypt: and lightning constantly flashed through the hail, such fierce hail as had never been seen in the land since Egypt became a nation. It struck down every man and beast that was in the open throughout the land of Egypt; it beat down every growing thing and splintered every tree in the fields. Only in the land of Gesen, where the Israelites dwelt, was there no hail.

Then Pharao summoned Moses and Aaron and said to them, "I have sinned again! The Lord is just; it is I and my subjects who are at fault. Pray to the Lord, for we have had enough of God's thunder and hail. Then I will let you go; you need stay no longer." Moses replied, "As soon as I leave the city I will extend my hands to the Lord; the thunder will cease, and there will be no more hail. Thus you shall learn that the earth is the Lord's. But you and your servants, I know, do not yet fear the Lord God."

When Moses had left Pharao's presence and had gone out of the city, he extended his hands to the Lord. Then the thunder and the hail ceased, and the rain no longer poured down upon the earth. But Pharao, seeing that the rain and hail and thunder had ceased, sinned again: he with his servants became obdurate, and in his obstinacy he would not let the Israelites go, as the Lord had foretold through Moses.

Then the Lord said to Moses, "Go to Pharao, for I have made him and his servants obdurate in order that I may perform these signs of mine among them and that you may recount to your son and grandson how ruthlessly I dealt with the Egyptians and what signs I wrought among them, so that you may know that I am the Lord."

So Moses and Aaron went to Pharao and told him, "Thus says the Lord, the God of the Hebrews: How long will you refuse to submit to me? Let my people go to worship me. If you refuse to let my people go, I warn you, tomorrow I will bring locusts into your country. They shall cover the ground, so that the ground itself will not be visible. They shall eat up the remnant you saved unhurt from the hail, as well as all the foliage that has since sprouted in your fields. They shall fill your houses and the houses of your servants and of all the Egyptians; such a sight your fathers or grandfathers have not seen from the day they first settled on this soil up to the present day." With that he turned and left Pharao.

But Pharao's servants said to him, "How long must he be a menace to us? Let the men go to worship the Lord, their God. Do you not realize that Egypt is being destroyed?" So Moses and Aaron were brought back to Pharao, who said to them, "You may go and worship the Lord, your God. But how many of you will go?" "Young and old must go with us," Moses answered, "our sons and daughters as well as our flocks and herds must accompany us. That is what a feast of the Lord means to us." "The Lord help you," Pharao replied, "if I ever let your little ones go with you! Clearly, you have some evil in mind. No, no! Just you men can go and worship the Lord. After all, that is what you want." With that they were driven from Pharao's presence.

The Lord then said to Moses, "Stretch out your hand over the land of Egypt, that locusts may swarm over it and eat up all the vegetation and whatever the hail has left." So Moses stretched out his staff over the land of Egypt, and the Lord set an east wind blowing over the land all that day and all that night. At dawn the east wind brought the locusts. They swarmed over the whole land of Egypt and settled down on every part of it. Never before had there been such a fierce swarm of locusts, nor will there ever be. They covered the surface of the whole land, till it was black with them. They ate up all the vegetation in the land and the fruit of whatever trees the hail had spared. Nothing green was left on any tree or plant throughout the land of Egypt.

Hastily Pharao summoned Moses and Aaron and said, "I have sinned against the Lord, your God, and against you. But now, do forgive me my sin once more, and pray the Lord, your God, to take at least this deadly pest from me." When Moses left the presence of Pharao, he prayed to the Lord, and the Lord changed the wind to a very strong west wind, which took up the locusts and hurled them into the Red Sea. But though not a single locust remained within the confines of Egypt, the Lord made Pharao obstinate, and he would not let the Israelites go.

Then the Lord said to Moses, "Stretch out your hand toward the sky, that over the land of Egypt there may be such intense darkness that one can feel it." So Moses stretched out his hand toward the sky, and there was dense darkness throughout the land of Egypt for three days. Men could not see one another, nor could they move from where they were, for three days. But all the Israelites had light where they dwelt.

Pharao then summoned Moses and Aaron and said, "Go and worship the Lord. Your little ones, too, may go with you. But your flocks and herds must remain." Moses replied, "You must also grant us sacrifices and holocausts to offer up to the Lord, our God. Hence, our livestock also must go with us. Not an animal must be left behind. Some of them we must sacrifice to the Lord, our God, but we ourselves shall not know which ones we must sacrifice to him until we arrive at the place itself." But the Lord made Pharao obstinate, and he would not let them go. "Leave my presence," Pharao said to him, "and see to it that you do not appear before me again! The day you appear before me you shall die!" Moses replied, "Well said! I will never appear before you again."

Then the Lord told Moses, "One more plague will I bring upon Pharao and upon Egypt. After that he will let you depart. In fact, he will not merely let you go; he will drive you away. Instruct your people that every man is to ask his neighbor, and every woman her neighbor, for silver and gold articles and for clothing." The Lord indeed made the Egyptians well-disposed toward the people; Moses himself was very highly regarded by Pharao's servants and the people in the land of Egypt.

Moses then said, "Thus says the Lord: At midnight I will go

forth through Egypt. Every first-born in this land shall die, from the first-born of Pharao on the throne to the first-born of the slave-girl at the handmill, as well as all the first-born of the animals. Then there shall be loud wailing throughout the land of Egypt, such as has never been, nor will ever be again. But among the Israelites and their animals not even a dog shall growl, so that you may know how the Lord distinguishes between the Egyptians and the Israelites. All these servants of yours shall then come down to me, and prostrate before me, they shall beg me, 'Leave us, you and all your followers!' Only then will I depart." With that he left Pharao's presence in hot anger.

THE PASSOVER OF THE LORD

The Lord said to Moses and Aaron, "This month shall stand at the head of your calendar; you shall reckon it the first month of the year. Tell the whole community of Israel: On the tenth of this month every one of your families must procure for itself a lamb, one apiece for each household. If a family is too small for a whole lamb, it shall join the nearest household in procuring one and shall share in the lamb in proportion to the number of persons who partake of it. The lamb must be a year-old male and without blemish. You may take it from either the sheep or the goats. You shall keep it until the fourteenth day of this month, and then, with the whole assembly of Israel present, it shall be slaughtered during the evening twilight. They shall take some of its blood and apply it to the two doorposts and the lintel of every house in which they partake of the lamb. That same night they shall eat its roasted flesh with unleavened bread and bitter herbs. It shall not be eaten raw or boiled, but roasted whole, with its head and shanks and inner organs. None of it must be kept beyond the next morning; whatever is left over in the morning shall be burned up.

"This is how you are to eat it: with your loins girt, sandals on your feet and your staff in hand, you shall eat like those who are in flight. It is the Passover of the Lord. For on this same night I will go through Egypt, striking down every first-born of the land, both man and beast, and executing judgment on all the gods of Egypt—I, the Lord! But the blood will mark the houses where you are. Seeing the blood, I will pass over you; thus, when I strike the land of Egypt, no destructive blow will come upon you. This day shall be a memorial feast for you, which all your generations shall celebrate with pilgrimage to the Lord, as a perpetual institution."

Moses called all the elders of Israel and said to them, "Go and procure lambs for your families, and slaughter them as Passover victims. Then take a bunch of hyssop, and dipping it in the blood that is in the basin, sprinkle the lintel and the two doorposts with this blood. But none of you shall go outdoors until morning. For the Lord will go by, striking down the Egyptians. Seeing the blood on the lintel and the two doorposts, the Lord will pass over that door and not let the destroyer come into your houses to strike you down.

"You shall observe this as a perpetual ordinance for yourselves and your descendants. Thus, you must also observe this rite when you have entered the land which the Lord will give you as he promised. When your children ask you, 'What does this rite of yours mean?' you shall reply, 'This is the Passover sacrifice of the Lord, who passed over the houses of the Israelites in Egypt; when he struck down the Egyptians, he spared our houses.'"

Then the people bowed down in worship, and the Israelites went and did as the Lord had commanded Moses and Aaron.

THE FIRST-BORN ARE KILLED

At midnight the Lord slew every first-born in the land of Egypt, from the first-born of Pharao on the throne to the first-born of the prisoner in the dungeon, as well as all the first-born of the animals. Pharao arose in the night, he and all his servants and all the Egyptians; and there was loud wailing throughout Egypt, for there was not a house without its dead.

PHARAO RELENTS

During the night Pharao summoned Moses and Aaron and said, "Leave my people at once, you and the Israelites with you! Go and worship the Lord as you said. Take your flocks, too, and your herds, as you demanded, and begone; and you will be doing me a favor."

The Egyptians likewise urged the people on, to hasten their departure from the land; they thought that otherwise they would all die. The people, therefore, took their dough before it was leavened, in their kneading bowls wrapped in their cloaks on their shoulders. The Israelites did as Moses had commanded: they asked the Egyptians for articles of silver and gold and for clothing. The Lord indeed had made the Egyptians so well-disposed toward the people that they let them have whatever they asked for. Thus did they despoil the Egyptians.

THE JEWS LEAVE EGYPT

The Israelites set out from Rameses for Socchoth, about six hundred thousand men on foot, not counting the children. A crowd of mixed ancestry also went up with them, besides their livestock, very numerous flocks and herds. Since the dough they had brought out of Egypt was not leavened, they baked it into unleavened loaves. They had been rushed out of Egypt and had no opportunity even to prepare food for the journey.

The time the Israelites had stayed in Egypt was four hundred and thirty years. At the end of four hundred and thirty years, all the hosts of the Lord left the land of Egypt on this very date. This was a night of vigil for the Lord, as he led them out of the land of Egypt; so on this same night all the Israelites must keep a vigil for the Lord throughout their generations.

Now, when Pharao let the people go, God did not lead them by way of the Philistines' land, though this was the nearest; for he thought, should the people see that they would have to fight, they might change their minds and return to Egypt. Instead, he rerouted them toward the Red Sea by way of the desert road. In battle array the Israelites marched out of Egypt. Moses also took Joseph's bones along, for Joseph had made the Israelites swear solemnly that, when God should come to them, they would carry his bones away with them.

Setting out from Socchoth, they camped at Etham near the edge of the desert.

The Lord preceded them, in the daytime by means of a column of cloud to show them the way, and at night by means of a column of fire to give them light. Thus they could travel both day and night. Neither the column of cloud by day nor the column of fire by night ever left its place in front of the people.

Then the Lord said to Moses, "Tell the Israelites to turn about and camp before Phi-hahiroth, between Magdol and the sea. You shall camp in front of Baal-Saphon, just opposite, by the sea. Pharao will then say, 'The Israelites are wandering about aimlessly in the land. The desert has closed in on them.' Thus will I make Pharao so obstinate that he will pursue them. Then I will receive glory through

Pharao and all his army, and the Egyptians will know that I am the Lord."

This the Israelites did. When it was reported to the king of Egypt that the people had fled, Pharao and his servants changed their minds about them. "What have we done!" they exclaimed. "Why, we have released Israel from our service!" So Pharao made his chariots ready and mustered his soldiers—six hundred first-class chariots and all the other chariots of Egypt, with warriors on them all. So obstinate had the Lord made Pharao that he pursued the Israelites even while they were marching away in triumph. The Egyptians, then, pursued them; Pharao's whole army, his horses, chariots and charioteers, caught up with them as they lay encamped by the sea, at Phi-hahiroth, in front of Baal-Saphon.

THE CROSSING OF THE RED SEA

Pharao was already near when the Israelites looked up and saw that the Egyptians were on the march in pursuit of them. In great fright they cried out to the Lord. And they complained to Moses, "Were there no burial places in Egypt that you had to bring us out here to die in the desert? Why did you do this to us? Why did you bring us out of Egypt? Did we not tell you this in Egypt, when we said, 'Leave us alone. Let us serve the Egyptians'? Far better for us to be the slaves of the Egyptians than to die in the desert." But Moses answered the people, "Fear not! Stand your ground, and you will see the victory the Lord will win for you today. These Egyptians whom you see today you will never see again. The Lord himself will fight for you; you have only to keep still."

Then the Lord said to Moses, "Why are you crying out to me? Tell the Israelites to go forward. And you, lift up your staff and, with hand outstretched over the sea, split the sea in two, that the Israelites may pass through it on dry land. But I will make the Egyptians so obstinate that they will go in after them. Then I will receive glory through Pharao and all his army."

The angel of God, who had been leading Israel's camp, now moved and went around behind them. The column of cloud also, leaving the front, took up its place behind them, so that it came between the camp of the Egyptians and that of Israel. But the cloud now became dark, and thus the night passed without the rival camps coming any closer together all night long. Then Moses stretched out his hand over the sea, and the Lord swept the sea with a strong east wind throughout the night and so turned it into dry land. When the water was thus divided, the Israelites marched into the midst of the sea on dry land, with the water like a wall to their right and to their left.

THE DESTRUCTION OF THE EGYPTIANS

The Egyptians followed in pursuit; all Pharao's horses and chariots and charioteers went after them right into the midst of the sea. In the night watch just before dawn the Lord cast through the column of the fiery cloud upon the Egyptian force a glance that threw it into a panic; and he so clogged their chariot wheels that they could hardly drive. With that the Egyptians sounded the retreat before Israel, because the Lord was fighting for them against the Egyptians.

Then the Lord told Moses, "Stretch out your hand over the sea, that the water may flow back upon the Egyptians, upon their chariots and their charioteers." So Moses stretched out his hand over the sea, and at dawn the sea flowed back to its normal depth. The Egyptians were fleeing head on toward the sea, when the Lord hurled them into its midst. As the water flowed back, it covered the chariots and the charioteers of Pharao's whole army which had followed the Israelites into the sea. Not a single one of them escaped. But the Israelites had marched on dry land through the midst of the sea, with the water like a wall to their right and to their left. Thus the Lord saved Israel on that day from the power of the Egyptians. When Israel saw the Egyptians lying dead on the seashore and beheld the great power that the Lord had shown against the Egyptians, they feared the Lord and believed in him and in his servant Moses.

SONG OF THE HEBREWS

Then Moses and the Israelites sang this song to the Lord:

I will sing to the Lord, for he is gloriously triumphant;
  horse and chariot he has cast into the sea.
My strength and my courage is the Lord,
  and he has been my savior.
He is my God, I praise him;
  the God of my father, I extol him.

59

The Lord is a warrior,
  Lord is his name!
Pharao's chariots and army he hurled into the sea;
  the elite of his officers were submerged in the Red Sea.

The flood waters covered them,
  they sank into the depths like a stone.

Your right hand, O Lord, magnificent in power,
  your right hand, O Lord, has shattered the enemy.
In your great majesty you overthrew your adversaries;
  you loosed your wrath to consume them like stubble.
At a breath of your anger the waters piled up,
  the flowing waters stood like a mound,
  the flood waters congealed in the midst of the sea.

The enemy boasted, "I will pursue and overtake them;
  I will divide the spoils and have my fill of them;
  I will draw my sword; my hand shall despoil them!"
When your wind blew, the sea covered them;
  like lead they sank in the mighty waters.

Who is like to you among the gods, O Lord?
  Who is like to you, magnificent in holiness?
O terrible in renown, worker of wonders,
  when you stretched out your right hand, the earth swallowed
    them!
In your mercy you led the people you redeemed;
  in your strength you guided them to your holy dwelling.
The nations heard and quaked;
  anguish gripped the dwellers in Philistia.
Then were the princes of Edom dismayed;
  trembling seized the chieftains of Moab;
All the dwellers in Chanaan melted away;
  terror and dread fell upon them.
By the might of your arm they were frozen like stone,
  while your people, O Lord, passed over,
  while the people you had made your own passed over.

And you brought them in and planted them on the moun-
    tain of your inheritance—

the place where you made your seat, O Lord,
the sanctuary, O Lord, which your hands established.

The Lord shall reign forever and ever.

They sang thus because Pharao's horses and chariots and chariot-eers had gone into the sea, and the Lord made the waters of the sea flow back upon them, though the Israelites had marched on dry land through the midst of the sea. So the prophetess Mariam, Aaron's sister, took a tambourine in her hand, while all the women went out after her with tambourines, dancing; and she answered them with the refrain:

Sing to the Lord, for he is gloriously triumphant;
horse and chariot he has cast into the sea.

THE JEWS BECOME IMPATIENT

Then Moses led Israel forward from the Red Sea, and they marched out to the desert of Sur. After traveling for three days through the desert without finding water, they arrived at Mara, where they could not drink the water, because it was too bitter. As the people grumbled against Moses, saying, "What are we to drink?" he appealed to the Lord, who pointed out to him a certain piece of wood. When he threw this into the water, the water became fresh.

It was here that the Lord, in making rules and regulations for them, put them to the test. "If you really listen to the voice of the Lord, your God," he told them, "and do what is right in his eyes: if you heed his commandments and keep all his precepts, I will not afflict you with any of the diseases with which I afflicted the Egyptians; for I, the Lord, am your healer."

Then they came to Elim, where there were twelve springs of water and seventy palm trees, and they camped there near the water.

Having set out from Elim, the whole Israelite community came into the desert of Sin, which is between Elim and Sinai, on the fifteenth day of the second month after their departure from the land of Egypt. Here in the desert the whole Israelite community grumbled against Moses and Aaron. The Israelites said to them, "Would that we had died at the Lord's hand in the land of Egypt, as we sat by our fleshpots and ate our fill of bread! But you had to lead us into this desert to make the whole community die of famine!"

Then the Lord said to Moses, "I will now rain down bread from heaven for you. Each day the people are to go out and gather their daily portion; thus will I test them, to see whether they follow my instructions or not. On the sixth day, however, when they prepare what they bring in, let it be twice as much as they gather on the other days." So Moses and Aaron told all the Israelites, "At evening you will know that it was the Lord who brought you out of the land of Egypt; and in the morning you will see the glory of the Lord, as he heeds your grumbling against him. But what are we that you should grumble against us? When the Lord gives you flesh to eat in the evening," continued Moses, "and in the morning your fill of bread, as he heeds the grumbling you utter against him, what then are we? Your grumbling is not against us, but against the Lord."

In the evening quail came up and covered the camp. In the morning a dew lay all about the camp, and when the dew evaporated, there on the surface of the desert were fine flakes like hoarfrost on the ground. On seeing it, the Israelites asked one another, "What is this?" for they did not know what it was. But Moses told them, "This is the bread which the Lord has given you to eat. Now, this is what the Lord has commanded. So gather it that everyone has enough to eat, a gomor for each person, as many of you as there are, each man providing for those of his own tent." Moses also told them, "Let no one keep any of it over until tomorrow morning." But they would not listen to him. When some kept a part of it over until the following morning, it became wormy and rotten. Therefore Moses was displeased with them.

Morning after morning they gathered it, till each had enough to eat; but when the sun grew hot, the manna melted away. On the sixth day they gathered twice as much food, two gomors for each person. When all the leaders of the community came and reported this to Moses, he told them, "That is what the Lord prescribed. Tomorrow is a day of complete rest, the Sabbath, sacred to the Lord. You may either bake or boil the manna, as you please; but whatever is left put away and keep for the morrow." When they put it away for the morrow, as Moses commanded, it did not become rotten or wormy. Moses then said, "Eat it today, for today is the Sabbath of the Lord. On this day you will not find any of it on the ground. On the other six days you can gather it, but on the seventh day, the Sabbath, none of it will be there." Still, on the seventh day some of the people went out to gather it, although they did not find any. Then the Lord said to Moses, "How long will you refuse to keep my commandments and laws? Take note!

The Lord has given you the Sabbath. That is why on the sixth day he gives you food for two days. On the seventh day everyone is to stay home and no one is to go out." After that the people rested on the seventh day.

From the desert of Sin the whole Israelite community journeyed by stages, as the Lord directed, and encamped at Raphidim. Here there was no water for the people to drink. They quarreled, therefore, with Moses and said, "Give us water to drink." Moses replied, "Why do you quarrel with me? Why do you put the Lord to a test?" So Moses cried out to the Lord, "What shall I do with this people? A little more and they will stone me!" The Lord answered Moses, "Go over there in front of the people, along with some of the elders of Israel, holding in your hand, as you go, the staff with which you struck the river. I will be standing there in front of you on the rock in Horeb. Strike the rock, and the water will flow from it for the people to drink." This Moses did, in the presence of the elders of Israel. The place was called Massa and Meriba, because the Israelites quarreled there and tested the Lord, saying, "Is the Lord in our midst or not?"

MOUNT SINAI AND THE TEN COMMANDMENTS

In the third month after their departure from the land of Egypt, on its first day, the Israelites came to the desert of Sinai. After the journey from Raphidim to the desert of Sinai, they pitched camp.

While Israel was encamped here in front of the mountain, Moses went up the mountain to God. Then the Lord called to him and said, "Thus shall you say to the house of Jacob; tell the Israelites: You have seen for yourselves how I treated the Egyptians and how I bore you up on eagle wings and brought you here to myself. Therefore, if you hearken to my voice and keep my covenant, you shall be my special possession, dearer to me than all other people, though all the earth is mine. You shall be to me a kingdom of priests, a holy nation. That is what you must tell the Israelites." So Moses went and summoned the elders of the people. When he set before them all that the Lord had ordered him to tell them, the people all answered together, "Everything the Lord has said, we will do." Then Moses brought back to the Lord the response of the people.

The Lord also told him, "I am coming to you in a dense cloud, so that when the people hear me speaking with you, they may always have faith in you also." When Moses, then, had reported to the Lord the response of the people, the Lord added, "Go to the people and have them sanctify themselves today and tomorrow. Make them wash their garments and be ready for the third day; for on the third day the Lord will come down on Mount Sinai before the eyes of all the people. Set limits for the people all around the mountain, and tell them: Take care not to go up the mountain, or even touch its base. If anyone touches the mountain he must be put to death. No hand shall touch him; he must be stoned to death or killed with arrows. Such a one, man or beast, must not be allowed to live. Only when the ram's horn resounds may they go up to the mountain." Then Moses came down from the mountain to the people and had them sanctify themselves and wash their garments. He warned them, "Be ready for the third day. Have no intercourse with any woman."

On the morning of the third day there were peals of thunder and lightning, and a heavy cloud over the mountain, and a very loud trumpet blast, so that all the people in the camp trembled. But Moses led the people out of the camp to meet God, and they stationed themselves at the foot of the mountain. Mount Sinai was all wrapped in smoke, for the Lord came down upon it in fire. The smoke rose from it as though from a furnace, and the whole mountain trembled violently. The trumpet blast grew louder and louder, while Moses was speaking and God answering him with thunder.

When the Lord came down to the top of Mount Sinai, he summoned Moses to the top of the mountain, and Moses went up to him. Then the Lord told Moses, "Go down and warn the people not to break through toward the Lord in order to see him; otherwise many of them will be struck down. The priests, too, who approach the Lord must sanctify themselves; else he will vent his anger upon them." Moses said to the Lord, "The people cannot go up to Mount Sinai, for you yourself warned us to set limits around the mountain to make it sacred." The Lord repeated, "Go down now! Then come up again along with Aaron. But the priests and the people must not break through to come up to the Lord; else he will vent his anger upon them." So Moses went down to the people and told them this.

Then God delivered all these commandments:

"I, the Lord, am your God, who brought you out of the land of Egypt, that place of slavery. You shall not have other gods besides me. You shall not carve idols for yourselves in the shape of anything in the sky above or on the earth below or in the waters beneath the earth; you shall not bow down before them or worship them. For I, the Lord, your God, am a jealous God, inflicting punishment for their fathers' wickedness on the children of those who hate me, down to the third and fourth generation; but bestowing mercy down to the thousandth generation, on the children of those who love me and keep my commandments.

"You shall not take the name of the Lord, your God, in vain. For the Lord will not leave unpunished him who takes his name in vain.

"Remember to keep holy the Sabbath day. Six days you may labor and do all your work, but the seventh day is the Sabbath of the Lord, your God. No work may be done then either by you, or your son or daughter, or your male or female slave, or your beast, or by the alien who lives with you. In six days the Lord made the heavens and the earth, the sea and all that is in them; but on the seventh day he rested. That is why the Lord has blessed the Sabbath day and made it holy.

"Honor your father and your mother, that you may have a long life in the land which the Lord, your God, is giving you.

"You shall not kill.

"You shall not commit adultery.

"You shall not steal.

"You shall not bear false witness against your neighbor.

"You shall not covet your neighbor's house. You shall not covet your neighbor's wife, nor his male or female slave, nor his ox or ass, nor anything else that belongs to him."

When the people witnessed the thunder and lightning, the trumpet blast and the mountain smoking, they all feared and trembled. So they took up a position much farther away and said to Moses, "You speak to us, and we will listen; but let not God speak to us, or we shall die." Moses answered the people, "Do not be afraid, for God has come to you only to test you and put his fear upon you, lest you should sin." Still the people remained at a distance, while Moses approached the cloud where God was.

The Lord said to Moses, "Come up to me on the mountain and, while you are there, I will give you the stone tablets on which I have written the commandments intended for their instruction." So Moses set out with Josue, his aide, and went up to the mountain of God. The elders, however, had been told by him, "Wait here for us until we return to you. Aaron and Hur are staying with you. If anyone has a complaint, let him refer the matter to them." After Moses had gone up, a cloud covered the mountain. The glory of the Lord settled upon Mount Sinai. The cloud covered it for six days, and on the seventh day he called to Moses from the midst of the cloud. To the Israelites the glory of the Lord was seen as a consuming fire on the mountaintop. But Moses passed into the midst of the cloud as he went up on the mountain; and there he stayed for forty days and forty nights.

GOD'S TENT IN THE DESERT

This is what the Lord then said to Moses: "Tell the Israelites to take up a collection for me. From every man you shall accept the contribution that his heart prompts him to give me. They shall make a sanctuary for me, that I may dwell in their midst. This Dwelling and all its furnishings you shall make exactly according to the pattern that I will now show you.

"You shall make an ark of acacia wood, two and a half cubits long, one and a half cubits wide, and one and a half cubits high. Plate it inside and outside with pure gold, and put a molding of gold around the top of it.

"You shall then make a propitiatory of pure gold, two cubits and a half long, and one and a half cubits wide. Make two cherubim of beaten gold for the two ends of the propitiatory, fastening them so that one cherub springs direct from each end. The cherubim shall have their wings spread out above, covering the propitiatory with them; they shall be turned toward each other, but with their faces looking toward the propitiatory. This propitiatory you shall then place on top of the ark. In the ark itself you are to put the Commandments which I will give you. There I will meet you and there, from above the propitiatory, between the two cherubim on the Ark of the Commandments, I will tell you all the commands that I wish you to give the Israelites.

"You shall also make a table of acacia wood, two cubits long, a cubit wide, and a cubit and a half high. Plate it with pure gold and make a molding of gold around it. On the table you shall always keep showbread set before me.

"You shall make a lampstand of pure beaten gold—its shaft and branches—with its cups and knobs and petals springing directly from it. You shall then make seven lamps for it and so set up the lamps that they shed their light on the space in front of the lampstand.

"The Dwelling itself you shall make out of sheets woven of fine linen twined and of violet, purple and scarlet yarn, with cherubim embroidered on them. Also make sheets woven of goat hair, to be used as a tent covering over the Dwelling. Over the tent itself you shall make a covering of rams' skins dyed red, and above that, a covering of thahas skins.

"You shall make boards of acacia wood as walls for the Dwelling. The length of each board is to be ten cubits, and its width one and a half cubits. You shall have a veil woven of violet, purple and scarlet yarn, and of fine linen twined, with cherubim embroidered on it. It is to be hung on four gold-plated columns of acacia wood, which shall have hooks of gold and shall rest on four silver pedestals. Hang the veil from clasps. The Ark of the Commandments you shall bring inside, behind this veil which divides the Holy Place from the Holy of Holies. Set the propitiatory on the Ark of the Commandments in the Holy of Holies.

"Outside the veil you shall place the table and the lampstand, the latter on the south side of the Dwelling, opposite the table, which is to be put on the north side.

"You shall make an altar of acacia wood, on a square, five cubits long and five cubits wide; it shall be three cubits high. At the four corners there are to be horns, so made that they spring directly from the altar. You shall then plate it with bronze. You shall also make a court for the Dwelling. On the south side the court shall have hangings a hundred cubits long, woven of fine linen twined, with twenty columns and twenty pedestals of bronze; the hooks and bands on the columns shall be of silver.

"You shall order the Israelites to bring you clear oil of crushed olives, to be used for the light, so that you may keep lamps burning regularly. From evening to morning Aaron and his sons shall maintain them before the Lord in the Meeting Tent, outside the veil which hangs in front of the Commandments. This shall be a perpetual ordinance for the Israelites throughout their generations.

"From among the Israelites have your brother Aaron, together with his sons Nadab, Abiu, Eleazar and Ithamar, brought to you, that they may be my priests. For the glorious adornment of your brother Aaron you shall have sacred vestments made. Therefore, to the various expert workmen whom I have endowed with skill, you shall give instructions to make such vestments for Aaron as will set him apart for his sacred service as my priest. These are the vestments they shall make: a breastpiece, an ephod, a robe, a brocaded tunic, a miter and a sash. In making these sacred vestments which your brother Aaron and his sons are to wear in serving as my priests, they shall use gold, violet, purple and scarlet yarn and fine linen.

"For burning incense you shall make an altar of acacia wood, with a square surface, a cubit long, a cubit wide, and a cubit high, with horns that spring directly from it. Its grate on top, its walls on all four sides, and its horns you shall plate with pure gold. Put a gold molding around it. Underneath the molding you shall put gold rings, two on one side and two on the opposite side, as holders for the poles used in carrying it. Make the poles, too, of acacia wood and plate them with gold. This altar you are to place in front of the veil that hangs before the Ark of the Commandments where I will meet you. On it Aaron shall burn fragrant incense. Morning after morning, when he prepares the lamps, and again in the evening twilight, when he lights the lamps, he shall burn incense. Throughout your generation this shall be the established incense offering before the Lord.

"And you shall blend a sacred anointing oil, perfumed ointment expertly prepared. With this sacred anointing oil you shall anoint the Meeting Tent and the Ark of the Commandments, the table, the lampstand, the altar of incense and the altar of holocausts, and the laver with its base. When you have consecrated them, they shall be most sacred; whatever touches them shall be sacred. Aaron and his sons you shall also anoint and consecrate as my priests. To the Israelites you shall say: As sacred anointing oil this shall belong to me throughout your generations. It may not be used in any ordinary anointing of the body, nor may you make any other oil of like mixture. It is sacred, and shall be treated as sacred by you. Whoever prepares a perfume like this, or whoever puts any of this on a layman, shall be cut off from his kinsmen."

THE JEWS WORSHIP AN IDOL

When the people became aware of Moses' delay in coming down from the mountain, they gathered around Aaron and said to him, "Come, make us a god who will be our leader; as for the man Moses who brought us out of the land of Egypt, we do not know what has happened to him." Aaron replied, "Have your wives and sons and daughters take off the golden earrings they are wearing, and bring them to me." So all the people took off their earrings and brought them to Aaron, who accepted their offering, and fashioning this gold with a graving tool, made a molten calf. Then they cried out, "This is your God, O Israel, who brought you out of the land of Egypt." On seeing this, Aaron built an altar before the calf and proclaimed, "Tomorrow is a feast of the Lord." Early the next day the people offered holocausts and brought peace offerings. Then they sat down to eat and drink, and rose up to revel.

Moses then turned and came down the mountain with the two tablets of the Commandments in his hands, tablets that were written on both sides, front and back; tablets that were made by God, having inscriptions on them that were engraved by God himself. Now, when Josue heard the noise of the people shouting, he said to Moses, "That sounds like a battle in the camp." But Moses answered, "It does not sound like cries of victory, nor does it sound like cries of defeat; the sounds that I hear are cries of revelry." As he drew near the camp, he saw the calf and the dancing. With that, Moses' wrath flared up, so that he threw the tablets down and broke them on the base of the mountain. Taking the calf they had made, he fused it in the fire and then ground it down to powder, which he scattered on the water and made the Israelites drink.

He stood at the gate of the camp and cried, "Whoever is for the Lord, let him come to me!" All the Levites then rallied to him, and he told them, "Thus says the Lord, the God of Israel: Put your sword on your hip, every one of you! Now go up and down the camp, from gate to gate, and slay your own kinsmen, your friends and neighbors!" The Levites carried out the command of Moses, and that day there fell about three thousand of the people.

THE TEN COMMANDMENTS ARE RENEWED

The Lord said to Moses, "Cut two stone tablets like the former, that I may write on them the Commandments which were on the former tablets that you broke. Get ready for tomorrow morning, when you are to go up Mount Sinai and there present yourself to me on the top of the mountain. No one shall come with you, and no one is even to be seen on any part of the mountain; even the flocks and the herds are not to go grazing toward this mountain." Moses then cut two stone tablets like the former, and early the next morning he went up Mount Sinai as the Lord had commanded him, taking along the two stone tablets.

Having come down in a cloud, the Lord stood with him there and proclaimed his name, "Lord." Thus the Lord passed before him and cried out, "The Lord, the Lord, a merciful and gracious God, slow to anger and rich in kindness and fidelity, continuing his kindness for a thousand generations, and forgiving wickedness and crime and sin; yet not declaring the guilty guiltless, but punishing children and grand-children to the third and fourth generation for their fathers' wicked-ness!" Moses at once bowed down to the ground in worship. Then he said, "If I find favor with you, O Lord, do come along in our company. This is indeed a stiff-necked people; yet pardon our wickedness and sins, and receive us as your own."

"Here, then," said the Lord, "is the covenant I will make. Before the eyes of all your people I will work such marvels as have never been wrought in any nation anywhere on earth, so that this people among whom you live may see how awe-inspiring are the deeds which I, the Lord, will do at your side. But you, on your part, must keep the commandments I am giving you today."

Then the Lord said to Moses, "Write down these words, for in accordance with them I have made a covenant with you and with Israel." So Moses stayed there with the Lord for forty days and forty nights, without eating any food or drinking any water, and he wrote on the tablets the words of the covenant, the Ten Commandments.

GOD'S CRAFTSMEN BUILD HIS DESERT DWELLING

Moses said to the Israelites, "See, the Lord had chosen Beseleel, son of Uri, son of Hur, of the tribe of Juda, and has filled him with a divine spirit of skill and understanding and knowledge in every craft: in the production of embroidery, in making things of gold, silver or bronze, in cutting and mounting precious stones, in carving wood, and in every other craft. He has also given both him and Oholiab, son of Achisamach, of the tribe of Dan, the ability to teach others. He has endowed them with skill to execute all types of work: engraving, embroidering, the making of variegated cloth of violet, purple and scarlet yarn and fine linen thread, weaving, and all other arts and crafts.

"Beseleel, therefore, will set to work with Oholiab and with all the experts whom the Lord has endowed with skill and understanding in knowing how to execute all the work for the service of the sanctuary, just as the Lord has commanded."

Moses then called Beseleel and Oholiab and all the other experts whom the Lord had endowed with skill, men whose hearts moved them to come and take part in the work. They received from Moses all the contributions which the Israelites had brought for establishing the service of the sanctuary. Still, morning after morning the people continued to bring their voluntary offerings to Moses. Thereupon the experts who were executing the various kinds of work for the sanctuary, all left the work they were doing, and told Moses, "The people are bringing much more than is needed to carry out the work which the Lord has commanded us to do." Moses, therefore, ordered a proclamation to be made throughout the camp: "Let neither man nor woman make any more contributions for the sanctuary." So the people stopped bringing their offerings; there was already enough at hand, in fact, more than enough, to complete the work to be done.

Moses did exactly as the Lord had commanded him. On the first day of the first month of the second year the Dwelling was erected. It was Moses who erected the Dwelling. He placed its pedestals, set up its boards, put in its bars, and set up its columns. He spread the tent over the Dwelling and put the covering on top of the tent. He took the Commandments and put them in the ark; he placed poles alongside the ark and set the propitiatory upon it. He brought the ark into the Dwelling and hung the curtain veil, thus screening off the Ark of the Commandments. He put the table in the Meeting Tent, on the north side of the Dwelling, outside the veil, and arranged the bread on it before the Lord. He placed the lampstand in the Meeting Tent, opposite the table, on the south side of the Dwelling, and he set up the lamps before the Lord. He placed the golden altar in the Meeting Tent, in front of the veil, and on it he burned fragrant incense. He hung the curtain at the entrance of the Dwelling. He put the altar of holocausts in front of the entrance of the Dwelling of the Meeting Tent, and offered holocausts and cereal offerings on it. He placed the laver between the Meeting Tent and the altar, and put water in it for washing. Moses and Aaron and his sons used to wash their hands and feet there, for they washed themselves whenever they went into the Meeting Tent or approached the altar. Finally, he set up the court around the Dwelling and the altar and hung the curtain at the entrance of the court. Thus Moses finished all the work.

On the day when the Dwelling was erected, the cloud covered the Dwelling, the Tent of the Commandments; but from evening until morning it took on the appearance of fire over the Dwelling. It was always so: during the day the Dwelling was covered by the cloud, which at night had the appearance of fire. Whenever the cloud rose from the Tent, the Israelites would break camp; wherever the cloud came to rest, they would pitch camp. At the bidding of the Lord the Israelites moved on, and at his bidding they encamped. As long as the cloud stayed over the Dwelling, they remained in camp.

CHAPTER THREE

Laws and Rituals

GOD INSTILLS FEAR

The Lord told Moses, "Thus shall you speak to the Israelites: You have seen for yourselves that I have spoken to you from heaven. Do not make anything to rank with me; neither gods of silver nor gods of gold shall you make for yourselves. Do not turn aside to idols, nor make molten gods for yourselves. I, the Lord, am your God. Whoever sacrifices to any god, except to the Lord alone, shall be doomed.

"An altar of earth you shall make for me, and upon it you shall sacrifice your holocausts and peace offerings, your sheep and your oxen. In whatever place I choose for the remembrance of my name I will come to you and bless you. If you make an altar of stone for me, do not build it of cut stone, for by putting a tool to it you desecrate it. You shall not go up by steps to my altar, on which you must not be indecently uncovered.

"When you sacrifice your peace offering to the Lord, if you wish it to be acceptable, it must be eaten on the very day of your sacrifice or on the following day. Whatever is left over until the third day shall be burned up in the fire. If any of it is eaten on the third day, the sacrifice will be unacceptable as refuse; whoever eats of it then shall pay the penalty for having profaned what is sacred to the Lord. Such a one shall be cut off from his people."

BODILY HARM

"Whoever strikes a man a mortal blow must be put to death. He, however, who did not hunt a man down, but caused his death by an act of God, may flee to a place which I will set apart for this purpose. But when a man kills another after maliciously scheming to do so, you must take him even from my altar and put him to death. Whoever strikes his father or mother shall be put to death.

72

"A kidnaper, whether he sells his victim or still has him when caught, shall be put to death.

"When men quarrel and one strikes the other with a stone or with his fist, not mortally, but enough to put him in bed, the one who struck the blow shall be acquitted, provided the other can get up and walk around with the help of his staff. Still, he must compensate him for his enforced idleness and provide for his complete cure.

"When a man strikes his male or female slave with a rod so hard that the slave dies under his hand, he shall be punished. If, however, the slave survives for a day or two, he is not to be punished, since the slave is his own property.

"When a man strikes his male or female slave in the eye and destroys the use of the eye, he shall let the slave go free in compensation for the eye. If he knocks out a tooth of his male or female slave, he shall let the slave go free in compensation for the tooth.

"When men have a fight and hurt a pregnant woman, so that she suffers a miscarriage, but not further injury, the guilty one shall be fined as much as the woman's husband demands of him, and he shall pay in the presence of the judges. But if injury ensues, you shall give life for life, eye for eye, tooth for tooth, hand for hand, foot for foot, burn for burn, wound for wound, stripe for stripe."

PERSONAL INTEGRITY

"When a man gives money or any article to another for safekeeping and it is stolen from the latter's house, the thief, if caught, must make twofold restitution. It the thief is not caught, the owner of the house shall be brought to God, to swear that he himself did not lay hands on his neighbor's property. In every question of dishonest appropriation, whether it be about an ox, or an ass, or a garment, or anything else that has disappeared, where another claims that the thing is his, both parties shall present their case before God; the one whom God convicts must make twofold restitution to the other.

"If you lend money to one of your poor neighbors among my people, you shall not act like an extortioner toward him by demanding interest from him. If you take your neighbor's cloak as a pledge, you shall return it to him before sunset; for this cloak of his is the only covering he has for his body. What else has he to sleep in? If he cries out to me, I will hear him; for I am compassionate.

"You shall not wrong any widow or orphan. If ever you wrong

them and they cry out to me, I will surely hear their cry. My wrath will flare up, and I will kill you with the sword; then your own wives will be widows, and your children orphans.

"You shall not repeat a false report. Do not join the wicked in putting your hand, as an unjust witness, upon anyone. Neither shall you allege the example of the many as an excuse for doing wrong, nor shall you, when testifying in a lawsuit, side with the many in perverting justice. You shall not favor a poor man in his lawsuit.

"You shall not deny one of your needy fellow men his rights in his lawsuit. You shall keep away from anything dishonest. The innocent and the just you shall not put to death, nor shall you acquit the guilty. Never take a bribe, for a bribe blinds even the most clear-sighted and twists the words even of the just.

"You shall not act dishonestly in rendering judgment. Show neither partiality to the weak nor deference to the mighty, but judge your fellow men justly. You shall not go about spreading slander among your kinsmen; nor shall you stand by idly when your neighbor's life is at stake."

VARIOUS RULES OF CONDUCT

The Lord said to Moses, "Speak to the whole Israelite community and tell them: Be holy, for I, the Lord, your God, am holy. Revere your mother and father, and keep my Sabbaths.

"Do not practice divination or soothsaying. Do not go to mediums or consult fortune tellers, for you will be defiled by them.

"Do not clip your hair at the temples, nor trim the edges of your beard. Do not lacerate your bodies for the dead, and do not tattoo yourselves.

"You shall not degrade your daughter by making a prostitute of her; else the land will become corrupt and full of lewdness. When a man seduces a virgin who is not betrothed, and lies with her, he shall pay her marriage price and marry her. If her father refuses to give her to him, he must still pay him the customary marriage price for virgins.

"Anyone who lies with an animal shall be put to death.

"Do not act dishonestly in using measures of length or weight or capacity. You shall have a true scale and true weights, an honest epha and an honest hin. You shall not defraud or rob your neighbor. You shall not withhold overnight the wages of your day laborer.

"When you come upon your enemy's ox or ass going astray, see to it that it is returned to him. When you notice the ass of one who hates you lying prostrate under its burden, by no means desert him; help him, rather, to raise it up.

"You shall not curse the deaf, or put a stumbling block in front of the blind.

"Stand up in the presence of the aged, and show respect for the old; thus shall you fear your God.

"Be careful, then, to observe all my statutes and decrees. Keep my Sabbaths, and reverence my sanctuary. I am the Lord."

THE SANCTITY OF SEX

The Lord said to Moses, "Speak to the Israelites and tell them: You shall not do as they do in the land of Egypt, where you once lived, nor shall you do as they do in the land of Chanaan, where I am bringing you; do not conform to their customs:

"None of you shall approach a close relative to have sexual intercourse with her. You shall not disgrace your father by having intercourse with your mother. Besides, since she is your own mother, you shall not have intercourse with her. If a man disgraces his father by lying with his father's wife, both the man and his stepmother shall be put to death; they have forfeited their lives. If a man lies with his daughter-in-law, both of them shall be put to death; since they have committed an abhorrent deed, they have forfeited their lives. If a man lies with a male as with a woman, both of them shall be put to death for their abominable deed; they have forfeited their lives. If a man marries a woman and her mother also, the man and the two women as well shall be burned to death for their shameful conduct, so that such shamefulness may not be found among you. If a man has carnal relations with an animal, the man shall be put to death, and the animal shall be slain. If a woman goes up to any animal to mate with it, the woman and the animal shall be slain; let them both be put to death; their lives are forfeit. If a man consummates marriage with his sister or his half-sister, they shall be publicly cut off from their people for this shameful deed; the man shall pay the penalty of having had intercourse with his own sister. If a man lies in sexual intercourse with a woman during her menstrual period, both of them shall be cut off from their people, because they have laid bare the flowing fountain of her blood. You shall not have intercourse with your mother's sister or your father's sister; whoever does so shall pay the penalty of incest. If a man disgraces his uncle by having intercourse with his uncle's wife, the man and his aunt shall pay the penalty by dying childless. If a man marries his brother's wife and thus disgraces his brother, they shall be childless because of this incest.

"Do not defile yourselves by any of these things by which the nations whom I am driving out of your way have defiled themselves. Because their land has become defiled, I am punishing it for its wickedness, by making it vomit out its inhabitants; otherwise the land will vomit you out also for having defiled it, just as it vomited out the nations before you. Everyone who does any of these abominations shall be cut off from among his people. Heed my charge, then, not to defile yourselves by observing the abominable customs that have been observed before you.

"If a man's wife goes astray and becomes unfaithful to him by having intercourse with another man, though her husband has not sufficient evidence of the fact, so that her impurity remains unproved for lack of a witness who might have caught her in the act; or if a man is overcome by a feeling of jealousy that makes him suspect his wife, whether she was actually impure or not: he shall bring his wife to the priest and shall take along as an offering for her a tenth of an epha of barley meal. However, he shall not pour oil on it nor put frankincense over it, since it is a cereal offering of jealousy, a cereal offering for an appeal in a question of guilt.

"The priest shall first have the woman come forward and stand before the Lord. In an earthen vessel he shall meanwhile put some holy water, as well as some dust that he has taken from the floor of the Dwelling. Then, as the woman stands before the Lord, the priest shall uncover her head and place in her hands the cereal offering of her appeal, that is, the cereal offering of jealousy, while he himself shall hold the bitter water that brings a curse. Then he shall adjure the woman, saying to her, 'If no other man has had intercourse with you, and you have not gone astray by impurity while under the authority of your husband, be immune to the curse brought by this bitter water. But if you have gone astray while under the authority of your husband and have acted impurely by letting a man other than your husband have intercourse with you'—so shall the priest adjure the woman with this oath of imprecation—'may the Lord make you an example of malediction and imprecation among your people by causing your thighs to waste away and your belly to swell! May this water, then, that brings a curse, enter your body to make your belly swell and your thighs waste away!' And the woman shall say, 'Amen, amen!' The priest shall put these imprecations in writing and shall then wash them off into the bitter water, which he is to have the woman drink, so that it may go into her with all its bitter curse. But first he shall take the cereal offering of jealousy from the woman's hand, and having waved this offering before the Lord, shall put it near the altar, where he shall take a handful of the cereal offering as its token offering and burn it on the altar. Only then shall he have the woman drink the water. Once she has done so, if she has been impure and unfaithful to her husband, this bitter water that brings a curse will go into her, and her belly will swell and her thighs will waste away, so that she will become an example of imprecation among her people. If, however, the woman has not defiled herself, but is still pure, she will be immune and will still be able to bear children.

"This, then, is the law for jealousy: When a woman goes astray while under the authority of her husband and acts impurely, or when such a feeling of jealousy comes over a man that he becomes suspicious of his wife, he shall have her stand before the Lord, and the priest shall apply this law in full to her. The man shall be free from guilt, but the woman shall bear such guilt as she may have.

"If a man, after marrying a woman and having relations with her, comes to dislike her, and makes monstrous charges against her and defames her by saying, 'I married this woman, but when I first had relations with her I did not find her a virgin,' the father and mother of the girl shall take the evidence of her virginity and bring it to the elders at the city gate. There the father of the girl shall say to the elders, 'I gave my daughter to this man in marriage, but he has come to dislike her, and now brings monstrous charges against her, saying: I did not find your daughter a virgin. But here is the evidence of my daughter's virginity!' And they shall spread out the cloth before the elders of the city. Then these city elders shall take the man and chastise him, besides fining him one hundred silver shekels, which they shall give to the girl's father, because the man defamed a virgin in Israel. Moreover, she shall remain his wife, and he may not divorce her as long as he lives.

"But if this charge is true, and evidence of the girl's virginity is not found, they shall bring the girl to the entrance of her father's house and there her townsmen shall stone her to death, because she committed a crime against Israel by her unchasteness in her father's house. Thus shall you purge the evil from your midst.

"You must be able to distinguish between what is sacred and what is profane, between what is clean and what is unclean; you must teach the Israelites all the laws that the Lord has given them through Moses."

OFFERING TO THE LORD

The Lord called Moses, and from the Meeting Tent gave him this message: "Speak to the Israelites and tell them: When any one of you wishes to bring an animal offering to the Lord, such an offering must be from the herd or from the flock.

"If his holocaust offering is from the herd, it must be a male without blemish. To find favor with the Lord, he shall bring it to the entrance of the Meeting Tent and there lay his hand on the head of the holocaust, so that it may be acceptable to make atonement for him. He shall then slaughter the bull before the Lord, but Aaron's sons, the priests, shall offer up its blood by splashing it on the sides of the altar which is at the entrance of the Meeting Tent. Then he shall skin the holocaust and cut it up into pieces. After Aaron's sons, the priests, have put some burning embers on the altar and laid some wood on them, they shall lay the pieces of meat, together with the head and the suet, on top of the wood and embers on the altar. The inner organs and the shanks, however, the offerer shall first wash with water. The priest shall then burn the whole offering on the altar as a holocaust, a sweet-smelling oblation to the Lord."

The Lord said to Moses, "Give Aaron and his sons the following command: This is the ritual for holocausts. The holocaust is to remain on the hearth of the altar all night until the next morning, and the fire is to be kept burning on the altar. The priest, clothed in his linen robe and wearing linen drawers on his body, shall take away the ashes to which the fire has reduced the holocaust on the altar, and lay them at the side of the altar. Then, having taken off these garments and put on other garments, he shall carry the ashes to a clean place outside the camp. The fire on the altar is to be kept burning; it must not go out. Every morning the priest shall put firewood on it. On this he shall lay out the holocaust and burn the fat of the peace offerings. The fire is to be kept burning continuously on the altar; it must not go out."

RESPONSIBILITY OF MOTHERHOOD

The Lord said to Moses, "Tell the Israelites: When a woman has conceived and gives birth to a boy, she shall be unclean for seven days, with the same uncleanness as at her menstrual period. On the eighth day, the flesh of the boy's foreskin shall be circumcised, and then she shall spend thirty-three days more in becoming purified of her blood; she shall not touch anything sacred nor enter the sanctuary till the days of her purification are fulfilled. If she gives birth to a girl, for fourteen days she shall be as unclean as at her menstruation, after which she shall spend sixty-six days in becoming purified of her blood. When the days of her purification for a son or for a daughter are fulfilled, she shall bring to the priest at the entrance of the Meeting Tent a yearling lamb for a holocaust and a pigeon or a turtledove for a sin offering. The priest shall offer them up before the Lord to make atonement for her, and thus she will be clean again after her flow of blood. Such is the law for the woman who gives birth to a boy or a girl child. If, however, she cannot afford a lamb, she may take two turtledoves or two pigeons, the one for a holocaust and the other for a sin offering. The priest shall make atonement for her, and thus she will again be clean."

THE DAY OF EXPIATION

After the death of Aaron's two sons, who died when they approached the Lord's presence, the Lord spoke to Moses and said to him, "Tell your brother Aaron that he is not to come whenever he pleases into the sanctuary, inside the veil, in front of the propitiatory on the ark; otherwise, when I reveal myself in a cloud above the propitiatory, he will die. Only in this way may Aaron enter the sanctuary. He shall bring a young bullock for a sin offering and a ram for a holocaust. He shall wear the sacred linen tunic, with the linen drawers next his flesh, gird himself with the linen sash and put on the linen miter. But since these vestments are sacred, he shall not put them on until he has first bathed his body in water. From the Israelite community he shall receive two male goats for a sin offering and one ram for a holocaust.

"Aaron shall bring in the bullock, his sin offering to atone for himself and for his household. Taking the two male goats and setting them before the Lord at the entrance of the Meeting Tent, he shall cast lots to determine which one is for the Lord and which for Azazel. The goat that is determined by lot for the Lord Aaron shall bring in and offer up as a sin offering. But the goat determined by lot for Azazel he shall set alive before the Lord, so that with it he may make atonement by sending it off to Azazel in the desert.

"Thus shall Aaron offer up the bullock, his sin offering, to atone for himself and for his family. When he has slaughtered it, he shall take a censer full of glowing embers from the altar before the Lord, as well as a double handful of finely ground fragrant incense, and bringing them inside the veil, there before the Lord he shall put incense on the fire, so that a cloud of incense may cover the propitiatory over the Commandments; else he will die. Taking some of the bullock's blood, he shall sprinkle it with his finger on the fore part of the propitiatory and likewise sprinkle some of the blood with his finger seven times in front of the propitiatory.

"Then he shall slaughter the people's sin-offering goat, and bringing its blood inside the veil, he shall do with it as he did with the bullock's blood, sprinkling it on the propitiatory and before it. Thus he shall make atonement for the sanctuary because of all the sinful defilements and faults of the Israelites. He shall do the same for the Meeting Tent, which is set up among them in the midst of their uncleanness. No one else may be in the Meeting Tent from the time he enters the sanctuary to make atonement until he departs. When he has made atonement for himself and his household, as well as for the whole Israelite community, he shall come out to the altar before the Lord and make atonement for it also. Taking some of the bullock's and the goat's blood, he shall put it on the horns around the altar, and with his finger sprinkle some of the blood on it seven times. Thus he shall render it clean and holy, purged of the defilements of the Israelites.

"When he has completed the atonement rite for the sanctuary, the Meeting Tent and the altar, Aaron shall bring forward the live goat. Laying both hands on its head, he shall confess over it all the sinful faults and transgressions of the Israelites, and so put them on the goat's head. He shall then have it led into the desert by an attendant. Since the goat is to carry off their iniquities to an isolated region, it must be sent away into the desert.

"This shall be an everlasting ordinance for you: on the tenth day of the seventh month every one of you, whether a native or a resident alien, shall mortify himself and shall do no work. Since on this day atonement is made for you to make you clean, so that you may be cleansed of all your sins before the Lord, by everlasting ordinance it shall be a most solemn sabbath for you, on which you must mortify yourselves.

"This atonement is to be made by the priest who has been anointed and ordained to the priesthood in succession to his father. He shall wear the linen garments, the sacred vestments, and make atonement for the sacred sanctuary, the Meeting Tent and the altar, as well as for the priests and all the people of the community. This, then, shall be an everlasting ordinance for you: once a year atonement shall be made for all the sins of the Israelites." Thus was it done, as the Lord had commanded Moses.

HOLY DAYS

The Lord said to Moses, "Speak to the Israelites and tell them: The following are the festivals of the Lord, my feast days, which you shall celebrate with a sacred assembly. For six days work may be done; but the seventh day is the sabbath rest, a day for sacred assembly, on which you shall do no work. The Sabbath shall belong to the Lord wherever you dwell.

"These, then, are the festivals of the Lord which you shall celebrate at their proper time with a sacred assembly. The Passover of the Lord falls on the fourteenth day of the first month, at the evening twilight. The fifteenth day of this month is the Lord's feast of Unleavened Bread. For seven days you shall eat unleavened bread. On the first of these days you shall hold a sacred assembly and do no sort of work. On each of the seven days you shall offer an oblation to the Lord. Then on the seventh day you shall again hold a sacred assembly and do no sort of work."

The Lord said to Moses, "Speak to the Israelites and tell them: When you come into the land which I am giving you, and reap your harvest, you shall bring a sheaf of the first fruits of your harvest to the priest, who shall wave the sheaf before the Lord that it may be acceptable for you. On the day after the Sabbath the priest shall do this. On this day, when your sheaf is waved, you shall offer to the Lord for a holocaust an unblemished yearling lamb. Its cereal offering shall be two tenths of an epha of fine flour mixed with oil, as a sweet-smelling oblation to the Lord; and its libation shall be a fourth of a hin of wine. Until this day, when you bring your God this offering, you shall not eat any bread or roasted grain or fresh kernels. This shall be a perpetual statute for you and your descendants wherever you dwell.

"Beginning with the day after the Sabbath, the day on which you bring the wave-offering sheaf, you shall count seven full weeks, and then on the day after the seventh week, the fiftieth day, you shall present the new cereal offering to the Lord. For the wave offering of your first fruits to the Lord, you shall bring with you from wherever you live two loaves of bread made of two tenths of an epha of fine flour and baked with leaven. Besides the bread, you shall offer to the Lord a holocaust of seven unblemished yearling lambs, one young bull, and two rams, along with their cereal offering and libations, as a sweet-smelling oblation to the Lord. One male goat shall be sacrificed as a sin offering, and two yearling lambs as a peace offering. The priest shall wave the bread of the first fruits and the two lambs as a wave offering before the Lord; these shall be sacred to the Lord and belong to the priest. On this same day you shall by proclamation have a sacred assembly, and no sort of work may be done. This shall be a perpetual statute for you and your descendants wherever you dwell.

"When you reap the harvest of your land, you shall not be so thorough that you reap the field to its very edge, nor shall you glean the stray ears of your grain. These things you shall leave for the poor and the alien. I, the Lord, am your God."

The Lord said to Moses, "Tell the Israelites: On the first day of the seventh month you shall keep a sabbath rest, with a sacred assembly and with the trumpet blasts as a reminder; you shall then do no sort of work, and you shall offer an oblation to the Lord."

The Lord said to Moses, "The tenth of this seventh month is the Day of Atonement, when you shall hold a sacred assembly and mortify yourselves and offer an oblation to the Lord. On this day you shall not do any work, because it is the Day of Atonement, when atonement is made for you before the Lord, your God. Anyone who does not mortify himself on this day shall be cut off from his people; and if anyone does any work on this day, I will remove him from the midst of his people. This is a perpetual statute for you and your descendants wherever you dwell: you shall do no work, but shall keep the sabbath of complete rest and mortify yourselves. Beginning on the evening of the ninth of the month, you shall keep this sabbath of yours from evening to evening."

The Lord said to Moses, "Tell the Israelites: The fifteenth day of this seventh month is the Lord's feast of Booths, which shall continue for seven days. On the first day there shall be a sacred assembly, and you shall do no sort of work. For seven days you shall offer an oblation to the Lord, and on the eighth day you shall again hold a sacred assembly and offer an oblation to the Lord. On that solemn closing you shall do no sort of work.

"These, therefore, are the festivals of the Lord on which you shall proclaim a sacred assembly, and offer as an oblation to the Lord holocausts and cereal offerings, sacrifices and libations, as prescribed for each day, in addition to those of the Lord's Sabbaths, your donations, your various votive offerings and the freewill offerings that you present to the Lord.

"On the fifteenth day, then, of the seventh month, when you have gathered in the produce of the land, you shall celebrate a pilgrim feast of the Lord for a whole week. The first and the eighth day shall be days of complete rest. On the first day you shall gather foliage from majestic trees, branches of palms and boughs of myrtles and of valley poplars, and then for a week you shall make merry before the Lord, your God. By perpetual statute for you and your descendants you shall keep this pilgrim feast of the Lord for one whole week in the seventh month of the year. During this week every native Israelite among you shall dwell in booths, that your descendants may realize that, when I led the Israelites out of the land of Egypt, I made them dwell in booths. I, the Lord, am your God."

Thus did Moses announce to the Israelites the festivals of the Lord.

DEDICATION TO THE LORD

Now the Lord said to Moses: "Summon the tribe of Levi and present them to Aaron the priest, as his assistants. They shall discharge his obligations and those of the whole community before the Meeting Tent by serving at the Dwelling. They shall have custody of all the furnishings of the Meeting Tent and discharge the duties of the Israelites in the service of the Dwelling. You shall give the Levites to Aaron and his sons; they have been set aside from among the Israelites as dedicated to me. But only Aaron and his descendants shall you appoint to have charge of the priestly functions. Any layman who comes near shall be put to death."

The Lord said to Moses: "Speak to the Israelites and tell them: When a man (or a woman) solemnly takes the Nazirite vow to dedicate himself to the Lord, he shall abstain from wine and strong drink; he may neither drink wine vinegar, other vinegar, or any kind of grape juice, nor eat either fresh or dried grapes. As long as he is a Nazirite he shall not eat anything of the produce of the vine; not even unripe grapes or grapeskins. While he is under the Nazirite vow, no razor shall touch his hair. Until the period of his dedication to the Lord is over, he shall be sacred, and shall let the hair of his head grow freely. As long as he is dedicated to the Lord, he shall not enter where a dead person is. Not even for his father or mother, his sister or brother, should they die, may he become unclean, since his head bears his dedication to God. As long as he is a Nazirite he is sacred to the Lord.

"If someone dies very suddenly in his presence, so that his dedicated head becomes unclean, he shall shave his head on the day of his purification, that is, on the seventh day. On the eighth day he shall bring two turtledoves or two pigeons to the priest at the entrance of the Meeting Tent. The priest shall offer up the one as a sin offering and the other as a holocaust, thus making atonement for him for the sin he has committed by reason of the dead person. On the same day he shall reconsecrate his head and begin anew the period of his dedication to the Lord as a Nazirite, bringing a yearling lamb as a guilt offering. The previous period is not valid, because his dedicated head became unclean.

"This is the ritual for the Nazirite: On the day he completes the period of his dedication he shall go to the entrance of the Meeting Tent, bringing as his offering to the Lord one unblemished yearling lamb for a holocaust, one unblemished yearling ewe lamb for a sin offering, one unblemished ram as a peace offering, along with their cereal offerings and libations, and a basket of unleavened cakes of fine flour mixed with oil and of unleavened wafers spread with oil. The priest shall present them before the Lord, and shall offer up the sin offering and the holocaust for him. He shall then offer up the ram as a peace offering to the Lord, with its cereal offering and libation, and the basket of unleavened cakes. Then at the entrance of the Meeting Tent the Nazirite shall shave his dedicated head, collect the hair, and put it in the fire that is under the peace offering. After the Nazirite has shaved off his dedicated hair, the priest shall take a boiled shoulder of the ram, as well as one unleavened cake and one unleavened wafer from the basket, and shall place them in the hands of the Nazirite. The priest shall then wave them as a wave offering before the Lord. They become sacred and shall belong to the priest, along with the breast of the wave offering and the leg of the raised offering. Only after this may the Nazirite drink wine.

"This, then, is the law for the Nazirite; this is the offering to the Lord which is included in his vow of dedication apart from anything else which his means may allow. Thus shall he carry out the law of his dedication in keeping with the vow he has taken."

84

MOSES EXPOUNDS THE COMMANDMENTS OF THE LORD

"These words, and nothing more, the Lord spoke with a loud voice to your entire assembly on the mountain from the midst of the fire and the dense cloud. He wrote them upon two tablets of stone and gave them to me. But when you heard the voice from the midst of the darkness, while the mountain was ablaze with fire, you came to me in the person of all your tribal heads and elders, and said, 'The Lord, our God, has indeed let us see his glory and his majesty! We have heard his voice from the midst of the fire and have found out today that a man can still live after God has spoken with him. But why should we die now? Surely this great fire will consume us. If we hear the voice of the Lord, our God, any more, we shall die. For what mortal has heard, as we have, the voice of the living God speaking from the midst of fire, and survived? Go closer, you, and hear all that the Lord, our God, will say, and then tell us what the Lord, our God, tells you; we will listen and obey.'

"The Lord heard your words as you were speaking to me and said to me, 'I have heard the words these people have spoken to you, which are all well said. Would that thy might always be of such a mind, to fear me and to keep all my commandments! Then they and their descendants would prosper forever.'

"These, then, are the commandments, the statutes and decrees which the Lord, your God, has ordered that you be taught to observe in the land into which you are crossing for conquest, so that you and your son and your grandson may fear the Lord, your God, and keep, throughout the days of your lives, all his statutes and commandments which I enjoin on you, and thus have long life. Hear then, Israel, and be careful to observe them, that you may grow and prosper the more, in keeping with the promise of the Lord, the God of your fathers, to give you a land flowing with milk and honey.

"Hear, O Israel! The Lord is our God, the Lord alone! Therefore, you shall love the Lord, your God, with all your heart, and with all your soul, and with all your strength. Take to heart these words which I enjoin on you today. Drill them into your children. Speak of them at home and abroad, whether you are busy or at rest. Bind them at your wrist as a sign and let them be as a pendant on your forehead. Write them on the doorposts of your houses and on your gates.

"When the Lord, your God, brings you into the land which he swore to your fathers that he would give you, a land with fine, large cities that you did not build, with houses full of goods of all sorts that you did not garner, with cisterns that you did not dig, with vineyards and olive groves that you did not plant; and when, therefore, you eat your fill, take care not to forget the Lord, who brought you out of the land of Egypt, that place of slavery. The Lord, your God, shall you fear, him shall you serve, and by his name shall you swear. You shall not follow other gods, such as those of the surrounding nations, lest the wrath of the Lord, your God, flare up against you and he destroy you from the face of the land; for the Lord, your God, who is in your midst, is a jealous God.

"You shall not put the Lord, your God, to the test, as you did at Massa. But keep the commandments of the Lord, your God, and the ordinances and statutes he has enjoined on you. Do what is right and good in the sight of the Lord, that you may, according to his word, prosper, and may enter in and possess the good land which the Lord promised on oath to your fathers, thrusting all your enemies out of your way.

"When the Lord, your God, brings you into the land which you are to enter and occupy, and dislodges great nations before you—the Hethites, Gergesites, Amorrites, Chanaanites, Pherezites, Hevites and Jebusites: seven nations more numerous and powerful than you—and when the Lord, your God, delivers them up to you and you defeat them, you shall doom them. Make no covenant with them and show them no mercy. You shall not intermarry with them, neither giving your daughters to their sons nor taking their daughters for your sons. For they would turn your sons from following me to serving other gods, and then the wrath of the Lord would flare up against you and quickly destroy you.

"But this is how you must deal with them: Tear down their altars, smash their sacred pillars, chop down their sacred poles, and destroy their idols by fire. For you are a people sacred to the Lord, your God; he has chosen you from all the nations on the face of the earth to be a people peculiarly his own.

"And now, Israel, what does the Lord, your God, ask of you but to fear the Lord, your God, and follow his ways exactly, to love and serve the Lord, your God, with all your heart and all your soul, to keep the commandments and statutes of the Lord which I enjoin on you today for your own good? Think! The heavens, even the highest heavens, belong to the Lord, your God, as well as the earth and everything on it.

Yet in his love for your fathers the Lord was so attached to them as to choose you, their descendants, in preference to all other peoples, as indeed he has now done.

"When you come into the land which the Lord, your God, is giving you, you shall not learn to imitate the abominations of the peoples there. Let there not be found among you anyone who immolates his son or daughter in the fire, nor a fortuneteller, soothsayer, charmer, diviner, or caster of spells, nor one who consults ghosts and spirits or seeks oracles from the dead. Anyone who does such things is an abomination to the Lord, and because of such abominations the Lord, your God, is driving these nations out of your way. You, however, must be altogether sincere toward the Lord, your God. Though these nations whom you are to dispossess listen to their soothsayers and fortunetellers, the Lord, your God, will not permit you to do so.

"A prophet like me will the Lord, your God, raise up for you from among your own kinsmen; to him you shall listen. This is exactly what you requested of the Lord, your God, at Horeb on the day of the assembly, when you said, 'Let us not again hear the voice of the Lord, our God, nor see this great fire any more, lest we die.' And the Lord said to me, 'This was well said. I will raise up for them a prophet like you from among their kinsmen, and will put my words into his mouth; he shall tell them all that I command him. If any man will not listen to my words which he speaks in my name, I myself will make him answer for it. But if a prophet presumes to speak in my name an oracle that I have not commanded him to speak, or speaks in the name of other gods, he shall die.'

"If you say to yourselves, 'How can we recognize an oracle which the Lord has spoken?', know that, even though a prophet speaks in the name of the Lord, if his oracle is not fulfilled or verified, it is an oracle which the Lord did not speak. The prophet has spoken it presumptuously, and you shall have no fear of him.

"Thus, then, shall it be: if you continue to heed the voice of the Lord and are careful to observe all his commandments, the Lord will raise you high above all the nations of the earth. When you hearken to the voice of the Lord, all these blessings will come upon you and overwhelm you:

"May you be blessed in the city,
and blessed in the country!

87

Blessed be the fruit of your womb,
   the produce of your soil and the offspring of your livestock,
   the issue of your herds and the young of your flocks!
Blessed be your grain bin and your kneading bowl!
May you be blessed in your coming in,
   and blessed in your going out!

"The Lord will beat down before you the enemies that rise up against you; though they come out against you from but one direction, they will flee before you in seven. The Lord will affirm his blessing upon you, on your barns and on all your undertakings, blessing you in the land that the Lord, your God, gives you. But if you do not hearken to the voice of the Lord and are not careful to observe all his commandments, all these curses shall come upon you and overwhelm you:

"May you be cursed in the city,
   and cursed in the country!
Cursed be your grain bin and your kneading bowl!
Cursed be the fruit of your womb,
   the produce of your soil and the offspring of your livestock,
   the issue of your herds and the young of your flocks!
May you be cursed in your coming in,
   and cursed in your going out!

"The Lord will put a curse on you, defeat and frustration in every enterprise you undertake, until you are speedily destroyed and perish for the evil you have done in forsaking me.

"When all these things which I have set before you, the blessings and the curses, are fulfilled in you, and from among whatever nations the Lord, your God, may have dispersed you, you ponder them in your heart: then, provided that you and your children return to the Lord, your God, and heed his voice with all your heart and all your soul, just as I now command you, the Lord, your God, will change your lot; and taking pity on you, he will again gather you from all the nations wherein he has scattered you. Though you may have been driven to the farthest corner of the world, even from there will the Lord gather you; even from there will he bring you back.

"For this command which I enjoin on you today is not too mysterious and remote for you. It is not up in the sky, that you should say, 'Who will go up in the sky to get it for us and tell us of it, that we may carry it out?' Nor is it across the sea, that you should say, 'Who will cross the sea to get it for us and tell us of it, that we may carry it out?' No, it is something very near to you, already in your mouths and in your hearts; you have only to carry it out.

"Here, then, I have today set before you life and prosperity, death and doom. If you obey the commandments of the Lord, your God, loving him, and walking in his ways, and keeping his statutes and decrees, you will live and grow numerous, and the Lord will bless you in the land you are entering to occupy. If, however, you turn away your hearts and will not listen, but are led astray and adore and serve other gods, I tell you now that you will certainly perish; you will not have a long life on the land which you are crossing the Jordan to enter and occupy. I call heaven and earth today to witness against you: I have set before you life and death, the blessing and the curse. Choose life, then, that you and your descendants may live, by loving the Lord, your God, heeding his voice, and holding fast to him. For that will mean life for you, a long life for you to live on the land which the Lord swore he would give to your fathers Abraham, Isaac and Jacob.

"Ask now of the days of old, before your time, ever since God created man upon the earth; ask from one end of the sky to the other: Did anything so great ever happen before? Was it ever heard of? Out of the heavens he let you hear his voice to discipline you; on earth he let you see his great fire, and you heard him speaking out of the fire. This is why you must now know, and fix in your heart, that the Lord is God in the heavens above and on earth below, and that there is no other."

CHAPTER FOUR

Rebellion in the Desert

A SURVEY IS MADE: FURTHER ANGUISH IN THE DESERT

The Lord said to Moses, "Send men to reconnoiter the land of Chanaan, which I am giving the Israelites. You shall send one man from each ancestral tribe, all of them princes." In sending them to the land of Chanaan, Moses said to them, "Go up here in the Negeb, up into the highlands, and see what kind of land it is. Are the people living there strong or weak, few or many? Is the country in which they live good or bad? Are the towns in which they dwell open or fortified? Is the soil fertile or barren, wooden or clear? And do your best to get some of the fruit of the land." It was then the season for early grapes. So they went up and reconnoitered the land from the desert of Sin as far as Rohob, at the entrance to Hamath.

After reconnoitering the land for forty days they returned, met Moses and Aaron and the whole community of the Israelites in the desert of Pharan at Cades, made a report to them all, and showed them the fruit of the country. They told Moses: "We went into the land to which you sent us. It does indeed flow with milk and honey, and here is its fruit. However, the people who are living in the land are fierce, and the towns are fortified and very strong. Besides, we saw descendants of the Enacim there. Amalecites live in the region of the Negeb; Hethites, Jebusites and Amorrites dwell in the highlands, and Chanaanites along the seacoast and the banks of the Jordan."

Caleb, however, to quiet the people toward Moses, said, "We ought to go up and seize the land, for we can certainly do so." But the men who had gone up with him said, "We cannot attack these people; they are too strong for us." So they spread discouraging reports among the Israelites about the land they had scouted, saying, "The land that we explored is a country that consumes its inhabitants. And all the people we saw there are huge men, veritable giants [the Enacim were a race of

90

giants]; we felt like mere grasshoppers, and so we must have seemed to them."

At this, the whole community broke out with loud cries, and even in the night the people wailed. All the Israelites grumbled against Moses and Aaron, the whole community saying to them, "Would that we had died in the land of Egypt, or that here in the desert we were dead! Why is the Lord bringing us into this land only to have us fall by the sword? Our wives and little ones will be taken as booty. Would it not be better for us to return to Egypt?" So they said to one another, "Let us appoint a leader and go back to Egypt."

But Moses and Aaron fell prostrate before the whole assembled community of the Israelites; while Josue, son of Nun, and Caleb, son of Jephonne, who had been in the party that scouted the land, tore their garments and said to the whole community of the Israelites, "The country which we went through and explored is a fine, rich land. If the Lord is pleased with us, he will bring us in and give us that land, a land flowing with milk and honey. But do not rebel against the Lord! You need not be afraid of the people of that land; they are but food for us! Their defense has left them, but the Lord is with us. Therefore, do not be afraid of them." In answer, the whole community threatened to stone them.

But then the glory of the Lord appeared at the Meeting Tent to all the Israelites. And the Lord said to Moses, "How long will this people spurn me? How long will they refuse to believe in me, despite all the signs I have performed among them? I will strike them with pestilence and wipe them out. Then I will make of you a nation greater and mightier than they."

"Pardon, then, the wickedness of this people in keeping with your great kindness, even as you have forgiven them from Egypt until now."

The Lord answered: "I pardon them as you have asked. Yet, by my life and the Lord's glory that fills the whole earth, of all the men who have seen my glory and the signs I worked in Egypt and in the desert, and who nevertheless have put me to the test ten times already and have failed to heed my voice, not one shall see the land which I promised on oath to their fathers. None of these who have spurned me shall see it."

BROTHER AGAINST BROTHER

Core, son of Isaar, son of Caath, son of Levi, [and Dathan and Abiram, sons of Eliab, son of Phallu, son of Ruben] took two hundred and fifty

Israelites who were leaders in the community, members of the council and men of note. They stood before Moses, and held an assembly against Moses and Aaron, to whom they said, "Enough from you! The whole community, all of them, are holy; the Lord is in their midst. Why then should you set yourselves over the Lord's congregation?"

When Moses heard this, he fell prostrate. Then he said to Core and to all his band, "May the Lord make known tomorrow morning who belongs to him and who is the holy one and whom he will have draw near to him! Whom he chooses, he will have draw near him."

Moses said to Core, "You and all your band shall appear before the Lord tomorrow—you and they and Aaron too. Then each of your two hundred and fifty followers shall take his own censer, put incense in it, and offer it to the Lord; and you and Aaron, each with his own censer, shall do the same." So they all took their censers, and laying incense on the fire they had put in them, they took their stand by the entrance of the Meeting Tent along with Moses and Aaron. Then, when Core had assembled all his band against them at the entrance of the Meeting Tent, the glory of the Lord appeared to the entire community, and the Lord said to Moses and Aaron, "Stand apart from this band, that I may consume them at once." But they fell prostrate and cried out, "O God, God of the spirits of all mankind, will one man's sin make you angry with the whole community?" The Lord answered Moses, "Speak to the community and tell them: Withdraw from the space around the Dwelling" [of Core, Dathan and Abiram].

Moses, followed by the elders of Israel, arose and went to Dathan and Abiram. Then he warned the community, "Keep away from the tents of these wicked men and do not touch anything that is theirs: otherwise you too will be swept away because of all their sins." When Dathan and Abiram had come out and were standing at the entrances of their tents with their wives and sons and little ones, Moses said, "This is how you shall know that it was the Lord who sent me to do all I have done, and that it was not I who planned it: if these men die an ordinary death, merely suffering the fate common to all mankind, then it was not the Lord who sent me. But if the Lord does something entirely new, and the ground opens its mouth and swallows them alive down into the nether world, with all belonging to them, then you will know that these men have defied the Lord." No sooner had he finished saying all this than the ground beneath them split open, and the earth opened its mouth and swallowed them and their families [and all of Core's men] and all their possessions. They went down alive to the nether world with all belonging to them; the earth closed over them, and they perished from the community. But all the Israelites near them fled at their shrieks, saying, "The earth might swallow us too!"

MOSES AND AARON LOSE FAITH

The whole Israelite community arrived in the desert of Sin in the first month, and the people settled at Cades. It was here that Mariam died, and here that she was buried.

As the community had no water, they held a council against Moses and Aaron. The people contended with Moses, exclaiming, "Would that we too had perished with our kinsmen in the Lord's presence! Why have you brought the Lord's community into this desert where we and our livestock are dying? Why did you lead us out of Egypt, only to bring us to this wretched place which has neither grain nor figs nor vines nor pomegranates? Here there is not even water to drink!" But Moses and Aaron went away from the assembly to the entrance of the Meeting Tent, where they fell prostrate.

Then the glory of the Lord appeared to them, and the Lord said to Moses, "Take the staff and assemble the community, you and your brother Aaron, and in their presence order the rock to yield its waters. From the rock you shall bring forth water for the community and their livestock to drink." So Moses took the staff from its place before the Lord, as he was ordered. He and Aaron assembled the community in front of the rock, where he said to them, "Listen to me, you rebels! Are we to bring water for you out of this rock?" Then, raising his hand, Moses struck the rock twice with his staff, and water gushed out in abundance for the community and their livestock to drink. But the Lord said to Moses and Aaron, "Because you were not faithful to me in showing forth my sanctity before the Israelites, you shall not lead this community into the land I will give them."

These are the waters of Meriba, where the Israelites contended against the Lord, and where he revealed his sanctity among them.

From Cades Moses sent men to the king of Edom with the message: "Your brother Israel has this to say: You know of all the hardships that have befallen us, how our fathers went down to Egypt, where we stayed a long time, how the Egyptians maltreated us and our fathers, and how, when we cried to the Lord, he heard our cry and sent an angel who led us out of Egypt. Now here we are at the town of Cades at the edge of your territory. Kindly let us pass through your country. We will not cross any fields or vineyards, nor drink any well water, but we will go straight along the royal road without turning to the right or to the left, until we have passed through your territory."

But Edom answered him, "You shall not pass through here; if you do, I will advance against you with the sword." The Israelites insisted, "We want only to go up along the highway. If we or our livestock drink any of your water, we will pay for it. Surely there is no harm in merely letting us march through." But Edom still said, "No, you shall not pass through," and advanced against them with a large and heavily armed force. Therefore, since Edom refused to let them pass through their territory, Israel detoured around them.

Setting out from Cades, the whole Israelite community came to Mount Hor. There at Mount Hor, on the border of the land of Edom, the Lord said to Moses and Aaron, "Aaron is about to be taken to his people; he shall not enter the land I am giving to the Israelites, because you both rebelled against my commandment at the waters of Meriba. Take Aaron and his son Eleazar and bring them up on Mount Hor. Then strip Aaron of his garments and put them on his son Eleazar; for there Aaron shall be taken in death."

Moses did as the Lord commanded. When they had climbed Mount Hor in view of the whole community, Moses stripped Aaron of his garments and put them on his son Eleazar. Then Aaron died there on top of the mountain. When Moses and Eleazar came down from the mountain, all the community understood that Aaron had passed away; and for thirty days the whole house of Israel mourned him.

A SERPENT KILLS AND CURES

From Mount Hor they set out on the Red Sea road, to by-pass the land of Edom. But with their patience worn out by the journey, the people complained against God and Moses, "Why have you brought us up from Egypt to die in this desert, where there is no food or water? We are disgusted with this wretched food!"

In punishment the Lord sent among the people saraph serpents, which bit the people so that many of them died. Then the people came to Moses and said, "We have sinned in complaining against the Lord and you. Pray the Lord to take the serpents from us." So Moses prayed for the people, and the Lord said to Moses, "Make a saraph and mount it on a pole, and if anyone who has been bitten looks at it, he will recover." Moses accordingly made a bronze serpent and mounted it on a pole, and whenever anyone who had been bitten by a serpent looked at the bronze serpent, he recovered.

BALAC ORDERS A CURSE TO STIFLE ISRAEL

Now Balac, son of Sepphor, saw all that Israel did to the Amorrites. Indeed, Moab feared the Israelites greatly because of their numbers, and detested them. So Moab said to the elders of Madian, "Soon this horde will devour all the country around us as an ox devours the grass of the field." And Balac, who was king of Moab at that time, sent messengers to Balaam, son of Beor, at Phathur on the Euphrates, in the land of the Amauites, summoning him with these words, "A people has come here from Egypt who now cover the face of the earth and are settling down opposite us! Please come and curse this people for us; they are stronger than we are. We may then be able to defeat them and drive them out of the country. For I know that whoever you bless is blessed and whoever you curse is cursed."

Here Balac slaughtered oxen and sheep, and sent portions to Balaam and to the princes who were with him. The next morning Balac took Balaam up on Bamoth-Baal, and from there he saw some of the clans. Then Balaam gave voice to his oracle:

> From Aram has Balac brought me here,
>> Moab's king, from the Eastern Mountains:
> "Come and lay a curse for me on Jacob,
>> come and denounce Israel."
> How can I curse whom God has not cursed?
>> How denounce whom the Lord has not denounced?
> For from the top of the crags I see him,
>> from the heights I behold him.
> Here is a people that lives apart
>> and does not reckon itself among the nations.
> Who has ever counted the dust of Jacob,
>> or numbered Israel's wind-borne particles?
> May I die the death of the just,
>> may my descendants be as many as theirs!

Then Balac said to him, "Please come with me to another place from which you can see only some and not all of them, and from there curse them for me." So he brought him to the lookout field on the top of Phasga, where he built seven altars and offered a bullock and a ram on each of them. Balaam then said to Balac, "Stand here by your holocaust, while I seek a meeting over there." Then the Lord met Balaam, and having put an utterance in his mouth, he said to him, "Go back to Balac, and speak accordingly." So he went back to Balac, who was still standing by his holocaust together with the princes of Moab. When Balac asked him, "What did the Lord say?" Balaam gave voice to his oracle:

> Be aroused, O Balac, and hearken;
>> give ear to my testimony, O son of Sepphor!
> God is not man that he should speak falsely,
>> nor human, that he should change his mind.
> Is he one to speak and not act,
>> to decree and not fulfill?
> It is a blessing I have been given to pronounce;
>> a blessing which I cannot restrain.
> Misfortune is not observed in Jacob,
>> nor misery seen in Israel.
> The Lord, his God, is with him;
>> with him is the triumph of his King.
> It is God who brought him out of Egypt,
>> a wild bull of towering might.
> No, there is no sorcery against Jacob,
>> nor omen against Israel.
> It shall yet be said of Jacob,
>> and of Israel, "Behold what God has wrought!"
> Here is a people that springs up like a lioness,
>> and stalks forth like a lion;
> It rests not till it has devoured its prey
>> and has drunk the blood of the slain.

Then Balac said to Balaam, "Come, let me bring you to another place; perhaps God will approve of your cursing them for me from there." So he took Balaam to the top of Phogor, that overlooks Jesimon. Balaam then said to him, "Here build me seven altars; and here prepare for me seven bullocks and seven rams." And Balac did as Balaam had ordered, offering a bullock and a ram on each altar. Balaam, however, perceiving that the Lord was pleased to bless Israel, did not go aside as before to seek omens, but turned his gaze toward the desert.

When he raised his eyes and saw Israel encamped, tribe by tribe, the spirit of God came upon him, and he gave voice to his oracle:

> The utterance of Balaam, son of Beor,
>   the utterance of the man whose eye is true,
> The utterance of one who hears what God says,
>   and knows what the Most High knows,
> Of one who sees what the Almighty sees,
>   enraptured, and with eyes unveiled:
> How goodly are your tents, O Jacob;
>   your encampments, O Israel!
> They are like gardens beside a stream,
>   like the cedars planted by the Lord.

Balac beat his palms together in a blaze of anger at Balaam and said to him, "It was to curse my foes that I summoned you here; yet three times now you have even blessed them instead! Be off at once, then, to your home. I promised to reward you richly, but the Lord has withheld the reward from you!" Balaam replied to Balac, "Did I not warn the very messengers whom you sent to me, 'Even if Balac gave me his house full of silver and gold, I could not of my own accord do anything, good or evil, contrary to the command of the Lord'? Whatever the Lord says I must repeat. But now that I am about to go to my own people, let me first warn you what this people will do to your people in the days to come." Then Balaam gave voice to his oracle:

> I see him, though not now;
>   I behold him, though not near:
> A star shall advance from Jacob,
>   and a staff shall rise from Israel,
> That shall smite the brows of Moab,
>   and the skulls of all the Suthites,
> Till Edom is dispossessed,
>   and no fugitive is left in Seir.
> Israel shall do valiantly,
>   and Jacob shall overcome his foes.

Then Balaam set out on his journey home; and Balac also went his way.

CHAPTER FIVE

The Song of Moses

THE WORDS OF A PROPHET

"If you are not careful to observe every word of the Law which is written in this book, and to revere the glorious and awesome name of the Lord, your God, he will smite you with severe and constant blows, malignant and lasting maladies. Should there be any kind of sickness or calamity not mentioned in this book, that too the Lord will bring upon you until you are destroyed. Of you who were numerous as the stars in the sky, only a few will be left, because you would not hearken to the voice of the Lord, your God."

When Moses had finished speaking these words to all Israel, he said to them, "I am now one hundred and twenty years old and am no longer able to move about freely; besides, the Lord has told me that I shall not cross this Jordan. It is the Lord who will cross before you; he will destroy these nations before you, that you may supplant them. [It is Josue who will cross before you, as the Lord promised.] The Lord will deal with them just as he dealt with Sehon and Og, the kings of the Amorrites whom he destroyed, and with their country. When, therefore, the Lord delivers them up to you, you must deal with them exactly as I have ordered you."

Then Moses summoned Josue and in the presence of all Israel said to him, "Be brave and steadfast, for you must bring this people into the land which the Lord swore to their fathers he would give them; you must put them in possession of their heritage. It is the Lord who marches before you; he will be with you and will never fail you or forsake you. So do not fear or be dismayed."

The Lord said to Moses, "The time is now approaching for you to die. Summon Josue, and present yourselves at the Meeting Tent that I may give him his commission." So Moses and Josue went and presented themselves at the Meeting Tent. And the Lord appeared at the

Tent in a column of cloud, which stood still at the entrance of the Tent.

Then the Lord commissioned Josue, and said to him, "Be brave and steadfast, for it is you who must bring the Israelites into the land which I promised them on oath. I myself will be with you."

"Now, this is what the Lord has commanded," Moses said to the people, "Be careful to observe all the commandments I enjoin on you today, that you may live and increase, and may enter in and possess the land which the Lord promised. Remember how for forty years now the Lord has directed all your journeying in the desert, so as to test you by affliction and find out whether or not it was your intention to keep his commandments. He therefore let you be afflicted with hunger, and then fed you with manna, a food unknown to you and your fathers, in order to show you that not by bread alone does man live, but by every word that comes forth from the mouth of the Lord. The clothing did not fall from you in tatters, nor did your feet swell these forty years. So you must realize that the Lord, your God, disciplines you even as a man disciplines his son."

The Lord said to Moses, "Soon you will be at rest with your fathers, and then this people will take to rendering wanton worship to the strange gods among whom they will live in the land they are about to enter. They will forsake me and break the covenant which I have made with them. At that time my anger will flare up against them; I will forsake them and hide my face from them, so that they will become a prey to be devoured, and many evils and troubles will befall them. At that time they will indeed say, 'Is it not because our God is not among us that these evils have befallen us?' Yet I will be hiding my face from them at that time only because of all the evil they have done in turning to other gods. Write out this song, then, for yourselves. Teach it to the Israelites and have them recite it, so that this song may be a witness for me against the Israelites. For when I have brought them into the land flowing with milk and honey which I promised on oath to their fathers, and they have eaten their fill and grown fat, if they turn to other gods and serve them, despising me and breaking my covenant; then, when many evils and troubles befall them, this song, which their descendants will not have forgotten to recite, will bear witness against them. For I know what they are inclined to do even at the present time, before I have brought them into the land which I promised on oath to their fathers." So Moses wrote this song that same day, and he taught it to the Israelites.

When Moses had finished writing out on a scroll the words of the law in their entirety, he gave the Levites who carry the Ark of the Covenant of the Lord this order: "Take this scroll of the law and put it beside the Ark of the Covenant of the Lord, your God, that there it may be a witness against you. For I already know how rebellious and stiff-necked you will be. Why, even now, while I am alive among you, you have been rebels against the Lord! How much more, then, after I am dead! Therefore, assemble all your tribal elders and your officials before me, that I may speak these words for them to hear, and so may call heaven and earth to witness against them. For I know that after my death you are sure to become corrupt and to turn aside from the way along which I directed you, so that evil will befall you in some future age because you have done evil in the Lord's sight, and provoked him by your deeds."

Then Moses recited the words of this song from beginning to end, for the whole assembly of Israel to hear:

> Give ear, O heavens, while I speak;
>> let the earth hearken to the words of my mouth!
> May my instruction soak in like the rain,
>> and my discourse permeate like the dew,
> Like a downpour upon the grass,
>> like a shower upon the crops:
>
> For I will sing the Lord's renown.
>> Oh, proclaim the greatness of our God!
> The Rock—how faultless are his deeds,
>> how right all his ways!
> A faithful God, without deceit,
>> how just and upright he is!
>
> Yet basely has he been treated by his degenerate children,
>> a perverse and crooked race!
> Is the Lord to be thus repaid by you,
>> O stupid and foolish people?
> Is he not your father who created you?
>> Has he not made you and established you?
>
> Think back on the days of old,
>> reflect on the years of age upon age.
> Ask your father and he will inform you,
>> ask your elders and they will tell you:

The Song of Moses

When the Most High assigned the nations their heritage,
    when he parceled out the descendants of Adam,
He set up the boundaries of the peoples
    after the number of the sons of God;
While the Lord's own portion was Jacob,
    His hereditary share was Israel.

He found them in a wilderness,
    a wasteland of howling desert.
He shielded them and cared for them,
    guarding them as the apple of his eye.

As an eagle incites its nestlings forth
    by hovering over its brood,
So he spread his wings to receive them
    and bore them up on his pinions.

The Lord alone was their leader,
    no strange god was with him.
He had them ride triumphant over the summits of the land
    and live off the products of its fields,
Giving them honey to suck from its rocks
    and olive oil from its hard, stony ground;

Butter from its cows and milk from its sheep,
    with the fat of its lambs and rams;
Its Basan bulls and its goats,
    with the cream of its finest wheat;
    and the foaming blood of its grapes you drank.

So Jacob ate his fill,
    the darling grew fat and frisky;
    you became fat and gross and gorged.
They spurned the God who made them
    and scorned their saving Rock.
They provoked him with strange gods
    and angered him with abominable idols.

They offered sacrifice to demons, to "no-gods,"
    to gods whom they had not known before,
To newcomers just arrived,
    of whom their fathers had never stood in awe.
You were unmindful of the Rock that begot you,
    You forgot the God who gave you birth.

When the Lord saw this, he was filled with loathing
    and anger toward his sons and daughters.
"I will hide my face from them," he said,
    "and see what will then become of them.
What a fickle race they are,
    sons with no loyalty in them!

"Since they have provoked me with their 'no-god'
    and angered me with their vain idols,
I will provoke them with a 'no-people';
    with a foolish nation I will anger them.

"For by my wrath a fire is enkindled
    that shall rage to the depths of the nether world,
Consuming the earth with its yield,
    and licking with flames the roots of the mountains.
I will spend on them woe upon woe
    and exhaust all my arrows against them:

"Emaciating hunger and consuming fever
    and bitter pestilence,
And the teeth of wild beasts I will send among them,
    with the venom of reptiles gliding in the dust.

"Snatched away by the sword in the street
    and by sheer terror at home
Shall be the youth and the maiden alike,
    the nursing babe as well as the hoary old man.

"I would have said, 'I will make an end of them
    and blot out their name from men's memories,'
Had I not feared the insolence of their enemies,
    feared that these foes would mistakenly boast,
'Our own hand won the victory;
    the Lord had nothing to do with it.' "

For they are a people devoid of reason,
    having no understanding.
If they had insight they would realize what happened,
    they would understand their success and say,

"How could one man rout a thousand,
    or two men put ten thousand to flight,

Unless it was because their Rock sold them
  and the Lord delivered them up?"
Indeed, their "rock" is not like our Rock,
  and our foes are under condemnation.

They are a branch of Sodom's vinestock,
  from the vineyards of Gomorra.
Poisonous are their grapes
  and bitter their clusters.
Their wine is the venom of dragons
  and the cruel poison of cobras.

"Is not this preserved in my treasury,
  sealed up in my storehouse,
Against the day of vengeance and requital,
  against the time they lose their footing?"
Close at hand is the day of their disaster,
  and their doom is rushing upon them!

Surely, the Lord shall do justice for his people;
  on his servants he shall have pity.
When he sees their strength failing,
  and their protected and unprotected alike disappearing,

He will say, "Where are their gods
  whom they relied on as their 'rock'?
Let those who ate the fat of your sacrifices
  and drank the wine of your libations
Rise up now and help you!
  Let them be your protection!

"Learn then that I, I alone, am God,
  and there is no god besides me.
It is I who bring both death and life,
  I who inflict wounds and heal them,
  and from my hand there is no rescue.

"To the heavens I raise my hand and swear:
  As surely as I live forever,
I will sharpen my flashing sword,
  and my hand shall lay hold of my quiver.

"With vengeance I will repay my foes
  and requite those who hate me.

103

I will make my arrows drunk with blood,
   and my sword shall gorge itself with flesh—
With the blood of the slain and the captured,
   Flesh from the heads of the enemy leaders."

Exult with him, you heavens,
   glorify him, all you angels of God;
For he avenges the blood of his servants
   and purges his people's land.

When Moses had finished speaking all these words to all Israel, he said, "Take to heart all the warning which I have now given you and which you must impress on your children, that you may carry out carefully every word of this law. For this is no trivial matter for you; rather, it means your very life, since it is by this means that you are to enjoy a long life on the land which you will cross the Jordan to occupy."

On that very day the Lord said to Moses, "Go up on Mount Nebo, here in the Abarim Mountains [it is in the land of Moab facing Jericho], and view the land of Chanaan, which I am giving to the Israelites as their possession. Then you shall die on the mountain you have climbed, and shall be taken to your people, just as your brother Aaron died on Mount Hor and there was taken to his people; because both of you broke faith with me among the Israelites at the waters of Meribath-Cades in the desert of Sin by failing to manifest my sanctity among the Israelites. You may indeed view the land at a distance, but you shall not enter that land which I am giving to the Israelites."

This is the blessing which Moses, the man of God, pronounced upon the Israelites before he died. He said:

"The Lord came from Sinai
   and dawned on his people from Seir;
He shone forth from Mount Pharan
   and advanced from Meribath-Cades,
While at his right hand a fire blazed forth
   and his wrath devastated the nations.
But all his holy ones were in his hand;
   they followed at his feet
   and he bore them up on his pinions.

A law he gave to us;
   he made the community of Jacob his domain,
   and he became king of his darling,
When the chiefs of the people assembled
   and the tribes of Israel came together.

"There is no god like the God of the darling,
   who rides the heavens in his power,
   and rides the skies in his majesty;
He spread out the primeval tent;
   he extended the ancient canopy.
He drove the enemy out of your way
   and the Amorrite he destroyed.
Israel has dwelt securely,
   and the fountain of Jacob has been undisturbed
In a land of grain and wine,
   where the heavens drip with dew.
How fortunate you are, O Israel!
   Where else is a nation victorious in the Lord?
The Lord is your saving shield,
   and his sword is your glory.
Your enemies fawn upon you,
   as you stride upon their heights."

THE DEATH OF MOSES

Then Moses went up from the plains of Moab to Mount Nebo, the headland of Phasga which faces Jericho, and the Lord showed him all the land—Galaad, and as far as Dan, all Nephthali, the land of Ephraim and Manasse, all the land of Juda as far as the Western Sea, the Negeb, the circuit of the Jordan with the lowlands at Jericho, city of palms, and as far as Segor. The Lord then said to him, "This is the land which I swore to Abraham, Isaac and Jacob that I would give to their descendants. I have let you feast your eyes upon it, but you shall not cross over." So there, in the land of Moab, Moses, the servant of the Lord, died as the Lord had said; and he was buried in the ravine opposite Beth-Phogor in the land of Moab, but to this day no one knows the place of his burial. Moses was one hundred and twenty years old when he died, yet his eyes were undimmed and his vigor unabated. For thirty days the Israelites wept for Moses in the plains of Moab, till they had completed the period of grief and mourning for Moses.

Now Josue, son of Nun, was filled with the spirit of wisdom, since Moses had laid his hands upon him; and so the Israelites gave him their obedience, thus carrying out the Lord's command to Moses.

Since then no prophet has arisen in Israel like Moses, whom the Lord knew face to face. He had no equal in all the signs and wonders the Lord sent him to perform in the land of Egypt against Pharao and all his servants and against all his land, and for the might and the terrifying power that Moses exhibited in the sight of all Israel.

CHAPTER SIX

The Jews Conquer the Promised Land

JOSUE SUCCEEDS MOSES

After Moses had died, the Lord said to Moses' aide Josue, son of Nun: "My servant Moses is dead. So prepare to cross the Jordan here, with all the people, into the land I will give the Israelites. As I promised Moses, I will deliver to you every place where you set foot. Your domain is to be all the land of the Hethites, from the desert and from Lebanon east to the great river Euphrates and west to the Great Sea. No one can withstand you while you live. I will be with you as I was with Moses; I will not leave you nor forsake you. Be firm and steadfast, so that you may give this people possession of the land which I swore to their fathers I would give them. Above all, be firm and steadfast, taking care to observe the entire Law which my servant Moses enjoined on you. Do not swerve from it either to the right or to the left, that you may succeed wherever you go. Keep this Book of the Law on your lips. Recite it by day and by night, that you may observe carefully all that is written in it; then you will successfully attain your goal. I command you: be firm and steadfast! Do not fear nor be dismayed, for the Lord is with you wherever you go."

So Josue commanded the officers of the people: "Go through the camp and instruct the people, 'Prepare your provisions, for three days from now you shall cross the Jordan here, to march in and take possession of the land which the Lord is giving you.' "

Josue reminded the Rubenites, the Gadites, and the half-tribe of Manasse: "Remember what Moses commanded you when he said, 'The Lord will permit you to settle in this land.' Your wives, your children, and your livestock shall remain in the land Moses gave you here beyond the Jordan. But all the warriors among you must cross over armed ahead of your kinsmen and you must help them until the Lord has settled your kinsmen, and they like you possess the land which the Lord is giving them. Afterward you may return and occupy your own land, which Moses has given you east of the Jordan." "We will do all you have commanded us," they answered Josue, "and we will go wherever you send us. We will obey you as completely as we obeyed Moses. But may the Lord, your God, be with you as he was with Moses. If anyone rebels against your orders and does not obey every command you give him, he shall be put to death. But be firm and steadfast."

A PROSTITUTE HELPS THE CHOSEN PEOPLE

Then Josue secretly sent out two spies from Sattim, saying, "Go, reconnoiter the land and Jericho." When the two reached Jericho, they went into the house of a harlot named Rahab, where they lodged. But a report was brought to the king of Jericho that some Israelites had come there that night to spy out the land. So the king of Jericho sent Rahab the order, "Put out the visitors who have entered your house, for they have come to spy out the entire land." The woman had taken the two men and hidden them, so she said, "True, the men you speak of came to me, but I did not know where they came from. At dark, when it was time for the gate to be shut, they left, and I do not know where they went. You will have to pursue them immediately to overtake them." Now, she had led them to the roof, and hidden them among her stalks of flax spread out there. But the pursuers set out along the way to the fords of the Jordan, and once they had left, the gate was shut.

Before the spies fell asleep, Rahab came to them on the roof and said: "I know that the Lord has given you the land, that a dread of you has come upon us, and that all the inhabitants of the land are overcome with fear of you. For we have heard how the Lord dried up the waters of the Red Sea before you when you came out of Egypt, and how you dealt with Sehon and Og, the two kings of the Amorrites beyond the Jordan, whom you doomed to destruction. At these reports, we are disheartened; everyone is discouraged because of you, since the Lord, your God, is God in heaven above and on earth below. Now then, swear to me by the Lord that, since I am showing kindness to you, you in turn will show kindness to my family; and give me an unmistakable token that you are to spare my father and mother, brothers and sisters, and all their kin, and save us from death." "We pledge our lives for yours," the men answered her. "If you do not betray this errand of ours, we will be faithful in showing kindness to you when the Lord gives us the land."

Then she let them down through the window with a rope; for she lived in a house built into the city wall. "Go up into the hill country," she suggested to them, "that your pursuers may not find you. Hide there for three days, until they return; then you may proceed on your way." The men answered her, "This is how we will fulfill the oath you made us take: When we come into the land, tie this scarlet cord in the window through which you are letting us down; and gather your father and mother, your brothers and all your family into your house. Should any of them pass outside the doors of your house, he will be responsible for his own death, and we shall be guiltless. But we shall be responsible if anyone in the house with you is harmed. If, however, you betray this errand of ours, we shall be quit of the oath you have made us take." "Let it be as you say," she replied, and bade them farewell. When they were gone, she tied the scarlet cord in the window.

They went up into the hills, where they stayed three days until their pursuers, who had sought them all along the road without finding them, returned. Then the two came back down from the hills, crossed the Jordan to Josue, and reported all that had befallen them. They assured Josue, "The Lord has delivered all this land into our power; indeed, all the inhabitants of the land are overcome with fear of us."

THE CROSSING OF THE JORDAN

Early the next morning, Josue moved with all the Israelites from Sattim to the Jordan, where they lodged before crossing over. Three days later the officers went through the camp and issued these instructions to the people: "When you see the Ark of the Covenant of the Lord, your God, which the Levitical priests will carry, you must also break camp and follow it, that you may know the way to take, for you have not gone over this road before. But let there be a space of two thousand cubits between you and the Ark. Do not come nearer to it." Josue also said to the people, "Sanctify yourselves, for tomorrow the Lord will perform wonders among you." And he directed the priests to take up the Ark of the Covenant and go on ahead of the people; and they did so.

Then the Lord said to Josue, "Today I will begin to exalt you in the sight of all Israel, that they may know I am with you, as I was with Moses. Now command the priests carrying the Ark of the Covenant to come to a halt in the Jordan when they reach the edge of the waters."

So Josue said to the Israelites, "Come here and listen to the words of the Lord, your God." He continued: "This is how you will know that there is a living God in your midst, who at your approach will dispossess the Chanaanites, Hethites, Hevites, Pherezites, Gergesites, Amorrites and Jebusites. The Ark of the Covenant of the Lord of the whole earth will precede you into the Jordan. [Now choose twelve men, one from each of the tribes of Israel.] When the soles of the feet of the priests carrying the Ark of the Lord, the Lord of the whole earth, touch the water of the Jordan, it will cease to flow; for the water flowing down from upstream will halt in a solid bank."

The people struck their tents to cross the Jordan, with the priests carrying the Ark of the Covenant ahead of them. No sooner had these priestly bearers of the Ark waded into the waters at the edge of the Jordan, which overflows all its banks during the entire season of the harvest, than the waters flowing from upstream halted, backing up in a solid mass for a very great distance indeed, from Adama, a city in the direction of Sarthan; while those flowing downstream toward the Salt Sea of the Araba disappeared entirely. Thus the people crossed over opposite Jericho. While all Israel crossed over on dry ground, the priests carrying the Ark of the Covenant remained motionless on dry ground in the bed of the Jordan until the whole nation had completed the passage.

THE FALL OF JERICHO

Now Jericho was in a state of siege because of the presence of the Israelites, so that no one left or entered. And to Josue the Lord said, "I have delivered Jericho and its king into your power. Have all the soldiers circle the city, marching once around it. Do this for six days, with seven priests carrying rams' horns ahead of the Ark. On the seventh day march around the city seven times, and have the priests blow the horns. When they give a long blast on the ram's horn and you hear that signal, all the people shall shout aloud. The wall of the city will collapse, and they will be able to make a frontal attack."

Summoning the priests, Josue then ordered them to take up the Ark of the Covenant with seven of the priests carrying rams' horns in front of the Ark. And he ordered the people to proceed in a circle around the city, with the picked troops marching ahead of the Ark. At this order they proceeded, with the seven priests who carried rams' horns before the Lord blowing their horns, and the Ark following them. In front of the priests with the horns marched the picked troops; the rear guard followed the Ark, and the blowing of horns was kept up continually as they marched. But the people had been commanded by Josue not to shout or make any noise or outcry until he gave the word: only then were they to shout. So he had the Ark circle the city, going once around it, after which they returned to camp for the night.

Early the next morning, Josue had the priests take up the Ark. The seven priests bearing the rams' horns marched in front of the Ark, blowing their horns. Ahead of these marched the picked troops, while the rear guard followed the Ark, and the blowing of horns was kept up continually. On this second day they again marched around the city once before returning to camp; and for six days in all they did the same.

On the seventh day, beginning at daybreak, they marched around the city seven times in the same manner; on that day only did they march around the city seven times. The seventh time around, the priests blew the horns and Josue said to the people, "Now shout, for the Lord has given you the city and everything in it. It is under the Lord's ban. Only the harlot Rahab and all who are in the house with her are to be spared, because she hid the messengers we sent. But be careful not to take, in your greed, anything that is under the ban; else you will bring upon the camp of Israel this ban and the misery of it. All silver and gold, and the articles of bronze or iron, are sacred to the Lord. They shall be put in the treasury of the Lord."

As the horns blew, the people began to shout. When they heard the signal horn, they raised a tremendous shout. The wall collapsed, and the people stormed the city in a frontal attack and took it. They observed the ban by putting to the sword all living creatures in the city: men and women, young and old, as well as oxen, sheep and asses.

Josue directed the two men who had spied out the land, "Go into the harlot's house and bring out the woman with all her kin, as you swore to her you would do." The spies entered and brought out Rahab, with her father, mother, brothers, and all her kin. Her entire family they led forth and placed them outside the camp of Israel. The city itself they burned with all that was in it, except the silver, gold, and articles of bronze and iron, which were placed in the treasury of the house of the Lord. Because Rahab the harlot had hidden the messengers whom Josue had sent to reconnoiter Jericho, Josue spared her with her family and all her kin, who continue in the midst of Israel to this day.

On that occasion Josue imposed the oath: Cursed before the Lord be the man who attempts to rebuild this city, Jericho. He shall lose his first-born when he lays its foundation, and he shall lose his youngest son when he sets up its gates. [And the Lord stood by Josue's side, till his fame spread abroad all over the land.]

THE DEFEAT OF HAI AND THE CAPTURE OF HAI

[But now Israel incurred guilt by turning the forfeited plunder to their own use. Achan, a man of Juda, descended from Zara through Charmi and Zabdi, took some of the plunder for himself, and God was angry with the people of Israel.]

Josue next sent men from Jericho to Hai, which is near Bethel on its eastern side, with instructions to go up and reconnoiter the land. When they had explored Hai, they returned to Josue and advised, "Do not send all the people up; if only about two or three thousand go up, they can overcome Hai. The enemy there are few; you need not call for an effort from all the people." About three thousand of the people made the attack, but they were defeated by those at Hai, who killed some thirty-six of them. They pressed them back across the clearing in front of the city gate till they broke ranks, and defeated them finally on the descent, so that the confidence of the people melted away like water.

Josue, together with the elders of Israel, rent his garments and lay prostrate before the Ark of the Lord until evening; and they threw dust on their heads. "Alas, O Lord God," Josue prayed, "why did you ever allow this people to pass over the Jordan, delivering us into the power of the Amorrites, that they might destroy us? Would that we had been content to dwell on the other side of the Jordan. Pray, Lord, what can I say, now that Israel has turned its back to its enemies? When the Chanaanites and the other inhabitants of the land hear of it, they will close in around us and efface our name from the earth. What will you do for your great name?"

The Lord replied to Josue: "Stand up. Why are you lying prostrate? Israel has sinned: they have violated the covenant which I enjoined on them. They have stealthily taken goods subject to the ban, and have deceitfully put them in their baggage. If the Israelites cannot stand up to their enemies, but must turn their back to them, it is because they are under the ban. I will not remain with you unless you remove from among you whoever has incurred the ban. Rise, sanctify the people. Tell them to sanctify themselves before tomorrow, for the Lord, the God of Israel, says: You are under the ban, O Israel. You cannot stand up to your enemies until you remove from among you whoever has incurred the ban. In the morning you must present yourselves by tribes. The tribe which the Lord designates shall come forward by clans; the clan which the Lord designates shall come forward by families; the family which the Lord designates shall come forward one by one. He who is designated as having incurred the ban shall be destroyed by fire, with all that is his, because he has violated the covenant of the Lord and has committed a shameful crime in Israel."

Early next morning Josue had Israel come forward by tribes, and the tribe of Juda was designated. Then he had the clans of Juda come forward, and the clan of Zara was designated. He had the clan of Zara come forward by families, and Zabdi was designated. Finally he had that family come forward one by one, and Achan was designated. Josue said to Achan, "My son, give to the Lord, the God of Israel, glory and honor by telling me what you have done; do not hide it from me." Achan answered Josue, "I have indeed sinned against the Lord. This is what I have done: Among the spoils, I saw a beautiful Babylonian mantle, two hundred shekels of silver, and a bar of gold fifty shekels in weight; in my greed I took them. They are now hidden in the ground inside my tent, with the silver underneath." The messengers whom Josue sent hastened to the tent and found them hidden there, with the silver underneath. They took them from the tent, brought them to Josue and all the Israelites, and spread them out before the Lord.

Then Josue and all Israel took Achan, with the silver, the mantle, and the bar of gold, and with his sons and daughters, his ox, his ass and his sheep, his tent, and all his possessions, and led them off to the Valley of Achor. Josue said, "The Lord bring upon you today the misery with which you have afflicted us!" And all Israel stoned him to death and piled a great heap of stones over him, which remains to the present day. Then the anger of the Lord relented. That is why the place is called the Valley of Achor to this day.

The Lord then said to Josue, "Do not be afraid or dismayed. Take all the army with you and prepare to attack Hai. I have delivered the king of Hai into your power, with his people, city and land. Do to Hai and its king what you did to Jericho and its king; except that you may take its spoil and livestock as booty. Set an ambush behind the city." So Josue and all the soldiers prepared to attack Hai. Picking out thirty thousand warriors, Josue sent them off by night with these orders: "See that you ambush the city from the rear, at no great distance; then all of you be on the watch. The rest of the people and I will come up to the city, and when they make a sortie against us as they did the last time, we will flee from them. They will keep coming out after us until we have drawn them away from the city, for they will think we are fleeing from them as we did the last time. When this occurs, rise from ambush and take possession of the city, which the Lord, your God, will deliver into your power. When you have taken the city, set it afire in obedience to the Lord's command. These are my orders to you." Then Josue sent them away. They went to the place of ambush, taking up their position to the west of Hai, toward Bethel. Josue, however, spent that night in the plain.

Early the next morning Josue mustered the army and went up to Hai at its head, with the elders of Israel. When all the troops he led were drawn up in position before the city, they pitched camp north of Hai, on the other side of the ravine. [He took about five thousand men and set them in ambush between Bethel and Hai, west of the city.] Thus the people took up their stations, with the main body north of the city and the ambush west of it, and Josue waited overnight among his troops. The king of Hai saw this, and he and all his army came out very early in the morning to engage Israel in battle at the descent toward the Araba, not knowing that there was an ambush behind the city. Josue and the main body of the Israelites fled in seeming defeat toward the desert, till the last of the soldiers in the city had been called out to pursue them. Since they were drawn away from the city, with every man engaged in this pursuit of Josue and the Israelites, not a soldier remained in Hai [or Bethel], and the city was open and unprotected.

Then the Lord directed Josue, "Stretch out the javelin in your hand toward Hai, for I will deliver it into your power." Josue stretched out the javelin in his hand toward the city, and as soon as he did so, the men in ambush rose from their post, rushed in, captured the city, and immediately set it on fire. By the time the men of Hai looked back, the smoke from the city was already sky-high. Escape in any direction was impossible, because the Israelites retreating toward the desert now turned on their pursuers; for when Josue and the main body of Israelites saw that the city had been taken from ambush and was going up in smoke, they struck back at the men of Hai. Since those in the city came out to intercept them, the men of Hai were hemmed in by Israelites on either side, who cut them down without any fugitives or survivors except the king, whom they took alive and brought to Josue.

All the inhabitants of Hai who had pursued the Israelites into the desert were slain by the sword there in the open, down to the last man. Then all Israel returned and put to the sword those inside the city. There fell that day a total of twelve thousand men and women, the entire population of Hai. Josue kept the javelin in his hand stretched out until he had fulfilled the doom on all the inhabitants of Hai. However, the Israelites took for themselves as booty the livestock and the spoil of that city, according to the command of the Lord issued to Josue. Then Josue destroyed the place by fire, reducing it to an everlasting mound of ruins, as it remains today. He had the king of Hai hanged on a tree until evening; then at sunset Josue ordered the body removed from the tree and cast at the entrance of the city gate, where a great heap of stones was piled up over it, which remains to the present day.

Later Josue built an altar to the Lord, the God of Israel, on Mount Ebal, of unhewn stones on which no iron tool had been used, in keeping with the command to the Israelites of Moses, the servant of the Lord, as recorded in the Book of the Law. On this altar they offered holocausts and peace offerings to the Lord. There, in the presence of the Israelites, Josue inscribed upon the stones a copy of the law written by Moses. And all Israel, stranger and native alike, with their elders, officers and judges, stood on either side of the Ark facing the Levitical priests who were carrying the Ark of the Covenant of the Lord. Half of them were facing Mount Garizim and half Mount Ebal, thus carrying out the instructions of Moses, the servant of the Lord, for the blessing of the people of Israel on this first occasion. Then were read aloud all the words of the law, the blessings and the curses, exactly as written in the Book of the Law. Every single word that Moses had commanded, Josue read aloud to the entire community, including the women and children, and the strangers who had accompanied Israel.

THE DAY THE SUN STOOD STILL; DEFEAT
OF THE FIVE KINGS

Now Adonisedec, king of Jerusalem, heard that, in the capture and destruction of Hai, Josue had done to that city and its king as he had done to Jericho and its king. He heard also that the inhabitants of Gabaon had made their peace with Israel, remaining among them, and that there was great fear abroad, because Gabaon was large enough for a royal city, larger even than the city of Hai, and all its men were brave. So Adonisedec, king of Jerusalem, sent for Oham, king of Hebron, Pharam, king of Jerimoth, Japhia, king of Lachis, and Dabir, king of Eglon, to come to his aid for an attack on Gabaon, since it had concluded peace with Josue and the Israelites. The five Amorrite kings united all their forces and marched against Gabaon, where they took up siege positions. Thereupon, the men of Gabaon sent an appeal to Josue in his camp at Galgal: "Do not abandon your servants. Come up here quickly and save us. Help us, because all the Amorrite kings of the mountain country have joined forces against us."

So Josue marched up from Galgal with his picked troops and the rest of his soldiers. Meanwhile the Lord said to Josue, "Do not fear them, for I have delivered them into your power. Not one of them will be able to withstand you." And when Josue made his surprise attack upon them after an all-night march from Galgal, the Lord threw them into disorder before him. The Israelites inflicted a great slaughter on them at Gabaon and pursued them down the Beth-Horon slope, harassing them as far as Azeca and Maceda.

While they fled before Israel along the descent from Beth-Horon, the Lord hurled great stones from the sky above them all the way to Azeca, killing many. More died from these hailstones than the Israelites slew with the sword. On this day, when the Lord delivered up the Amorrites to the Israelites,

> Josue prayed to the Lord,
>   and said in the presence of Israel:
> Stand still, O sun, at Gabaon,
>   O moon, in the valley of Aialon!
> And the sun stood still,
>   and the moon stayed,
>   while the nation took vengeance on its foes.

Is this not recorded in the Book of Jashar? The sun halted in the middle of the sky; not for a whole day did it resume its swift course. Never before or since was there a day like this, when the Lord obeyed the voice of a man; for the Lord fought for Israel. [Then Josue and all Israel returned to the camp at Galgal.]

Meanwhile the five kings who had fled, hid in a cave at Maceda. When Josue was told that the five kings had been discovered hiding in a cave at Maceda, he said, "Roll large stones to the mouth of the cave and post men over it to guard them. But do not remain there yourselves. Pursue your enemies, and harry them in the rear. Do not allow them to escape to their cities, for the Lord, your God, has delivered them into your power."

Once Josue and the Israelites had finally inflicted the last blows in this very great slaughter, and the survivors had escaped from them into the fortified cities, all the army returned safely to Josue and the camp at Maceda, no man uttering a sound against the Israelites. Then Josue said, "Open the mouth of the cave and bring out those five kings to me." Obediently, they brought out to him from the cave the five kings. When they had done so, Josue summoned all the men of Israel and said to the commanders of the soldiers who had marched with him, "Come forward and put your feet on the necks of these kings." They came forward and put their feet upon their necks. Then Josue said to them, "Do not be afraid or dismayed, be firm and steadfast. This is what the Lord will do to all the enemies against whom you fight." Thereupon Josue struck and killed them, and hanged them on five trees, where they remained hanging until evening. At sunset they were removed from the trees at the command of Josue and cast into the cave where they had hidden; over the mouth of the cave large stones were placed, which remain until this very day.

OTHER BATTLES IN CHANAAN

Maceda, too, Josue captured and put to the sword at that time. He fulfilled the doom on the city, on its king, and on every person in it, leaving no survivors. Thus he did to the king of Maceda what he had done to the king of Jericho. Josue then passed on with all Israel from Maceda to Lebna, which he attacked. Lebna also, with its king, the Lord delivered into the power of Israel. He put it to the sword with every person there, leaving no survivors. Thus he did to its king what he had done to the king of Jericho. Josue next passed on with all

Israel from Lebna to Lachis, where they set up a camp during the attack. The Lord delivered Lachis into the power of Israel, so that on the second day Josue captured it and put it to the sword with every person in it, just as he had done to Lebna. At that time Horam, king of Gazer, came up to help Lachis, but Josue defeated him and his people, leaving no survivors. From Lachis, Josue passed on with all Israel to Eglon; encamping near it, they attacked it and captured it the same day, putting it to the sword. He fulfilled the doom that day on every person in it, just as he had done at Lachis. From Eglon, Josue went up with all Israel to Hebron, which they attacked and captured. They put it to the sword with its king, all its towns, and every person there, leaving no survivors, just as Josue had done to Eglon. He fulfilled the doom on it and on every person there. Then Josue and all Israel turned back to Dabir and attacked it, capturing it with its king and all its towns. They put them to the sword and fulfilled the doom on every person there, leaving no survivors. Thus was done to Dabir and its king what had been done to Hebron, as well as to Lebna and its king.

Josue conquered the entire country; the mountain regions, the Negeb, the foothills, and the mountain slopes, with all their kings. He left no survivors, but fulfilled the doom on all who lived there, just as the Lord, the God of Israel, had commanded. Josue conquered from Cadesbarne to Gaza, and all the land of Gosen to Gabaon. All these kings and their lands Josue captured in a single campaign, for the Lord fought for Israel. Thereupon Josue with all Israel returned to the camp at Galgal.

JOSUE'S FINAL PLEA

Many years later, after the Lord had given the Israelites rest from all their enemies round about them, and when Josue was old and advanced in years, he summoned all Israel (including their elders, leaders, judges and officers) and said to them: "I am old and advanced in years. You have seen all that the Lord, your God, has done for you against all these nations; for it has been the Lord himself who fought for you. Bear in mind that I have apportioned among your tribes as their heritage the nations that survive [as well as those I destroyed] between the Jordan and the Great Sea in the west. The Lord will drive them out and dislodge them at your approach, so that you will take possession of their land as the Lord promised you. Therefore strive hard to observe and carry out all that is written in the Book of the Law of Moses, not straying from it in any way, or mingling with these nations while they survive among you. You must not invoke their gods, or swear by them, or serve them, or worship them, but you must remain loyal to the Lord as you have been to this day. At your approach the Lord has driven out large and strong nations, and to this day no one has withstood you. One of you puts to flight a thousand, because it is the Lord himself who fights for you, as he promised you. Take great care, however, to love the Lord. For if you ever abandon him and ally yourselves with the remnant of these nations while they survive among you, by intermarrying and intermingling with them, know for certain that the Lord will no longer drive these nations out of your way. Instead they will be a snare and a trap for you, a scourge for your sides and thorns for your eyes, until you perish from this good land which the Lord has given you.

"Today, as you see, I am going the way of all men. So now acknowledge with your whole heart and soul that not one of all the promises the Lord made to you has remained unfulfilled. Every promise has been fulfilled for you, with not one single exception. But just as every promise the Lord made to you has been fulfilled for you, so will he fulfill every threat, even so far as to exterminate you from this land. If you transgress the covenant of the Lord which he enjoined on you, serve other gods and worship them, the anger of the Lord will flare up against you and you will quickly perish from the good land which he has given you."

A PERTINENT REMINDER

Josue gathered together all the tribes of Israel at Sichem, summoning their elders, their leaders, their judges and their officers. When they stood in ranks before God, Josue addressed all the people: "Thus says the Lord, the God of Israel: In times past your fathers, down to Thare, father of Abraham and Nahor, dwelt beyond the River and served other gods. But I brought your father Abraham from the region beyond the River and led him through the entire land of Chanaan. I made his descendants numerous, and gave him Isaac. To Isaac I gave Jacob and Esau. To Esau I assigned the mountain region of Seir in which to settle, while Jacob and his children went down to Egypt.

"Then I sent Moses and Aaron, and smote Egypt with the prodigies which I wrought in her midst. Afterward I led you out of Egypt, and when you reached the sea, the Egyptians pursued your fathers to the

Red Sea with chariots and horsemen. Because they cried out to the Lord, he put darkness between your people and the Egyptians, upon whom he brought the sea so that it engulfed them. After you witnessed what I did to Egypt, and dwelt a long time in the desert, I brought you into the land of the Amorrites who lived east of the Jordan. They fought against you, but I delivered them into your power. You took possession of their land, and I destroyed them [the two kings of the Amorrites] before you. Then Balac, son of Sepphor, king of Moab, prepared to war against Israel. He summoned Balaam, son of Beor, to curse you; but I would not listen to Balaam. On the contrary, he had to bless you and I saved you from him. Once you crossed the Jordan and came to Jericho, the men of Jericho fought against you, but I delivered them also into your power.

"I gave you a land which you had not tilled and cities which you had not built, to dwell in; you have eaten of vineyards and olive groves which you did not plant.

"Now, therefore, fear the Lord and serve him completely and sincerely. Cast out the gods your fathers served beyond the River and in Egypt, and serve the Lord. If it does not please you to serve the Lord, decide today whom you will serve, the gods your fathers served beyond the River or the gods of the Amorrites in whose country you are dwelling. As for me and my household, we will serve the Lord."

But the people answered, "Far be it from us to forsake the Lord for the service of other gods. For it was the Lord, our God, who brought us and our fathers up out of the land of Egypt, out of a state of slavery. He performed those great miracles before our very eyes and protected us along our entire journey and among all the peoples through whom we passed. At our approach the Lord drove out [all the peoples, in cluding] the Amorrites who dwelt in the land. Therefore we also will serve the Lord, for he is our God."

Josue in turn said to the people, "You may not be able to serve the Lord, for he is a holy God; he is a jealous God who will not forgive your transgressions or your sins. If, after the good he has done for you, you forsake the Lord and serve strange gods, he will do evil to you and destroy you."

But the people answered Josue, "We will still serve the Lord." Josue therefore said to the people, "You are your own witnesses that you have chosen to serve the Lord." They replied, "We are, indeed!" "Now, therefore, put away the strange gods that are among you and turn your hearts to the Lord." Then the people promised Josue, "We will serve the Lord, our God, and obey his voice."

So Josue made a covenant with the people that day and made statutes and ordinances for them at Sichem, which he recorded in the Book of the Law of God. Then he took a large stone and set it up there under the oak that was in the sanctuary of the Lord. And Josue said to all the people, "This stone shall be our witness, for it has heard all the words which the Lord spoke to us. It shall be a witness against you, should you wish to deny your God." Then Josue dismissed the people, each to his own heritage.

THE DEATH OF JOSUE

After these events Josue, son of Nun, servant of the Lord, died at the age of a hundred and ten. He was buried within the limits of his heritage at Thamnath-Sare in the mountain region of Ephraim north of Mount Gaas. Israel served the Lord during the entire lifetime of Josue and that of the elders who outlived Josue and knew all that the Lord had done for Israel. The bones of Joseph, which the Israelites had brought up from Egypt, were buried in Sichem in the plot of ground Jacob had bought from the sons of Hemor, father of Sichem, for a hundred pieces of money. This was a heritage of the descendants of Joseph. When Eleazar, son of Aaron, also died, he was buried on the hill which had been given to his son Phinees in the mountain region of Ephraim.

CHAPTER SEVEN

God's People and
Their Ungodly Neighbors

THE JEWS TURN FROM GOD

But once the rest of that generation were gathered to their fathers, and a later generation arose that did not know the Lord, or what he had done for Israel, the Israelites offended the Lord by serving the Baals. Abandoning the Lord, the God of their fathers, who had led them out of the land of Egypt, they followed the other gods of the various nations around them, and by their worship of these gods provoked the Lord.

Because they had thus abandoned him and served Baal and the Astharthes, the anger of the Lord flared up against Israel, and he delivered them over to plunderers who despoiled them. He allowed them to fall into the power of their enemies round about whom they were no longer able to withstand. Whatever they undertook, the Lord turned into disaster for them, as in his warning he had sworn he would do, till they were in great distress. They were quick to stray from the way their fathers had taken, and did not follow their example of obedience to the commandments of the Lord. Whenever the Lord raised up judges for them, he would be with the judge and save them from the power of their enemies as long as the judge lived; it was thus the Lord took pity on their distressful cries of affliction under their oppressors. But when the judge died, they would relapse and do worse than their fathers, following other gods in service and worship, relinquishing none of their evil practices or stubborn conduct.

[So the children of Israel] were living among the Chanaanites, Hethites, Amorrites, Pherezites, Hevites and Jebusites. In fact, they took their daughters in marriage, and gave their own daughters to their sons in marriage, and served their gods.

Because the Israelites had offended the Lord by forgetting the Lord, their God, and serving the Baals and the Asheras, the anger of the Lord flared up against them, and he allowed them to fall into the power of Chusan-Rasathaim, king of Aram Naharaim, whom they served for eight years. But when the Israelites cried out to the Lord, he raised up for them a savior, Othoniel, son of Caleb's younger brother Cenez, who rescued them. The spirit of the Lord came upon him, and he judged Israel. When he went out to war, the Lord delivered Chusan-Rasathaim, king of Aram, into his power, so that he made him a subject. The land then was at rest for forty years, until Othoniel, son of Cenez, died.

Again the Israelites offended the Lord, who because of this offense strengthened Eglon, king of Moab, against Israel. In alliance with the Ammonites and Amalecites, he attacked and defeated Israel, taking possession of the city of palms. The Israelites then served Eglon, king of Moab, for eighteen years. But when the Israelites cried out to the Lord, he raised up for them a savior, the Benjaminite Aod, son of Gera, who was left-handed. After him there was Samgar, son of Anath, who slew six hundred Philistines with an oxgoad. He, too, rescued Israel. After Aod's death, however, the Israelites again offended the Lord. So the Lord allowed them to fall into the power of the Chanaanite king, Jabin, who reigned in Hasor. The general of his army was Sisara, who dwelt in Haroseth-Goim. But the Israelites cried out to the Lord; for with his nine hundred iron chariots he sorely oppressed the Israelites for twenty years.

DEBORA AND BARAC

At this time the prophetess Debora, wife of Laphidoth, was judging Israel. She used to sit under Debora's palm tree, situated between Rama and Bethel in the mountain region of Ephraim, and there the Israelites came up to her for judgment. She sent and summoned Barac, son of Abinoem, from Cedes of Nephthali. "This is what the Lord, the God of Israel, commands," she said to him; "go, march on Mount Thabor, and take with you ten thousand Nephthalites and Zabulonites. I will lead Sisara, the general of Jabin's army, out to you at the Wadi Cison, together with his chariots and troops, and will deliver them into your power." But Barac answered her, "If you come with me, I will go; if you do not come with me, I will not go." "I will certainly go with you," she replied, "but you shall not gain the glory in the expedition on which you are setting out, for the Lord will have Sisara fall into the power of a woman." So Debora joined Barac and journeyed with him to Cedes.

Barac summoned Zabulon and Nephthali to Cedes, and ten thousand men followed him. Debora also went up with him. Now the Cinite Heber had detached himself from his own people, the descendants of Hobab, Moses' brother-in-law, and had pitched his tent by the terebinth of Saananim, which was near Cedes.

It was reported to Sisara that Barac had gone up to Mount Thabor. So Sisara assembled from Haroseth-Goim at the Wadi Cison all nine hundred of his iron chariots and all his forces. Debora then said to Barac, "Be off, for this is the day on which the Lord has delivered Sisara into your power. The Lord marches before you." So Barac went down Mount Thabor, followed by his ten thousand men. And the Lord put Sisara and all his chariots and all his forces to rout before Barac. Sisara himself dismounted from his chariot and fled on foot. Barac, however, pursued the chariots and the army as far as Haroseth-Goim. The entire army of Sisara fell beneath the sword, not even one man surviving.

Sisara, in the meantime, had fled on foot to the tent of Jahel, wife of the Cinite Heber, since Jabin, king of Hasor, and the family of the Cinite Heber were at peace with one another. Jahel went out to meet Sisara and said to him, "Come in, my lord, come in with me; do not be afraid." So he went into her tent, and she covered him with a rug. He said to her, "Please give me a little water to drink. I am thirsty." But she opened a jug of milk for him to drink, and then covered him over. "Stand at the entrance of the tent," he said to her. "If anyone comes and asks, 'Is there someone here?' say, 'No!'" Instead Jahel, wife of Heber, got a tent peg and took a mallet in her hand. While Sisara was sound asleep, she stealthily approached him and drove the peg through his temple down into the ground, so that he perished in death. Then when Barac came in pursuit of Sisara, Jahel went out to meet him and said to him, "Come, I will show you the man you seek." So he went in with her, and there lay Sisara dead, with the tent peg through his temple.

Thus on that day God humbled the Chanaanite king, Jabin, before the Israelites; their power weighed ever heavier upon him, till at length they destroyed the king; and the land was at rest for forty years.

THE CALL OF GEDEON, DEFENDER OF ISRAEL

The Israelites offended the Lord, who therefore delivered them into the power of Madian for seven years.

Then the angel of the Lord came and sat under the terebinth in Ephra that belonged to Joas the Abiezerite. While his son Gedeon was beating out wheat in the wine press to save it from the Madianites, the angel of the Lord appeared to him and said, "The Lord is with you, O champion!" "My lord," Gedeon said to him, "if the Lord is with us, why has all this happened to us? Where are his wondrous deeds of which our fathers told us when they said, 'Did not the Lord bring us up from Egypt?' For now the Lord has abandoned us and has delivered us into the power of Madian." The Lord turned to him and said, "Go with the strength you have and save Israel from the power of Madian. It is I who send you." But he answered him, "Please, my lord, how can I save Israel? My family is the meanest in Manasse, and I am the most insignificant in my father's house." "I shall be with you," the Lord said to him, "and you will cut down Madian to the last man."

Then all Madian and Amalec and the Cedemites mustered and crossed over into the valley of Jezrael, where they encamped. The spirit of the Lord enveloped Gedeon; he blew the horn that summoned Abiezer to follow him. He sent messengers, too, throughout Manasse, which also obeyed his summons; through Aser, Zabulon and Nephthali, likewise, he sent messengers and these tribes advanced to meet the others. Gedeon said to God, "If indeed you are going to save Israel through me, as you promised, I am putting this woolen fleece on the threshing floor. If dew comes on the fleece alone, while all the ground is dry, I shall know that you will save Israel through me, as you promised." This is what took place. Early the next morning he wrung the dew from the fleece, squeezing out of it a bowlful of water. Gedeon then said to God, "Do not be angry with me if I speak once more. Let me make just one more test with the fleece. Let the fleece alone be dry, but let there be dew on all the ground." That night God did so; the fleece alone was dry, but there was dew on all the ground.

The Lord said to Gedeon, "You have too many soldiers with you for me to deliver Madian into their power, lest Israel vaunt itself against me and say, 'My own power brought me the victory.' Now proclaim to all the soldiers, 'If anyone is afraid or fearful, let him leave.' " When Gedeon put them to this test on the mountain, twenty-two thousand of the soldiers left, but ten thousand remained. The Lord said to Gedeon, "There are still too many soldiers. Lead them down to the water and I will test them for you there. If I tell you that a certain man is to go with you, he must go with you. But no one is to go if I tell you he must not." When Gedeon led the soldiers down to the water, the Lord said to him, "You shall set to one side everyone who laps up the water as a dog does with its tongue; to the other, everyone who kneels down to drink." Those who lapped up the water raised to their mouths by hand numbered three hundred, but all the rest of the soldiers knelt down to drink the water. The Lord said to Gedeon, "By means of the three hundred who lapped up the water I will save you and will deliver Madian into your power. So let all the other soldiers go home." Their horns, and such supplies as the soldiers had with them, were taken up, and Gedeon ordered the rest of the Israelites to their tents, but kept the three hundred men. Now the camp of Madian was beneath him in the valley.

He divided the three hundred men into three companies, and provided them all with horns and with empty jars and torches inside the jars. "Watch me and follow my lead," he told them. "I shall go to the edge of the camp, and as I do, you must do also. When I and those with me blow horns, you too must blow horns all around the camp and cry out, 'For the Lord and for Gedeon!' " So Gedeon and the hundred men who were with him came to the edge of the camp at the beginning of the middle watch, just after the posting of the guards. They blew the horns and broke the jars they were holding. All three companies blew horns and broke their jars. They held the torches in their left hands, and in their right the horns they were blowing, and cried out, "A sword for the Lord and Gedeon!" They all remained standing in place around the camp, while the whole camp fell to running and shouting and fleeing. But the three hundred men kept blowing the horns, and throughout the camp the Lord set the sword of one against another. The army fled as far as Beth-Setta in the direction of Sarera, as far as the border of Abel-Mehula near Tebbath. [But the men of Israel shouting from Nephthali and Aser, and from all Manasse pursued after Madian.]

JEPHTE, ANOTHER PROTECTOR

The Israelites again offended the Lord, serving the Baals and Astharthes, the gods of Aram, the gods of Sidon, the gods of Moab, the gods of the Ammonites, and the gods of the Philistines. Since they had abandoned the Lord and would not serve him, the Lord became angry with Israel and allowed them to fall into the power of [the Philistines and] the Ammonites.

There was a chieftain, the Galaadite Jephte, born to Galaad of a harlot. Galaad's wife had also borne him sons, and on growing up the sons of the wife had driven Jephte away, saying to him, "You shall inherit nothing in our family, for you are the son of another woman." So Jephte had fled from his brothers and had taken up residence in the land of Tob. A rabble had joined company with him, and went out with him on raids.

Some time later, the Ammonites warred on Israel. When this occurred the elders of Galaad went to bring Jephte from the land of Tob. "Come," they said to Jephte, "be our commander that we may be able to fight the Ammonites." "Are you not the ones who hated me and drove me from my father's house?" Jephte replied to the elders of Galaad. "Why do you come to me now, when you are in distress?" The elders of Galaad said to Jephte, "In any case, we have now come back to you; if you go with us to fight against the Ammonites, you shall be the leader of all of us who dwell in Galaad." Jephte answered the elders of Galaad, "If you bring me back to fight against the Ammonites and the Lord delivers them up to me, I shall be your leader." The elders of Galaad said to Jephte, "The Lord is witness between us that we will do as you say."

So Jephte went with the elders of Galaad, and the people made him their leader and commander. In Maspha, Jephte settled all his affairs before the Lord. Then he sent messengers to the king of the Ammonites to say, "What have you against me that you come to fight with me in my land?" But the king of the Ammonites paid no heed to the message Jephte sent him. The spirit of the Lord came upon Jephte. He passed through Galaad and Manasse, and through Maspha-Galaad as well, and from there he went on to the Ammonites. Jephte made a vow to the Lord. "If you deliver the Ammonites into my power," he said, "whoever comes out of the doors of my house to meet me when I return in triumph from the Ammonites shall belong to the Lord. I shall offer him up as a holocaust."

Jephte then went on to the Ammonites to fight against them, and the Lord delivered them into his power, so that he inflicted a severe defeat on them, from Aroer to the approach to Mennith (twenty cities in all) and as far as Abel-cheramim. Thus were the Ammonites brought into subjection by the Israelites. When Jephte returned to his house in Maspha, it was his daughter who came forth, playing the tambourines and dancing. She was an only child: he had neither son nor daughter besides her. When he saw her, he rent his garments and said, "Alas, daughter, you have struck me down and brought calamity upon me. For I have made a vow to the Lord and I cannot retract." "Father," she replied, "you have made a vow to the Lord. Do with me as you have vowed, because the Lord has wrought vengeance for you on your enemies the Ammonites." Then she said to her father, "Let me have this favor. Spare me for two months, that I may go off down the mountains to mourn my virginity with my companions." "Go," he replied, and sent her away for two months. So she departed with her companions and mourned her virginity on the mountains. At the end of the two months she returned to her father, who did to her as he had vowed. She had not been intimate with man. It then became a custom in Israel for Israelite women to go yearly to mourn the daughter of Jephte the Galaadite for four days of the year.

THE STORY OF SAMSON

The Israelites again offended the Lord, who therefore delivered them into the power of the Philistines for forty years.

There was a certain man from Saraa, of the clan of the Danites, whose name was Manoe. His wife was barren and had borne no children. An angel of the Lord appeared to the woman and said to her, "Though you are barren and have no children, yet you will conceive and bear a son. Now, then, be careful to take no wine or strong drink and to eat nothing unclean. As for the son you will conceive and bear, no razor shall touch his head, for this boy is to be consecrated to God from the womb. It is he who will begin the deliverance of Israel from the power of the Philistines." The woman bore a son and named him Samson. The boy grew up and the Lord blessed him; the spirit of the Lord first stirred him in Mahane-Dan, which is between Saraa and Esthaol.

Samson went down to Thamna and saw there one of the Philistine women. On his return he told his father and mother, "There is a Philistine woman I saw in Thamna whom I wish you to get as a wife for me." His father and mother said to him, "Can you find no wife among your kinsfolk or among all our people, that you must go and take a wife from the uncircumcised Philistines?" But Samson answered his father, "Get her for me, for she pleases me." Now his father and mother did not know that this had been brought about by the Lord, who was providing an opportunity against the Philistines; for at that time they had dominion over Israel.

After some time, in the season of the wheat harvest, Samson visited his wife, bringing a kid. But when he said, "Let me be with my wife in private," her father would not let him enter, saying, "I thought it certain you wished to repudiate her; so I gave her to your best man. Her younger sister is more beautiful than she; you may have her instead." Samson said to them, "This time the Philistines cannot blame me if I harm them." So Samson left and caught three hundred foxes. Turning them tail to tail, he tied between each pair of tails one of the torches he had at hand. He then kindled the torches and set the foxes loose in the standing grain of the Philistines, thus burning both the shocks and the standing grain, and the vineyards and olive orchards as well.

When the Philistine asked who had done this, they were told, "Samson, the son-in-law of the Thamnaite, because his wife was taken and given to his best man." So the Philistines went up and destroyed her and her family by fire. Samson said to them, "If this is how you act, I will not stop until I have taken revenge on you." And with repeated blows, he inflicted a great slaughter on them. Then he went down and remained in a cavern of the cliff of Etam.

The Philistines went up and, from a camp in Juda, deployed against Lehi. When the men of Judah asked, "Why have you come up against us?" they answered, "To take Samson prisoner; to do to him as he has done to us." Three thousand men of Juda went down to the cavern in the cliff of Etam and said to Samson, "Do you not know that the Philistines are our rulers? Why, then, have you done this to us?" He answered them, "As they have done to me, so have I done to them." They said to him, "We have come to take you prisoner, to deliver you over to the Philistines." Samson said to them, "Swear to me that you will not kill me yourselves." "No," they replied, "we will certainly not kill you but will only bind you and deliver you over to them." So they bound him with two new ropes and brought him up from the cliff. When he reached Lehi, and the Philistines came shouting to meet him, the spirit of the Lord came upon him: the ropes around his arms became as flax that is consumed by fire and his bonds melted away from his hands. Near him was the fresh jawbone of an ass; he reached out, grasped it, and with it killed a thousand men. Then Samson said,

> "With the jawbone of an ass
> I have piled them in a heap;
> With the jawbone of an ass
> I have slain a thousand men."

As he finished speaking he threw the jawbone from him; and so that place was named Ramath-Lehi. Being very thirsty, he cried to the Lord and said, "You have granted this great victory by the hand of your servant. Must I now die of thirst or fall into the hands of the uncircumcised?" Then God split the cavity in Lehi, and water issued from it, which Samson drank till his spirit returned and he revived. Hence that spring in Lehi is called En-Haccore to this day.

Samson judged Israel for twenty years in the days of the Philistines.

After that he fell in love with a woman in the Wadi Sorec whose name was Dalila. The lords of the Philistines came to her and said, "Beguile him and find out the secret of his great strength, and how we may overcome and bind him so as to keep him helpless. We will each give you eleven hundred shekels of silver."

So Dalila said to Samson, "Tell me the secret of your great strength and how you may be bound so as to be kept helpless." She importuned him continually and vexed him with her complaints till he was deathly weary of them. So he took her completely into his confidence and told her, "No razor has touched my head, for I have been consecrated to God from my mother's womb. If I am shaved, my strength will leave me, and I shall be as weak as any other man." When Dalila saw that he had taken her completely into his confidence, she summoned the lords of the Philistines, saying, "Come up this time, for he has opened his heart to me." So the lords of the Philistines came and brought up the money with them. She had him sleep on her lap, and called for a man who shaved off his seven locks of hair. Then she began to mistreat him, for his strength had left him. When she said, "The Philistines are upon you, Samson!", and he awoke from his sleep, he thought he could make good his escape as he had done time and again, for he did not realize that the Lord had left him. But the Philistines seized him and gouged out his eyes. Then they brought him down to Gaza and bound him with bronze fetters, and he was put to grinding in the prison. But the hair of his head began to grow as soon as it was shaved off.

The lords of the Philistines assembled to offer a great sacrifice to their god Dagon and to make merry. They said,

> "Our god has delivered into our power
> Samson our enemy."

When their spirits were high, they said, "Call Samson that he may amuse us." So they called Samson from the prison, and he played the buffoon before them. When the people saw him, they praised their god. For they said,

> "Our god has delivered into our power
> our enemy, the ravager of our land,
> the one who has multiplied our slain."

Then they stationed him between the columns. Samson said to the attendant who was holding his hand, "Put me where I may touch the columns that support the temple and may rest against them." The temple was full of men and women: all the lords of the Philistines were there, and from the roof about three thousand men and women looked on as Samson provided amusement. Samson cried out to the Lord and said, "O Lord God, remember me! Strengthen me, O God, this last time that for my two eyes I may avenge myself once and for all on the Philistines." Samson grasped the two middle columns on which the temple rested and braced himself against them, one at his right hand, the other at his left. And Samson said, "Let me die with the Philistines!" He pushed hard, and the temple fell upon the lords and all the people who were in it. Those he killed at his death were more than those he had killed during his lifetime.

All his family and kinsmen went down and bore him up for burial in the grave of his father Manoe between Saraa and Esthaol. He had judged Israel for twenty years.

[And when they were back in their own domain they built new cities to dwell in. And each son of Israel went back to the dwelling-place of his own clan, his own family. This was in the days before any king ruled in Israel, when men lived by the best light they had.]

CHAPTER EIGHT

A Beautiful Example of Filial Piety

RUTH AND NOEMI

Once in the time of the judges there was a famine in the land; so a man from Bethlehem of Juda departed with his wife and two sons to reside on the plateau of Moab. The man was named Elimelech, his wife Noemi, and his sons Mahalon and Chelion; they were Ephrathites from Bethlehem of Juda. Some time after their arrival on the Moabite plateau, Elimelech, the husband of Noemi, died, and she was left with her two sons, who married Moabite women, one named Orpha, the other Ruth. When they had lived there about ten years, both Mahalon and Chelion died also, and the woman was left with neither her two sons nor her husband. She then made ready to go back from the plateau of Moab because word reached her there that the Lord had visited his people and given them food. She and her two daughters-in-law left the place where they had been living. Then as they were on the road back to the land of Juda, Noemi said to her two daughters-in-law, "Go back, each of you, to your mother's house! May the Lord be kind to you as you were to the departed and to me!" She kissed them good-by, but they wept with loud sobs, and told her they would return with her to her people.

Again they sobbed aloud and wept; and Orpha kissed her mother-in-law good-by, but Ruth stayed with her. "See now!" she said, "your sister-in-law has gone back to her people and her god. Go back after your sister-in-law!" But Ruth said, "Do not ask me to abandon or forsake you! for wherever you go I will go, wherever you lodge I will lodge, your people shall be my people, and your God my God. Wherever you die I will die, and there be buried. May the Lord do so and so to me, and more besides, if aught but death separates me from you!"

Noemi then ceased to urge her, for she saw she was determined to go with her.

RUTH AND BOOZ

Noemi had a prominent kinsman named Booz, of the clan of her husband Elimelech. Ruth the Moabite said to Noemi, "Let me go and glean ears of grain in the field of anyone who will allow me that favor." Noemi said to her, "Go, my daughter," and she went. The field she entered to glean after the harvester happened to be the section belonging to Booz. Booz himself came from Bethlehem and said to the harvesters, "The Lord be with you!" and they replied, "The Lord bless you!" Booz asked the overseer of his harvesters, "Whose girl is this?" The overseers answered, "She is the Moabite girl who returned from the plateau of Moab with Noemi. She asked leave to gather the gleanings into sheaves after the harvesters; and ever since she came this morning she has remained here until now, with scarcely a moment's rest."

Booz said to Ruth, "Listen, my daughter! Do not go to glean in anyone else's field; you are not to leave here. Stay here with my women servants. Watch to see which field is to be harvested, and follow them; I have commanded the young men to do you no harm. When you are thirsty, you may go and drink from the vessels the young men have filled."

At mealtime Booz said to her, "Come here and have some food; dip your bread in the sauce." Then as she sat near the reapers, he handed her some roasted grain and she ate her fill and had some left over. She rose to glean, and Booz instructed his servants to let her glean among the sheaves themselves without scolding her, and even to let drop some handfuls and leave them for her to glean without being rebuked.

She gleaned in the field until evening, and when she beat out what she had gleaned it came to about an epha of barley, which she took into the city and showed to her mother-in-law. Next she brought out and gave her what she had left over from lunch. So Noemi said to her, "Where did you glean today? Where did you go to work? May he who took notice of you be blessed!" Then she told her mother-in-law with whom she had worked. "The man at whose place I worked today is named Booz," she said. "May he be blessed by the Lord, who is ever

133

merciful to the living and to the dead," Noemi exclaimed to her daughter-in-law; and she continued, "He is a relative of ours, one of our next of kin. So bathe and anoint yourself; then put on your best attire and go down to the threshing floor. Do not make yourself known to the man before he has finished eating and drinking. But when he lies down, take note of the place where he does so. Then go, uncover a place at his feet, and lie down. He will tell you what to do." "I will do whatever you advise," Ruth replied. So she went down to the threshing floor and did just as her mother-in-law had instructed her.

Booz ate and drank to his heart's content. Then when he went and lay down at the edge of the sheaves, she stole up, uncovered a place at his feet, and lay down. In the middle of the night, however, the man gave a start and turned around to find a woman lying at his feet. He asked, "Who are you?" And she replied, "I am your servant Ruth. Spread the corner of your cloak over me, for you are my next of kin." He said, "May the Lord bless you, my daughter! You have been even more loyal now than before in not going after the young men, whether poor or rich. So be assured, daughter, I will do for you whatever you say; all my townspeople know you for a worthy woman. Now, though indeed I am closely related to you, you have another relative still closer. Stay as you are for tonight, and tomorrow, if he wishes to claim you, good! let him do so. But if he does not wish to claim you, as the Lord lives, I will claim you myself. Lie there until morning." So she lay at his feet until morning, but rose before men could recognize one another. Booz said, "Let it not be known that this woman came to the threshing floor." Then he said to her, "Take off your cloak and hold it out." When she did so, he poured out six measures of barley, helped her lift the bundle, and left for the city.

Ruth went home to her mother-in-law, who asked, "How have you fared, my daughter?" So she told her all the man had done for her, and concluded, "He gave me these six measures of barley because he did not wish me to come back to my mother-in-law empty-handed!" Noemi then said, "Wait here, my daughter, until you learn what happens, for the man will not rest, but will settle the matter today."

THE MARRIAGE OF RUTH

Booz went and took a seat at the gate; and when he saw the closer relative of whom he had spoken come along, he called to him by name, "Come and sit beside me!" And he did so. Then Booz picked out ten of the elders of the city and asked them to sit nearby. When they had done this, he said to the near relative: "Noemi, who has come back from the Moabite plateau, is putting up for sale the piece of land that belonged to our kinsman Elimelech. So I thought I would inform you, bidding you before those here present, including the elders of my people, to put in your claim for it if you wish to acquire it as next of kin. But if you do not wish to claim it, tell me so, that I may be guided accordingly, for no one has a prior claim to yours, and mine is next." He answered, "I will put in my claim."

Booz continued, "Once you acquire the field from Noemi, you must take also Ruth the Moabite, the widow of the late heir, and raise up a family for the departed on his estate." The near relative replied, "I cannot exercise my claim lest I depreciate my own estate. Put in a claim yourself in my stead, for I cannot exercise my claim." Now it used to be the custom in Israel that, to make binding a contract of redemption or exchange, one party would take off his sandal and give it to the other. This was the form of attestation in Israel. So the near relative, in saying to Booz, "Acquire it for yourself," drew off his sandal. Booz then said to the elders and to all the people, "You are witnesses today that I have acquired from Noemi all the holdings of Elimelech, Chelion and Mahalon. I also take Ruth the Maobite, the widow of Mahalon, as my wife, in order to raise up a family for her late husband on his estate, so that the name of the departed may not perish among his kinsmen and fellow citizens. Do you witness this today?" All those at the gate, including the elders, said, "We do so. May the Lord make this wife come into your house like Rachel and Lia, who between them built up the house of Israel. May you do well in Ephratha and win fame in Bethlehem. With the offspring the Lord will give you from this girl, may your house become like the house of Phares, whom Thamar bore to Juda."

Booz took Ruth. When they came together as man and wife, the Lord enabled her to conceive and she bore a son. Then the women said to Noemi, "Blessed is the Lord who has not failed to provide you today with an heir! May he become famous in Israel! He will be your comfort and the support of your old age, for his mother is the daughter-in-law who loves you. She is worth more to you than seven sons!" Noemi took the child, placed him on her lap, and became his nurse. And the neighbor women gave him his name, at the news that a grandson had been born to Noemi. They called him Obed.

CHAPTER NINE

The Chosen People
Plead for a King

THE BIRTH OF SAMUEL; HIS VOCATION

There was a man of Ramathaimsophim, of mount Ephraim, and his name was Elcana, the son of Jeroham, the son of Eliu, the son of Thohu, the son of Suph, an Ephraimite. And he had two wives, the name of one was Anna, and the name of the other Phenenna. Phenenna had children, but Anna had no children. And this man went up out of his city upon the appointed days, to adore and to offer sacrifice to the Lord of hosts in Silo. And the two sons of Heli, Ophni and Phinees, were there priests of the Lord. Now the day came, and Elcana offered sacrifice, and gave to Phenenna his wife, and to all her sons and daughters, portions; but to Anna he gave one portion with sorrow, because he loved Anna. And the Lord had shut up her womb.

. . . And she made a vow, saying: "O Lord of hosts, if thou wilt look down on the affliction of thy servant, and wilt be mindful of me, and not forget thy handmaid, and wilt give to thy servant a man child, I will give him to the Lord all the days of his life, and no razor shall come upon his head." And it came to pass when the time was come about, Anna conceived and bore a son, and called his name Samuel: because she had asked him of the Lord. And after she had weaned him, she carried him with her, with three calves, and three bushels of flour, and a bottle of wine, and she brought him to the house of the Lord in Silo. Now the child was as yet very young. And they immolated a calf, and offered the child to Heli and Anna said: "For this child did I pray, and the Lord hath granted me my petition, which I asked of him. Therefore I also have lent him to the Lord: all the days of his life, he shall be lent to the Lord." And they adored the Lord there.

The Chosen People Plead for a King

ANNA SINGS FOR JOY

And Anna prayed, and said: "My heart hath rejoiced in the Lord, and my horn is exalted in my God: my mouth is enlarged over my enemies, because I have joyed in thy salvation. There is none holy as the Lord is; for there is no other besides thee, and there is none strong like our God. Do not multiply to speak lofty things, boasting. Let old matters depart from your mouth; for the Lord is a God of all knowledge, and to him are thoughts prepared. The bow of the mighty is overcome, and the weak are girt with strength. They that were full before have hired out themselves for bread: and the hungry are filled, so that the barren hath borne many; and she that had many childen is weakened.

"The Lord killeth and maketh alive, he bringeth down to hell and bringeth back again. The Lord maketh poor and maketh rich, he humbleth and he exalteth. He raiseth up the needy from the dust, and lifteth up the poor from the dunghill, that he may sit with princes, and hold the throne of glory. For the poles of the earth are the Lord's, and upon them he hath set the world. He will keep the feet of his saints, and the wicked shall be silent in darkness, because no man shall prevail by his own strength. The adversaries of the Lord shall fear him: and upon them shall be thunder in the heavens. The Lord shall judge the ends of the earth, and he shall give empire to his king, and shall exalt the horn of his Christ."

And Elcana went to Ramatha, to his house: but the child ministered in the sight of the Lord before the face of Heli the priest. Now the sons of Heli were children of Belial, not knowing the Lord. Now Heli was very old, and he heard all that his sons did to all Israel: and how they lay with the women that waited at the door of the tabernacle. And he said to them: "Why do ye these kinds of things, which I hear, very wicked things, from all the people? Do not so, my sons, for it is no good report that I hear, that you make the people of the Lord to transgress. If one man shall sin against another, God may be appeased in his behalf; but if a man shall sin against the Lord, who shall pray for him?" And they hearkened not to the voice of their father, because the Lord would slay them. But the child Samuel advanced, and grew on, and pleased both the Lord and men.

GOD BECKONS SAMUEL

Now the child Samuel ministered to the Lord before Heli, and the word of the Lord was precious in those days: there was no manifest vision. And it came to pass one day when Heli lay in his place, and his eyes were grown dim, that he could not see, before the lamp of God went out, Samuel slept in the temple of the Lord, where the ark of God was. And the Lord called Samuel. And he answered: "Here am I." And he ran to Heli and said: "Here am I, for thou didst call me." He said: "I did not call; go back and sleep." And he went and slept. And the Lord called Samuel again. And Samuel arose and went to Heli, and said: "Here am I, for thou calledst me." He answered: "I did not call thee, my son; return and sleep."

Now Samuel did not yet know the Lord, neither had the word of the Lord been revealed to him. And the Lord called Samuel again the third time. And he arose and went to Heli, and said: "Here am I, for thou didst call me." Then Heli understood that the Lord called the child, and he said to Samuel: "Go, and sleep; and if he shall call thee any more, thou shalt say: 'Speak, Lord, for thy servant heareth.'"

So Samuel went and slept in his place. And the Lord came and stood; and he called, as he had called the other times: "Samuel, Samuel." And Samuel said: "Speak, Lord, for thy servant heareth." And the Lord said to Samuel: "Behold I do a thing in Israel, and whosoever shall hear it, both his ears shall tingle. In that day I will raise up against Heli all the things I have spoken concerning his house; I will begin, and I will make an end. For I have foretold unto him, that I will judge his house forever, for iniquity, because he knew that his sons did wickedly, and did not chastise them. Therefore have I sworn to the house of Heli, that the iniquity of his house shall not be expiated with victims nor offerings forever." So Samuel told him all the words, and did not hide them from him. And he answered: "It is the Lord. Let him do what is good in his sight." And Samuel grew, and the Lord was with him, and not one of his words fell to the ground. And all Israel from Dan to Bersabee, knew that Samuel was a faithful prophet of the Lord. And the Lord again appeared in Silo, for the Lord revealed himself to Samuel in Silo, according to the word of the Lord. And the word of Samuel came to pass to all Israel.

The Chosen People Plead for a King

THE PHILISTINES VANQUISH THE ISRAELITES

And it came to pass in those days, that the Philistines gathered themselves together to fight: and Israel went out to war against the Philistines, and camped by the Stone of help. And the Philistines came to Aphec, and put their army in array against Israel. And when they had joined battle, Israel turned their backs to the Philistines, and there were slain in the fields about four thousand men. And the people returned to the camp; and the ancients of Israel said: "Why hath the Lord defeated us today before the Philistines? Let us fetch unto us the ark of the covenant of the Lord from Silo, and let it come in the midst of us, that it may save us from the hand of our enemies." So the people sent to Silo, and they brought from thence the ark of the covenant of the Lord of hosts sitting upon the cherubims: and the two sons of Heli, Ophni and Phinees, were with the ark of the covenant of God. And when the ark of the covenant of the Lord was come into the camp, all Israel shouted with a great shout, and the earth rang again. And the Philistines heard the noise of the shout, and they said: "What is this noise of a great shout in the camp of the Hebrews?" And they understood that the ark of the Lord was come into the camp. And the Philistines were afraid, saying: "God is come into the camp." And sighing, they said: "Woe to us, for there was no such great joy yesterday and the day before. Woe to us. Who shall deliver us from the hand of these high gods? These are the gods that struck Egypt with all the plagues in the desert. Take courage and behave like men, ye Philistines; lest you come to be servants to the Hebrews, as they have served you. Take courage and fight." So the Philistines fought, and Israel was overthrown, and every man fled to his own dwelling: and there was an exceeding great slaughter; for there fell of Israel thirty thousand footmen. And the ark of God was taken: and the two sons of Heli, Ophni and Phinees, were slain. And there ran a man of Benjamin out of the army, and came to Silo the same day, with his clothes rent, and his head strewed with dust. And when he was come, Heli sat upon a stool over against the way watching. For his heart was fearful for the ark of God. And when the man was come into the city, he told it: and all the city cried out. And Heli heard the noise of the cry, and he said: "What meaneth the noise of this uproar?" But he made haste, and came, and told Heli. Now Heli was ninety and eight years old, and his eyes were dim, and he could not see. And he said to

Heli: "I am he that came from the battle, and have fled out of the field this day." And he said to him: "What is there done, my son?" And he that brought the news answered, and said: "Israel has fled before the Philistines, and there has been a great slaughter of the people; moreover, thy two sons, Ophni and Phinees, are dead; and the ark of God is taken." And when he had named the ark of God, he fell from his stool backwards by the door, and broke his neck, and died. For he was an old man, and far advanced in years; and he judged Israel forty years.

THE VICTORY OF GOD'S PEOPLE

And the Philistines took the ark of God and carried it from the Stone of help into Azotus. And the hand of the Lord was heavy upon the Azotians, and he destroyed them, and afflicted Azotus and the lands thereof with emerods. And in the villages and fields in the midst of that country, there came forth a multitude of mice, and there was the confusion of a great mortality in the city. Now the ark of God was in the land of the Philistines seven months. And the Philistines called for the priests and the diviners, saying: "What shall we do with the ark of the Lord? Tell us how we are to send it back to its place?" And they said: "If you send back the ark of the God of Israel, send it not away empty, but render unto him what you owe for sin, and then you shall be healed: and you shall know why his hand departeth not from you." They answered: "What is it we ought to render unto him for sin?" And they answered: "Why do you harden your hearts, as Egypt and Pharao hardened their hearts? Did not he, after he was struck, then let them go, and they departed? Now therefore take and make a new cart: and two kine that have calved, on which there hath come no yoke, tie to the cart, and shut up their calves at home. And you shall take the ark of the Lord, and lay it on the cart, and the vessels of gold, which you have paid him for sin, you shall put into a little box, at the side thereof: and send it away that it may go. And you shall look: and if it go up by the way of his own coasts towards Bethsames, then he hath done us this great evil; but if not, we shall know that it is not his hand hath touched us, but it hath happened by chance."

They did therefore in this manner: and taking two kine that had suckling calves, they yoked them to the cart, and shut up their calves at home. And they laid the ark of God upon the cart, and the little box that had in it the golden mice and the likeness of the emerods. And the kine took the straight way that leadeth to Bethsames, and they went along the way, lowing as they went, and turned not aside neither to the right hand nor to the left: and the lords of the Philistines followed them as far as the borders of Bethsames. And the men of Cariathiarim came and fetched up the ark of the Lord and carried it into the house of Abinadab in Gabaa: and they sanctified Eleazar his son, to keep the ark of the Lord. And it came to pass that from the day the ark of the Lord abode in Cariathiarim days were multiplied (for it was now the twentieth year), and all the house of Israel rested following the Lord.

And Samuel spoke to all the house of Israel, saying: "If you turn to the Lord with all your heart, put away the strange gods from among you, Baalim and Astaroth: and prepare your hearts unto the Lord, and serve him only, and he will deliver you out of the hand of the Philistines." Then the children of Israel put away Baalim and Astaroth, and served the Lord only. And Samuel said: "Gather all Israel to Masphath, that I may pray to the Lord for you." And they gathered together to Masphath. And they drew water, and poured it out before the Lord, and they fasted on that day, and they said there: "We have sinned against the Lord." And Samuel judged the children of Israel in Masphath.

And the Philistines heard that the children of Israel were gathered together to Masphath, and the lords of the Philistines went up against Israel. And when the children of Israel heard this, they were afraid of the Philistines. And they said to Samuel: "Cease not to cry to the Lord our God for us, that he may save us out of the hand of the Philistines." And Samuel took a sucking lamb, and offered it whole for a holocaust to the Lord: and Samuel cried to the Lord for Israel, and the Lord heard him. And it came to pass, when Samuel was offering the holocaust, the Philistines began to battle against Israel; but the Lord thundered with a great thunder on that day upon the Philistines, and terrified them, and they were overthrown before the face of Israel. And the men of Israel going out of Masphath pursued after the Philistines, and made slaughter of them till they came under Bethchar.

And Samuel judged Israel all the days of his life. And he went every year about to Bethel and to Galgal and to Masphath, and he judged Israel in the aforesaid places. And he returned to Ramatha, for there was his house, and there he judged Israel. He built also there an altar to the Lord.

THE JEWS CLAMOR FOR A KING

And it came to pass when Samuel was old, that he appointed his sons to be judges over Israel. Now the name of his firstborn son was Joel, and the name of the second was Abia, judges in Bersabee. And his sons walked not in his ways; but they turned aside after lucre, and took bribes, and perverted judgment. Then all the ancients of Israel being assembled, came to Samuel to Ramatha, and they said to him: "Behold thou art old, and thy sons walk not in thy ways. Make us a king, to judge us, as all nations have."

And the word was displeasing in the eyes of Samuel, that they should say: "Give us a king, to judge us." And Samuel prayed to the Lord. And the Lord said to Samuel: "Hearken to the voice of the people in all that they say to thee. For they have not rejected thee, but me, that I should not reign over them. According to all their works, they have done from the day that I brought them out of Egypt until this day: as they have forsaken me, and served strange gods, so do they also unto thee. Now therefore hearken to their voice; but yet testify to them, and foretell them the right of the king that shall reign over them." Then Samuel told all the words of the Lord to the people that had desired a king of him, and said: "This will be the right of the king that shall reign over you: He will take your sons, and put them in his chariots, and will make them his horsemen, and his running footmen to run before his chariots; and he will appoint of them to be his tribunes, and centurions, and to plough his fields, and to reap his corn, and to make him arms and chariots. Your daughters also he will take to make him ointments, and to be his cooks, and bakers. And he will take your fields, and your vineyards, and your best oliveyards, and give them to his servants. Moreover he will take the tenth of your corn, and of the revenues of your vineyards, to give his eunuchs and servants. Your servants also and handmaids, and your goodliest young men, and your asses he will take away, and put them to his work. Your flocks also he will tithe, and you shall be his servants. And you shall cry out in that day from the face of the king, whom you have chosen to yourselves: and the Lord will not hear you in that day, because you desired unto yourselves a king."

But the people would not hear the voice of Samuel, and they said: "Nay: but there shall be a king over us. And we also will be like all nations; and our king shall judge us, and go out before us, and fight our battles for us." And Samuel heard all the words of the people, and rehearsed them in the ears of the Lord. And the Lord said to Samuel: "Hearken to their voice, and make them a king." And Samuel said to the men of Israel: "Let every man go to his city."

SAMUEL MEETS SAUL

Now there was a man of Benjamin whose name was Cis, valiant and strong. And he had a son whose name was Saul, a choice and goodly man, and there was not among the children of Israel a goodlier person than he: from his shoulders and upwards he appeared above all the people.

And the asses of Cis, Saul's father, were lost; and Cis said to his son Saul: "Take one of the servants with thee, and arise, go, and seek the asses." And when they had passed through mount Ephraim, and through the land of Salisa, and had not found them, they passed also through the land of Salim, and they were not there: and through the land of Jemini, and found them not. And when they were come to the land of Suph, Saul said to the servant that was with him: "Come, let us return, lest perhaps my father forget the asses, and be concerned for us." And he said to him: "Behold there is a man of God in this city, a famous man: all that he saith, cometh certainly to pass. Now therefore let us go thither, perhaps he may tell us of our way, for which we are come." And they went up into the city. And when they were walking in the midst of the city, behold Samuel was coming out over against them, to go up to the high place. Now the Lord had revealed to the ear of Samuel the day before Saul came, saying: "Tomorrow about this same hour I will send thee a man of the land of Benjamin, and thou shalt anoint him to be ruler over my people Israel: and he shall save my people out of the hand of the Philistines, for I have looked down upon my people, because their cry is come to me." And when Samuel saw Saul, the Lord said to him: "Behold the man, of whom I spoke to thee, this man shall reign over my people." And they went down from the high place into the town, and he spoke with Saul upon the top of the house: and he prepared a bed for Saul on the top of the house, and he slept. And when they were risen in the morning, and it began now to be light, Samuel called Saul on the top of the house, saying: "Arise, that I may let thee go." And Saul arose; and they went out both of them, to wit, he and Samuel. And as they were going down in the end of the city, Samuel said to Saul: "Speak to the servant to go before us, and pass on; but stand thou still a while, that I may tell thee the word of the Lord."

SAUL IS ANOINTED

And Samuel took a little vial of oil, and poured it upon his head, and kissed him, and said: "Behold, the Lord hath anointed thee to be prince over his inheritance, and thou shalt deliver his people out of the hands of their enemies, that are round about them. And this shall be a sign unto thee, that God hath anointed thee to be prince. When thou shalt depart from me this day, thou shalt find two men by the sepulchre of Rachel in the borders of Benjamin to the south, and they shall say to thee: The asses are found which thou wentest to seek; and thy father thinking no more of the asses is concerned for you, and saith: What shall I do for my son?"

SAUL IS PROCLAIMED KING

[And now Samuel bade the whole people gather in the Divine presence at Maspha, and this message he gave them from the Lord God of Israel: "It was I that rescued you from Egypt, I that protected you from the clutches of these and of all your oppressors. And now you have cast away your God, your only shield against so many misfortunes and afflictions: A king, you say, appoint a king to reign over us! Come then, present yourselves before the Lord, tribe by tribe, clan by clan." Then Samuel brought forward all the tribes of Israel by name, and the lot fell on Benjamin; brought forward all the families of Benjamin by name, and the lot fell on Metri's; and in the end he reached Saul, the son of Cis. When they looked for him, he was nowhere to be found; was he on his way to Maspha? They asked the Lord, and the answer came that Saul was there, hiding in his tent. Whereupon they ran to fetch him, and before long he stood in their midst, a head and shoulders taller than any of them. "The Lord's chosen!" cried Samuel. "Look at him, and see if he has his like in Israel!" And all the people shouted, "Long live the king!"

And now Samuel proclaimed to the people what the king's rights were; wrote it down, too, in a book, which he laid up in the Lord's presence; then he bade them disperse to their homes. Saul went back to Gabaa, and with him went some of the fighting men, whom God so inspired. There were others, graceless folk, who asked contemptuously whether such a man as this could bring them victory; and no gift would they offer him. But Saul made as if he could not hear their mutterings.]

SAUL DEFEATS THE AMMONITES

And it came to pass about a month after this that Naas the Ammonite came up, and began to fight against Jabes Galaad. And all the men of Jabes said to Naas: "Make a covenant with us, and we will serve thee." And Naas the Ammonite answered them: "On this condition will I make a covenant with you, that I may pluck out all your right eyes, and make you a reproach in all Israel." And the ancients of Jabes said to him: "Allow us seven days, that we may send messengers to all the coasts of Israel; and if there be no one to defend us we will come out to thee." The messengers therefore came to Gabaa of Saul; and they spoke these words in the hearing of the people: and all the people lifted up their voices and wept.

And behold Saul came, following oxen out of the field, and he said: "What aileth the people that they weep?" And they told him the words of the men of Jabes. And the spirit of the Lord came upon Saul, when he had heard these words, and his anger was exceedingly kindled. And taking both the oxen, he cut them in pieces, and sent them into all the coasts of Israel by messengers, saying: "Whosoever shall not come forth, and follow Saul and Samuel, so shall it be done to his oxen." And the fear of the Lord fell upon the people, and they went out as one man. And he numbered them in Bezech, and there were of the children of Israel three hundred thousand, and of the men of Juda thirty thousand. And they said to the messengers that came: "Thus shall you say to the men of Jabes Galaad: Tomorrow, when the sun shall be hot, you shall have relief." The messengers therefore came, and told the men of Jabes: and they were glad. And they said: "In the morning we will come out to you: and you shall do what you please with us." And it came to pass, when the morrow was come that Saul put the people in three companies: and he came into the midst of the camp in the morning watch, and he slew the Ammonites until the day grew hot, and the rest were scattered, so that two of them were not left together.

And the people said to Samuel: "Who is he that said: Shall Saul reign over us? Bring the men and we will kill them." And Saul said: "No man shall be killed this day, because the Lord this day hath wrought salvation in Israel." And Samuel said to the people: "Come and let us go to Galgal, and let us renew the kingdom there." And all the people went to Galgal, and there they made Saul king before the Lord in Galgal, and they sacrificed there victims of peace before the Lord. And there Saul and all the men of Israel rejoiced exceedingly.

SAMUEL RESIGNS HIS JUDGESHIP

And Samuel said to all Israel: "Behold I have hearkened to your voice in all that you said to me, and have made a king over you. And now the king goeth before you. But I am old and greyheaded, and my sons are with you. Having then conversed with you from my youth unto this day, behold here I am. Speak of me before the Lord, and before his anointed, whether I have taken any man's ox, or ass: if I have wronged any man, if I have oppressed any man, if I have taken a bribe at any man's hand: and I will despise it this day, and will restore it to you." And they said: "Thou hast not wronged us, nor oppressed us, nor taken aught at any man's hand."

And he said to them: "The Lord is witness against you, and his anointed is witness this day, that you have not found anything in my hand." And they said: "He is witness." And Samuel said to the people: "It is the Lord, who made Moses and Aaron, and brought our fathers out of the land of Egypt. Now therefore stand up, that I may plead in judgment against you before the Lord, concerning all the kindness of the Lord, which he hath shown to you, and to your fathers: How Jacob went into Egypt, and your fathers cried to the Lord, and the Lord sent Moses and Aaron, and brought your fathers out of Egypt, and made them dwell in this place. And they forgot the Lord their God, and he delivered them into the hands of Sisara, captain of the army of Hasor, and into the hands of the Philistines, and into the hand of the king of Moab, and they fought against them. But afterwards they cried to the Lord, and said: We have sinned, because we have forsaken the Lord, and have served Baalim and Astaroth; but now deliver us from the hand of our enemies, and we will serve thee. And the Lord sent Jerobaal, and Badan, and Jephte, and Samuel, and delivered you from the hand of your enemies round about, and you dwelt securely. But seeing that Naas king of the children of Ammon was come against you, you said to me: Nay, but a king shall reign over us, whereas the Lord your God was your king. Now therefore your king is here, whom you have chosen and desired: Behold the Lord hath given you a king. If you will fear the Lord, and serve him, and hearken to his voice, and not provoke the mouth of the Lord, then shall both you, and the king who reigneth over you, be followers of the Lord your God. But if you will not hearken to the voice of the Lord, but will rebel against his words, the hand of the Lord shall be upon you, and upon your fathers."

SAMUEL'S FINAL WARNING

"Now then stand, and see this great thing which the Lord will do in your sight. Is it not wheat harvest today? I will call upon the Lord, and he shall send thunder and rain; and you shall know and see that you yourselves have done a great evil in the sight of the Lord, in desiring a king over you." And Samuel cried unto the Lord, and the Lord sent thunder and rain that day. And all the people greatly feared the Lord and Samuel. And all the people said to Samuel: "Pray for thy servants to the Lord thy God, that we may not die, for we have added to all our sins this evil, to ask for a king." And Samuel said to the people: "Fear not. You have done all this evil; but yet depart not from following the Lord, but serve the Lord with all your heart. And turn not aside after vain things which shall never profit you, nor deliver you, because they are vain. And the Lord will not forsake his people for his great name's sake, because the Lord hath sworn to make you his people. And far from me be this sin against the Lord, that I should cease to pray for you, and I will teach you the good and the right way. Therefore, fear the Lord, and serve him in truth and with your whole heart, for you have seen the great works which he hath done among you. But if you will still do wickedly, both you and your king shall perish together."

CHAPTER TEN

The History of Saul's Reign

SAUL GOES TO WAR

Saul chose three thousand men of Israel; two thousand were with Saul in Michmash and the hill country of Bethel, and a thousand were with Jonathan in Gibe-ah of Benjamin; the rest of the people he sent home, every man to his tent. Jonathan defeated the garrison of the Philistines which was at Geba; and the Philistines heard of it. And Saul blew the trumpet throughout all the land, saying, "Let the Hebrews hear." And all Israel heard it said that Saul had defeated the garrison of the Philistines, and also that Israel had become odious to the Philistines. And the people were called out to join Saul at Gilgal. And the Philistines mustered to fight with Israel, thirty thousand chariots, and six thousand horseman, and troops like the sand on the seashore in multitude; they came up and encamped in Michmash, to the east of Beth-aven.

One day Jonathan the son of Saul said to the young man who bore his armor, "Come, let us go over to the Philistine garrison on yonder side." But he did not tell his father. Saul was staying in the outskirts of Gibe-ah under the pomegranate tree which is at Migron; the people who were with him were about six hundred men.

And Jonathan said to the young man who bore his armor, "Come, let us go over to the garrison of these uncircumcised; it may be that the Lord will work for us; for nothing can hinder the Lord from saving by many or by few."

Then Jonathan climbed up on his hands and feet, and his armor-bearer after him. And they fell before Jonathan, and his armor-bearer killed them after him; and that first slaughter, which Jonathan and his armor-bearer made, was of about twenty men within as it were half a furrow's length in an acre of land. And there was panic in the camp, in the field, and among all the people; the garrison and even the raiders trembled; the earth quaked; and it became a very great panic.

The History of Saul's Reign

Likewise, when all the men of Israel who had hid themselves in the hill country of Ephraim heard that the Philistines were fleeing, they too followed after them in battle. So the Lord delivered Israel that day; and the battle passed beyond Beth-aven.

When Saul had taken the kingship over Israel, he fought against all his enemies on every side, against Moab, against the Ammonites, against Edom, against the kings of Zobah, and against the Philistines; wherever he turned he put them to the worse.

THE REBELLION OF SAUL; DAVID BECOMES KING

And Samuel said to Saul, "The Lord sent me to anoint you king over his people Israel; now therefore hearken to the words of the Lord. Thus says the Lord of hosts, 'I will punish what Amalek did to Israel in opposing them on the way, when they came up out of Egypt. Now go and smite Amalek, and utterly destroy all that they have; do not spare them, but kill both man and woman, infant and suckling, ox and sheep, camel and ass.' "

So Saul summoned the people, and numbered them in Telaim, two hundred thousand men on foot, and ten thousand men of Judah. And Saul came to the city of Amalek, and lay in wait in the valley. And Saul said to the Kenites, "Go, depart, go down from among the Amalekites, lest I destroy you with them; for you showed kindness to all the people of Israel when they came up out of Egypt." So the Kenites departed from among the Amalekites. And Saul defeated the Amalekites, from Havilah as far as Shur, which is east of Egypt. And he took Agag the king of the Amalekites alive, and utterly destroyed all the people with the edge of the sword. But Saul and the people spared Agag, and the best of the sheep and of the oxen and of the fatlings, and the lambs, and all that was good, and would not utterly destroy them; all that was despised and worthless they utterly destroyed.

The word of the Lord came to Samuel: "I repent that I have made Saul king; for he has turned back from following me, and has not performed my commandments." And Samuel was angry; and he cried to the Lord all night. And Samuel rose early to meet Saul in the morning; and it was told Samuel, "Saul came to Carmel, and behold, he set up a monument for himself and turned, and passed on, and went down to Gilgal." And Samuel came to Saul, and Saul said to him, "Blessed be you to the Lord; I have performed the commandment of the Lord." And Samuel said, "What then is this bleating of the sheep in my ears,

149

and the lowing of oxen which I hear?" Saul said, "They have brought them from the Amalekites; for the people spared the best of the sheep and of the oxen, to sacrifice to the Lord your God; and the rest we have utterly destroyed."

And Samuel said, "Has the Lord as great delight in burnt offerings and sacrifices, as in obeying the voice of the Lord? Behold, to obey is better than sacrifice, and to hearken than the fat of rams. For rebellion is as the sin of divination, and stubbornness is as iniquity and idolatry. Because you have rejected the word of the Lord, he has also rejected you from being king."

Then Samuel said, "Bring here to me Agag the king of the Amalekites." And Agag came to him cheerfully. Agag said, "Surely the bitterness of death is past." And Samuel said, "As your sword has made women childless, so shall your mother be childless among women." And Samuel hewed Agag in pieces before the Lord in Gilgal.

Then Samuel went to Ramah; and Saul went up to his house in Gibe-ah of Saul. And Samuel did not see Saul again until the day of his death, but Samuel grieved over Saul. And the Lord repented that he had made Saul king over Israel.

The Lord said to Samuel, "How long will you grieve over Saul, seeing I have rejected him from being king over Israel? Fill your horn with oil, and go; I will send you to Jesse the Bethlehemite, for I have provided for myself a king among his sons." And Samuel said, "How can I go? If Saul hears it, he will kill me." And the Lord said, "Take a heifer with you, and say, 'I have come to sacrifice to the Lord.' And invite Jesse to the sacrifice, and I will show you what you shall do; and you shall anoint for me him whom I name to you." Samuel did what the Lord commanded, and came to Bethlehem. The elders of the city came to meet him trembling, and said, "Do you come peaceably?" And he said, "Peaceably; I have come to sacrifice to the Lord; consecrate yourselves, and come with me to the sacrifice." And he consecrated Jesse and his sons, and invited them to the sacrifice.

When they came, he looked on Eliab and thought, "Surely the Lord's anointed is before him." But the Lord said to Samuel, "Do not look on his appearance or on the height of his stature, because I have rejected him; for the Lord sees not as man sees; man looks on the outward appearance, but the Lord looks on the heart." Then Jesse called Abinadab, and made him pass before Samuel. And he said, "Neither has the Lord chosen this one." And Jesse made seven of his sons pass before Samuel. And Samuel said to Jesse, "The Lord has not chosen these."

And Samuel said to Jesse, "Are all your sons here?" And he said, "There remains yet the youngest, but behold, he is keeping the sheep." And Samuel said to Jesse, "Send and fetch him; for we will not sit down till he comes here." And he sent, and brought him in. Now he was ruddy, and had beautiful eyes, and was handsome. And the Lord said, "Arise, anoint him; for this is he." Then Samuel took the horn of oil, and anointed him in the midst of his brothers; and the Spirit of the Lord came mightily upon David from that day forward. And Samuel rose up, and went to Ramah.

Now the Spirit of the Lord departed from Saul, and an evil spirit from the Lord tormented him. And Saul's servants said to him, "Behold now, an evil spirit from God is tormenting you. Let our lord now command your servants, who are before you, to seek out a man who is skilful in playing the lyre; and when the evil spirit from God is upon you, he will play it, and you will be well." So Saul said to his servants, "Provide for me a man who can play well, and bring him to me." One of the young men answered, "Behold, I have seen a son of Jesse the Bethlehemite, who is skilful in playing, a man of valor, a man of war, prudent in speech, and a man of good presence; and the Lord is with him." Therefore Saul sent messengers to Jesse, and said, "Send me David your son, who is with the sheep." And Jesse took an ass laden with bread, and a skin of wine and a kid, and sent them by David his son to Saul. And David came to Saul, and entered his service. And Saul loved him greatly, and he became his armor-bearer. And Saul sent to Jesse, saying, "Let David remain in my service, for he has found favor in my sight." And whenever the evil spirit from God was upon Saul, David took the lyre and played it with his hand; so Saul was refreshed, and was well, and the evil spirit departed from him.

DAVID AND GOLIATH

Now the Philistines gathered their armies for battle; and they were gathered at Socoh, which belongs to Judah, and encamped between Socoh and Azekah, in Ephes-dammim. And Saul and the men of Israel were gathered, and encamped in the valley of Elah, and drew up in line of battle against the Philistines. And the Philistines stood on the mountain on the one side, and Israel stood on the mountain on the other side, with a valley between them. And there came out from the camp of the Philistines a champion named Goliath, of Gath, whose height was six cubits and a span. He had a helmet of bronze on his head, and he was armed with a coat of mail, and the weight of the coat was five thousand shekels of bronze. And he had greaves of bronze upon his legs, and a javelin of bronze slung between his shoulders. And the shaft of his spear was like a weaver's beam, and his spear's head weighed six hundred shekels of iron; and his shield-bearer went before him. He stood and shouted to the ranks of Israel, "Why have you come out to draw up for battle? Am I not a Philistine, and are you not servants of Saul? Choose a man for yourselves, and let him come down to me. If he is able to fight with me and kill me, then we will be your servants; but if I prevail against him and kill him, then you shall be our servants and serve us." And the Philistine said, "I defy the ranks of Israel this day; give me a man, that we may fight together." When Saul and all Israel heard these words of the Philistine, they were dismayed and greatly afraid.

Now David was the son of an Ephrathite of Bethlehem in Judah, named Jesse, who had eight sons. In the days of Saul the man was already old and advanced in years. The three eldest sons of Jesse had followed Saul to the battle; and the names of his three sons who went to battle were Eliab the first-born, and next to him Abinadab, and the third Shammah. David was the youngest; the three eldest followed Saul, but David went back and forth from Saul to feed his father's sheep at Bethlehem. For forty days the Philistine came forward and took his stand, morning and evening.

And Jesse said to David his son, "Take for your brothers an ephah of this parched grain, and these ten loaves, and carry them quickly to the camp to your brothers; also take these ten cheeses to the commander of their thousand. See how your brothers fare, and bring some token from them."

And the men of Israel said, "Have you seen this man who has come up? Surely he has come up to defy Israel; and the man who kills him, the king will enrich with great riches, and will give him his daughter, and make his father's house free in Israel." And David said to the men who stood by him, "What shall be done for the man who kills this Philistine, and takes away the reproach from Israel? For who is this uncircumcised Philistine, that he should defy the armies of the living God?" And the people answered him in the same way, "So shall it be done to the man who kills him."

Now Eliab his eldest brother heard when he spoke to the men; and Eliab's anger was kindled against David, and he said, "Why have you come down? And with whom have you left those few sheep in the wilderness? I know your presumption, and the evil of your heart; for you have come down to see the battle." And David said, "What have I done now? Was it not but a word?" And he turned away from him toward another, and spoke in the same way; and the people answered him again as before.

When the words which David spoke were heard, they repeated them before Saul; and he sent for him. And David said to Saul, "Let no man's heart fail because of him; your servant will go and fight with this Philistine." And Saul said to David, "You are not able to go against this Philistine to fight with him; for you are but a youth, and he has been a man of war from his youth." But David said to Saul, "Your servant used to keep sheep for his father; and when there came a lion, or a bear, and took a lamb from the flock, I went after him and smote him and delivered it out of his mouth; and if he arose against me, I caught him by his beard, and smote him and killed him. Your servant has killed both lions and bears; and this uncircumcised Philistine shall be like one of them, seeing he has defied the armies of the living God." And David said, "The Lord who delivered me from the paw of the lion and from the paw of the bear, will deliver me from the hand of this Philistine." And Saul said to David, "Go, and the Lord be with you!" Then Saul clothed David with his armor; he put a helmet of bronze on his head, and clothed him with a coat of mail. And David girded his sword over his armor, and he tried in vain to go, for he was not used to them. Then David said to Saul, "I cannot go with these; for I am not used to them." And David put them off. Then he took his staff in his hand, and chose five smooth stones from the brook, and put them in his shepherd's bag or wallet; his sling was in his hand, and he drew near to the Philistine.

And the Philistine came on and drew near to David, with his shield-bearer in front of him. And when the Philistine looked, and saw David, he disdained him; for he was but a youth, ruddy and comely in appearance. And the Philistine said to David, "Am I a dog, that you come to me with sticks?" And the Philistine cursed David by his gods. The Philistine said to David, "Come to me, and I will give your flesh to the birds of the air and to the beasts of the field." Then David said to the Philistine, "You come to me with a sword and with a spear and with a javelin; but I come to you in the name of the Lord of hosts, the God of the armies of Israel, whom you have defied. This day the Lord will deliver you into my hand, and I will strike you down, and cut off your head; and I will give the dead bodies of the host of the Philistines this day to the birds of the air and to the wild beasts of the earth; that all the earth may know that there is a God in Israel, and that all this assembly may know that the Lord saves not with sword and spear; for the battle is the Lord's and he will give you into our hand."

When the Philistine arose and came and drew near to meet David, David ran quickly toward the battle line to meet the Philistine. And David put his hand in his bag and took out a stone, and slung it, and struck the Philistine on his forehead; the stone sank into his forehead, and he fell on his face to the ground.

So David prevailed over the Philistine with a sling and with a stone, and struck the Philistine, and killed him; there was no sword in the hand of David. Then David ran and stood over the Philistine, and took his sword and drew it out of its sheath, and killed him, and cut off his head with it. When the Philistines saw that their champion was dead, they fled.

THE FRIENDSHIP OF JONATHAN AND DAVID

When he had finished speaking to Saul, the soul of Jonathan was knit to the soul of David, and Jonathan loved him as his own soul. And Saul took him that day, and would not let him return to his father's house. Then Jonathan made a covenant with David, because he loved him as his own soul. And Jonathan stripped himself of the robe that was upon him, and gave it to David, and his armor, and even his sword and his bow and his girdle. And David went out and was successful wherever Saul sent him; so that Saul set him over the men of war. And this was good in the sight of all the people and also in the sight of Saul's servants.

As they were coming home, when David returned from slaying the Philistine, the women came out of all the cities of Israel, singing and dancing, to meet King Saul, with timbrels, with songs of joy, and with instruments of music. And the women sang to one another as they made merry,

"Saul has slain his thousands,
and David his ten thousands."

And Saul was very angry, and this saying displeased him; he said, "They have ascribed to David ten thousands, and to me they have ascribed thousands; and what more can he have but the kingdom?" And Saul eyed David from that day on.

And on the morrow an evil spirit from God rushed upon Saul, and he raved within his house, while David was playing the lyre, as he did day by day. Saul had his spear in his hand; and Saul cast the spear, for he thought, "I will pin David to the wall." But David evaded him twice.

Saul was afraid of David, because the Lord was with him but had departed from Saul. So Saul removed him from his presence, and made him a commander of a thousand; and he went out and came in before the people. And David had success in all his undertakings; for the Lord was with him.

But when Saul saw and knew that the Lord was with David, and that all Israel loved him, Saul was still more afraid of David. So Saul was David's enemy continually.

Then the princes of the Philistines came out to battle, and as often as they came out David had more success than all the servants of Saul; so that his name was highly esteemed.

And Saul spoke to Jonathan his son and to all his servants, that they should kill David. But Jonathan, Saul's son, delighted much in David. And Jonathan told David, "Saul my father seeks to kill you; therefore take heed to yourself in the morning, stay in a secret place and hide yourself; and I will go out and stand beside my father in the field where you are, and I will speak to my father about you; and if I learn anything I will tell you." And Jonathan spoke well of David to Saul his father, and said to him, "Let not the king sin against his servant David; because he has not sinned against you, and because his deeds have been of good service to you; for he took his life in his hand and he slew the Philistine, and the Lord wrought a great victory for all Israel. You saw it, and rejoiced; why then will you sin against innocent blood by killing David without cause?" And Saul hearkened to the voice of Jonathan; Saul swore, "As the Lord lives, he shall not be put to death."

Then David fled from Naioth in Ramah, and came and said before Jonathan, "What have I done? What is my guilt? And what is my sin before your father, that he seeks my life?" And he said to him, "Far from it! You shall not die. Behold, my father does nothing either great or small without disclosing it to me; and why should my father hide this from me? It is not so." But David replied, "Your father knows well that I have found favor in your eyes; and he thinks, 'Let not

Jonathan know this, lest he be grieved.' But truly, as the Lord lives and as your soul lives, there is but a step between me and death." Then said Jonathan to David, "Whatever you say, I will do for you." David said to Jonathan, "Behold, tomorrow is the new moon, and I should not fail to sit at table with the king; but let me go, that I may hide myself in the field till the third day at evening. If your father misses me at all, then say, 'David earnestly asked leave of me to run to Bethlehem his city; for there is a yearly sacrifice there for all the family.' If he says, 'Good!' it will be well with your servant; but if he is angry, then know that evil is determined by him."

And Jonathan said to David, "The Lord, the God of Israel, be witness! When I have sounded my father, about this time tomorrow, or the third day, behold, if he is well disposed toward David, shall I not then send and disclose it to you? But should it please my father to do you harm, the Lord do so to Jonathan, and more also, if I do not disclose it to you, and send you away, that you may go in safety. May the Lord be with you, as he has been with my father."

Then Jonathan said to him, "Tomorrow is the new moon; and you will be missed, because your seat will be empty. And on the third day you will be greatly missed; then go to the place where you hid yourself when the matter was in hand, and remain beside yonder stone heap. And I will shoot three arrows to the side of it, as though I shot at a mark. And behold, I will send the lad, saying, 'Go, find the arrows.' If I say to the lad, 'Look, the arrows are on this side of you, take them,' then you are to come, for, as the Lord lives, it is safe for you and there is no danger. But if I say to the youth, 'Look, the arrows are beyond you,' then go; for the Lord has sent you away."

In the morning Jonathan went out into the field to the appointment with David, and with him a little lad. And he said to his lad, "Run and find the arrows which I shoot." As the lad ran, he shot an arrow beyond him. And when the lad came to the place of the arrow which Jonathan had shot, Jonathan called after the lad and said, "Is not the arrow beyond you?" And Jonathan called after the lad, "Hurry, make haste, stay not." So Jonathan's lad gathered up the arrows, and came to his master. But the lad knew nothing; only Jonathan and David knew the matter. And Jonathan gave his weapons to his lad, and said to him, "Go and carry them to the city." And as soon as the lad had gone, David rose from beside the stone heap and fell on his face to the ground, and bowed three times; and they kissed one another, and wept with one another, until David recovered himself. Then Jonathan said to David, "Go in peace, forasmuch as we have sworn both of us in the name of the Lord, saying, 'The Lord shall be between me and you, and between my descendants and your descendants, for ever.'" And he rose and departed; and Jonathan went into the city.

DAVID'S FLIGHT

Then came David to Nob to Ahimelech the priest; and Ahimelech came to meet David trembling, and said to him, "Why are you alone, and no one with you?" And David said to Ahimelech the priest, "The king has charged me with a matter, and said to me, 'Let no one know anything of the matter about which I send you, and with which I have charged you.' I have made an appointment with the young men for such and such a place. Now then, what have you at hand? Give me five loaves of bread, or whatever is here."

So the priest gave him the holy bread; for there was no bread there but the bread of the Presence, which is removed from before the Lord, to be replaced by hot bread on the day it is taken away.

Now a certain man of the servants of Saul was there that day, detained before the Lord; his name was Doeg the Edomite, the chief of Saul's herdsmen. And David said to Ahimelech, "And have you not here a spear or a sword at hand? For I have brought neither my sword nor my weapons with me, because the king's business required haste." And the priest said, "The sword of Goliath the Philistine, whom you killed in the valley of Elah, behold, it is here wrapped in a cloth behind the ephod; if you will take that, take it, for there is none but that here." And David said, "There is none like that; give it to me."

David departed from there and escaped to the cave of Adullam; and when his brothers and all his father's house heard it, they went down there to him. And every one who was in distress, and every one who was in debt, and every one who was discontented, gathered to him; and he became captain over them. And there were with him about four hundred men. And David went from there to Mizpeh of Moab; and he said to the king of Moab, "Pray let my father and my mother stay with you, till I know what God will do for me." And he left them with the king of Moab, and they stayed with him all the time that David was in the stronghold.

Then the prophet Gad said to David, "Do not remain in the stronghold; depart, and go into the land of Judah." So David departed, and went into the forest of Hereth. Now Saul heard that David was discovered, and the men who were with him. Saul was sitting at Gibe-ah, under the tamarisk tree on the height, with his spear in his hand, and all his servants were standing about him. And Saul said to his servants who stood about him, "Hear now, you Benjaminites; will the son of Jesse give every one of you fields and vineyards, will he make you all commanders of thousands and commanders of hundreds, that all of you have conspired against me? No one discloses to me when my son makes a league with the son of Jesse, none of you is sorry for me or discloses to me that my son has stirred up my servant against me, to lie in wait, as at this day."

Then answered Doeg the Edomite, who stood by the servants of Saul, "I saw the son of Jesse coming to Nob, to Ahimelech the son of Ahitub, and he inquired of the Lord for him, and gave him provisions, and gave him the sword of Goliath the Philistine." Then the king sent to summon Ahimelech the priest, the son of Ahitub, and all his father's house, the priests who were at Nob; and all of them came to the king. And Saul said, "Hear now, son of Ahitub." And he answered, "Here I am, my lord." And Saul said to him, "Why have you conspired against me, you and the son of Jesse, in that you have given him bread and sword, and have inquired of God for him, so that he has risen against me, to lie in wait, as at this day?" Then the king said to Doeg, "You turn and fall upon the priests." And Doeg the Edomite turned and fell upon the priests, and he killed on that day eighty-five persons who wore the linen ephod. And Nob, the city of the priests, he put to the sword; both men and women, children and sucklings, oxen, asses, and sheep, he put to the sword.

But one of the sons of Ahimelech the son of Ahitub, named Abiathar, escaped and fled after David. And Abiathar told David that Saul had killed the priests of the Lord. And David said to Abiathar, "I knew on that day, when Doeg the Edomite was there, that he would surely tell Saul. I have occasioned the death of all the persons of your father's house. Stay with me, fear not; for he that seeks my life seeks your life; with me you shall be in safekeeping."

DAVID IN EXILE

Now Samuel died; and all Israel assembled and mourned for him, and they buried him in his house at Ramah. Then David rose and went down to the wilderness of Paran. Saul had given Michal his daughter, David's wife, to Palti the son of Laish, who was of Gallim. And Saul encamped on the hill of Hachilah, which is beside the road on the east of Jeshimon. But David remained in the wilderness; and when he saw that Saul came after him into the wilderness, David sent out spies, and learned of a certainty that Saul had come. Then David rose and came to the place where Saul had encamped; and David saw the place where Saul lay, with Abner the son of Ner, the commander of his army; Saul was lying within the encampment, while the army was encamped around him.

Then David said to Ahimelech the Hittite, and to Joab's brother Abishai the son of Zeruiah, "Who will go down with me into the camp to Saul?" And Abishai said, "I will go down with you." So David and Abishai went to the army by night; and there lay Saul sleeping within the encampment, with his spear stuck in the ground at his head; and Abner and the army lay around him. Then said Abishai to David, "God has given your enemy into your hand this day; now therefore let me pin him to the earth with one stroke of the spear, and I will not strike him twice." But David said to Abishai, "Do not destroy him; for who can put forth his hand against the Lord's anointed, and be guiltless?" And David said, "As the Lord lives, the Lord will smite him; or his day shall come to die; or he shall go down into battle and perish. The Lord forbid that I should put forth my hand against the Lord's anointed; but take now the spear that is at his head, and the jar of water, and let us go." So David took the spear and the jar of water from Saul's head; and they went away. No man saw it, or knew it, nor did any awake; for they were all asleep, because a deep sleep from the Lord had fallen upon them.

Then David went over to the other side, and stood afar off on the top of the mountain, with a great space between them; and David called to the army, and to Abner the son of Ner, saying, "Will you not answer, Abner?" Then Abner answered, "Who are you that calls to the king?" And David said to Abner, "Are you not a man? Who is like you in Israel? Why then have you not kept watch over your lord the king? For one of the people came in to destroy the king your lord. This thing that you have done is not good. As the Lord lives, you deserve to die, because you have not kept watch over your lord, the Lord's anointed. And now see where the king's spear is, and the jar of water that was at his head."

Saul recognized David's voice, and said, "Is this your voice, my son David?" And David said, "It is my voice, my lord, O king." And he said, "Why does my lord pursue after his servant? For what have I done? What guilt is on my hands? Now therefore let my lord the king hear the words of his servant. If it is the Lord who has stirred you up against me, may he accept an offering; but if it is men, may they be cursed before the Lord, for they have driven me out this day that I should have no share in the heritage of the Lord, saying, 'Go, serve other gods.' Now therefore, let not my blood fall to the earth away from the presence of the Lord; for the king of Israel has come out to seek my life, like one who hunts a partridge in the mountains."

Then Saul said, "I have done wrong; return, my son David, for I will no more do you harm, because my life was precious in your eyes this day; behold, I have played the fool, and have erred exceedingly."

THE DEFEAT AND DEATH OF SAUL

In those days the Philistines gathered their forces for war, to fight against Israel.

Now Samuel had died, and all Israel had mourned for him and buried him in Ramah, his own city. And Saul had put the mediums and the wizards out of the land. The Philistines assembled, and came and encamped at Shunem; and Saul gathered all Israel, and they encamped at Gilboa. When Saul saw the army of the Philistines, he was afraid, and his heart trembled greatly. And when Saul inquired of the Lord, the Lord did not answer him, either by dreams, or by Urim, or by prophets. Then Saul said to his servants, "Seek out for me a woman who is a medium, that I may go to her and inquire of her." And his servants said to him, "Behold, there is a medium at Endor."

So Saul disguised himself and put on other garments, and went, he and two men with him; and they came to the woman by night. And he said, "Divine for me by a spirit, and bring up for me whomever I shall name to you." The woman said to him, "Surely you know what Saul has done, how he has cut off the mediums and the wizards from the land. Why then are you laying a snare for my life to bring about my death?" But Saul swore to her by the Lord, "As the Lord lives, no punishment shall come upon you for this thing." Then the woman said, "Whom shall I bring up for you?" He said, "Bring up Samuel for me." When the woman saw Samuel, she cried out with a loud voice; and the woman said to Saul, "Why have you deceived me? You are Saul." The king said to her, "Have no fear; what do you see?" And the woman said to Saul, "I see a god coming up out of the earth." He said to her, "What is his appearance?" And she said, "An old man is coming up;

and he is wrapped in a robe." And Saul knew that it was Samuel, and he bowed with his face to the ground, and did obeisance.

Then Samuel said to Saul, "Why have you disturbed me by bringing me up?" Saul answered, "I am in great distress; for the Philistines are warring against me, and God has turned away from me and answers me no more, either by prophets or by dreams; therefore I have summoned you to tell me what I shall do." And Samuel said, "Why then do you ask me, since the Lord has turned from you and become your enemy? The Lord has done to you as he spoke by me; for the Lord has torn the kingdom out of your hand, and given it to your neighbor, David. Because you did not obey the voice of the Lord, and did not carry out his fierce wrath against Amalek, therefore the Lord has done this thing to you this day. Moreover the Lord will give Israel also with you into the hand of the Philistines; and tomorrow you and your sons shall be with me; the Lord will give the army of Israel also into the hand of the Philistines."

Then Saul fell at once full length upon the ground, filled with fear because of the words of Samuel; and there was no strength in him, for he had eaten nothing all day and all night. And the woman came to Saul, and when she saw that he was terrified, she said to him, "Behold, your handmaid has hearkened to you; I have taken my life in my hand, and have hearkened to what you have said to me. Now therefore, you also hearken to your handmaid; let me set a morsel of bread before you; and eat, that you may have strength when you go on your way." He refused, and said, "I will not eat." But his servants, together with the woman, urged him; and he hearkened to their words. So he rose from the earth, and sat upon the bed. Now the woman had a fatted calf in the house, and she quickly killed it, and she took flour, and kneaded it and baked unleavened bread of it, and she put it before Saul and his servants; and they ate. Then they rose and went away that night.

Now the Philistines fought against Israel; and the men of Israel fled before the Philistines, and fell slain on Mount Gilboa. And the Philistines overtook Saul and his sons; and the Philistines slew Jonathan and Abinadab and Malchishua, the sons of Saul. The battle pressed hard upon Saul, and the archers found him; and he was badly wounded by the archers. Then Saul said to his armor-bearer, "Draw your sword, and thrust me through with it, lest these uncircumcised come and thrust me through, and make sport of me." But his armor-bearer would not; for he feared greatly. Therefore Saul took his own sword, and fell upon it. And when his armor-bearer saw that Saul was dead, he also fell upon his sword, and died with him. Thus Saul died, and his three sons, and his armor-bearer, and all his men, on the same day together. And when the men of Israel who were on the other side of the valley and those beyond the Jordan saw that the men of Israel had fled and that Saul and his sons were dead, they forsook their cities and fled; and the Philistines came and dwelt in them.

On the morrow, when the Philistines came to strip the slain, they found Saul and his three sons fallen on Mount Gilboa. And they cut off his head, and stripped off his armor, and sent messengers throughout the land of the Philistines, to carry the good news to their idols and to the people. They put his armor in the temple of Ashtaroth; and they fastened his body to the wall of Beth-shan. But when the inhabitants of Jabesh-gilead heard what the Philistines had done to Saul, all the valiant men arose, and went all night, and took the body of Saul and the bodies of his sons from the wall of Beth-shan; and they came to Jabesh and burnt them there. And they took their bones and buried them under the tamarisk tree in Jabesh, and fasted seven days.

CHAPTER ELEVEN

The Kingdom of David

DAVID MOURNS FOR SAUL AND JONATHAN

After the death of Saul, when David had returned from the slaughter of the Amalekites, David remained two days in Ziklag; and on the third day, behold, a man came from Saul's camp, with his clothes rent and earth upon his head. And when he came to David, he fell to the ground and did obeisance. David said to him, "Where do you come from?" And he said to him, "I have escaped from the camp of Israel." And David said to him, "How did it go? Tell me." And he answered, "The people have fled from the battle, and many of the people also have fallen and are dead; and Saul and his son Jonathan are also dead." Then David said to the young man who told him, "How do you know that Saul and his son Jonathan are dead?" And the young man who told him said, "By chance I happened to be on Mount Gilboa; and there was Saul leaning upon his spear; and lo, the chariots and the horsemen were close upon him. And when he looked behind him, he saw me, and called to me. And I answered, 'Here I am.' And he said to me, 'Who are you?' I answered him, 'I am an Amalekite.' And he said to me, 'Stand beside me and slay me; for anguish has seized me, and yet my life still lingers.' So I stood beside him, and slew him, because I was sure that he could not live after he had fallen; and I took the crown which was on his head and the armlet which was on his arm, and I have brought them here to my lord."

Then David took hold of his clothes and rent them; and so did all the men who were with him; and they mourned and wept and fasted until evening for Saul and for Jonathan his son and for the people of the Lord and for the house of Israel, because they had fallen by the sword. And David said to the young man who told him, "Where do you come from?" And he answered, "I am the son of a sojourner, an Amalekite." David said to him, "How is it you were not afraid to put forth your hand to destroy the Lord's anointed?" Then David called one of the young men and said, "Go, fall upon him." And he smote him so that he died. And David said to him, "Your blood be upon your head; for your own mouth has testified against you, saying, 'I have slain the Lord's anointed.'"

And David lamented with this lamentation over Saul and Jonathan his son, and he said it should be taught to the people of Judah; behold, it is written in the Book of Jashar. He said:

"Thy glory, O Israel, is slain upon thy high places! How are the mighty fallen! Tell it not in Gath, publish it not in the streets of Ashkelon; lest the daughters of the Philistines rejoice, lest the daughters of the uncircumcised exult.

"Ye mountains of Gilboa, let there be no dew or rain upon you, nor upsurging of the deep! For there the shield of the mighty was defiled, the shield of Saul, not anointed with oil.

"From the blood of the slain, from the fat of the mighty, the bow of Jonathan turned not back, and the sword of Saul returned not empty.

"Saul and Jonathan, beloved and lovely! In life and in death they were not divided; they were swifter than eagles, they were stronger than lions.

"Ye daughters of Israel, weep over Saul, who clothed you daintily in scarlet, who put ornaments of gold upon your apparel.

"How are the mighty fallen in the midst of the battle!

"Jonathan lies slain upon thy high places. I am distressed for you, my brother Jonathan; very pleasant have you been to me; your love to me was wonderful, passing the love of women.

"How are the mighty fallen, and the weapons of war perished!"

DAVID ANOINTED KING OF JUDAH

After this David inquired of the Lord, "Shall I go up into any of the cities of Judah?" And the Lord said to him, "Go up." David said, "To which shall I go up?" And he said, "To Hebron." So David went up there, and his two wives also, Ahinoam of Jezreel, and Abigail the widow of Nabal of Carmel. And David brought up his men who were with him, every one with his household; and they dwelt in the towns of Hebron.

And the men of Judah came, and there they anointed David king over the house of Judah. When they told David, "It was the men of Jabesh-gilead who buried Saul," David sent messengers to the men of

Jabesh-gilead, and said to them, "May you be blessed by the Lord, because you showed this loyalty to Saul your lord, and buried him! Now may the Lord show steadfast love and faithfulness to you! And I will do good to you because you have done this thing. Now therefore let your hands be strong, and be valiant; for Saul your lord is dead, and the house of Judah has anointed me king over them."

Now Abner the son of Ner, commander of Saul's army, had taken Ish-bosheth the son of Saul, and brought him over to Mahanaim; and he made him king over Gilead and the Ashurites and Jezreel and Ephraim and Benjamin and all Israel. Ish-bosheth, Saul's son, was forty years old when he began to reign over Israel, and he reigned two years. But the house of Judah followed David. And the time that David was king in Hebron over the house of Judah was seven years and six months.

Abner the son of Ner, and the servants of Ish-bosheth the son of Saul, went out from Mahanaim to Gibeon. And the battle was very fierce that day; and Abner and the men of Israel were beaten before the servants of David. And the three sons of Zeruiah were there, Joab, Abishai, and Asahel. Now Asahel was as swift of foot as a wild gazelle; and Asahel pursued Abner, and as he went he turned neither to the right hand nor to the left from following Abner. Then Abner looked behind him and said, "Is it you, Asahel?" And he answered, "It is I." Abner said to him, "Turn aside from following me; why should I smite you to the ground? How then could I lift up my face to your brother Joab?" But he refused to turn aside; therefore Abner smote him in the belly with the butt of his spear, so that the spear came out at his back; and he fell there, and died where he was. And all who came to the place where Asahel had fallen and died, stood still.

But Joab and Abishai pursued Abner; and as the sun was going down they came to the hill of Ammah, which lies before Giah on the way to the wilderness of Gibeon. And the Benjaminites gathered themselves together behind Abner, and became one band, and took their stand on the top of a hill. Then Abner called to Joab, "Shall the sword devour for ever? Do you not know that the end will be bitter? How long will it be before you bid your people turn from the pursuit of their brethren?" And Joab said, "As God lives, if you had not spoken, surely the men would have given up the pursuit of their brethren in the morning." So Joab blew the trumpet; and all the men stopped, and pursued Israel no more, nor did they fight any more.

And Abner and his men went all that night through the Arabah;

they crossed the Jordan, and marching the whole forenoon they came to Mahanaim. Joab returned from the pursuit of Abner; and when he had gathered all the people together, there were missing of David's servants nineteen men besides Asahel. But the servants of David had slain of Benjamin three hundred and sixty of Abner's men. And they took up Asahel, and buried him in the tomb of his father, which was at Bethlehem. And Joab and his men marched all night, and the day broke upon them at Hebron.

There was a long war between the house of Saul and the house of David; and David grew stronger and stronger, while the house of Saul became weaker and weaker. And sons were born to David at Hebron: his first-born was Amnon, of Ahinoam of Jezreel; and his second, Chile-ab, of Abigail the widow of Nabal of Carmel; and the third, Absalom the son of Maacah.

FURTHER ADVENTURES OF DAVID

And Abner conferred with the elders of Israel, saying, "For some time past you have been seeking David as king over you. Now then bring it about; for the Lord has promised David, saying, 'By the hand of my servant David I will save my people Israel from the hand of the Philistines, and from the hand of all their enemies.' " Abner also spoke to Benjamin; and then Abner went to tell David at Hebron all that Israel and the whole house of Benjamin thought good to do. When Abner came with twenty men to David at Hebron, David made a feast for Abner and the men who were with him.

And Abner said to David, "I will arise and go, and will gather all Israel to my lord the king, that they may make a covenant with you, and that you may reign over all that your heart desires." So David sent Abner away; and he went in peace. Just then the servants of David arrived with Joab from a raid, bringing much spoil with them. But Abner was not with David at Hebron, for he had sent him away, and he had gone in peace. When Joab and all the army that was with him came, it was told Joab, "Abner the son of Ner came to the king, and he has let him go, and he has gone in peace." Then Joab went to the king and said, "What have you done? Behold, Abner came to you; why is it that you have sent him away, so that he is gone? You know that Abner the son of Ner came to deceive you, and to know your going out and your coming in, and to know all that you are doing."

When Joab came out from David's presence, he sent messengers after Abner, and they brought him back from the cistern of Sirah; but David did not know about it. And when Abner returned to Hebron, Joab took him aside into the midst of the gate to speak with him privately, and there he smote him in the belly, so that he died, for the blood of Asahel his brother. Afterward, when David heard of it, he said, "I and my kingdom are for ever guiltless before the Lord for the blood of Abner the son of Ner. The Lord requite the evildoer according to his wickedness!"

When Ish-bosheth, Saul's son, heard that Abner had died at Hebron, his courage failed, and all Israel was dismayed. Now Saul's son had two men who were captains of raiding bands; the name of the one was Bannah, and the name of the other Rechab, sons of Rimmon a man of Benjamin from Be-eroth (for Be-eroth also is reckoned to Benjamin; the Be-erothites fled to Gittaim, and have been sojourners there to this day). Jonathan, the son of Saul, had a son who was crippled in his feet. He was five years old when the news about Saul and Jonathan came from Jezreel; and his nurse took him up, and fled; and, as she fled in her haste, he fell, and became lame. And his name was Mephibosheth.

Now the sons of Rimmon the Be-erothite, Rechab and Baanah, set out, and about the heat of the day they came to the house of Ish-bosheth, as he was taking his noonday rest. And behold, the doorkeeper of the house had been cleaning wheat, but she grew drowsy and slept; so Rechab and Baanah his brother slipped in. When they came into the house, as he lay on his bed in his bedchamber, they smote him, and slew him, and beheaded him. They took his head, and went by the way of the Arabah all night, and brought the head of Ish-bosheth to David at Hebron. And they said to the king, "Here is the head of Ish-bosheth, the son of Saul, your enemy, who sought your life; the Lord has avenged my lord the king this day on Saul and on his offspring."

But David answered Rechab and Baanah his brother, the sons of Rimmon the Be-erothite, "As the Lord lives, who has redeemed my life out of every adversity, when one told me, 'Behold, Saul is dead,' and thought he was bringing good news, I seized him and slew him at Ziklag, which was the reward I gave him for his news. How much more, when wicked men have slain a righteous man in his own house upon his bed, shall I not now require his blood at your hand, and destroy you from the earth?" And David commanded his young men, and they killed them, and cut off their hands and feet, and hanged them beside the pool at Hebron. But they took the head of Ish-bosheth, and buried it in the tomb of Abner at Hebron.

Then all the tribes of Israel came to David at Hebron, and said, "Behold, we are your bone and flesh. In times past, when Saul was king over us, it was you that led out and brought in Israel; and the Lord said to you, 'You shall be shepherd of my people Israel, and you shall be prince over Israel.'" So all the elders of Israel came to the king at Hebron; and King David made a covenant with them at Hebron before the Lord, and they anointed David king over Israel. David was thirty years old when he began to reign, and he reigned forty years. At Hebron he reigned over Judah seven years and six months; and at Jerusalem he reigned over all Israel and Judah thirty-three years.

And the king and his men went to Jerusalem against the Jebusites, the inhabitants of the land, who said to David, "You will not come in here, but the blind and the lame will ward you off"—thinking, "David cannot come in here." Nevertheless David took the stronghold of Zion, that is, the city of David.

When the Philistines heard that David had been anointed king over Israel, all the Philistines went up in search of David; but David heard of it and went down to the stronghold. Now the Philistines had come and spread out in the valley of Rephaim. Three of the thirty chief men went down to the rock to David at the cave of Adullam, when the army of Philistines was encamped in the valley of Rephaim. David was then in the stronghold; and the garrison of the Philistines was then at Bethlehem. And David said longingly, "O that some one would give me water to drink from the well of Bethlehem which is by the gate!" Then the three mighty men broke through the camp of the Philistines, and drew water out of the well of Bethlehem which was by the gate, and took and brought it to David. But David would not drink of it; he poured it out to the Lord, and said, "Far be it from me before my God that I should do this. Shall I drink the lifeblood of these men? For at the risk of their lives they brought it." Therefore he would not drink it. These things did the three mighty men.

And when David inquired of the Lord, he said, "You shall not go up; go around to their rear, and come upon them opposite the balsam trees. And when you hear the sound of marching in the tops of the balsam trees, then bestir yourself; for then the Lord has gone out before you to smite the army of the Philistines." And David did as the Lord commanded him, and smote the Philistines from Geba to Gezer.

THE ARK IS RECOVERED

David again gathered all the chosen men of Israel, thirty thousand. And David arose and went with all the people who were with him from Baale-judah, to bring up from there the ark of God, which is called by the name of the Lord of hosts who sits enthroned on the cherubim. And when those who bore the ark of the Lord had gone six paces, he sacrificed an ox and a fatling. And David danced before the Lord with all his might; and David was girded with a linen ephod. So David and all the house of Israel brought up the ark of the Lord with shouting, and with the sound of the horn.

As the ark of the Lord came into the city of David, Michal the daughter of Saul looked out of the window, and saw King David leaping and dancing before the Lord; and she despised him in her heart. And they brought in the ark of the Lord, and set it in its place, inside the tent which David had pitched for it; and David offered burnt offerings and peace offerings before the Lord. And when David had finished offering the burnt offerings and the peace offerings, he blessed the people in the name of the Lord of hosts, and distributed among all the people, the whole multitude of Israel, both men and women, to each a cake of bread, a portion of meat, and a cake of raisins. Then all the people departed, each to his house.

And David returned to bless his household. But Michal the daughter of Saul came out to meet David, and said, "How the king of Israel honored himself today, uncovering himself today before the eyes of his servants' maids, as one of the vulgar fellows shamelessly uncovers himself!" And David said to Michal, "It was before the Lord, who chose me above your father, and above all his house, to appoint me as prince over Israel, the people of the Lord—and I will make merry before the Lord. I will make myself yet more contemptible than this, and I will be abased in your eyes; but by the maids of whom you have spoken, by them I shall be held in honor." And Michal the daughter of Saul had no child to the day of her death.

Now when the king dwelt in his house, and the Lord had given him rest from all his enemies round about, the king said to Nathan the prophet, "See now, I dwell in a house of cedar, but the ark of God dwells in a tent." And Nathan said to the king, "Go, do all that is in your heart; for the Lord is with you."

But that same night the word of the Lord came to Nathan, "Go and tell my servant David, 'Thus says the Lord: Would you build me a house to dwell in? I have not dwelt in a house since the day I brought up the people of Israel from Egypt to this day, but I have been moving about in a tent for my dwelling. In all places where I have moved with all the people of Israel, did I speak a word with any of the judges of Israel, whom I commanded to shepherd my people Israel, saying, "Why have you not built me a house of cedar?"' Now therefore thus you shall say to my servant David, 'Thus says the Lord of hosts, I took you from the pasture, from following the sheep, that you should be prince over my people Israel; and I have been with you wherever you went, and have cut off all your enemies from before you; and I will make for you a great name, like the name of the great ones of the earth. When your days are fulfilled and you lie down with your fathers, I will raise up your offspring after you, who shall come forth from your body, and I will establish his kingdom. He shall build a house for my name, and I will establish the throne of his kingdom for ever. I will be his father, and he shall be my son. When he commits iniquity, I will chasten him with the rod of men; but I will not take my steadfast love from him, as I took it from Saul, whom I put away from before you. And your house and your kingdom shall be made sure for ever before me; your throne shall be established for ever.'" In accordance with all these words, and in accordance with all this vision, Nathan spoke to David.

PEACE COMES TO DAVID

After this David defeated the Philistines and subdued them, and David took Metheg-ammah out of the hand of the Philistines. And he defeated Moab, and measured them with a line, making them lie down on the ground; two lines he measured to be put to death, and one full line to be spared. And the Moabites became servants to David and brought tribute. David also defeated Hadadezer the son of Rehob, king of Zobah, as he went to restore his power at the river Euphrates. And David took from him a thousand and seven hundred horsemen, and twenty thousand foot soldiers; and David hamstrung all the chariot horses, but left enough for a hundred chariots. And when the Syrians of Damascus came to help Hadadezer king of Zobah, David slew twenty-two thousand men of the Syrians. Then David put garrisons in Aram of

Damascus; and the Syrians became servants to David and brought tribute. And the Lord gave victory to David wherever he went.

And David said, "Is there still any one left of the house of Saul, that I may show him kindness for Jonathan's sake?" Now there was a servant of the house of Saul whose name was Ziba, and they called him to David; and the king said to him, "Are you Ziba?" And he said, "Your servant is he." And the king said, "Is there not still some one of the house of Saul, that I may show the kindness of God to him?" Ziba said to the king, "There is still a son of Jonathan; he is crippled in his feet." The king said to him, "Where is he?" And Ziba said to the king, "He is in the house of Machir the son of Ammiel, at Lo-debar." Then King David sent and brought him from the house of Machir the son of Ammiel, at Lo-debar. And Mephibosheth the son of Jonathan, son of Saul, came to David, and fell on his face and did obeisance. And David said, "Mephibosheth!" And he answered, "Behold, your servant." And David said to him, "Do not fear; for I will show you kindness for the sake of your father Jonathan, and I will restore to you all the land of Saul your father; and you shall eat at my table always." And he did obeisance, and said, "What is your servant, that you should look upon a dead dog such as I?"

Then the king called Ziba, Saul's servant, and said to him, "All that belonged to Saul and to all his house I have given to your master's son. And you and your sons and your servants shall till the land for him, and shall bring in the produce, that your master's son may have bread to eat; but Mephibosheth your master's son shall always eat at my table."

And Mephibosheth had a young son, whose name was Mica. And all who dwelt in Ziba's house became Mephibosheth's servants. So Mephibosheth dwelt in Jerusalem; for he ate always at the king's table. Now he was lame in both his feet.

THE TRANSGRESSION OF DAVID

In the spring of the year, the time when kings go forth to battle, David sent Joab, and his servants with him, and all Israel; and they ravaged the Ammonites, and besieged Rabbah. But David remained at Jerusalem.

It happened, late one afternoon, when David arose from his couch and was walking upon the roof of the king's house, that he saw from the roof a woman bathing; and the woman was very beautiful. And David sent and inquired about the woman. And one said, "Is not this Bathsheba, the daughter of Eliam, the wife of Uriah the Hittite?" So David sent messengers, and took her; and she came to him, and he lay with her. (Now she was purifying herself from her uncleanness.) Then she returned to her house. And the woman conceived; and she sent and told David, "I am with child."

So David sent word to Joab, "Send me Uriah the Hittite." And Joab sent Uriah to David. When Uriah came to him, David asked how Joab was doing, and how the people fared, and how the war prospered. Then David said to Uriah, "Go down to your house, and wash your feet." And Uriah went out of the king's house, and there followed him a present from the king. But Uriah slept at the door of the king's house with all the servants of his lord, and did not go down to his house. When they told David, "Uriah did not go down to his house," David said to Uriah, "Have you not come from a journey? Why did you not go down to your house?" Uriah said to David, "The ark and Israel and Judah dwell in booths; and my lord Joab and the servants of my lord are camping in the open field; shall I then go to my house, to eat and to drink, and to lie with my wife? As you live, and as your soul lives, I will not do this thing." Then David said to Uriah, "Remain here today also, and tomorrow I will let you depart." So Uriah remained in Jerusalem that day, and the next. And David invited him, and he ate in his presence and drank, so that he made him drunk; and in the evening he went out to lie on his couch with the servants of his lord, but he did not go down to his house.

In the morning David wrote a letter to Joab, and sent it by the hand of Uriah. In the letter he wrote, "Set Uriah in the forefront of the hardest fighting, and then draw back from him, that he may be struck down, and die." And as Joab was besieging the city, he assigned Uriah to the place where he knew there were valiant men. And the men of the city came out and fought with Joab; and some of the servants of David among the people fell. Uriah the Hittite was slain also. Then Joab sent and told David all the news about the fighting; and he instructed the messenger, "When you have finished telling all the news about the fighting to the king, then, if the king's anger rises, and if he says to you, 'Why did you go so near the city to fight? Did you not know that they would shoot from the wall? Who killed Abimelech the son of Jerubbesheth? Did not a woman cast an upper millstone upon him from the wall, so that he died at Thebez? Why did you go so near the wall?' then you shall say, 'Your servant Uriah the Hittite is dead also.' "

So the messenger went, and came and told David all that Joab had sent him to tell. The messenger said to David, "The men gained an advantage over us, and came out against us in the field; but we drove them back to the entrance of the gate. Then the archers shot at your servants from the wall; some of the king's servants are dead; and your servant Uriah the Hittite is dead also." David said to the messenger, "Thus shall you say to Joab, 'Do not let this matter trouble you, for the sword devours now one and now another; strengthen your attack upon the city, and overthrow it.' And encourage him."

When the wife of Uriah heard that Uriah her husband was dead, she made lamentation for her husband. And when the mourning was over, David sent and brought her to his house, and she became his wife, and bore him a son. But the thing that David had done displeased the Lord.

And the Lord sent Nathan to David. He came to him, and said to him, "There were two men in a certain city, the one rich and the other poor. The rich man had very many flocks and herds; but the poor man had nothing but one little ewe lamb, which he had bought. And he brought it up, and it grew up with him and with his children; it used to eat of his morsel, and drink from his cup, and lie in his bosom, and it was like a daughter to him. Now there came a traveler to the rich man, and he was unwilling to take one of his own flock or herd to prepare for the wayfarer who had come to him, but he took the poor man's lamb, and prepared it for the man who had come to him." Then David's anger was greatly kindled against the man; and he said to Nathan, "As the Lord lives, the man who has done this deserves to die; and he shall restore the lamb fourfold, because he did this thing, and because he had no pity."

Nathan said to David, "You are the man. Thus says the Lord, the God of Israel, 'I anointed you king over Israel, and I delivered you out of the hand of Saul; and I gave you your master's house, and your master's wives into your bosom, and gave you the house of Israel and of Judah; and if this were too little, I would add to you as much more. Why have you despised the word of the Lord, to do what is evil in his sight? You have smitten Uriah the Hittite with the sword, and have taken his wife to be your wife, and have slain him with the sword of the Ammonites. Now therefore the sword shall never depart from your house, because you have despised me, and have taken the wife of Uriah the Hittite to be your wife.' Thus says the Lord, 'Behold, I will raise up evil against you out of your own house; and I will take your wives before your eyes, and give them to your neighbor, and he shall lie with your wives in the sight of this sun. For you did it secretly; but I will do this thing before all Israel, and before the sun.'" David said to Nathan, "I have sinned against the Lord." And Nathan said to David, "The Lord also has put away your sin; you shall not die. Nevertheless, because by this deed you have utterly scorned the Lord, the child that is born to you shall die." Then Nathan went to his house.

And the Lord struck the child that Uriah's wife bore to David, and it became sick. David therefore besought God for the child; and David fasted, and went in and lay all night upon the ground. And the elders of his house stood beside him, to raise him from the ground; but he would not, nor did he eat food with them. On the seventh day the child died. And the servants of David feared to tell him that the child was dead; for they said, "Behold, while the child was yet alive, we spoke to him, and he did not listen to us; how then can we say to him the child is dead? He may do himself some harm." But when David saw that his servants were whispering together, David perceived that the child was dead; and David said to his servants, "Is the child dead?" They said, "He is dead." Then David arose from the earth, and washed, and anointed himself, and changed his clothes; and he went into the house of the Lord, and worshiped; he then went to his own house; and when he asked, they set food before him, and he ate. Then his servants said to him, "What is this thing that you have done? You fasted and wept for the child while it was alive; but when the child died, you arose and ate food." He said, "While the child was still alive, I fasted and wept; for I said, 'Who knows whether the Lord will be gracious to me, that the child may live?' But now he is dead; why should I fast? Can I bring him back again? I shall go to him, but he will not return to me."

Then David comforted his wife, Bathsheba, and went in to her, and lay with her; and she bore a son, and he called his name Solomon. And the Lord loved him.

DAVID'S FLIGHT BEFORE HIS SON ABSALOM

Now in all Israel there was no one so much to be praised for his beauty as Absalom; from the sole of his foot to the crown of his head there was no blemish in him. And when he cut the hair of his head (for at the end of every year he used to cut it; when it was heavy on him, he cut it), he weighed the hair of his head, two hundred shekels by the king's weight.

And Absalom used to rise early and stand beside the way of the gate; and when any man had a suit to come before the king for judgment, Absalom would call to him, and say, "From what city are you?" And when he said, "Your servant is of such and such a tribe in Israel," Absalom would say to him, "See, your claims are good and right; but there is no man deputed by the king to hear you." Absalom said moreover, "Oh that I were judge in the land! Then every man with a suit or cause might come to me, and I would give him justice." And whenever a man came near to do obeisance to him, he would put out his hand, and take hold of him, and kiss him. Thus Absalom did to all of Israel who came to the king for judgment; so Absalom stole the hearts of the men of Israel.

And at the end of four years Absalom said to the king, "Pray let me go and pay my vow, which I have vowed to the Lord, in Hebron. For your servant vowed a vow while I dwelt at Geshur in Aram, saying, 'If the Lord will indeed bring me back to Jerusalem, then I will offer worship to the Lord.'" The king said to him, "Go in peace." So he arose, and went to Hebron. But Absalom sent secret messengers throughout all the tribes of Israel, saying, "As soon as you hear the sound of the trumpet, then say, 'Absalom is king at Hebron!'" With Absalom went two hundred men from Jerusalem who were invited guests, and they went in their simplicity, and knew nothing. And while Absalom was offering the sacrifices, he sent for Ahithophel the Gilonite, David's counselor, from his city Giloh. And the conspiracy grew strong, and the people with Absalom kept increasing.

And a messenger came to David, saying, "The hearts of the men of Israel have gone after Absalom." Then David said to all his servants who were with him at Jerusalem, "Arise, and let us flee; or else there will be no escape for us from Absalom; go in haste, lest he overtake us quickly, and bring down evil upon us, and smite the city with the edge of the sword." And the king's servants said to the king, "Behold, your servants are ready to do whatever my lord the king decides." So the king went forth, and all his household after him. And the king left ten concubines to keep the house. And the king went forth, and all the people after him; and they halted at the last house. And all his

175

servants passed by him; and all the Cherethites, and all the Pelethites, and all the six hundred Gittites who had followed him from Gath, passed on before the king.

But David went up the ascent of the Mount of Olives, weeping as he went, barefoot and with his head covered; and all the people who were with him covered their heads, and they went up, weeping as they went. And it was told David, "Ahithophel is among the conspirators with Absalom." And David said, "O Lord, I pray thee, turn the counsel of Ahithophel into foolishness."

When David came to the summit, where God was worshiped, behold, Hushai the Archite came to meet him with his coat rent and earth upon his head. David said to him, "If you go on with me, you will be a burden to me. But if you return to the city, and say to Absalom, 'I will be your servant, O king; as I have been your father's servant in time past, so now I will be your servant,' then you will defeat for me the counsel of Ahithophel. Are not Zadok and Abiathar the priests with you there? So whatever you hear from the king's house, tell it to Zadok and Abiathar the priests. Behold, their two sons are with them there, Ahima-az, Zadok's son, and Jonathan, Abiathar's son; and by them you shall send to me everything you hear." So Hushai, David's friend, came into the city, just as Absalom was entering Jerusalem.

When King David came to Bahurim, there came out a man of the family of the house of Saul, whose name was Shime-i, the son of Gera; and as he came he cursed continually. And he threw stones at David, and at all the servants of King David; and all the people and all the mighty men were on his right hand and on his left. And Shime-i said as he cursed, "Begone, begone, you man of blood, you worthless fellow! The Lord has avenged upon you all the blood of the house of Saul, in whose place you have reigned; and the Lord has given the kingdom into the hand of your son Absalom. See, your ruin is on you; for you are a man of blood."

Then Abishai the son of Zeruiah said to the king, "Why should this dead dog curse my lord the king? Let me go over and take off his head." But the king said, "What have I to do with you, you sons of Zeruiah? If he is cursing because the Lord has said to him, 'Curse David,' who then shall say, 'Why have you done so?'" And David said to Abishai and to all his servants, "Behold, my own son seeks my life; how much more now may this Benjaminite! Let him alone, and let him curse; for the Lord has bidden him. It may be that the Lord will look upon my affliction, and that the Lord will repay me with good for this cursing of me today." So David and his men went on the road, while Shime-i went along on the hillside opposite him and cursed as he went, and threw stones at him and flung dust. And the king, and all the people who were with him, arrived weary at the Jordan; and there he refreshed himself.

ABSALOM REACHES HIS END

Now Absalom and all the people, the men of Israel, came to Jerusalem, and Ahithophel with him. And when Hushai the Archite, David's friend, came to Absalom, Hushai said to Absalom, "Long live the king! Long live the king!" And Absalom said to Hushai, "Is this your loyalty to your friend?" And Hushai said to Absalom, "No; for whom the Lord and this people have chosen, his I will be, and with him I will remain. And again, whom should I serve? Should it not be his son? As I have served your father, so I will serve you."

Then Absalom said to Ahithophel, "Give your counsel; what shall we do?" Ahithophel said to Absalom, "Go in to your father's con-cubines, whom he has left to keep the house; and all Israel will hear that you have made yourself odious to your father, and the hands of all who are with you will be strengthened." So they pitched a tent for Absalom upon the roof; and Absalom went in to his father's con-cubines in the sight of all Israel. Now in those days the counsel which Ahithophel gave was as if one consulted the oracle of God; so was all the counsel of Ahithophel esteemed, both by David and by Absalom.

Moreover Ahithophel said to Absalom, "Let me choose twelve thousand men, and I will set out and pursue David tonight. I will come upon him while he is weary and discouraged, and throw him into a panic; and all the people who are with him will flee. I will strike down the king only, and I will bring all the people back to you as a bride comes home to her husband. You seek the life of only one man, and all the people will be at peace." And the advice pleased Absalom and all the elders of Israel.

Then Absalom said, "Call Hushai the Archite also, and let us hear what he has to say." And when Hushai came to Absalom, Absalom said to him, "Thus has Ahithophel spoken; shall we do as he advises? If not, you speak." Then Hushai said to Absalom, "This time the counsel which Ahithophel has given is not good." Hushai said moreover, "You know that your father and his men are mighty men, and that they are enraged, like a bear robbed of her cubs in the field. Besides, your father is expert in war; he will not spend the night with the people. Behold, even now he has hidden himself in one of the pits, or in some other place. And when some of the people fall at the first attack, whoever hears it will say, 'There has been a slaughter among the people who follow Absalom.' Then even the valiant man, whose heart is like the heart of a lion, will utterly melt with fear; for all Israel knows that your father is a mighty man, and that those who are with him are valiant men. But my counsel is that all Israel be gathered to you, from Dan to Beer-sheba, as the sand by the sea for multitude, and that you go to battle in person. So we shall come upon him in some place where he is to be found, and we shall light upon him as the dew falls on the ground; and of him and all the men with him not one will be left. If he withdraws into a city, then all Israel will bring ropes to that city, and we shall drag it into the valley, until not even a pebble is to be found there." And Absalom and all the men of Israel said, "The counsel of Hushai the Archite is better than the counsel of Ahithophel." For the Lord had ordained to defeat the good counsel of Ahithophel, so that the Lord might bring evil upon Absalom.

When Ahithophel saw that his counsel was not followed, he saddled his ass, and went off home to his own city. And he set his house in order, and hanged himself; and he died, and was buried in the tomb of his father.

Then David came to Mahanaim. And Absalom crossed the Jordan with all the men of Israel. Now Absalom had set Amasa over the army instead of Joab. Amasa was the son of a man named Ithra the Ish-maelite, who had married Abigail the daughter of Nahash, sister of Zeruiah, Joab's mother. And Israel and Absalom encamped in the land of Gilead.

When David came to Mahanaim, Shobi the son of Nahash from Rabbah of the Ammonites, and Machir the son of Ammi-el from Lo-debar, and Barzillai the Gileadite from Rogelim, brought beds, basins, and earthen vessels, wheat, barley, meal, parched grains, beans and lentils, honey and curds and sheep and cheese from the herd, for David and the people with him to eat; for they said, "The people are hungry and weary and thirsty in the wilderness."

Then David mustered the men who were with him, and set over them commanders of thousands and commanders of hundreds. And the king ordered Joab and Abishai and Ittai, "Deal gently for my sake with the young man Absalom." And all the people heard when the king gave orders to all the commanders about Absalom. So the army went out into the field against Israel; and the battle was fought in the forest of Ephraim. And the men of Israel were defeated there by the servants of David, and the slaughter there was great on that day, twenty thousand men. The battle spread over the face of all the country; and the forest devoured more people that day than the sword.

And Absalom chanced to meet the servants of David. Absalom was riding upon his mule, and the mule went under the thick branches of a great oak, and his head caught fast in the oak, and he was left hanging between heaven and earth, while the mule that was under him went on. And a certain man saw it, and told Joab, "Behold, I saw Absalom hanging in an oak." Joab said to the man who told him, "What, you saw him! Why then did you not strike him there to the ground? I would have been glad to give you ten pieces of silver and a girdle." But the man said to Joab, "Even if I felt in my hand the weight of a thousand pieces of silver, I would not put forth my hand against the king's son; for in our hearing the king commanded you and Abishai and Ittai, 'For my sake protect the young man Absalom.' On the other hand, if I had dealt treacherously against his life (and there is nothing hidden from the king), then you yourself would have stood aloof." Joab said, "I will not waste time like this with you." And he took three darts in his hand, and thrust them into the heart of Absalom, while he was still alive in the oak. And ten young men, Joab's armor-bearers, surrounded Absalom and struck him, and killed him.

Then Joab blew the trumpet, and the troops came back from pursuing Israel; for Joab restrained them. And they took Absalom, and threw him into a great pit in the forest, and raised over him a very great heap of stones; and all Israel fled every one to his own home. Now Absalom in his lifetime had taken and set up for himself the pillar which is in the King's Valley, for he said, "I have no son to keep my name in remembrance"; he called the pillar after his own name, and it is called Absalom's monument to this day.

Then said Ahima-az the son of Zadok, "Let me run, and carry tidings to the king that the Lord has delivered him from the power of his enemies." And Joab said to him, "You are not to carry tidings to-day; you may carry tidings another day, but today you shall carry no tidings, because the king's son is dead." Then Joab said to the Cushite, "Go, tell the king what you have seen." The Cushite bowed before Joab, and ran. Then Ahima-az the son of Zadok said again to Joab, "Come what may, let me also run after the Cushite." And Joab said,

"Why will you run, my son, seeing that you will have no reward for the tidings?" "Come what may," he said, "I will run." So he said to him, "Run." Then Ahima-az ran by the way of the plain and outran the Cushite.

Now David was sitting between the two gates; and the watchman went up to the roof of the gate by the wall, and when he lifted up his eyes and looked, he saw a man running alone. And the watchman called out and told the king. And the king said, "If he is alone, there are tidings in his mouth." And he came apace, and drew near. And the watchman saw another man running; and the watchman called to the gate and said, "See, another man running alone!" The king said, "He also brings tidings." And the watchman said, "I think the running of the foremost is like the running of Ahima-az the son of Zadok." And the king said, "He is a good man, and comes with good tidings."

Then Ahima-az cried out to the king, "All is well." And he bowed before the king with his face to the earth, and said, "Blessed be the Lord your God, who has delivered up the men who raised their hand against my lord the king." And the king said, "Is it well with the young man Absalom?" Ahima-az answered, "When Joab sent your servant, I saw a great tumult but I do not know what it was." And the king said, "Turn aside, and stand here." So he turned aside, and stood still.

And behold, the Cushite came; and the Cushite said, "Good tidings for my lord the king! For the Lord has delivered you this day from the power of all who rose up against you." The king said to the Cushite, "Is it well with the young man Absalom?" And the Cushite answered, "May the enemies of my lord the king, and all who rise up against you for evil, be like that young man." And the king was deeply moved, and went up to the chamber over the gate, and wept; and as he went, he said, "O my son Absalom, my son, my son Absalom! Would I had died instead of you, O Absalom, my son, my son!"

So the king came back to the Jordan; and Judah came to Gilgal to meet the king and to bring the king over the Jordan. And Shime-i the son of Gera, the Benjaminite, from Bahurim, made haste to come down with the men of Judah to meet King David; and with him were a thousand men from Benjamin. And Ziba the servant of the house of Saul, with his fifteen sons and his twenty servants, rushed down to the Jordan before the king, and they crossed the ford to bring over the king's household, and to do his pleasure. And Shime-i the son of Gera fell down before the king, as he was about to cross the Jordan, and said to the king, "Let not my lord hold me guilty or remember how your servant did wrong on the day my lord the king left Jerusalem; let not the king bear it in mind. For your servant knows that I have sinned; therefore, behold, I have come this day, the first of all the house of Joseph to come down to meet my lord the king." Abishai the son of Zeruiah answered, "Shall not Shime-i be put to death for this, because he cursed the Lord's anointed?" But David said, "What have I to do with you, you sons of Zeruiah, that you should this day be as an adversary to me? Shall any one be put to death in Israel to this day? For do I not know that I am this day king over Israel?" And the king said to Shime-i, "You shall not die." And the king gave him his oath.

THE TRAGEDIES OF KING DAVID'S REIGN

Now there was a famine in the days of David for three years, year after year; and David sought the face of the Lord. And the Lord said, "There is bloodguilt on Saul and on his house, because he put the Gibeonites to death." So the king called the Gibeonites. Now the Gibeonites were not of the people of Israel, but of the remnant of the Amorites; although the people of Israel had sworn to spare them, Saul had sought to slay them in his zeal for the people Israel and Judah. And David said to the Gibeonites, "What shall I do for you? And how shall I make expiation, that you may bless the heritage of the Lord?" The Gibeonites said to him, "It is not a matter of silver or gold between us and Saul or his house; neither is it for us to put any man to death in Israel." And he said, "What do you say that I shall do for you?" They said to the king, "The man who consumed us and planned to destroy us, so that we should have no place in all the territory of Israel, let seven of his sons be given to us, so that we may hang them up before the Lord at Gibeon on the mountain of the Lord." And the king said, "I will give them."

But the king spared Mephibosheth, the son of Saul's son Jonathan, because of the oath of the Lord which was between them, between David and Jonathan the son of Saul. The king took the two sons of Rizpah the daughter of Aiah, whom she bore to Saul, Armoni and Mephibosheth; and the five sons of Merab the daughter of Saul, whom she bore to Adri-el the son of Barzillai the Meholathite; and he gave them into the hands of the Gibeonites, and they hanged them on the mountain before the Lord, and the seven of them perished together. They were put to death in the first days of harvest, at the beginning of barley harvest.

Then Rizpah the daughter of Aiah took sackcloth, and spread it for herself on the rock, from the beginning of harvest until rain fell upon them from the heavens; and she did not allow the birds of the air to come upon them by day, or the beasts of the field by night. When David was told what Rizpah the daughter of Aiah, the concubine of Saul, had done, David went and took the bones of Saul and the bones of his son Jonathan from the men of Jabesh-gilead, who had stolen them from the public square of Beth-shan, where the Philistines had hanged them, on the day the Philistines killed Saul on Gilboa; and he brought up from there the bones of Saul and the bones of his son Jonathan; and they gathered the bones of those who were hanged. And they buried the bones of Saul and his son Jonathan in the land of Benjamin in Zela, in the tomb of Kish his father; and they did all that the king commanded. And after that God heeded supplications for the land.

Again the anger of the Lord was kindled against Israel, and he incited David against them, saying, "Go, number Israel and Judah." So the king said to Joab and the commanders of the army, who were with him, "Go through all the tribes of Israel, from Dan to Beer-sheba, and number the people, that I may know the number of the people." But Joab said to the king, "May the Lord your God add to the people a hundred times as many as they are, while the eyes of my lord the king still see it; but why does my lord the king delight in this thing?" But the king's word prevailed against Joab and the commanders of the army. So Joab and the commanders of the army went out from the presence of the king to number the people of Israel. They crossed the Jordan, and began from Aroer, and from the city that is in the middle of the valley, toward Gad and on to Jazer. Then they came to Gilead, and to Kadesh in the land of the Hittites; and they came to Dan, and from Dan they went around to Sidon, and came to the fortress of Tyre and to all the cities of the Hivites and Canaanites; and they went out to the Negeb of Judah at Beer-sheba. So when they had gone through all the land, they came to Jerusalem at the end of nine months and twenty days. And Joab gave the sum of the numbering of the people to the king: in Israel there were eight hundred thousand valiant men who drew the sword, and the men of Judah were five hundred thousand.

But David's heart smote him after he had numbered the people. And David said to the Lord, "I have sinned greatly in what I have done. But now, O Lord, I pray thee, take away the iniquity of thy servant; for I have done very foolishly." And when David arose in the morning, the word of the Lord came to the prophet Gad, David's seer, saying, "Go and say to David, 'Thus says the Lord, Three things I offer you; choose one of them, that I may do it to you.'" So Gad came to David and told him, and said to him, "Shall three years of famine come to you in your land? Or will you flee three months before your foes while they pursue you? Or shall there be three days' pestilence in your land? Now consider, and decide what answer I shall return to him who sent me." Then David said to Gad, "I am in great distress; let us fall into the hand of the Lord, for his mercy is great; but let me not fall into the hand of man."

So the Lord sent a pestilence upon Israel from the morning until the appointed time; and there died of the people from Dan to Beersheba seventy thousand men. And when the angel stretched forth his hand toward Jerusalem to destroy it, the Lord repented of the evil, and said to the angel who was working destruction among the people, "It is enough; now stay your hand." And the angel of the Lord was by the threshing floor of Araunah the Jebusite. Then David spoke to the Lord when he saw the angel who was smiting the people, and said, "Lo, I have sinned, and I have done wickedly; but these sheep, what have they done? Let thy hand, I pray thee, be against me and against my father's house."

And Gad came that day to David, and said to him, "Go up, rear an altar to the Lord on the threshing floor of Araunah the Jebusite." So David went up at Gad's word, as the Lord commanded. And when Araunah looked down, he saw the king and his servants coming on toward him; and Araunah went forth, and did obeisance to the king with his face to the ground. And Araunah said, "Why has my lord the king come to his servant?" David said, "To buy the threshing floor of you, in order to build an altar to the Lord, that the plague may be averted from the people." Then Araunah said to David, "Let my lord the king take and offer up what seems good to him; here are the oxen for the burnt offering, and the threshing sledges and the yokes of the oxen for the wood. All this, O king, Araunah gives to the king." And Araunah said to the king, "The Lord your God accept you." But the king said to Araunah, "No, but I will buy it of you for a price; I will not offer burnt offerings to the Lord my God which cost me nothing." So David bought the threshing floor and the oxen for fifty shekels of silver. And David built there an altar to the Lord, and offered burnt offerings and peace offerings. So the Lord heeded supplications for the land, and the plague was averted from Israel.

DAVID'S FINAL MOMENTS

David assembled at Jerusalem all the officials of Israel, the officials of the tribes, the officers of the divisions that served the king, the commanders of thousands, the commanders of hundreds, the stewards of all the property and cattle of the king and his sons, together with the palace officials, the mighty men, and all the seasoned warriors. Then King David rose to his feet and said: "Hear me, my brethren and my people. I had it in my heart to build a house of rest for the ark of the covenant of the Lord, and for the footstool of our God; and I made preparations for building. But God said to me, 'You may not build a house for my name, for you are a warrior and have shed blood.' Yet the Lord God of Israel chose me from all my father's house to be king over Israel for ever; for he chose Judah as leader, and in the house of Judah my father's house, and among my father's sons he took pleasure in me to make me king over all Israel. And of all my sons (for the Lord has given me many sons) he has chosen Solomon my son to sit upon the throne of the kingdom of the Lord over Israel. He said to me, 'It is Solomon your son who shall build my house and my courts, for I have chosen him to be my son, and I will be his father. I will establish his kingdom for ever if he continues resolute in keeping my commandments and ordinances, as he is today.' Now therefore in the sight of all Israel, the assembly of the Lord, and in the hearing of our God, observe and seek out all the commandments of the Lord your God; that you may possess this good land, and leave it for an inheritance to your children after you for ever.

"And you, Solomon my son, know the God of your father, and serve him with a whole heart and with a willing mind; for the Lord searches all hearts, and understands every plan and thought. If you seek him, he will be found by you; but if you forsake him, he will cast you off for ever. Take heed now, for the Lord has chosen you to build a house for the sanctuary; be strong, and do it."

And David the king said to all the assembly, "Solomon my son, whom alone God has chosen, is young and inexperienced, and the work is great; for the palace will not be for man but for the Lord God. So I have provided for the house of my God, so far as I was able, the gold for the things of gold, the silver for the things of silver, and the bronze for the things of bronze, the iron for the things of iron, and wood for the things of wood, besides great quantities of onyx and stones for setting, antimony, colored stones, all sorts of precious stones, and marble. Moreover, in addition to all that I have provided for the holy house, I have a treasure of my own of gold and silver, and because of my devotion to the house of my God I give it to the house of my God: three thousand talents of gold, of the gold of Ophir, and seven thousand talents of refined silver, for overlaying the walls of the house, and for all the work to be done by craftsmen, gold for the things of gold and silver for the things of silver. Who then will offer willingly, consecrating himself today to the Lord?"

Then the heads of fathers' houses made their freewill offerings, as did also the leaders of the tribes, the commanders of thousands and of hundreds, and the officers over the king's work. They gave for the service of the house of God five thousand talents and ten thousand darics of gold, ten thousand talents of silver, eighteen thousand talents of bronze, and a hundred thousand talents of iron. And whoever had precious stones gave them to the treasury of the house of the Lord, in the care of Jehiel the Gershonite. Then the people rejoiced because these had given willingly, for with a whole heart they had offered freely to the Lord; David the king also rejoiced greatly.

Therefore David blessed the Lord in the presence of all the assembly; and David said: "Blessed art thou, O Lord, the God of Israel our father, for ever and ever. Thine, O Lord, is the greatness, and the power, and the glory, and the victory, and the majesty; for all that is in the heavens and in the earth is thine; thine is the kingdom, O Lord, and thou art exalted as head above all. Both riches and honor come from thee, and thou rulest over all. In thy hand are power and might; and in thy hand it is to make great and to give strength to all. And now we thank thee, our God, and praise thy glorious name.

"But who am I, and what is my people, that we should be able thus to offer willingly? For all things come from thee, and of thy own have we given thee. For we are strangers before thee, and sojourners, as all our fathers were; our days on the earth are like a shadow, and there is no abiding. O Lord our God, all this abundance that we have provided for building thee a house for thy holy name comes from thy hand and is all thy own. I know, my God, that thou triest the heart, and hast pleasure in uprightness; in the uprightness of my heart I have freely offered all these things, and now I have seen thy people, who are present here, offering freely and joyously to thee. O Lord, the God of Abraham, Isaac, and Israel, our fathers, keep for ever such purposes and thoughts in the hearts of thy people, and direct their hearts toward thee. Grant to Solomon my son that with a whole heart he may keep thy commandments, thy testimonies, and thy statutes, performing all, and that he may build the palace for which I have made provision."

Then David said to all the assembly, "Bless the Lord your God." And all the assembly blessed the Lord, the God of their fathers, and bowed their heads, and worshiped the Lord, and did obeisance to the king. And they performed sacrifices to the Lord, and on the next day offered burnt offerings to the Lord, a thousand bulls, a thousand rams, and a thousand lambs, with their drink offerings, and sacrifices in abundance for all Israel; and they ate and drank before the Lord on that day with great gladness.

And they made Solomon the son of David king the second time, and they anointed him as prince for the Lord, and Zadok as priest. Then Solomon sat on the throne of the Lord as king instead of David his father; and he prospered, and all Israel obeyed him. All the leaders and the mighty men, and also all the sons of King David, pledged their allegiance to King Solomon. And the Lord gave Solomon great repute in the sight of all Israel, and bestowed upon him such royal majesty as had not been on any king before him in Israel.

Thus David the son of Jesse reigned over all Israel. The time that he reigned over Israel was forty years; he reigned seven years in Hebron, and thirty-three years in Jerusalem. Then he died in a good old age, full of days, riches, and honor; and Solomon his son reigned in his stead.

CHAPTER TWELVE

The Psalms of King David

PSALM 2

Why do the nations rage and the peoples utter folly? The kings of the earth rise up, and the princes conspire together against the Lord and against his anointed: "Let us break their fetters and cast their bonds from us!"

He who is throned in heaven laughs; the Lord derides them. Then in anger he speaks to them; he terrifies them in his wrath: "I myself have set up my king on Sion, my holy mountain."

I will proclaim the decree of the Lord: the Lord said to me, "You are my son; this day I have begotten you. Ask of me and I will give you the nations for an inheritance and the ends of the earth for your possession. You shall rule them with an iron rod; you shall shatter them like an earthen dish."

And now, O kings, give heed; take warning, you rulers of the earth. Serve the Lord with fear, and rejoice before him; with trembling pay homage to him, lest he be angry and you perish from the way, when his anger blazes suddenly. Happy are all who take refuge in him!

PSALM 3

O Lord, how many are my adversaries! Many rise up against me! Many are saying of me, "There is no salvation for him in God." But you, O Lord, are my shield; my glory, you lift up my head!

When I call out to the Lord, he answers me from his holy mountain. When I lie down in sleep, I wake again, for the Lord sustains me. I fear not the myriads of people arrayed against me on every side.

Rise up, O Lord! Save me, my God! For you strike all my enemies on the cheek; the teeth of the wicked you break. Salvation is the Lord's! Upon your people be your blessing!

PSALM 4

When I call, answer me, O my just God, you who relieve me when I am in distress; have pity on me, and hear my prayer!

Men of rank, how long will you be dull of heart? Why do you love what is vain and seek after falsehood? Know that the Lord does wonders for his faithful one; the Lord will hear me when I call upon him. Tremble, and sin not; reflect, upon your beds, in silence. Offer just sacrifices, and trust in the Lord.

Many say, "Oh, that we might see better times!" O Lord, let the light of your countenance shine upon us! You put gladness into my heart, more then when grain and wine abound. As soon as I lie down, I fall peacefully asleep, for you alone, O Lord, bring security to my dwelling.

PSALM 8

O Lord, our Lord, how glorious is your name over all the earth! You have exalted your majesty above the heavens. Out of the mouths of babes and sucklings you have fashioned praise because of your foes, to silence the hostile and the vengeful. When I behold your heavens, the work of your fingers, the moon and the stars which you set in place —what is man that you should be mindful of him, or the son of man that you should care for him?

You have made him little less than the angels, and crowned him with glory and honor. You have given him rule over the works of your hands, putting all things under his feet: all sheep and oxen, yes, and the beasts of the field, the birds of the air, the fishes of the sea, and whatever swims the paths of the seas. O Lord, our Lord, how glorious is your name over all the earth!

PSALM 15

Keep me, O God, for in you I take refuge; I say to the Lord, "My Lord are you. Apart from you I have no good." How wonderfully has he made me cherish the holy ones who are in his land! They multiply their sorrows who court other gods. Blood libations to them I will not pour out, nor will I take their names upon my lips. O Lord, my allotted portion and my cup, you it is who hold fast my lot. For me the measuring lines have fallen on pleasant sites; fair to me indeed is my inheritance.

I bless the Lord who counsels me; even in the night my heart exhorts me. I set the Lord ever before me; with him at my right hand I shall not be disturbed. Therefore my heart is glad and my soul rejoices, my body, too, abides in confidence; because you will not abandon my soul to the nether world, nor will you suffer your faithful one to undergo corruption. You will show me the path to life, fullness of joys in your presence, the delights at your right hand forever.

PSALM 18

The heavens declare the glory of God, and the firmament proclaims his handiwork. Day pours out the word to day, and night to night imparts knowledge; not a word nor a discourse whose voice is not heard; through all the earth their voice resounds, and to the ends of the world, their message.

He has pitched a tent there for the sun, which comes forth like the groom from his bridal chamber and, like a giant, joyfully runs its course. At one end of the heavens it comes forth, and its course is to their other end; nothing escapes its heat.

The law of the Lord is perfect, refreshing the soul; the decree of the Lord is trustworthy, giving wisdom to the simple. The precepts of the Lord are right, rejoicing the heart; the command of the Lord is clear, enlightening the eye; the fear of the Lord is pure, enduring forever; the ordinances of the Lord are true, all of them just; they are more precious than gold, than a heap of purest gold; sweeter also than syrup or honey from the comb.

Though your servant is careful of them, very diligent in keeping them, yet who can detect failings? Cleanse me from my unknown faults! From wanton sin especially, restrain your servant; let it not rule over me. Then shall I be blameless and innocent of serious sin. Let the words of my mouth and the thought of my heart find favor before you, O Lord, my rock and my redeemer.

PSALM 21

My God, my God, why have you forsaken me, far from my prayer, from the words of my cry? O my God, I cry out by day, and you answer not; by night, and there is no relief for me. Yet you are enthroned in the holy place, O glory of Israel! In you our fathers trusted; they trusted, and you delivered them. To you they cried, and they escaped; in you they trusted, and they were not put to shame.

But I am a worm, not a man; the scorn of men, despised by the people. All who see me scoff at me; they mock me with parted lips, they wag their heads: "He relied on the Lord; let him deliver him, let him rescue him, if he loves him." You have been my guide since I was first formed, my security at my mother's breast. To you I was committed at birth, from my mother's womb you are my God.

Be not far from me, for I am in distress; be near, for I have no one to help me. Many bullocks surround me; the strong bulls of Basan encircle me. They open their mouths against me like ravening and roaring lions.

I am like water poured out; all my bones are racked. My heart has become like wax melting away within my bosom. My throat is dried up like baked clay, my tongue cleaves to my jaws; to the dust of death you have brought me down.

Indeed, many dogs surround me, a pack of evildoers closes in upon me; they have pierced my hands and my feet; I can count all my bones. They look on and gloat over me; they divide my garments among them, and for my vesture they cast lots.

But you, O Lord, be not far from me; O my help, hasten to aid me. Rescue my soul from the sword, my loneliness from the grip of the dog. Save me from the lion's mouth; from the horns of the wild bulls, my wretched life.

I will proclaim your name to my brethren; in the midst of the assembly I will praise you: "You who fear the Lord, praise him; all you descendants of Jacob, give glory to him; revere him, all you descendants of Israel! For he has not spurned nor disdained the wretched man in his misery, nor did he turn his face away from him, but when he cried out to him, he heard him." So by your gift will I utter praise in the vast assembly; I will fulfill my vows before those who fear him. The lowly shall eat their fill; they who seek the Lord shall praise him: "May your hearts be ever merry!"

All the ends of the earth shall remember and turn to the Lord; all the families of the nations shall bow down before him. For dominion is the Lord's, and he rules the nations. To him alone shall bow down all who sleep in the earth; before him shall bend all who go down into the dust. And to him my soul shall live; my descendants shall serve him. Let the coming generation be told of the Lord that they may proclaim to a people yet to be born the justice he has shown.

PSALM 22

The Lord is my shepherd; I shall not want. In verdant pastures he gives me repose; beside restful waters he leads me; he refreshes my soul. He guides me in right paths for his name's sake. Even though I walk in the dark valley I fear no evil; for you are at my side with your rod and your staff that give me courage.

You spread the table before me in the sight of my foes; you anoint my head with oil; my cup overflows. Only goodness and kindness follow me all the days of my life; and I shall dwell in the house of the Lord for years to come.

PSALM 23

The Lord's are the earth and its fullness; the world and those who dwell in it. For he founded it upon the seas and established it upon the rivers.

Who can ascend the mountain of the Lord? or who may stand in his holy place? He whose hands are sinless, whose heart is clean, who desires not what is vain, nor swears deceitfully to his neighbor. He shall receive a blessing from the Lord, a reward from God his savior. Such is the race that seeks for him, that seeks the face of the God of Jacob.

Lift up, O gates, your lintels; reach up, you ancient portals, that the king of glory may come in! Who is this king of glory? The Lord, strong and mighty, the Lord, mighty in battle. Lift up, O gates, your lintels; reach up, you ancient portals, that the king of glory may come in! Who is this king of glory? The Lord of hosts; he is the king of glory.

PSALM 25

Do me justice, O Lord! for I have walked in integrity, and in the Lord I trust without wavering. Search me, O Lord, and try me; test my soul and my heart.

For your kindness is before my eyes, and I walk in your truth. I stay not with worthless men, nor do I consort with hypocrites. I hate the assembly of evildoers, and with the wicked I will not stay. I wash my hands in innocence, and I go around your altar, O Lord, giving voice to my thanks, and recounting all your wondrous deeds. O Lord, I love the house in which you dwell, the tenting-place of your glory.

Gather not my soul with those of sinners, nor with men of blood my life. On their hands are crimes, and their right hands are full of bribes. But I walk in integrity; redeem me, and have pity on me. My foot stands on level ground; in the assemblies I will bless the Lord.

PSALM 30

In you, O Lord, I take refuge; let me never be put to shame. In your justice rescue me, incline your ear to me, make haste to deliver me! Be my rock of refuge, a stronghold to give me safety. You are my rock and my fortress; for your name's sake you will lead and guide me. You will free me from the snare they set for me, for you are my refuge. Into your hands I commend my spirit; you will redeem me, O Lord, O faithful God. You hate those who worship vain idols, but my trust is in the Lord. I will rejoice and be glad of your kindness, when you have seen my affliction and watched over me in my distress, not shutting me up in the grip of the enemy but enabling me to move about at large.

Have pity on me, O Lord, for I am in distress; with sorrow my eye is consumed; my soul also, and my body. For my life is spent with grief and my years with sighing; my strength has failed through affliction, and my bones are consumed. For all my foes I am an object of reproach, a laughingstock to my neighbors, and a dread to my friends; they who see me abroad flee from me. I am forgotten like the unremembered dead; I am like a dish that is broken. I hear the whispers of the crowd, that frighten me from every side, as they consult together against me, plotting to take my life. But my trust is in you, O Lord; I say, "You are my God." In your hands is my destiny; rescue me from the clutches of my enemies and my persecutors. Let your face shine upon your servant; save me in your kindness. O Lord, let me not be put to shame, for I call upon you; let the wicked be put to shame; let them be reduced to silence in the nether world. Let dumbness strike their lying lips that speak insolence against the just in pride and scorn.

How great is the goodness, O Lord, which you have in store for those who fear you, and which, toward those who take refuge in you, you show in the sight of men. You hide them in the shelter of your presence from the plottings of men; you screen them within your abode from the strife of tongues. Blessed be the Lord whose wondrous kindness he has shown me in a fortified city. Once I said in my anguish, "I am cut off from your sight"; yet you heard the sound of my pleading when I cried out to you. Love the Lord, all you his faithful ones! The Lord keeps those who are constant, but more than requites those who act proudly. Take courage and be stouthearted, all you who hope in the Lord.

PSALM 33

I will bless the Lord at all times; his praise shall be ever in my mouth. Let my soul glory in the Lord; the lowly will hear me and be glad. Glorify the Lord with me, let us together extol his name.

I sought the Lord, and he answered me and delivered me from all my fears. Look to him that you may be radiant with joy, and your faces may not blush with shame. When the afflicted man called out, the Lord heard, and from all his distress he saved him. The angel of the Lord encamps around those who fear him, and delivers them. Taste and see how good the Lord is; happy the man who takes refuge in him. Fear the Lord, you his holy ones, for nought is lacking to those who fear him. The great grow poor and hungry; but those who seek the Lord want for no good thing.

Come, children, hear me; I will teach you the fear of the Lord. Which of you desires life, and takes delight in prosperous days? Keep your tongue from evil and your lips from speaking guile; turn from evil, and do good; seek peace, and follow after it. The Lord has eyes for the just, and ears for their cry. The Lord confronts the evildoers, to destroy remembrance of them from the earth. When the just cry out, the Lord hears them, and from all their distress he rescues them. The Lord is close to the brokenhearted; and those who are crushed in spirit he saves. Many are the troubles of the just man, but out of them all the Lord delivers him; he watches over all his bones; not one of them shall be broken. Vice slays the wicked, and the enemies of the just pay for their guilt. But the Lord redeems the lives of his servants; no one incurs guilt who takes refuge in him.

PSALM 40

Happy is he who has regard for the lowly and the poor; in the day of misfortune the Lord will deliver him. The Lord will keep and preserve him; he will make him happy on the earth, and not give him over to the will of his enemies. The Lord will help him on his sickbed, he will take away all his ailment when he is ill.

Once I said, "O Lord, have pity on me; heal me, though I have sinned against you. My enemies say the worst of me: 'When will he die and his name perish?' When one comes to see me, he speaks without sincerity; his heart stores up malice; when he leaves he gives voice to it outside. All my foes whisper together against me; against me they imagine the worst: 'A malignant disease fills his frame'; and 'Now that he lies ill, he will not rise again.' Even my friend who had my trust and partook of my bread, has raised his heel against me. But you, O Lord, have pity on me, and raise me up, that I may repay them." That you love me I know by this, that my enemy does not triumph over me, but because of my integrity you sustain me and let me stand before you forever.

Blessed be the Lord, the God of Israel, from all eternity and forever. Amen. Amen.

PSALM 42

Do me justice, O God, and fight my fight against a faithless people; from the deceitful and impious man rescue me. For you, O God, are my strength. Why do you keep me so far away? Why must I go about in mourning, with the enemy oppressing me? Send forth your light and your fidelity; they shall lead me on and bring me to your holy mountain, to your dwelling-place. Then will I go to the altar of God, the God of my gladness and joy; then will I give you thanks upon the harp, O God, my God! Why are you so downcast, O my soul? Why do you sigh within me? Hope in God! For I shall again be thanking him, in the presence of my savior and my God.

PSALM 44

My heart overflows with a goodly theme; as I sing my ode to the king, my tongue is nimble as the pen of a skillful scribe.

Fairer in beauty are you than the sons of men; grace is poured out upon your lips; thus God has blessed you forever. Gird your sword upon your thigh, O mighty one! In your splendor and your majesty ride on triumphant in the cause of truth and for the sake of justice; and may your right hand show you wondrous deeds. Your arrows are sharp; peoples are subject to you; the king's enemies lose heart. Your throne, O God, stands forever and ever; a tempered rod is your royal scepter. You love justice and hate wickedness; therefore, God, your God, has anointed you with the oil of gladness above your fellow kings. With myrrh and aloes and cassia your robes are fragrant; from ivory palaces string music brings you joy. The daughters of kings come to meet you; the queen takes her place at your right hand in gold of Ophir.

Hear, O daughter, and see; turn your ear, forget your people and your father's house. So shall the king desire your beauty; for he is your lord, and you must worship him. And the city of Tyre is here with gifts; the rich among the people seek your favor. All glorious is the king's daughter as she enters; her raiment is threaded with spun gold. In embroidered apparel she is borne in to the king; behind her the virgins of her train are brought to you. They are borne in with gladness and joy; they enter the palace of the king.

The place of your fathers your sons shall have; you shall make them princes through all the land. I will make your name memorable through all generations; therefore shall nations praise you forever and ever.

PSALM 50

Have mercy on me, O God, in your goodness; in the greatness of your compassion wipe out my offense. Thoroughly wash me from my guilt and of my sin cleanse me.

For I acknowledge my offense, and my sin is before me always: "Against you only have I sinned, and done what is evil in your sight"— that you may be justified in your sentence, vindicated when you condemn. Indeed, in guilt was I born, and in sin my mother conceived me; behold, you are pleased with sincerity of heart, and in my inmost being you teach me wisdom.

Cleanse me of sin with hyssop, that I may be purified; wash me, and I shall be whiter than snow. Let me hear the sounds of joy and gladness; the bones you have crushed shall rejoice. Turn away your face from my sins, and blot out all my guilt.

A clean heart create for me, O God, and a steadfast spirit renew within me. Cast me not out from your presence, and your holy spirit take not from me. Give me back the joy of your salvation, and a willing spirit sustain in me.

I will teach transgressors your ways, and sinners shall return to you. Free me from blood guilt, O God, my saving God; then my tongue shall revel in your justice. O Lord, open my lips, and my mouth shall proclaim your praise. For you are not pleased with sacrifices; should I offer a holocaust, you would not accept it. My sacrifice, O God, is a contrite spirit; a heart contrite and humbled, O God, you will not spurn. Be bountiful, O Lord, to Sion in your kindness by rebuilding the walls of Jerusalem; then shall you be pleased with due sacrifices, burnt offerings and holocausts; then shall they offer up bullocks on your altar.

PSALM 54

Hearken, O God, to my prayer; turn not away from my pleading; give heed to me, and answer me. I rock with grief, and am troubled at the voice of the enemy and the clamor of the wicked. For they bring down evil upon me, and with fury they persecute me. My heart quakes within me; the terror of death has fallen upon me. Fear and trembling come upon me, and horror overwhelms me, and I say, "Had I but wings like a dove, I would fly away and be at rest. Far away I would flee; I would lodge in the wilderness. I would hasten to find shelter from the violent storm and the tempest."

Engulf them, O Lord; divide their counsels, for in the city I see violence and strife; day and night they prowl about upon its walls. Evil and mischief are in its midst; [treachery is in its midst;] oppression and fraud never depart from its streets. If an enemy had reviled me, I could have borne it; if he who hates me had vaunted himself against me, I might have hidden from him. But you, my other self, my companion and my bosom friend! You, whose comradeship I enjoyed; at whose side I walked in procession in the house of God!

Let death surprise them; let them go down alive to the nether world, for evil is in their dwellings, in their very midst. But I will call upon God, and the Lord will save me. In the evening, and at dawn, and at noon, I will grieve and moan, and he will hear my voice. He will give me freedom and peace from those who war against me, for many there are who oppose me. God will hear me and will humble them from his eternal throne; for improvement is not in them, nor do they fear God. Each one lays hands on his associates, and violates his pact. Softer than butter is his speech, but war is in his heart; his words are smoother than oil, but they are drawn swords. Cast your care upon the Lord, and he will support you; never will he permit the just man to be disturbed. And you, O God, will bring them down into the pit of destruction; men of blood and deceit shall not live out half their days. But I trust in you, O Lord.

PSALM 68

Save me, O God, for the waters threaten my life; I am sunk in the abysmal swamp where there is no foothold; I have reached the watery depths; the flood overwhelms me. I am wearied with calling, my throat is parched; my eyes have failed with looking for my God. Those outnumber the hairs of my head who hate me without cause. Too many for my strength are they who wrongfully are my enemies. Must I restore what I did not steal?

O God, you know my folly, and my faults are not hid from you. Let not those who wait for you be put to shame through me, O Lord, God of hosts. Let not those who seek you blush for me, O God of Israel, since for your sake I bear insult, and shame covers my face. I have become an outcast to my brothers, a stranger to my mother's sons, because zeal for your house consumes me, and the insults of those who blaspheme you fall upon me. I humbled myself with fasting, and this was made a reproach to me. I made sackcloth my garment, and I became a byword for them. They who sit at the gate gossip about me, and drunkards make me the butt of their songs.

But I pray to you, O Lord, for the time of your favor, O God! In your great kindness answer me with your constant help. Rescue me out of the mire; may I not sink! may I be rescued from my foes, and from the watery depths. Let not the flood-waters overwhelm me, nor the abyss swallow me up, nor the pit close its mouth over me. Answer me, O Lord, for bounteous is your kindness; in your great mercy turn toward me. Hide not your face from your servant; in my distress, make haste to answer me. Come and ransom my life; as an answer for my enemies, redeem me. You know my reproach, my shame and my ignominy; before you are all my foes. Insult has broken my heart, and

I am weak, I looked for sympathy, but there was none; for comforters, and I found none. Rather they put gall in my food, and in my thirst they gave me vinegar to drink.

Let their own table be a snare before them, and a net for their friends. Let their eyes grow dim so that they cannot see, and keep their backs always feeble. Pour out your wrath upon them; let the fury of your anger overtake them. Let their encampment become desolate; in their tents let there be no one to dwell. For they kept after him whom you smote, and added to the pain of him you wounded. Heap guilt upon their guilt, and let them not attain to your reward. May they be erased from the book of the living, and not be recorded with the just!

But I am afflicted and in pain; let your saving help, O God, protect me. I will praise the name of God in song, and I will glorify him with thanksgiving; this will please the Lord more than oxen or bullocks with horns and divided hooves: "See, you lowly ones, and be glad; you who seek God, may your hearts be merry! For the Lord hears the poor, and his own who are in bonds he spurns not. Let the heavens and the earth praise him, the seas and whatever moves in them!"

For God will save Sion and rebuild the cities of Juda. They shall dwell in the land and own it, and the descendants of his servants shall inherit it, and those who love his name shall inhabit it.

PSALM 71

O God, with your judgment endow the king, and with your justice, the king's son; he shall govern your people with justice and your afflicted ones with judgment. The mountains shall yield peace for the people, and the hills justice. He shall defend the afflicted among the people, save the children of the poor, and crush the oppressor.

May he endure as long as the sun, and like the moon through all generations. He shall be like rain coming down on the meadow, like showers watering the earth. Justice shall flower in his days, and profound peace, till the moon be no more.

May he rule from sea to sea, and from the River to the ends of the earth. His foes shall bow before him, and his enemies shall lick the dust. The kings of Tharsis and the Isles shall offer gifts; the kings of Arabia and Saba shall bring tribute. All kings shall pay him homage, all nations shall serve him.

For he shall rescue the poor man when he cries out, and the afflicted when he has no one to help him. He shall have pity for the lowly and the poor; the lives of the poor he shall save. From fraud and violence he shall redeem them, and precious shall their blood be in his sight.

May he live to be given the gold of Arabia, and to be prayed for continually; day by day shall they bless him. May there be an abundance of grain upon the earth; on the tops of the mountains the crops shall rustle like Lebanon; the city dwellers shall flourish like the verdure of the fields. May his name be blessed forever; as long as the sun his name shall remain. In him shall all the tribes of the earth be blessed; all the nations shall proclaim his happiness.

Blessed be the Lord, the God of Israel, who alone does wondrous deeds. And blessed forever be his glorious name; may the whole earth be filled with his glory. Amen. Amen.

PSALM 79

O shepherd of Israel, hearken, O guide of the flock of Joseph! From your throne upon the cherubim, shine forth before Ephraim, Benjamin and Manasse. Rouse your power, and come to save us. O Lord of hosts, restore us; if your face shine upon us, then we shall be safe.

O Lord of hosts, how long will you burn with anger while your people pray? You have fed them with the bread of tears and given them tears to drink with ample measure. You have left us to be fought over by our neighbors, and our enemies mock us. O Lord of hosts, restore us; if your face shine upon us, then we shall be safe.

A vine from Egypt you transplanted; you drove away the nations and planted it. You cleared the ground for it, and it took root and filled the land. The mountains were hidden in its shadow; by its branches, the cedars of God. It put forth its foliage to the Sea, its shoots as far as the River.

Why have you broken down its walls, so that every passer-by plucks its fruit, the boar from the forest lays it waste, and the beasts of the field feed upon it? Once again, O Lord of hosts, look down from heaven, and see; take care of this vine, and protect what your right hand has planted.

Let those who would burn it with fire or cut it down perish before you at your rebuke. May your help be with the man of your right hand, with the son of man whom you yourself made strong. Then we will no more withdraw from you; give us new life, and we will call upon your name. O Lord of hosts, restore us; if your face shine upon us, then we shall be safe.

PSALM 81

God arises in the divine assembly; he judges in the midst of the gods.

"How long will you judge unjustly and favor the cause of the wicked? Defend the lowly and the fatherless; render justice to the afflicted and the destitute. Rescue the lowly and the poor; from the hand of the wicked deliver them.

"They know not, neither do they understand; they go about in darkness; all the foundations of the earth are shaken. I said: You are gods, all of you sons of the Most High; yet like men you shall die, and fall like any prince." Rise, O God; judge the earth, for yours are all the nations.

PSALM 83

How lovely is your dwelling place, O Lord of hosts! My soul yearns and pines for the courts of the Lord. My heart and my flesh cry out for the living God. Even the sparrow finds a home, and the swallow a nest in which she puts her young—your altars, O Lord of hosts, my king and my God!

Happy they who dwell in your house! continually they praise you. Happy the men whose strength you are! their hearts are set upon the pilgrimage: when they pass through the arid valley, they make a spring of it; the early rain clothes it with generous growth. They go from strength to strength; they shall see the God of gods in Sion.

O Lord of hosts, hear my prayer; hearken, O God of Jacob! O God, behold our shield, and look upon the face of your anointed. I had rather one day in your courts than a thousand elsewhere; I had rather lie at the threshold of the house of my God than dwell in the tents of the wicked. For a sun and a shield is the Lord God; grace and glory he bestows; the Lord withholds no good thing from those who walk in sincerity. O Lord of hosts, happy the men who trust in you!

PSALM 90

You who dwell in the shelter of the Most High, who abide in the shadow of the Almighty, say to the Lord, "My refuge and my fortress, my God, in whom I trust." For he will rescue you from the snare of the fowler, from the destroying pestilence. With his pinions he will cover you, and under his wings you shall take refuge; his faithfulness is a buckler and a shield. You shall not fear the terror of the night nor the arrow that flies by day; not the pestilence that roams in darkness nor the devastating plague at noon. Though a thousand fall at your side, ten thousand at your right side, near you it shall not come. Rather with your eyes shall you behold and see the requital of the wicked, because you have the Lord for your refuge; you have made the Most High your stronghold. No evil shall befall you, nor shall affliction come near your tent, for to his angels he has given command about you, that they guard you in all your ways. Upon their hands they shall bear you up, lest you dash your foot against a stone. You shall tread upon the asp and the viper; you shall trample down the lion and the dragon.

Because he clings to me, I will deliver him; I will set him on high because he acknowledges my name. He shall call upon me, and I will answer him; I will be with him in distress; I will deliver him and glorify him; with length of days I will gratify him and will show him my salvation.

PSALM 94

Come, let us sing joyfully to the Lord; let us acclaim the Rock of our salvation. Let us greet him with thanksgiving; let us joyfully sing psalms to him. For the Lord is a great God, and a great king above all gods; in his hands are the depths of the earth, and the tops of the mountains are his. His is the sea, for he has made it, and the dry land, which his hands have formed.

Come, let us bow down in worship; let us kneel before the Lord who made us. For he is our God, and we are the people he shepherds, the flock he guides.

Oh, that today you would hear his voice: "Harden not your hearts as at Meriba, as in the day of Massa in the desert, where your fathers tempted me; they tested me though they had seen my works. Forty years I loathed that generation, and I said: They are a people of erring heart, and they know not my ways. Therefore I swore in my anger: They shall not enter into my rest."

PSALM 102

Bless the Lord, O my soul; and all my being, bless his holy name. Bless the Lord, O my soul, and forget not all his benefits; he pardons all your iniquities, he heals all your ills. He redeems your life from destruction, he crowns you with kindness and compassion, he fills your lifetime with good; your youth is renewed like the eagle's.

The Lord secures justice and the rights of all the oppressed. He has made known his ways to Moses, and his deeds to the children of Israel. Merciful and gracious is the Lord, slow to anger and abounding in kindness. He will not always chide, nor does he keep his wrath forever. Not according to our sins does he deal with us, nor does he requite us according to our crimes.

For as the heavens are high above the earth, so surpassing is his kindness toward those who fear him. As far as the east is from the west, so far has he put our transgressions from us. As a father has compassion on his children, so the Lord has compassion on those who fear him, for he knows how we are formed; he remembers that we are dust. Man's days are like those of grass; like a flower of the field he blooms; the wind sweeps over him and he is gone, and his place knows him no more. But the kindness of the Lord is from eternity to eternity toward those who fear him, and his justice toward children's children among those who keep his covenant and remember to fulfill his precepts.

The Lord has established his throne in heaven, and his kingdom rules over all. Bless the Lord, all you his angels, you mighty in strength, who do his bidding, obeying his spoken word. Bless the Lord, all you his hosts, his ministers, who do his will. Bless the Lord, all his works, everywhere in his domain. Bless the Lord, O my soul!

PSALM 108

O God, whom I praise, be not silent, for they have opened wicked and treacherous mouths against me. They have spoken to me with lying tongues, and with words of hatred they have encompassed me and attacked me without cause. In return for my love they slandered me, but I prayed. They repaid me evil for good and hatred for my love.

Raise up a wicked man against him, and let the accuser stand at his right hand. When he is judged, let him go forth condemned, and may his plea be in vain. May his days be few; may another take his office. May his children be fatherless, and his wife a widow. May his children be roaming vagrants and beggars; may they be cast out of the ruins of their homes. May the usurer ensnare all his belongings, and strangers plunder the fruit of his labors. May there be no one to do him a kindness, nor anyone to pity his orphans. May his posterity meet with destruction; in the next generation may their name be blotted out. May the guilt of his fathers be remembered by the Lord; let not his mother's sin be blotted out; may they be continually before the Lord, till he banish the memory of these parents from the earth, because he remembered not to show kindness, but persecuted the wretched and poor and the brokenhearted, to do them to death. He loved cursing; may it come upon him; he took no delight in blessing; may it be far from him. And may he be clothed with cursing as with a robe; may it penetrate into his entrails like water and like oil into his bones; may it be for him like a garment which covers him, like a girdle which is always about him.

May this be the recompense from the Lord upon my accusers and upon those who speak evil against me. But do you, O God, my Lord, deal kindly with me for your name's sake; in your generous kindness rescue me; for I am wretched and poor, and my heart is pierced within me. Like a lengthening shadow I pass away; I am swept away like the locust. My knees totter from my fasting, and my flesh is wasted of its substance. And I am become a mockery to them; when they see me, they shake their heads. Help me, O Lord, my God; save me, in your kindness, and let them know that this is your hand; that you, O Lord, have done this. Let them curse, but do you bless; may my adversaries be put to shame, but let your servant rejoice. Let my accusers be clothed with disgrace and let them wear their shame like a mantle. I will speak my thanks earnestly to the Lord, and in the midst of the throng I will praise him, for he stood at the right hand of the poor man, to save him from those who would condemn him.

PSALM 109

The Lord said to my Lord: "Sit at my right hand till I make your enemies your footstool." The scepter of your power the Lord will stretch forth from Sion: "Rule in the midst of your enemies. Yours is princely power in the day of your birth, in holy splendor; before the daystar, like the dew, I have begotten you."

The Lord has sworn, and he will not repent: "You are a priest forever, according to the order of Melchisedec."

The Lord is at your right hand; he will crush kings on the day of his wrath. He will do judgment on the nations, heaping up corpses; he will crush heads over the wide earth. From the brook by the wayside he will drink; therefore will he lift up his head.

PSALM 113

When Israel came forth from Egypt, the house of Jacob from a people of alien tongue, Juda became his sanctuary, Israel his domain. The sea beheld and fled; Jordan turned back. The mountains skipped like rams, the hills like the lambs of the flock. Why is it, O sea, that you flee? O Jordan, that you turn back? You mountains, that you skip like rams? You hills, like the lambs of the flock? Before the face of the Lord, tremble, O earth, before the face of the God of Jacob, who turned the rock into pools of water, the flint into flowing springs.

Not to us, O Lord, not to us but to your name give glory because of your kindness, because of your truth. Why should the pagans say, "Where is their God?" Our God is in heaven; whatever he wills, he does.

Their idols are silver and gold, the handiwork of men. They have mouths but speak not; they have eyes but see not; they have ears but hear not; they have noses but smell not; they have hands but feel not; they have feet but walk not; they utter no sound from their throat. Their makers shall be like them, everyone that trusts in them.

The house of Israel trusts in the Lord; he is their help and their shield. The house of Aaron trusts in the Lord; he is their help and their shield. Those who fear the Lord trust in the Lord; he is their help and their shield. The Lord remembers us and will bless us: he will bless the house of Israel; he will bless the house of Aaron; he will bless those who fear the Lord, both the small and the great. May the Lord bless you more and more, both you and your children. May you be blessed by the Lord, who made heaven and earth. Heaven is the heaven of the Lord, but the earth he has given to the children of men. It is not the dead who praise the Lord, nor those who go down into silence; but we bless the Lord, both now and forever.

PSALM 115

I believed even when I said, "I am greatly afflicted"; I said in my alarm, "No man is dependable." How shall I make a return to the Lord for all the good he has done for me? The cup of salvation I will take up, and I will call upon the name of the Lord; my vows to the Lord I will pay in the presence of all his people. Precious in the eyes of the Lord is the death of his faithful ones. O Lord, I am your servant; I am your servant, the son of your handmaid; you have loosed my bonds. To you will I offer sacrifice of thanksgiving, and I will call upon the name of the Lord. My vows to the Lord I will pay in the presence of all his people, in the courts of the house of the Lord, in your midst, O Jerusalem.

PSALM 116

Praise the Lord, all you nations; glorify him, all you peoples! For steadfast is his kindness toward us, and the fidelity of the Lord endures forever.

PSALM 117

Give thanks to the Lord, for he is good, for his mercy endures forever. Let the house of Israel say, "His mercy endures forever." Let the house of Aaron say, "His mercy endures forever." Let those who fear the Lord say, "His mercy endures forever."

In my straits I called upon the Lord; the Lord answered me and set me free. The Lord is with me; I fear not; what can man do against me? The Lord is with me to help me, and I shall look down upon my foes. It is better to take refuge in the Lord than to trust in man. It is better to take refuge in the Lord than to trust in princes.

All the nations encompassed me; in the name of the Lord I crushed them. They encompassed me on every side; in the name of the Lord I crushed them. They encompassed me like bees, they flared up like fire among thorns; in the name of the Lord I crushed them. I was hard pressed and was falling, but the Lord helped me. My strength and my courage is the Lord, and he has been my savior.

The joyful shout of victory in the tents of the just: "The right hand of the Lord has struck with power: the right hand of the Lord is exalted; the right hand of the Lord has struck with power." I shall not die, but live, and declare the works of the Lord. Though the Lord has indeed chastised me, yet he has not delivered me to death.

Open to me the gates of justice; I will enter them and give thanks to the Lord. This gate is the Lord's; the just shall enter it. I will give thanks to you, for you have answered me and have been my savior. The stone which the builders rejected has become the cornerstone. By the Lord has this been done; it is wonderful in our eyes. This is the day the Lord has made; let us be glad and rejoice in it. O Lord, grant salvation! O Lord, grant prosperity!

Blessed is he who comes in the name of the Lord; we bless you from the house of the Lord. The Lord is God, and he has given us light. Join in procession with leafy boughs up to the horns of the altar. You are my God, and I give thanks to you; O my God, I extol you. Give thanks to the Lord, for he is good; for his kindness endures forever.

PSALM *121*

I rejoiced because they said to me, "We will go up to the house of the Lord." And now we have set foot within your gates, O Jerusalem— Jerusalem, built as a city with compact unity.

To it the tribes go up, the tribes of the Lord, according to the decree for Israel, to give thanks to the name of the Lord. In it are set up judgment seats, seats for the house of David.

Pray for the peace of Jerusalem! May those who love you prosper! May peace be within your walls, prosperity in your buildings. Because of my relatives and friends I will say, "Peace be within you!" Because of the house of the Lord, our God, I will pray for your good.

PSALM *123*

Had not the Lord been with us, let Israel say, had not the Lord been with us—when men rose up against us, then would they have swallowed us alive. When their fury was inflamed against us, then would the waters have overwhelmed us; the torrent would have swept over us; over us then would have swept the raging waters.

Blessed be the Lord, who did not leave us a prey to their teeth. We were rescued like a bird from the fowlers' snare; broken was the snare, and we were freed. Our help is in the name of the Lord, who made heaven and earth.

PSALM *129*

Out of the depths I cry to you, O Lord; Lord, hear my voice! Let your ears be attentive to my voice in supplication:

If you, O Lord, mark iniquities, Lord, who can stand? But with you is forgiveness, that you may be revered.

I trust in the Lord; my soul trusts in his word. My soul waits for the Lord more than sentinels wait for the dawn.

More than sentinels wait for the dawn, let Israel wait for the Lord, for with the Lord is kindness and with him is plenteous redemption; and he will redeem Israel from all their iniquities.

PSALM 131

Remember, O Lord, for David all his anxious care: how he swore to the Lord, vowed to the Mighty One of Jacob: "I will not enter the house I live in, nor lie on the couch where I sleep; I will give my eyes no sleep, my eyelids no rest, till I find a place for the Lord, a dwelling for the Mighty One of Jacob."

Behold, we heard of it in Ephratha; we found it in the fields of Jaar. Let us enter into his dwelling, let us worship at his footstool. Advance, O Lord, to your resting place, you and the ark of your majesty. May your priests be clothed with justice; let your faithful ones shout merrily for joy. For the sake of David your servant, reject not the plea of your anointed.

The Lord swore to David a firm promise from which he will not withdraw: "Your own offspring I will set upon your throne; if your sons keep my covenant and the decrees which I shall teach them, their sons, too, forever shall sit upon your throne." For the Lord has chosen Sion; he prefers her for his dwelling.

"Sion is my resting place forever; in her will I dwell, for I prefer her. I will bless her with abundant provision, her poor I will fill with bread. Her priests I will clothe with salvation, and her faithful ones shall shout merrily for joy. In her will I make a horn to sprout forth for David; I will place a lamp for my anointed. His enemies I will clothe with shame, but upon him my crown shall shine."

PSALM 133

Come, bless the Lord, all you servants of the Lord who stand in the house of the Lord during the hours of night. Lift up your hands toward the sanctuary, and bless the Lord. May the Lord bless you from Sion, the maker of heaven and earth.

PSALM *136*

By the streams of Babylon we sat and wept when we remembered Sion. On the aspens of that land we hung up our harps, though there our captors asked of us the lyrics of our songs, and our despoilers urged us to be joyous: "Sing for us the songs of Sion!"

How could we sing a song of the Lord in a foreign land? If I forget you, Jerusalem, may my right hand be forgotten! May my tongue cleave to my palate if I remember you not, if I place not Jerusalem ahead of my joy.

Remember, O Lord, against the children of Edom, the day of Jerusalem, when they said, "Raze it, raze it down to its foundations!" O daughter of Babylon, you destroyer, happy the man who shall repay you the evil you have done us! Happy the man who shall seize and smash your little ones against the rock!

PSALM *150*

Praise the Lord in his sanctuary, praise him in the firmament of his strength. Praise him for his mighty deeds, praise him for his sovereign majesty. Praise him with the blast of the trumpet, praise him with lyre and harp, praise him with timbrel and dance, praise him with strings and pipe. Praise him with sounding cymbals, praise him with clanging cymbals. Let everything that has breath praise the Lord! Alleluia.

CHAPTER THIRTEEN

The Kingdom of Solomon

THE WISDOM OF SOLOMON

And the kingdom was established in the hand of Solomon, and he made a marriage alliance with Pharaoh king of Egypt; he took Pharaoh's daughter, and brought her into the city of David, until he had finished building his own house and the house of the Lord and the wall around Jerusalem. The people were sacrificing at the high places, however, because no house had yet been built for the name of the Lord.

Solomon loved the Lord, walking in the statutes of David his father; only, he sacrificed and burnt incense at the high places. And the king went to Gibeon to sacrifice there, for that was the great high place; Solomon used to offer a thousand burnt offerings upon that altar. At Gibeon the Lord appeared to Solomon in a dream by night; and God said, "Ask what I shall give you." And Solomon said, "Thou hast shown great and steadfast love to thy servant David my father, because he walked before thee in faithfulness, in righteousness, and in uprightness of heart toward thee; and thou hast kept for him this great and steadfast love, and hast given him a son to sit on his throne this day. And now, O Lord my God, thou hast made thy servant king in place of David my father, although I am but a little child; I do not know how to go out or come in. And thy servant is in the midst of thy people whom thou hast chosen, a great people, that cannot be numbered or counted for multitude. Give thy servant therefore an understanding mind to govern thy people, that I may discern between good and evil; for who is able to govern this thy great people?"

It pleased the Lord that Solomon had asked this. And God said to him, "Because you have asked this, and have not asked for yourself long life or riches or the life of your enemies, but have asked for yourself understanding to discern what is right, behold, I now do according to your word. Behold, I give you a wise and discerning mind, so that none like you has been before you and none like you shall arise after you. I give you also what you have not asked, both riches and honor, so that no other king shall compare with you, all your days. And if you will walk in my ways, keeping my statutes and my commandments, as your father David walked, then I will lengthen your days."

And Solomon awoke, and behold, it was a dream. Then he came to Jerusalem, and stood before the ark of the covenant of the Lord, and offered up burnt offerings and peace offerings, and made a feast for all his servants.

Then two harlots came to the king, and stood before him. The one woman said, "Oh, my lord, this woman and I dwell in the same house; and I gave birth to a child while she was in the house. Then on the third day after I was delivered, this woman also gave birth; and we were alone; there was no one else with us in the house, only we two were in the house. And this woman's son died in the night, because she lay on it. And she arose at midnight, and took my son from beside me, while your maidservant slept, and laid it in her bosom, and laid her dead son in my bosom. When I rose in the morning to nurse my child, behold, it was dead; but when I looked at it closely in the morning, behold, it was not the child that I had borne." But the other woman said, "No, the living child is mine, and the dead child is yours." The first said, "No, the dead child is yours, and the living child is mine." Thus they spoke before the king.

Then the king said, "The one says, 'This is my son that is alive, and your son is dead'; and the other says, 'No; but your son is dead, and my son is the living one.'" And the king said, "Bring me a sword." So a sword was brought before the king. And the king said, "Divide the living child in two, and give half to the one, and half to the other." Then the woman whose son was alive said to the king, because her heart yearned for her son, "Oh, my lord, give her the living child, and by no means slay it." But the other said, "It shall be neither mine nor yours; divide it." Then the king answered and said, "Give the living child to the first woman, and by no means slay it; she is its mother." And all Israel heard of the judgment which the king had rendered; and they stood in awe of the king, because they perceived that the wisdom of God was in him, to render justice.

Solomon ruled over all the kingdoms from the Euphrates to the land of the Philistines and to the border of Egypt; they brought tribute and served Solomon all the days of his life. Solomon's provision for one day was thirty cors of fine flour, and sixty cors of meal, ten fat oxen, and twenty pasture-fed cattle, a hundred sheep, besides harts, gazelles, roebucks, and fatted fowl. For he had dominion over all the region west of the Euphrates from Tiphsah to Gaza, over all the kings west of the Euphrates; and he had peace on all sides round about him. And Judah and Israel dwelt in safety, from Dan even to Beer-sheba, every man under his vine and under his fig tree, all the days of Solomon.

Solomon also had forty thousand stalls of horses for his chariots, and twelve thousand horsemen. And those officers supplied provisions for King Solomon, and for all who came to King Solomon's table, each one in his month; they let nothing be lacking. Barley also and straw for the horses and swift steeds they brought to the place where it was required, each according to his charge.

And God gave Solomon wisdom and understanding beyond measure, and largeness of mind like the sand on the seashore, so that Solomon's wisdom surpassed the wisdom of all the people of the east, and all the wisdom of Egypt. For he was wiser than all other men, wiser than Ethan the Ezrahite, and Heman, Calcol, and Darda, the sons of Mahol; and his fame was in all the nations round about. He also uttered three thousand proverbs; and his songs were a thousand and five. He spoke of trees, from the cedar that is in Lebanon to the hyssop that grows out of the wall; he spoke also of beasts, and of birds, and of reptiles, and of fish. And men came from all peoples to hear the wisdom of Solomon, and from all the kings of the earth, who had heard of his wisdom.

PLANS FOR THE TEMPLE AND THE PALACE

Now Hiram king of Tyre sent his servants to Solomon, when he heard that they had anointed him king in place of his father; for Hiram always loved David. And Solomon sent word to Hiram, "You know that David my father could not build a house for the name of the Lord his God because of the warfare with which his enemies surrounded him, until the Lord put them under the soles of his feet. But now the Lord my God has given me rest on every side; there is neither adversary nor misfortune. And so I purpose to build a house for the name of the Lord my God, as the Lord said to David my father, 'Your son, whom I will set upon your throne in your place, shall build the house for my name.' Now therefore command that cedars of Lebanon be cut for me; and my servants will join your servants, and I will pay you for your servants such wages as you set; for you know that there is no one among us who knows how to cut timber like the Sidonians."

When Hiram heard the words of Solomon, he rejoiced greatly, and said, "Blessed be the Lord this day, who has given to David a wise son to be over this great people." And Hiram sent to Solomon, saying, "I have heard the message which you have sent to me; I am ready to do all you desire in the matter of cedar and cypress timber. My servants shall bring it down to the sea from Lebanon; and I will make it into rafts to go by sea to the place you direct, and I will have them broken up there, and you shall receive it; and you shall meet my wishes by providing food for my household." So Hiram supplied Solomon with all the timber of cedar and cypress that he desired, while Solomon gave Hiram twenty thousand cors of wheat as food for his household, and twenty thousand cors of beaten oil. Solomon gave this to Hiram year by year. And the Lord gave Solomon wisdom, as he promised him; and there was peace between Hiram and Solomon; and the two of them made a treaty.

King Solomon raised a levy of forced labor out of all Israel; and the levy numbered thirty thousand men. And he sent them to Lebanon, ten thousand a month in relays; they would be a month in Lebanon and two months at home; Adoniram was in charge of the levy. Solomon also had seventy thousand burden-bearers and eighty thousand hewers of stone in the hill country, besides Solomon's three thousand three hundred chief officers who were over the work, who had charge of the people who carried on the work. At the king's command, they quarried out great, costly stones in order to lay the foundation of the house with dressed stones. So Solomon's builders and Hiram's builders and the men of Gebal did the hewing and prepared the timber and the stone to build the house.

THE FULFILLMENT OF A DREAM

In the four hundred and eightieth year after the people of Israel came out of the land of Egypt, in the fourth year of Solomon's reign over Israel, in the month of Ziv, which is the second month, he began to build the house of the Lord. The house which King Solomon built for the Lord was sixty cubits long, twenty cubits wide, and thirty cubits high. The vestibule in front of the nave of the house was twenty cubits long, equal to the width of the house, and ten cubits deep in front of the house. And he made for the house windows with recessed frames. He also built a structure against the wall of the house, running round the walls of the house, both the nave and the inner sanctuary; and he made side chambers all around. The lowest story was five cubits broad, the middle one was six cubits broad, and the third was seven cubits broad; for around the outside of the house he made offsets on the wall in order that the supporting beams should not be inserted into the walls of the house.

When the house was built, it was with stone prepared at the quarry; so that neither hammer nor axe nor any tool of iron was heard in the temple, while it was being built.

The entrance for the lowest story was on the south side of the house; and one went up by stairs to the middle story, and from the middle story to the third. So he built the house, and finished it; and he made the ceiling of the house of beams and planks of cedar. He built the structure against the whole house, each story five cubits high, and it was joined to the house with timbers of cedar.

Now the word of the Lord came to Solomon, "Concerning this house which you are building, if you will walk in my statutes and obey my ordinances and keep all my commandments and walk in them, then I will establish my word with you, which I spoke to David your father. And I will dwell among the children of Israel, and will not forsake my people Israel."

So Solomon built the house, and finished it. He lined the walls of the house on the inside with boards of cedar; from the floor of the house to the rafters of the ceiling, he covered them on the inside with wood; and he covered the floor of the house with boards of cypress. He built twenty cubits of the rear of the house with boards of cedar from the floor to the rafters, and he built this within as an inner sanctuary, as the most holy place. The house, that is, the nave in front of the inner sanctuary, was forty cubits long. The cedar within the house was carved in the form of gourds and open flowers; all was cedar, no stone was seen. The inner sanctuary he prepared in the innermost part of the house, to set there the ark of the covenant of the Lord. The inner sanctuary was twenty cubits long, twenty cubits wide, and twenty cubits high; and he overlaid it with pure gold. He also made an altar of cedar. And Solomon overlaid the inside of the house with pure gold, and he drew chains of gold across, in front of the inner sanctuary, and overlaid it with gold. And he overlaid the whole house with gold, until all the house was finished. Also the whole altar that belonged to the inner sanctuary he overlaid with gold. In the inner sanctuary he made two cherubim of olivewood, each ten cubits high.

Solomon was building his own house thirteen years, and he finished his entire house. He built the House of the Forest of Lebanon; its length was a hundred cubits, and its breadth fifty cubits, and its height thirty cubits, and it was built upon three rows of cedar pillars.

So Solomon made all the vessels that were in the house of the Lord: the golden altar, the golden table for the bread of the Presence, the lampstands of pure gold, five on the south side and five on the north, before the inner sanctuary; the flowers, the lamps, and the tongs, of gold; the cups, snuffers, basins, dishes for incense, and firepans, of pure gold; and the sockets of gold, for the doors of the innermost part of the house, the most holy place, and for the doors of the nave of the temple. Thus all the work that King Solomon did on the house of the Lord was finished. And Solomon brought in the things which David his father had dedicated, the silver, the gold, and the vessels, and stored them in the treasuries of the house of the Lord.

THE DEDICATION OF THE TEMPLE

Then Solomon assembled the elders of Israel and all the heads of the tribes, the leaders of the fathers' houses of the people of Israel, before King Solomon in Jerusalem, to bring up the ark of the covenant of the Lord out of the city of David, which is Zion. And all the men of Israel assembled to King Solomon at the feast in the month Ethanim, which is the seventh month. And all the elders of Israel came, and the priests took up the ark. And they brought up the ark of the Lord, the tent of meeting, and all the holy vessels that were in the tent; the priests and the Levites brought them up. And King Solomon and all the congregation of Israel, who had assembled before him, were with him before the ark, sacrificing so many sheep and oxen that they could not be counted or numbered. Then the priests brought the ark of the covenant of the Lord to its place, in the inner sanctuary of the house, in the most holy place, underneath the wings of the cherubim. For the cherubim spread out their wings over the place of the ark, so that the cherubim made a covering above the ark and its poles. And the poles were so long that the ends of the poles were seen from the holy place before the inner sanctuary; but they could not be seen from outside; and they are there to this day. There was nothing in the ark except the two tables of stone which Moses put there at Horeb, where the Lord made a covenant with the people of Israel, when they came out of the land of Egypt. And when the priests came out of the holy place, a cloud filled the house of the Lord, so that the priests could not stand to minister because of the cloud; for the glory of the Lord filled the house of the Lord.

Then Solomon said, "The Lord has set the sun in the heavens, but has said that he would dwell in thick darkness. I have built thee an exalted house, a place for thee to dwell in for ever." Then the king faced about, and blessed all the assembly of Israel, while all the assembly of Israel stood. And he said, "Blessed be the Lord, the God of Israel, who with his hand has fulfilled what he promised with his mouth to David my father, saying, 'Since the day that I brought my people Israel out of Egypt, I chose no city in all the tribes of Israel in which to build a house, that my name might be there; but I chose David to be over my people Israel.' Now it was in the heart of David my father to build a house for the name of the Lord, the God of Israel. But the Lord said to David my father, 'Whereas it was in your heart to build a house for my name, you did well that it was in your heart; nevertheless you shall not build the house, but your son who shall be born to you shall build the house for my name.' Now the Lord has fulfilled his promise which he made; for I have risen in the place of David my father, and sit on the throne of Israel, as the Lord promised, and I have built the house for the name of the Lord, the God of Israel. And there I have provided a place for the ark, in which is the covenant of the Lord which he made with our fathers, when he brought them out of the land of Egypt."

Then Solomon stood before the altar of the Lord in the presence of all the assembly of Israel, and spread forth his hands toward heaven; and said, "O Lord, God of Israel, there is no God like thee, in heaven above or on earth beneath, keeping covenant and showing steadfast love to thy servants who walk before thee with all their heart; who hast kept with thy servant David my father what thou didst declare to him; yea, thou didst speak with thy mouth, and with thy hand hast fulfilled it this day. Now therefore, O Lord, God of Israel, keep with thy servant David my father what thou hast promised him, saying, 'There shall never fail you a man before me to sit upon the throne of Israel, if only your sons take heed to their way, to walk before me as you have walked before me.' Now therefore, O God of Israel, let thy word be confirmed, which thou hast spoken to thy servant David my father.

"But will God indeed dwell on the earth? Behold, heaven and the highest heaven cannot contain thee; how much less this house which I have built! Yet have regard to the prayer of thy servant and to his supplication, O Lord my God, hearkening to the cry and to the prayer which thy servant prays before thee this day; that thy eyes may be open night and day toward this house, the place of which thou hast said, 'My name shall be there,' that thou mayest hearken to the prayer which thy servant offers toward this place. And hearken thou to the supplication of thy servant and of thy people Israel, when they pray toward this place; yea, hear thou in heaven thy dwelling place, and when thou hearest, forgive.

"If a man sins against his neighbor and is made to take an oath, and comes and swears his oath before thine altar in this house, then hear thou in heaven, and act, and judge thy servants, condemning the guilty by bringing his conduct upon his own head, and vindicating the righteous by rewarding him according to his righteousness.

"When thy people Israel are defeated before the enemy because they have sinned against thee, if they turn again to thee, and acknowledge thy name, and pray and make supplication to thee in this house; then hear thou in heaven, and forgive the sin of thy people Israel, and bring them again to the land which thou gavest to their fathers.

"When heaven is shut up and there is no rain because they have sinned against thee, if they pray toward this place, and acknowledge thy name, and turn from their sin, when thou dost afflict them, then hear thou in heaven, and forgive the sin of thy servants, thy people Israel, when thou dost teach them the good way in which they should walk; and grant rain upon thy land, which thou hast given to thy people as an inheritance.

"If there is famine in the land, if there is pestilence or blight or mildew or locust or caterpillar; if their enemy besieges them in any of their cities; whatever plague, whatever sickness there is; whatever prayer, whatever supplication is made by any man or by all the people Israel, each knowing the affliction of his own heart and stretching out his hands toward this house; then hear thou in heaven thy dwelling place, and forgive, and act, and render to each whose heart thou knowest, according to all his ways (for thou, thou only, knowest the hearts of all the children of men); that they may fear thee all the days that they live in the land which thou gavest to our fathers.

"Likewise when a foreigner, who is not of thy people Israel, comes from a far country for thy name's sake (for they shall hear of thy great name, and thy mighty hand, and of thy outstretched arm), when he comes and prays toward this house, hear thou in heaven thy dwelling place, and do according to all for which the foreigner calls to thee; in order that all the peoples of the earth may know thy name and fear thee, as do thy people Israel, and that they may know that this house which I have built is called by thy name.

"If thy people go out to battle against their enemy, by whatever way thou shalt send them, and they pray to the Lord toward the city which thou hast chosen and the house which I have built for thy name, then hear thou in heaven their prayer and their supplication, and maintain their cause.

"If they sin against thee—for there is no man who does not sin—and thou art angry with them, and dost give them to an enemy, so that they are carried away captive to the land of the enemy, far off or near; yet if they lay it to heart in the land to which they have been carried captive, and repent, and make supplication to thee in the land of their captors, saying, 'We have sinned, and have acted perversely and wickedly'; if they repent with all their mind and with all their heart in the land of their enemies, who carried them captive, and pray to thee toward their land, which thou gavest to their fathers, the city which thou hast chosen, and the house which I have built for thy name; then hear thou in heaven thy dwelling place their prayer and their supplication, and maintain their cause and forgive thy people who have sinned against thee, and all their transgressions which they have committed against thee; and grant them compassion in the sight of those who carried them captive, that they may have compassion on them (for they are thy people, and thy heritage, which thou didst bring out of Egypt, from the midst of the iron furnace). Let thy eyes be open to the supplication of thy servant, and to the supplication of thy people Israel, giving ear to them whenever they call to thee. For thou didst separate them from among all the peoples of the earth, to be thy heritage, as thou didst declare through Moses, thy servant, when thou didst bring our fathers out of Egypt, O Lord God."

Now as Solomon finished offering all this prayer and supplication to the Lord, he arose from before the altar of the Lord, where he had knelt with hands outstretched toward heaven; and he stood and blessed all the assembly of Israel with a loud voice, saying, "Blessed be the Lord who has given rest to his people Israel, according to all that he promised; not one word has failed of all his good promise, which he uttered by Moses his servant. The Lord our God be with us, as he was with our fathers; may he not leave us or forsake us; that he may incline our hearts to him, to walk in all his ways, and to keep his commandments, his statutes, and his ordinances, which he commanded our fathers. Let these words of mine, wherewith I have made supplication before the Lord, be near to the Lord our God day and night, and may he maintain the cause of his servant, and the cause of his people Israel, as each day requires; that all the peoples of the earth may know that the Lord is God; there is no other. Let your heart therefore be wholly true to the Lord our God, walking in his statutes, and keeping his commandments, as at this day."

Then the king, and all Israel with him, offered sacrifice before the Lord. Solomon offered as peace offerings to the Lord twenty-two thousand oxen and a hundred and twenty thousand sheep. So the king and all the people of Israel dedicated the house of the Lord. The same day the king consecrated the middle of the court that was before the house of the Lord; for there he offered the burnt offering and the cereal offering and the fat pieces of the peace offerings, because the bronze altar that was before the Lord was too small to receive the burnt offering and the cereal offering and the fat pieces of the peace offerings.

So Solomon held the feast at that time, and all Israel with him, a great assembly, from the entrance of Hamath to the Brook of Egypt, before the Lord our God, seven days. On the eighth day he sent the people away; and they blessed the king, and went to their homes joyful and glad of heart for all the goodness that the Lord had shown to David his servant and to Israel his people.

When Solomon had finished building the house of the Lord and the king's house and all that Solomon desired to build, the Lord appeared to Solomon a second time, as he had appeared to him at Gibeon. And the Lord said to him, "I have heard your prayer and supplication, which you have made before me; I have consecrated this house which you have built, and put my name there for ever; my eyes and my heart will be there for all time. And as for you, if you will walk before me, as David your father walked, with integrity of heart and uprightness, doing according to all that I have commanded you, and keeping my statutes and my ordinances, then I will establish your royal throne over Israel for ever, as I promised David your father, saying, 'There shall not fail you a man upon the throne of Israel.' But if you turn aside from following me, you or your children, and do not keep my commandments and my statutes which I have set before you, but go and serve other gods and worship them, then I will cut off Israel from the land which I have given them; and the house which I have consecrated for my name I will cast out of my sight; and Israel will become a proverb and a byword among all peoples. And this house will become a heap of ruins; everyone passing by it will be astonished, and will hiss; and they will say, 'Why has the Lord done thus to this land and to this house?' Then they will say, 'Because they forsook the Lord their God who brought their fathers out of the land of Egypt, and laid hold on other gods, and worshiped them and served them; therefore the Lord has brought all this evil upon them.' "

King Solomon built a fleet of ships at Ezion-geber, which is near Eloth on the shore of the Red Sea, in the land of Edom. And Hiram sent with the fleet his servants, seamen who were familiar with the sea, together with the servants of Solomon; and they went to Ophir, and brought from there gold, to the amount of four hundred and twenty talents; and they brought it to King Solomon.

THE RICHES OF SOLOMON'S COURT; HIS DEATH

Now when the queen of Sheba heard of the fame of Solomon concerning the name of the Lord, she came to test him with hard questions. She came to Jerusalem with a very great retinue, with camels bearing spices, and very much gold, and precious stones; and when she came to Solomon, she told him all that was on her mind. And Solomon answered all her questions; there was nothing hidden from the king which he could not explain to her. And when the queen of Sheba had seen all the wisdom of Solomon, the house that he had built, the food of his table, the seating of his officials, and the attendance of his servants, their clothing, his cupbearers, and his burnt offerings which he offered at the house of the Lord, there was no more spirit in her.

And she said to the king, "The report was true which I heard in my own land of your affairs and of your wisdom, but I did not believe the reports until I came and my own eyes had seen it; and, behold, the half was not told me; your wisdom and prosperity surpass the report which I heard. Happy are your wives! Happy are these your servants, who continually stand before you and hear your wisdom! Blessed be the Lord your God, who has delighted in you and set you on the throne of Israel! Because the Lord loved Israel for ever, he has made you king, that you may execute justice and righteousness." Then she gave the king a hundred and twenty talents of gold, and a very great quantity of spices, and precious stones; never again came such an abundance of spices as these which the queen of Sheba gave to King Solomon.

Moreover the fleet of Hiram, which brought gold from Ophir, brought from Ophir a very great amount of almug wood and precious stones. And the king made of the almug wood supports for the house of the Lord, and for the king's house, lyres also and harps for the singers; no such almug wood has come or been seen, to this day.

And King Solomon gave to the queen of Sheba all that she desired, whatever she asked besides what was given her by the bounty of King Solomon. So she turned and went back to her own land, with her servants.

Now the weight of gold that came to Solomon in one year was six hundred and sixty-six talents of gold, besides that which came from the traders and from the traffic of the merchants, and from all the kings of Arabia and from the governors of the land.

Thus King Solomon excelled all the kings of the earth in riches and in wisdom. And the whole earth sought the presence of Solomon to hear his wisdom, which God had put into his mind. Every one of them brought his present, articles of silver and gold, garments, myrrh, spices, horses, and mules, so much year by year. And Solomon gathered together chariots and horsemen; he had fourteen hundred chariots and twelve thousand horsemen, whom he stationed in the chariot cities and with the king in Jerusalem. And the king made silver as common in Jerusalem as stone, and he made cedar as plentiful as the sycamore of the Shephelah.

Now King Solomon loved many foreign women: the daughter of Pharaoh, and Moabite, Ammonite, Edomite, Sidonian, and Hittite women, from the nations concerning which the Lord had said to the people of Israel, "You shall not enter into marriage with them, neither shall they with you, for surely they will turn away your heart after their gods"; Solomon clung to these in love. He had seven hundred wives, princesses, and three hundred concubines; and his wives turned away his heart. For when Solomon was old his wives turned away his heart after other gods; and his heart was not wholly true to the Lord his God, as was the heart of David his father. For Solomon went after Ashtoreth the goddess of the Sidonians, and after Milcom the abomination of the Ammonites. So Solomon did what was evil in the sight of the Lord, as David his father had done. Then Solomon built a high place for Chemosh the abomination of Moab, and for Molech the abomination of the Ammonites, on the mountain east of Jerusalem. And so he did for all his foreign wives, who burned incense and sacrificed to their gods.

And the Lord was angry with Solomon, because his heart had turned away from the Lord, the God of Israel, who had appeared to him twice, and had commanded him concerning this thing, that he should not go after other gods; but he did not keep what the Lord commanded. Therefore the Lord said to Solomon, "Since this has been your mind and you have not kept my covenant and my statutes which I have commanded you, I will surely tear the kingdom from you and I will give it to your servant. Yet for the sake of David your father I will not do it in your days. However I will not tear away all the kingdom; but I will give one tribe to your son, for the sake of David my servant and for the sake of Jerusalem which I have chosen." And the Lord raised up an adversary against Solomon, Hadad the Edomite; he was of the royal house in Edom.

Jeroboam the son of Nebat, an Ephraimite of Zeredah, a servant of Solomon, whose mother's name was Zeruah, a widow, also lifted up his hand against the king. And this was the reason why he lifted up his hand against the king. Solomon built the Millo, and closed up the breach of the city of David his father. The man Jeroboam was very able, and when Solomon saw that the young man was industrious he gave him charge over all the forced labor of the house of Joseph. And at that time, when Jeroboam went out of Jerusalem, the prophet Ahijah the Shilonite found him on the road. Now Ahijah had clad himself with a new garment; and the two of them were alone in the open country. Then Ahijah laid hold of the new garment that was on him, and tore it into twelve pieces. And he said to Jeroboam, "Take for yourself ten pieces; for thus says the Lord, the God of Israel, 'Behold, I am about to tear the kingdom from the hand of Solomon, and will give you ten tribes (but he shall have one tribe, for the sake of my servant David and for the sake of Jerusalem, the city which I have chosen out of all the tribes of Israel), because he has forsaken me, and worshiped Ashtoreth the goddess of the Sidonians, Chemosh the god of Moab, and Milcom the god of the Ammonites, and has not walked in my ways, doing what is right in my sight and keeping my statutes and my ordinances, as David his father did. Nevertheless I will not take the whole kingdom out of his hand; but I will make him ruler all the days of his life, for the sake of David my servant whom I chose, who kept my commandments and my statutes; but I will take the kingdom out of his son's hand, and will give it to you, ten tribes. Yet to his son I will give one tribe, that David my servant may always have a lamp before me in Jerusalem, the city where I have chosen to put my name. And I will take you, and you shall reign over all that your soul desires, and you shall be king over Israel. And if you will hearken to all that I command you, and will walk in my ways, and do what is right in my eyes by keeping my statutes and my commandments, as David my servant did, I will be with you, and will build you a sure house, as I built for David, and I will give Israel to you. And I will for this afflict the descendants of David, but not for ever.'" Solomon sought therefore to kill Jeroboam; but Jeroboam arose, and fled into Egypt, to Shishak king of Egypt, and was in Egypt until the death of Solomon.

Now the rest of the acts of Solomon, and all that he did, and his wisdom, are they not written in the book of the acts of Solomon? And the time that Solomon reigned in Jerusalem over Israel was forty years. And Solomon slept with his fathers, and was buried in the city of David his father; and Rehoboam his son reigned in his stead.

CHAPTER FOURTEEN

The Literature of King Solomon

A LESSON IN WISDOM AND REASON

The proverbs of Solomon, the son of David, king of Israel: That men may appreciate wisdom and discipline, may understand words of intelligence; may receive training in wise conduct, in what is right, just and honest; that resourcefulness may be imparted to the simple, to the young man knowledge and discretion. A wise man by hearing them will advance in learning, an intelligent man will gain sound guidance, that he may comprehend proverb and parable, the words of the wise and their riddles.

The fear of the Lord is the beginning of knowledge; wisdom and instruction fools despise.

Hear, my son, your father's instruction, and reject not your mother's teaching; a graceful diadem will they be for your head; a torque for your neck.

My son, forget not my teaching, keep in mind my commands; for many days, and years of life, and peace, will they bring you.

Let not kindness and fidelity leave you; bind them around your neck; then will you win favor and good esteem before God and man.

Trust in the Lord with all your heart, on your own intelligence rely not; in all your ways be mindful of him, and he will make straight your paths.

Be not wise in your own eyes, fear the Lord and turn away from evil; this will mean health for your flesh and vigor for your bones.

Honor the Lord with your wealth, with first fruits of all your produce; then will your barns be filled with grain, with new wine your vats will overflow.

The discipline of the Lord, my son, disdain not; spurn not his reproof; for whom the Lord loves he reproves, and he chastises the son he favors.

Happy the man who finds wisdom, the man who gains understanding! For her profit is better than profit in silver, and better than gold is her revenue; she is more precious than corals, and none of your choice possessions can compare with her.

Long life is in her right hand, in her left are riches and honor; her ways are pleasant ways, and all her paths are peace.

Does not Wisdom call, and Understanding raise her voice? On the top of the heights along the road, at the crossroads she takes her stand; by the gates at the approaches of the city, in the entryways she cries aloud: "To you, O men, I call; my appeal is to the children of men. You simple ones, gain resource, you fools, gain sense.

"Give heed! for noble things I speak; honesty opens my lips. Yes, the truth my mouth recounts, but wickedness my lips abhor. Sincere are all the words of my mouth, no one of them is wily or crooked; all of them are plain to the man of intelligence, and right to those who attain knowledge. Receive my instruction in preference to silver, and knowledge rather than choice gold. [For Wisdom is better than corals, and no choice possessions can compare with her.]

"I Wisdom, dwell with experience, and judicious knowledge I attain. [The fear of the Lord is to hate evil;] pride, arrogance, the evil way, and the perverse mouth I hate. Mine are counsel and advice; mine is strength; I am understanding. By me kings reign, and lawgivers establish justice; by me princes govern, and nobles; all the rulers of the earth.

"Those who love me I also love, and those who seek me find me. With me are riches and honor, enduring wealth and prosperity. My fruit is better than gold, yes, than pure gold, and my revenue than choice silver. On the way of duty I walk, along the paths of justice, granting wealth to those who love me, and filling their treasuries.

"The Lord begot me, the firstborn of his ways, the forerunner of his prodigies of long ago; from of old I was poured forth, at the first, before the earth. When there were no depths I was brought forth, when there were no fountains or springs of water; before the mountains were settled into place, before the hills, I was brought forth; while as yet the earth and the fields were not made, nor the first clods of the world.

"When he established the heavens I was there, when he marked out the vault over the face of the deep; when he made firm the skies above, when he fixed fast the foundations of the earth; when he set for the sea its limit, so that the waters should not transgress his command; then was I beside him as his craftsman, and I was his delight day by day, playing before him all the while, playing on the surface of his earth [and I found delight in the sons of men].

"So now, O children, listen to me; instruction and wisdom do not reject! Happy the man who obeys me, and happy those who keep my ways, happy the man watching daily at my gates, waiting at my doorposts; for he who finds me finds life, and wins favor from the Lord; but he who misses me harms himself; all who hate me love death."

Wisdom has built her house, she has set up her seven columns; she has dressed her meat, mixed her wine, yes, she has spread her table. She has sent out her maidens; she calls from the heights out over the city: "Let whoever is simple turn in here; to him who lacks understanding, I say, Come, eat of my food, and drink of the wine I have mixed! Forsake foolishness that you may live; advance in the way of understanding."

He who corrects an arrogant man earns insult; and he who reproves a wicked man incurs opprobrium. Reprove not an arrogant man, lest he hate you; reprove a wise man, and he will love you. Instruct a wise man, and he becomes still wiser; teach a just man, and he advances in learning.

The beginning of wisdom is the fear of the Lord, and knowledge of the Holy One is understanding; for by me your days will be multiplied and the years of your life increased.

THE WISDOM OF PRUDENCE

God has glory in what he conceals, kings have glory in what they fathom.

As the heavens in height, and the earth in depth, the heart of kings is unfathomable.

Remove the dross from silver, and it comes forth perfectly purified; remove the wicked from the presence of the king, and his throne is made firm through righteousness.

Claim no honor in the king's presence, nor occupy the place of great men; for it is better that you be told, "Come up closer!" than that you be humbled before the prince.

If your enemy be hungry, give him food to eat, if he be thirsty, give him to drink; for live coals you will heap on his head, and the Lord will vindicate you.

When one finds a worthy wife, her value is far beyond pearls. Her husband, entrusting his heart to her, has an unfailing prize. She brings him good, and not evil, all the days of her life. She obtains wool and flax, and makes cloth with skillful hands. Like merchant ships, she secures her provisions from afar. She rises while it is still night, and distributes food to her household. She picks out a field to purchase; out of her earnings she plants a vineyard. She is girt about with strength, and sturdy are her arms. She enjoys the success of her dealings; at night her lamp is undimmed. She puts her hands to the distaff, and her fingers ply the spindle. She reaches out her hands to the poor, and extends her arms to the needy. She fears not the snow for her household; all her charges are doubly clothed. She makes her own coverlets; fine linen and purple are her clothing. Her husband is prominent at the city gates as he sits with the elders of the land. She makes garments and sells them, and stocks the merchants with belts. She is clothed with strength and dignity, and she laughs at the days to come. She opens her mouth in wisdom, and on her tongue is kindly counsel. She watches the conduct of her household, and eats not her food in idleness. Her children rise up and praise her; her husband, too, extols her: "Many are the women of proven worth, but you have excelled them all." Charm is deceptive and beauty fleeting; the woman who fears the Lord is to be praised. Give her a reward of her labors, and let her works praise her at the city gates.

ALL IS VANITY

The words of David's son, Coheleth, king in Jerusalem: Vanity of vanities, says Coheleth, vanity of vanities! All things are vanity! What profit has man from all the labor which he toils at under the sun? One generation passes and another comes, but the world forever stays. The sun rises and the sun goes down; then it presses on to the place where it rises. Blowing now toward the south, then toward the north, the wind turns again and again, resuming its rounds. All rivers go to the sea, yet never does the sea become full. To the place where they go, the rivers keep on going. All speech is labored; there is nothing man can say. The eye is not satisfied with seeing nor is the ear filled with hearing.

What has been, that will be; what has been done, that will be done. Nothing is new under the sun. Even the thing of which we say, "See, this is new!" has already existed in the ages that preceded us. There is no remembrance of the men of old; nor of those to come will there be any remembrance among those who come after them.

I said to myself, "Come, now, let me try you with pleasure and the enjoyment of good things." But behold, this too was vanity. Of laughter I said: "Mad!" and of mirth: "What good does this do?"

I amassed for myself silver and gold, and the wealth of kings and provinces. I got for myself male and female singers and all human luxuries. I became great, and I stored up more than all others before me in Jerusalem; my wisdom, too, stayed with me. Nothing that my eyes desired did I deny them, nor did I deprive myself of any joy, but my heart rejoiced in the fruit of all my toil. This was my share for all my toil. But when I turned to all the works that my hands had wrought, and to the toil at which I had taken such pains, behold! all was vanity and a chase after wind, with nothing gained under the sun. For what will the man do who is to come after the king? What men have already done!

I went on to the consideration of wisdom, madness and folly. And I saw that wisdom had the advantage over folly as much as light has the advantage over darkness. The wise man has eyes in his head, but the fool walks in darkness. Yet I knew that one lot befalls both of them. So I said to myself, if the fool's lot is to befall me also, why then should I be wise? Where is the profit for me? And I concluded in my heart that this too is vanity. Neither of the wise man nor of the fool will there be an abiding remembrance, for in days to come both will have been forgotten. How is it that the wise man dies as well as the fool!

Again I considered all the oppressions that take place under the sun: the tears of the victims with none to comfort them! From the hand of their oppressors comes violence, and there is none to comfort them! And those now dead, I declared more fortunate in death than are the living to be still alive. And better off than both is the yet unborn, who has not seen the wicked work that is done under the sun. Then I saw that all toil and skillful work is the rivalry of one man for another. This also is vanity and a chase after wind.

Cast your bread upon the waters; after a long time you may find it again. Make seven or eight portions; you know not what misfortune may come upon the earth. When the clouds are full, they pour out rain upon the earth. Whether a tree falls to the south or to the north, wherever it falls, there shall it lie.

The last word, when all is heard: Fear God and keep his commandments, for this is man's all; because God will bring to judgment every work, with all its hidden qualities, whether good or bad.

THE ERROR OF MAN

Love justice, you who judge the earth; think of the Lord in goodness, and seek him in integrity of heart, because he is found by those who test him not, and he manifests himself to those who do not disbelieve in him.

Because God did not make death, nor does he rejoice in the destruction of the living. For he fashioned all things that they might have being; and the creatures of the world are wholesome, and there is not a destructive drug among them nor any domain of the nether world on earth, for justice is immortal. It was the wicked who with hands and words invited death, considered it a friend and pined for it; they made a covenant with it, because they deserve to be in its possession.

For they said among themselves, thinking not aright: "Brief and troublous is our lifetime; neither is there any remedy for man's dying, nor is anyone known to have come back from the nether world. For haphazard were we born, and hereafter we shall be as though we had not been; because the breath in our nostrils is a smoke and reason is a spark at the beating of our hearts, and when this is quenched, our body will be ashes and our spirit will be poured abroad like unresisting air. Even our name will be forgotten in time, and no one will recall our deeds. So our life will pass away like the traces of a cloud, and will be dispersed like a mist pursued by the sun's rays and overpowered by its heat. For our lifetime is the passing of a shadow; and our dying cannot be deferred because it is fixed with a seal; and no one returns. Come, therefore, let us enjoy the good things that are real, and use the freshness of creation avidly. Let us have our fill of costly wine and perfumes, and let no springtime blossom pass us by. Let us crown ourselves with rosebuds ere they wither; let no meadow be free from our wantonness. Everywhere let us leave tokens of our rejoicing, for this our portion is, and this our lot. Let us oppress the needy just man; let us neither spare the widow nor revere the old man for his hair grown white with time. But let our strength be our norm of justice; for weakness proves itself worthless. Let us beset the just one, because he is obnoxious to us; he sets himself against our doings, reproaches us for transgressions of the Law and charges us with violations of our training.

"He professes to have knowledge of God and styles himself as a child of the Lord. To us he is the censure of our thoughts; merely to see him is a hardship for us, because his life is not like other men's, and different are his ways. He judges us debased; he holds aloof from our paths as from things impure. He calls blest the destiny of the just and boasts that God is his Father. Let us see whether his words be true; let us find out what will happen to him. For if the just one be the son of God, he will defend him and deliver him from the hand of his foes. With revilement and torture let us put him to the test that we may have proof of his gentleness and try his patience. Let us condemn him to a shameful death; for according to his own words, God will take care of him."

These were their thoughts, but they erred; for their wickedness blinded them.

THE JUST ARE IN THE HAND OF GOD

But the souls of the just are in the hand of God, and no torment shall touch them. They seemed, in the view of the foolish, to be dead; and their passing away was judged an affliction and their going forth from us, utter destruction. But they are in peace. For if before men, indeed, they be punished, yet is their hope full of immortality; chastised a little, they shall be greatly blessed, because God tried them and found them worthy of himself. As gold in the furnace, he proved them, and as sacrificial offerings he took them to himself.

Better is childlessness with virtue; for immortal is its memory: because both by God is it acknowledged, and by men.

But the just man, though he die early, shall be at rest. For the age that is honorable comes not with the passing of time, nor can it be measured in terms of years. Rather, understanding is the hoary crown for men, and an unsullied life, the attainment of old age. He who pleased God was loved; he who lived among sinners was transported— snatched away, lest wickedness pervert his mind or deceit beguile his soul; for the witchery of paltry things obscures what is right and the whirl of desire transforms the innocent mind. Having become perfect in a short while, he reached the fullness of a long career; for his soul was pleasing to the Lord, therefore he sped him out of the midst of wickedness. But the people saw and did not understand; nor did they take this into account: That God's grace and mercy are with his holy ones and his care is with his elect. Yes, the just man dead condemns the sinful who live, and youth swiftly completed condemns the many years of the wicked man grown old. For they see the death of the wise man and do not understand what the Lord intended for him, or why he made him secure. They see, and hold him in contempt; but the Lord laughs them to scorn. And they shall afterward become dishonored corpses and an unceasing mockery among the dead. For he shall strike them down speechless and prostrate and rock them to their foundations; they shall be utterly laid waste and shall be in grief and their memory shall perish.

Then shall the just one with great assurance stand before his oppressors who set at nought his labors. Seeing this, they shall be shaken with dreadful fear, and amazed at the unlooked-for salvation. They shall say among themselves, rueful and groaning through anguish of spirit: "This is he whom once we held as a laughingstock and as a type for mockery, fools that we were! His life we deemed madness, and his death dishonored. See how he is accounted among the sons of God; how his lot is with the saints!"

Yes, the hope of the wicked is like thistledown borne on the wind, and like fine, tempest-driven foam; like smoke scattered by the wind, and like the passing memory of the nomad camping for a single day. But the just live forever, and in the Lord is their recompense, and the thought of them is with the Most High. Therefore shall they receive the splendid crown, the beauteous diadem, from the hand of the Lord— for he shall shelter them with his right hand, and protect them with his arm.

THE STRENGTH OF WISDOM

Hear, therefore, kings, and understand; learn, you magistrates of the earth's expanse! Hearken, you who rule the multitude and lord it over throngs of peoples! Because authority was given you by the Lord and sovereignty by the Most High, who shall probe your works and scrutinize your counsels! Because, though you were ministers of his kingdom, you judged not rightly, and did not keep the Law, nor walk according to the will of God, terribly and swiftly shall he come against you, because judgment is stern for the exalted—for the lowly may be pardoned out of mercy but the mighty shall be mightily put to the test. For the Lord of all shows no partiality, nor does he fear greatness, because he himself made the great as well as the small, and he provides for all alike; but for the powerful a rigorous scrutiny impends. To you, therefore, O princes, are my words addressed that you may learn wisdom and that you may not sin.

I too am a mortal man, like all the rest, and a descendant of the first man formed of earth. And in my mother's womb I was molded into flesh. Therefore I prayed, and prudence was given me; I pleaded, and the spirit of Wisdom came to me. Beyond health and comeliness I loved her, and I chose to have her rather than the light, because the splendor of her never yields to sleep. Yet all good things together came to me in her company, and countless riches at her hands; and I rejoiced in them all, because Wisdom is their leader, though I had not known that she is the mother of these. Simply I learned about her, and ungrudgingly do I share—her riches I do not hide away. For she is the refulgence of eternal light, the spotless mirror of the power of God, the image of his goodness. And she, who is one, can do all things, and renews everything while herself perduring; and passing into holy souls from age to age, she produces friends of God and prophets. For there is nought God loves, be it not one who dwells with Wisdom. For she is fairer than the sun and surpasses every constellation of the stars. Compared to light, she takes precedence; for that, indeed, night supplants, but wickedness prevails not over Wisdom.

Indeed, she reaches from end to end mightily and governs all things well.

Her I loved and sought after from my youth; I sought to take her for my bride and was enamored of her beauty. So I determined to draw her into fellowship, knowing that she would be my counselor while all was well, and my comfort in care and grief. And knowing that I could not otherwise possess her except God gave it—and this, too, was prudence, to know whose is the gift—I went to the Lord and besought him, and said with all my heart: God of my fathers, Lord of mercy, you who have made all things by your word and in your wisdom have established man to rule the creatures produced by you, to govern the world in holiness and justice, and to render judgment in integrity of heart: Give me Wisdom, the attendant at your throne, and reject me not from among your children; for I am your servant, the son of your handmaid, a man weak and short-lived and lacking in comprehension of judgment and of laws. Indeed, though one be perfect among the sons of men, if Wisdom, who comes from you, be not with him, he shall be held in no esteem. You have chosen me king over your people and magistrate for your sons and daughters. You have bid me build a temple on your holy mountain and an altar in the city that is your dwelling place, a copy of the holy tabernacle which you had established from of old. Now with you is Wisdom, who knows your works and was present when you made the world; who understands what is pleasing in your eyes and what is conformable with your commands. Send her forth from your holy heavens and from your glorious throne dispatch her that she may be with me and work with me, that I may know what is pleasing to you. For she knows and understands all things, and will guide me discreetly in my affairs and safeguard me by her glory; thus my deeds will be acceptable, and I shall judge your people justly and be worthy of my father's throne. For what man knows God's counsel, or who can conceive what the Lord intends? For the deliberations of mortals are timid, and unsure are our plans. For the corruptible body burdens the soul and the earthen shelter weighs down the mind that has many concerns. And scarce do we guess the things on earth, and what is within our grasp we find with difficulty; but when things are in heaven, who can search them out? Or who ever knew your counsel, except you had given Wisdom and sent your holy spirit from on high? And thus were the paths of those on earth made straight, and men learned what was your pleasure, and were saved by Wisdom.

THE USES OF WISDOM

She preserved the first-formed father of the world when he alone had been created; and she raised him up from his fall, and gave him power to rule all things. She did not abandon the just man when he was sold, but delivered him from sin. She went down with him into the dungeon, and did not desert him in his bonds, until she brought him the scepter of royalty and authority over his oppressors, showed those who had defamed him false, and gave him eternal glory. The holy people and blameless race—it was she who delivered them from the nation that oppressed them. She entered the soul of the Lord's servant, and withstood fearsome kings with signs and portents. She gave the holy ones the recompense of their labors, conducted them by a wondrous road, and became a shelter for them by day and a starry flame by night. She took them across the Red Sea and brought them through the deep waters —but their enemies she overwhelmed, and cast them up from the bottom of the depths. Therefore the just despoiled the wicked; and they sang, O Lord, your holy name and praised in unison your conquering hand—because Wisdom opened the mouths of the dumb, and gave ready speech to infants.

For all men were by nature foolish who were in ignorance of God, and who from the good things seen did not succeed in knowing him who is, and from studying the works did not discern the artisan; but either fire, or wind, or the swift air, or the circuit of the stars, or the mighty water, or the luminaries of heaven, the governors of the world, they considered gods. Now if out of joy in their beauty they thought them gods, let them know how far more excellent is the Lord than these; for the original source of beauty fashioned them. Or if they were struck by their might and energy, let them from these things realize how much more powerful is he who made them. For from the greatness and the beauty of created things their original author, by analogy, is seen. But yet, for these the blame is less; for they indeed have gone astray perhaps, though they seek God and wish to find him. For they search busily among his works, but are distracted by what they see, because the things seen are fair. But again, not even these are pardonable. For if they so far succeeded in knowledge that they could speculate about the world, how did they not more quickly find its Lord? But doomed are they, and in dead things are their hopes, who termed gods the works of human hands: Gold and silver, the product of art, and likenesses of beasts, or useless stone, the work of an ancient hand. Therefore they were fittingly punished by similar creatures, and were tormented by a swarm of insects.

When they determined to put to death the infants of the holy ones, and when a single boy had been cast forth but saved, as a reproof you carried off their multitude of sons and destroyed them all at once in the mighty water. That night was known beforehand to our fathers, that, with sure knowledge of the oaths in which they put their faith, they might have courage. Your people awaited the salvation of the just and the destruction of their foes. For when peaceful stillness compassed everything and the night in its swift course was half spent, your all-powerful word from heaven's royal throne bounded, a fierce warrior, into the doomed land, bearing the sharp sword of your inexorable decree. And as he alighted, he filled every place with death; he still reached to heaven, while he stood upon the earth. But the trial of death touched at one time even the just, and in the desert a plague struck the multitude; yet not for long did the anger last. For the blameless man hastened to be their champion, bearing the weapon of his special office, prayer and the propitiation of incense; he withstood the wrath and put a stop to the calamity, showing that he was your servant. And he overcame the bitterness not by bodily strength, not by force of arms; but by word he overcame the smiter, recalling the sworn covenant with their fathers. For when corpses had already fallen one on another in heaps, he stood in the midst and checked the anger, and cut off the way to the living. For on his full-length robe was the whole world, and the glories of the fathers were carved in four rows upon the stones, and your grandeur was on the crown upon his head.

A WAY OF LIFE

Be sincere of heart and steadfast, undisturbed in time of adversity. Cling to him, forsake him not; thus will your future be great. Accept whatever befalls you, in crushing misfortune be patient; for in fire gold is tested, and worthy men in the crucible of humiliation. Trust God and he will help you; make straight your ways and hope in him.

You who fear the Lord, wait for his mercy, turn not away lest you fall. You who fear the Lord, trust him, and your reward will not be lost. You who fear the Lord, hope for good things, for lasting joy and mercy. Study the generations long past and understand; has anyone hoped in the Lord and been disappointed? Has anyone persevered in his fear and been forsaken? has anyone called upon him and been rebuffed? Compassionate and merciful is the Lord; he forgives sins, he saves in time of trouble.

My son, conduct your affairs with humility, and you will be loved more than a giver of gifts. Humble yourself the more, the greater you are, and you will find favor with God. For great is the power of God; by the humble he is glorified. What is too sublime for you, seek not, into things beyond your strength search not. What is committed to you, attend to; for what is hidden is not your concern.

With what is too much for you meddle not, when shown things beyond human understanding. Their own opinion has misled many, and false reasoning unbalanced their judgment.

Say not: "I have sinned, yet what has befallen me?" for the Lord bides his time. Of forgiveness be not overconfident, adding sin upon sin. Say not: "Great is his mercy; my many sins he will forgive." For mercy and anger alike are with him; upon the wicked alights his wrath. Delay not your conversion to the Lord, put it not off from day to day; for suddenly his wrath flames forth; at the time of vengeance, you will be destroyed.

With your whole heart honor your father; your mother's birth-pangs forget not. Remember, of these parents you were born; what can you give them for all they gave you? With all your soul, fear God, revere his priests. With all your strength, love your Creator, forsake not his ministers. Honor God and respect the priest; give him his portion as you have been commanded: first fruits and contributions, due sacrifices and holy offerings. Avoid not those who weep, but mourn with those who mourn; neglect not to visit the sick—for these things you will be loved. In whatever you do, remember your last days, and you will never sin.

A man may become rich through a miser's life, and this is his allotted reward: When he says: "I have found rest, now I will feast on my possessions," he does not know how long it will be till he dies and leaves them to others.

The Eternal is the judge of all things without exception; the Lord alone is just. Whom has he made equal to describing his works, and who can probe his mighty deeds? Who can measure his majestic power, or exhaust the tale of his mercies? One cannot lessen, nor increase, nor penetrate the wonders of the Lord. When a man ends he is only beginning, and when he stops he is still bewildered. What is man, of what worth is he? the good, the evil in him, what are these? The sum of a man's days is great if it reaches a hundred years: Like a drop of sea water, like a grain of sand, so are these few years among the days of eternity. That is why the Lord is patient with men and showers upon them his mercy. He sees and understands that their death is grievous, and so he forgives them all the more. Man may be merciful to his fellow man, but the Lord's mercy reaches all flesh, reproving, admonishing, teaching, as a shepherd guides his flock; merciful to those who accept his guidance, who are diligent in his precepts.

Before you have fallen, humble yourself; when you have sinned, show repentance. Delay not to forsake sins, neglect it not till you are in distress. Let nothing prevent the prompt payment of your vows; wait not to fulfill them when you are dying. Before making a vow have the means to fulfill it; be not one who tries the Lord. Think of wrath and the day of death, the time of vengeance when he will hide his face. Remember the time of hunger in the time of plenty, poverty and want in the day of wealth. Between morning and evening the weather changes; before the Lord all things are fleeting.

Who will set a guard over my mouth, and upon my lips an effective seal, that I may not fail through them, that my tongue may not destroy me?

Lord, Father and Master of my life, permit me not to fall by them! Who will apply the lash to my thoughts, to my mind the rod of discipline, that my failings may not be spared, nor the sins of my heart overlooked; lest my failings increase, and my sins be multiplied; lest I succumb to my foes, and my enemy rejoice over me? Lord, Father and God of my life, abandon me not into their control! A brazen look allow me not; ward off passion from my heart, let not the lustful cravings of the flesh master me, surrender me not to shameless desires.

THE PROVIDENCE OF GOD

Wisdom sings her own praises, before her own people she proclaims her glory; in the assembly of the Most High she opens her mouth, in the presence of his hosts she declares her worth: "From the mouth of the Most High I came forth, and mistlike covered the earth. In the highest heavens did I dwell, my throne on a pillar of cloud. The vault of heaven I compassed alone, through the deep abyss I wandered. Over waves of the sea, over all the land, over every people and nation I held sway. Among all these I sought a resting place; in whose inheritance should I abide?

"Then the Creator of all gave me his command, and he who formed me chose the spot for my tent, saying, 'In Jacob make your dwelling, in Israel your inheritance.' Before all ages, in the beginning, he created me, and through all ages I shall not cease to be. In the holy Tent I ministered before him, and in Sion I fixed my abode. Thus in the chosen city he has given me rest, in Jerusalem is my domain. I have struck root among the glorious people, in the portion of the Lord, his heritage.

"Like a cedar on Lebanon I am raised aloft, like a cypress on Mount Hermon, like a palm tree in En-gaddi, like a rosebush in Jericho, like a fair olive tree in the field, like a plane tree growing beside the water. Like cinnamon, or fragrant balm, or precious myrrh, I give forth perfume; like galbanum and onycha and sweet spices, like the odor of incense in the Holy Place. I spread out my branches like a terebinth, my branches so bright and so graceful. I bud forth delights like the vine, my blossoms become fruit fair and rich. Come to me, all you that yearn for me, and be filled with my fruits; you will remember me as sweeter than honey, better to have than the honeycomb. He who eats of me will hunger still, he who drinks of me will thirst for more; he who obeys me will not be put to shame, he who serves me will never fail."

Come to our aid, O God of the universe, and put all the nations in dread of you! Raise your hand against the heathen, that they may realize your power. As you have used us to show them your holiness, so now use them to show us your glory. Thus they will know, as we know, that there is no God but you.

Give new signs and work new wonders; show forth the splendor of your right hand and arm; rouse your anger, pour out wrath, humble the enemy, scatter the foe. Hasten the day, bring on the time; crush the heads of the hostile rulers. Let raging fire consume the fugitive, and your people's oppressors meet destruction.

Gather all the tribes of Jacob, that they may inherit the land as of old, show mercy to the people called by your name; Israel, whom you named your first-born. Take pity on your holy city, Jerusalem, your dwelling place. Fill Sion with your majesty, your temple with your glory.

Give evidence of your deeds of old; fulfill the prophecies spoken in your name, reward those who have hoped in you, and let your prophets be proved true. Hear the prayer of your servants, for you are ever gracious to your people; thus it will be known to the very ends of the earth that you are the eternal God.

THE TRIUMPH OF WISDOM

How different the man who devotes himself to the study of the Law of the Most High! He explores the wisdom of men of old and occupies himself with the prophecies; he treasures the discourses of famous men, and goes to the heart of involved sayings; he studies obscure parables, and is busied with the hidden meanings of the sages. He is in attendance on the great, and has entrance to the ruler. He travels among the peoples of foreign lands to learn what is good and evil among men. His care is to seek the Lord, his Maker, to petition the Most High, to open his lips in prayer, to ask pardon for his sins. Then, if it pleases the Lord Almighty, he will be filled with the spirit of understanding; he will pour forth his words of wisdom and in prayer give thanks to the Lord, who will direct his knowledge and his counsel, as he meditates upon his mysteries. He will show the wisdom of what he has learned and glory in the Law of the Lord's covenant. Many will praise his understanding; his fame can never be effaced; unfading will be his memory, through all generations his name will live; peoples will speak of his wisdom, and in assembly sing his praises.

Now will I praise those godly men, our ancestors, each in his own time. Rulers of the earth by their authority, men of renown for their might, or counselors in their wisdom, or seers of all things in prophecy; resolute governors of peoples, or judges with discretion; authors skilled in composition, or poets with collected proverbs; composers of melodious psalms, or discoursers on lyric themes; stalwart men, solidly established and at peace in their own estates—all these were glorious in their time, each illustrious in his day. Some of them have left behind a name that is remembered to their praise; but of others there is no memory, for it perished when they perished, and they are as though they had never lived, they and their children after them. Yet these also were godly men whose virtues have not been forgotten; their wealth remains in their families, their heritage with their descendants; through God's covenant with them their family endures, and their hopes are never shattered.

All these are buried in peace, but their name lives on and on. At gatherings their wisdom is retold, and the assembly sings their praises.

Henoch walked with the Lord and was taken up, that succeeding generations might learn by his example. Noe, found just and perfect, renewed the race in the time of devastation. Because of his worth there were survivors, and with a sign to him the deluge ended; a lasting agreement was made with him, that never should all flesh be destroyed. Abraham, father of many peoples, kept his glory without stain: He observed the precepts of the Most High, and entered into an agreement with him; in his own flesh he incised the ordinance, and when tested he was found loyal.

From him was to spring the man who won the favor of all: dear to God and men, Moses, whose memory is held in benediction. God's honor devolved upon him, and the Lord strengthened him with fearful powers; God wrought swift miracles at his words and sustained him in the king's presence. He gave him the Commandments for his people, and revealed to him his glory. For his trustworthiness and meekness God selected him from all mankind; he permitted him to hear his voice, and led him into the cloud, where, face to face, he gave him the Commandments, the law of life and understanding, that he might teach his precepts to Jacob, his judgments and decrees to Israel.

Valiant leader was Josue, son of Nun, assistant to Moses in the prophetic office, formed to be, as his name implies, the great savior of God's chosen ones, to punish the enemy and to win the inheritance for Israel. What glory was his when he raised his arm, to brandish his javelin against the city!

After him came Nathan who served in the presence of David. Like the choice fat of the sacred offerings, so was David in Israel. He made sport of lions as though they were kids, and of bears, like lambs of the flock. As a youth he slew the giant and wiped out the people's disgrace, when his hand let fly the slingstone that crushed the pride of Goliath.

With his every deed he offered thanks to God Most High, in words of praise. With his whole being he loved his Maker and daily had his praises sung; he added beauty to the feasts and solemnized the seasons of each year with string music before the altar, providing sweet melody for the psalms so that when the Holy Name was praised, before daybreak the sanctuary would resound. The Lord forgave him his sins and exalted his strength forever; he conferred on him the rights of royalty and established his throne in Israel.

Because of his merits he had as his successor a wise son, who lived in security: Solomon reigned during an era of peace, for God made tranquil all his borders. He built a house to the name of God, and established a lasting sanctuary. How wise you were when you were young, overflowing with instruction, like the Nile in flood! Your understanding covered the whole earth, and, like a sea, filled it with knowledge. Your fame reached distant coasts, and their peoples came to hear you; with song and story and riddle, and with your answers, you astounded the nations. You were called by that glorious name which was conferred upon Israel. Gold you gathered like so much iron, you heaped up silver as though it were lead; but you abandoned yourself to women and gave them dominion over your body. You brought dishonor upon your reputation, shame upon your marriage, wrath upon your descendants, and groaning upon your domain; thus two governments came into being, when in Ephraim kingship was usurped. But God does not withdraw his mercy, nor permit even one of his promises to fail. He does not uproot the posterity of his chosen one, nor destroy the offspring of his friend. So he gave to Jacob a remnant, to David a root from his own family. Solomon finally slept with his fathers, and left behind him one of his sons, expansive in folly, limited in sense, Roboam, who by his policy made the people rebel; until one arose who should not be remembered, the sinner who led Israel into sin, who brought ruin to Ephraim and caused them to be exiled from their land.

Till like a fire there appeared the prophet whose words were as a flaming furnace. Their staff of bread he shattered, in his zeal he reduced them to straits; by God's word he shut up the heavens and three times brought down fire. How awesome are you, Elias! Whose glory is equal to yours? Blessed is he who shall have seen you before he dies, O Elias, enveloped in the whirlwind!

How can we fittingly praise Zorobabel, who was like a signet ring on God's right hand, and Josue, Josedec's son? In their time they built the house of God; they erected the holy temple, destined for everlasting glory. Extolled be the memory of Nehemias! He rebuilt our ruined walls, restored our shattered defenses, and set up gates and bars.

I give you thanks, O God of my father; I praise you, O God my savior! I will make known your name, refuge of my life; you have been my helper against my adversaries. You have saved me from death, and kept back my body from the pit, from the clutches of the nether world you have snatched my feet; you have delivered me, in your great mercy from the scourge of a slanderous tongue, and from lips that went over to falsehood; from the snare of those who watched for my downfall, and from the power of those who sought my life; from many a danger you have saved me, from flames that hemmed me in on every side; from the midst of unremitting fire, from the deep belly of the nether world; from deceiving lips and painters of lies, from the arrows of dishonest tongues. I was at the point of death, my soul was nearing the depths of the nether world; I turned every way, but there was no one to help me, I looked for one to sustain me, but could find no one. But then I remembered the mercies of the Lord, his kindness through ages past; for he saves those who take refuge in him, and rescues them from every evil. So I raised my voice from the very earth, from the gates of the nether world, my cry. I called out: O Lord, you are my father, you are my champion and my savior; do not abandon me in time of trouble, in the midst of storms and dangers. I will ever praise your name and be constant in my prayers to you. Thereupon the Lord heard my voice, he listened to my appeal; he saved me from evil of every kind and preserved me in time of trouble. For this reason I thank him and I praise him; I bless the name of the Lord.

See for yourselves! I labored but a little for her sake, and found great rest. Listen, children, to my teaching! you will win silver and gold through me. If you make my lessons your joy, you need feel no shame when you hear my song! Do your work in due season, and in his own time God will give you your reward.

CHAPTER FIFTEEN

A Jewish Love Poem

THE SONG OF SONGS BY SOLOMON

Let him kiss me with kisses of his mouth! More delightful is your love than wine! Your name spoken is a spreading perfume: that is why the maidens love you. Draw me: we will follow you eagerly! Bring me, O king, to your chambers. With you we rejoice and exult, we extol your love; it is beyond wine: how rightly you are loved! I am as dark—but lovely, O daughters of Jerusalem—as the tents of Cedar, as the curtains of Salma. Do not stare at me because I am swarthy, because the sun has burned me. My brothers have been angry with me; they charged me with the care of the vineyards: my own vineyard I have not cared for. Tell me, you whom my heart loves, where you pasture your flock, where you give them rest at midday, lest I be found wandering after the flocks of your companions.

For the king's banquet my nard gives forth its fragrance. My lover is for me a sachet of myrrh to rest in my bosom. My lover is for me a cluster of henna from the vineyards of En-gaddi. Ah, you are beautiful, my beloved, ah, you are beautiful; your eyes are doves! Ah, you are beautiful, my lover—yes, you are lovely. Our couch, too, is verdant; the beams of our house are cedars, our rafters, cypresses.

I am a flower of Saron, a lily of the valley. As a lily among thorns, so is my beloved among women. As an apple tree among the trees of the woods, so is my lover among men. I delight to rest in his shadow, and his fruit is sweet to my mouth. He brings me into the banquet hall and his emblem over me is love. Strengthen me with raisin cakes, refresh me with apples, for I am faint with love. His left hand is under my head and his right arm embraces me.

I adjure you, daughters of Jerusalem, by the gazelles and hinds of the field, do not arouse, do not stir up love before its own time. Hark! my lover—here he comes springing across the mountains, leaping across the hills. My lover is like a gazelle or a young stag. Here he stands

241

behind our wall, gazing through the windows, peering through the lattices. My lover speaks; he says to me, "Arise, my beloved, my beautiful one, and come! For see, the winter is past, the rains are over and gone. The flowers appear on the earth, the time of pruning the vines has come, and the song of the dove is heard in our land. The fig tree puts forth its figs, and the vines, in bloom, give forth fragrance. Arise, my beloved, my beautiful one, and come! O my dove in the clefts of the rock, in the secret recesses of the cliff, let me see you, let me hear your voice, for your voice is sweet, and you are lovely."

Catch us the foxes, the little foxes that damage the vineyards; for our vineyards are in bloom! My lover belongs to me and I to him; he browses among the lilies. Until the day breathes cool and the shadows lengthen, roam, my lover, like a gazelle or a young stag upon the mountains of Bether.

On my bed at night I sought him whom my heart loves—I sought him but I did not find him. I will rise then and go about the city; in the streets and crossings I will seek him whom my heart loves. I sought him but I did not find him. The watchmen came upon me as they made their rounds of the city: Have you seen him whom my heart loves? I had hardly left them when I found him whom my heart loves. I took hold of him and would not let him go till I should bring him to the home of my mother, to the room of my parent.

I adjure you, daughters of Jerusalem, by the gazelles and hinds of the field, do not arouse, do not stir up love before its own time. What is this coming up from the desert, like a column of smoke laden with myrrh, with frankincense, and with the perfume of every exotic dust?

Ah, you are beautiful, my beloved, ah, you are beautiful! Your eyes are doves behind your veil. Your hair is like a flock of goats streaming down the mountains of Galaad. You are beautiful, my beloved, and there is no blemish in you.

Come from Lebanon, my bride, come from Lebanon, come! Descend from the top of Amana, from the top of Sanir and Hermon, from the haunts of lions, from the leopards' mountains. You have ravished my heart, my sister, my bride; you have ravished my heart with one glance of your eyes, with one bead of your necklace. You are an enclosed garden, my sister, my bride, an enclosed garden, a fountain sealed. Arise, north wind! Come, south wind! blow upon my garden that its perfumes may spread abroad.

I was sleeping, but my heart kept vigil; I heard my lover knocking:

A Jewish Love Poem

"Open to me, my sister, my beloved, my dove, my perfect one! For my head is wet with dew, my locks with the moisture of the night."

My lover put his hand through the opening; my heart trembled within me, and I grew faint when he spoke. I rose to open to my lover, with my hands dripping myrrh: with my fingers dripping choice myrrh upon the fittings of the lock. I opened to my lover—but my lover had departed, gone. I sought him but I did not find him; I called to him but he did not answer me. The watchmen came upon me as they made their rounds of the city; they struck me, and wounded me, and took my mantle from me, the guardians of the walls. I adjure you, daughters of Jerusalem, if you find my lover—what shall you tell him? —that I am faint with love.

How does your lover differ from any other, O most beautiful among women? How does your lover differ from any other, that you adjure us so? My lover is radiant and ruddy; he stands out among thousands. Where has your lover gone, O most beautiful among women? Where has your lover gone that we may seek him with you? My lover has come down to his garden, to the beds of spice, to browse in the garden and to gather lilies. My lover belongs to me and I to him; he browses among the lilies.

You are as beautiful as Thersa, my beloved, as lovely as Jerusalem, as awe-inspiring as bannered troops. Who is this that comes forth like the dawn, as beautiful as the moon, as resplendent as the sun, as awe-inspiring as bannered troops?

His left hand is under my head and his right arm embraces me. I adjure you, daughters of Jerusalem, by the gazelles and hinds of the field, do not arouse, do not stir up love, before its own time. Who is this coming up from the desert, leaning upon her lover? Under the apple tree I awakened you; it was there that your mother conceived you, it was there that your parent conceived. Set me as a seal on your heart, as a seal on your arm; for stern as death is love, relentless as the nether world is devotion; its flames are a blazing fire. Deep waters cannot quench love, nor floods sweep it away. Were one to offer all he owns to purchase love, he would be roundly mocked. Be swift, my lover, like a gazelle or a young stag on the mountains of spices!

CHAPTER SIXTEEN

A Divided Kingdom:
The Eleven Reigns in Judah

"O ISRAEL, LOOK TO THY OWN HOUSE . . ."

Rehoboam went to Shechem, for all Israel had come to Shechem to make him king. And when Jeroboam the son of Nebat heard of it (for he was still in Egypt, whither he had fled from King Solomon), then Jeroboam returned from Egypt. And they sent and called him; and Jeroboam and all the assembly of Israel came and said to Rehoboam, "Your father made our yoke heavy. Now therefore lighten the hard service of your father and his heavy yoke upon us, and we will serve you." He said to them, "Depart for three days, then come again to me." So the people went away.

Then King Rehoboam took counsel with the old men, who had stood before Solomon his father while he was yet alive, saying, "How do you advise me to answer this people?" And they said to him, "If you will be a servant to this people today and serve them, and speak good words to them when you answer them, then they will be your servants for ever." But he forsook the counsel which the old men gave him, and took counsel with the young men who had grown up with him and stood before him. And he said to them, "What do you advise that we answer this people who have said to me, 'Lighten the yoke that your father put upon us'?" And the young men who had grown up with him said to him, "Thus shall you speak to this people who said to you, 'Your father made our yoke heavy, but do you lighten it for us'; thus shall you say to them, 'My little finger is thicker than my father's loins. And now, whereas my father laid upon you a heavy yoke, I will add to your yoke. My father chastised you with whips, but I will chastise you with scorpions.'"

So Jeroboam and all the people came to Rehoboam the third day, as the king said, "Come to me again the third day." And the king answered the people harshly, and forsaking the counsel which the old men had given him, he spoke to them according to the counsel of the young men, saying, "My father made your yoke heavy, but I will add to your yoke; my father chastised you with whips, but I will chastise you with scorpions." So the king did not hearken to the people; for it was a turn of affairs brought about by the Lord that he might fulfill his word, which the Lord spoke by Ahijah the Shilonite to Jeroboam the son of Nebat.

And when all Israel saw that the king did not hearken to them, the people answered the king, "What portion have we in David? We have no inheritance in the son of Jesse. To your tents, O Israel! Look now to your own house, David." So Israel departed to their tents. But Rehoboam reigned over the people of Israel who dwelt in the cities of Judah. Then King Rehoboam sent Adoram, who was taskmaster over the forced labor, and all Israel stoned him to death with stones. And King Rehoboam made haste to mount his chariot, to flee to Jerusalem. So Israel has been in rebellion against the house of David to this day. And when all Israel heard that Jeroboam had returned, they sent and called him to the assembly and made him king over all Israel. There was none that followed the house of David, but the tribe of Judah only.

THE LORD REMEMBERS HIS PEOPLE

Rehoboam dwelt in Jerusalem, and he built cities for defense in Judah. And the priests and the Levites that were in all Israel resorted to him from all places where they lived. For the Levites left their common lands and their holdings and came to Judah and Jerusalem, because Jeroboam and his sons cast them out from serving as priests of the Lord, and he appointed his own priests for the high places, and for the satyrs, and for the calves which he had made. And those who had set their hearts to seek the Lord God of Israel came after them from all the tribes of Israel to Jerusalem to sacrifice to the Lord, the God of their fathers. They strengthened the kingdom of Judah, and for three years they made Rehoboam the son of Solomon secure, for they walked for three years in the way of David and Solomon.

When the rule of Rehoboam was established and was strong, he forsook the law of the Lord, and all Israel with him. In the fifth year of King Rehoboam, because they had been unfaithful to the Lord, Shishak king of Egypt came up against Jerusalem with twelve hundred chariots and sixty thousand horsemen. And the people were without number who came with him from Egypt—Libyans, Sukkiim, and Ethiopians. And he took the fortified cities of Judah and came as far as

Jerusalem. Then Shemaiah the prophet came to Rehoboam and to the princess of Judah, who had gathered at Jerusalem because of Shishak, and said to them, "Thus says the Lord, 'You abandoned me, so I have abandoned you to the hand of Shishak.' " Then the princes of Israel and the king humbled themselves and said, "The Lord is righteous." When the Lord saw that they humbled themselves, the word of the Lord came to Shemaiah: "They have humbled themselves; I will not destroy them, but I will grant them some deliverance, and my wrath shall not be poured out upon Jerusalem by the hand of Shishak. Nevertheless they shall be servants to him, that they may know my service and the service of the kingdoms of the countries."

So Shishak king of Egypt came up against Jerusalem; he took away the treasures of the house of the Lord and the treasures of the king's house; he took away everything. He also took away the shields of gold which Solomon had made; and King Rehoboam made in their stead shields of bronze, and committed them to the hands of the officers of the guard, who kept the door of the king's house. And as often as the king went into the house of the Lord, the guard came and bore them, and brought them back to the guardroom. And when he humbled himself the wrath of the Lord turned from him, so as not to make a complete destruction; moreover, conditions were good in Judah.

So King Rehoboam established himself in Jerusalem and reigned. Rehoboam was forty-one years old when he began to reign, and he reigned seventeen years in Jerusalem, the city which the Lord had chosen out of all the tribes of Israel to put his name there. His mother's name was Naamah the Ammonitess. And he did evil, for he did not set his heart to seek the Lord.

Now the acts of Rehoboam, from first to last, are they not written in the chronicles of Shemaiah the prophet and Iddo the seer? There were continual wars between Rehoboam and Jeroboam. And Rehoboam slept with his fathers, and was buried in the city of David; and Abijah his son reigned in his stead.

In the eighteenth year of King Jeroboam Abijah began to reign over Judah. He reigned for three years in Jerusalem. His mother's name was Micaiah the daughter of Uriel of Gibe-ah.

Now there was war between Abijah and Jeroboam. Abijah went out to battle having an army of valiant men of war, four hundred thousand picked men; and Jeroboam drew up his line of battle against him with eight hundred thousand picked mighty warriors. Then Abijah stood up on Mount Zemaraim which is in the hill country of Ephraim, and said, "Hear me, O Jeroboam and all Israel! Ought you not to know that the Lord God of Israel gave the kingship over Israel for ever to David and his sons by a covenant of salt? Yet Jeroboam the son of Nebat, a servant of Solomon the son of David, rose up and rebelled against his lord; and certain worthless scoundrels gathered about him and defied Rehoboam the son of Solomon, when Rehoboam was young and irresolute and could not withstand them.

"And now you think to withstand the kingdom of the Lord in the hand of the sons of David, because you are a great multitude and have with you the golden calves which Jeroboam made you for gods. Have you not driven out the priests of the Lord, the sons of Aaron, and the Levites, and made priests for yourselves like the peoples of other lands? Whoever comes to consecrate himself with a young bull or seven rams becomes a priest of what are no gods. But as for us, the Lord is our God, and we have not forsaken him. We have priests ministering to the Lord who are sons of Aaron, and Levites for their service. They offer to the Lord every morning and every evening burnt offerings and incense of sweet spices, set out the showbread on the table of pure gold, and care for the golden lampstand that its lamps may burn every evening; for we keep the charge of the Lord our God, but you have forsaken him. Behold, God is with us at our head, and his priests with their battle trumpets to sound the call to battle against you. O sons of Israel, do not fight against the Lord, the God of your fathers; for you cannot succeed."

Jeroboam had sent an ambush around to come on them from behind; thus his troops were in front of Judah, and the ambush was behind them; and they cried to the Lord, and the priests blew the trumpets. Then the men of Judah raised the battle shout. And when the men of Judah shouted, God defeated Jeroboam and all Israel before Abijah and Judah. The men of Israel fled before Judah, and God gave them into their hand.

ISRAEL INSTRUCTED IN THE WAYS OF GOD

So Abijah slept with his fathers, and they buried him in the city of David; and Asa his son reigned in his stead. In his days the land had rest for ten years. And Asa did what was good and right in the eyes of the Lord his God. He took away the foreign altars and the high places, and broke down the pillars and hewed down the Asherim, and commanded Judah to seek the Lord, the God of their fathers, and to keep the law and the commandment.

And there was war between Asa and Baasha king of Israel all their days. Baasha king of Israel went up against Judah, and built Ramah, that he might permit no one to go out or come in to Asa king of Judah. Then Asa took all the silver and the gold that were left in the treasures of the house of the Lord and the treasures of the king's house, and gave them into the hands of his servants; and King Asa sent them to Ben-hadad the son of Tabrimmon, the son of Hezi-on, king of Syria, who dwelt in Damascus, saying, "Let there be a league between me and you, as between my father and your father: behold, I am sending to you a present of silver and gold; go, break your league with Baasha king of Israel, that he may withdraw from me." And Ben-hadad hearkened to King Asa, and sent the commanders of his armies against the cities of Israel, and conquered Ijon, Dan, Abel-beth-maacah, and all Chinneroth, with all the land of Naphtali. And when Baasha heard of it, he stopped building Ramah, and he dwelt in Tirzah. Then King Asa made a proclamation to all Judah, none was exempt, and they carried away the stones of Ramah and its timber, with which Baasha had been building; and with them King Asa built Geba of Benjamin and Mizpah. Now the rest of all the acts of Asa, all his might, and all that he did, and the cities which he built, are they not written in the Book of the Chronicles of the Kings of Judah? But in his old age he was diseased in his feet. And Asa slept with his fathers, and was buried with his fathers in the city of David his father.

Jehoshaphat his son reigned in his stead, and strengthened himself against Israel. He placed forces in all the fortified cities of Judah, and set garrisons in the land of Judah, and in the cities of Ephraim which Asa his father had taken. The Lord was with Jehoshaphat, because he walked in the earlier ways of his father; he did not seek the Baals, but sought the God of his father and walked in his commandments, and not according to the ways of Israel. Therefore the Lord established the kingdom in his hand; and all Judah brought tribute to Jehoshaphat; and he had great riches and honor.

After this the Moabites and Ammonites, and with them some of the Me-unites, came against Jehoshaphat for battle. Some men came and told Jehoshaphat, "A great multitude is coming against you from Edom, from beyond the sea; and, behold, they are in Hazazon-tamar" (that is, En-gedi). Then Jehoshaphat feared, and set himself to seek the Lord, and proclaimed a fast throughout all Judah. And Judah assembled to seek help from the Lord; from all the cities of Judah they came to seek the Lord.

And they rose early in the morning and went out into the wilderness of Tekoa; and as they went out, Jehoshaphat stood and said, "Hear me, Judah and inhabitants of Jerusalem! Believe in the Lord your God, and you will be established; believe his prophets, and you will succeed." And when he had taken counsel with the people, he appointed those who were to sing to the Lord and praise him in holy array, as they went before the army, and say, "Give thanks to the Lord, for his steadfast love endures for ever." And when they began to sing and praise, the Lord set an ambush against the men of Ammon, Moab, and Mount Seir, who had come against Judah, so that they were routed. For the men of Ammon and Moab rose against the inhabitants of Mount Seir, destroying them utterly, and when they had made an end of the inhabitants of Seir, they all helped to destroy one another.

After this Jehoshaphat king of Judah joined with Ahaziah king of Israel, who did wickedly. He joined him in building ships to go to Tarshish, and they built the ships in Ezion-geber. Then Eliezer the son of Dodavahu of Mareshah prophesied against Jehoshaphat, saying, "Because you have joined with Ahaziah, the Lord will destroy what you have made." And the ships were wrecked and were not able to go to Tarshish.

A PROPHECY COMES TRUE

Jehoshaphat slept with his fathers, and was buried with his fathers in the city of David; and Jehoram his son reigned in his stead. Jehoram was thirty-two years old when he became king, and he reigned eight years in Jerusalem. And he walked in the way of the kings of Israel, as the house of Ahab had done; for the daughter of Ahab was his wife. And he did what was evil in the sight of the Lord. Yet the Lord would not destroy the house of David, because of the covenant which he had made with David, and since he had promised to give a lamp to him and to his sons for ever.

In his days Edom revolted from the rule of Judah, and set up a king of their own. Then Jehoram passed over with his commanders and all his chariots, and he rose by night and smote the Edomites who had surrounded him and his chariot commanders. So Edom revolted from the rule of Judah to this day. At that time Libnah also revolted from his rule, because he had forsaken the Lord, the God of his fathers.

Moreover he made high places in the hill country of Judah, and led the inhabitants of Jerusalem into unfaithfulness, and made Judah go astray. And a letter came to him from Elijah the prophet, saying, "Thus says the Lord, the God of David your father, 'Because you have not walked in the ways of Jehoshaphat your father, or in the ways of Asa king of Judah, but have walked in the way of the kings of Israel, and have led Judah and the inhabitants of Jerusalem into unfaithfulness, as the house of Ahab led Israel into unfaithfulness, and also you have killed your brothers, of your father's house, who were better than yourself; behold, the Lord will bring a great plague on your people, your children, your wives, and all your possessions, and you yourself will have a severe sickness with a disease of your bowels, until your bowels come out because of the disease, day by day.' "

And the Lord stirred up against Jehoram the anger of the Philistines and of the Arabs who are near the Ethiopians; and they came up against Judah, and invaded it, and carried away all the possessions they found that belonged to the king's house, and also his sons and his wives, so that no son was left to him except Jehoahaz, his youngest son.

And after all this the Lord smote him in his bowels with an incurable disease. In course of time, at the end of two years, his bowels came out because of the disease, and he died in great agony. His people made no fire in his honor, like the fires made for his fathers. He was thirty-two years old when he began to reign, and he reigned eight years in Jerusalem; and he departed with no one's regret. They buried him in the city of David, but not in the tombs of the kings.

And the inhabitants of Jerusalem made Ahaziah his youngest son king in his stead; for the band of men that came with the Arabs to the camp had slain all the older sons. So Ahaziah the son of Jehoram king of Judah reigned. Ahaziah was forty-two years old when he began to reign, and he reigned one year in Jerusalem. His mother's name was Athaliah, the granddaughter of Omri. He also walked in the ways of the house of Ahab, for his mother was his counselor in doing wickedly. He did what was evil in the sight of the Lord, as the house of Ahab had done; for after the death of his father they were his counselors, to his undoing. He even followed their counsel, and went with Jehoram the son of Ahab king of Israel to make war against Hazael king of Syria at Ramoth-gilead. And the Syrians wounded Joram.

And when Jehu was executing judgment upon the house of Ahab, he met the princes of Judah and the sons of Ahaziah's brothers, who attended Ahaziah, and he killed them. He searched for Ahaziah, and he was captured while hiding in Samaria, and he was brought to Jehu and put to death. They buried him, for they said, "He is the grandson of Jehoshaphat, who sought the Lord with all his heart."

A WOMAN IS PUT TO DEATH

Now when Athaliah the mother of Ahaziah saw that her son was dead, she arose and destroyed all the royal family. But Jehosheba, the daughter of King Joram, sister of Ahaziah, took Joash the son of Ahaziah, and stole him away from among the king's sons who were about to be slain, and she put him and his nurse in a bedchamber. Thus she hid him from Athaliah, so that he was not slain; and he remained with her six years, hid in the house of the Lord, while Athaliah reigned over the land.

But in the seventh year Jehoiada sent and brought the captains of the Carites and of the guards, and had them come to him in the house of the Lord; and he made a covenant with them and put them under the oath in the house of the Lord, and he showed them the king's son. And he commanded them, "This is the thing that you shall do: one third of you, those who come off duty on the sabbath and guard the king's house (another third being at the gate Sur and a third at the gate behind the guards), shall guard the palace; and the two divisions of you, which come on duty in force on the sabbath and guard the house of the Lord, shall surround the king, each with his weapons in his hand; and whoever approaches the ranks is to be slain. Be with the king when he goes out and when he comes in."

The captains did according to all that Jehoiada the priest commanded, and each brought his men who were to go off duty on the sabbath, with those who were to come on duty on the sabbath, and came to Jehoiada the priest. And the priest delivered to the captains the spears and shields that had been King David's, which were in the house of the Lord; and the guards stood, every man with his weapons in his hand, from the south side of the house to the north side of the house, around the altar and the house. Then he brought out the king's son, and put the crown upon him, and gave him the testimony; and they proclaimed him king, and anointed him; and they clapped their hands, and said, "Long live the king!"

When Athaliah heard the noise of the guard and of the people, she went into the house of the Lord to the people; and when she looked, there was the king standing by the pillar, according to the custom, and the captains and the trumpeters beside the king, and all the people of the land rejoicing and blowing trumpets. And Athaliah rent her clothes, and cried, "Treason! Treason!" Then Jehoiada the priest commanded the captains who were set over the army, "Bring her out between the ranks; and slay with the sword any one who follows her." For the priest said, "Let her not be slain in the house of the Lord." So they laid hands on her; and she went through the horses' entrance to the king's house, and there she was slain.

In the seventh year of Jehu Jehoash began to reign, and he reigned forty years in Jerusalem. His mother's name was Zibiah of Beer-sheba. And Jehoash did what was right in the eyes of the Lord all his days, because Jehoiada the priest instructed him. Nevertheless the high places were not taken away; the people continued to sacrifice and burn incense on the high places.

But Jehoiada grew old and full of days, and died; he was a hundred and thirty years old at his death. And they buried him in the city of David among the kings, because he had done good in Israel, and toward God and his house.

Now after the death of Jehoiada the princes of Judah came and did obeisance to the king; then the king hearkened to them. And they forsook the house of the Lord, the God of their fathers, and served the Asherim and the idols. And wrath came upon Judah and Jerusalem for this their guilt. Yet he sent prophets among them to bring them back to the Lord; these testified against them, but they would not give heed.

Then the Spirit of God took possession of Zechariah the son of Jehoiada the priest; and he stood above the people, and said to them, "Thus says God, 'Why do you transgress the commandments of the Lord, so that you cannot prosper? Because you have forsaken the Lord, he has forsaken you.'" But they conspired against him, and by command of the king they stoned him with stones in the court of the house of the Lord. Thus Joash the king did not remember the kindness which Jehoiada, Zechariah's father, had shown him, but killed his son. And when he was dying, he said, "May the Lord see and avenge!"

At the end of the year the army of the Syrians came up against Joash. They came to Judah and Jerusalem, and destroyed all the princes of the people from among the people, and sent all their spoil to the king of Damascus. Though the army of the Syrians had come with few men, the Lord delivered into their hand a very great army, because they had forsaken the Lord, the God of their fathers. Thus they executed judgment on Joash.

When they had departed from him, leaving him severely wounded, his servants conspired against him because of the blood of the son of Jehoiada the priest, and slew him on his bed. So he died; and they buried him in the city of David, but they did not bury him in the tombs of the kings. Those who conspired against him were Zabad the son of Shime-ath the Ammonitess, and Jehozabad the son of Shimrith the Moabitess. Accounts of his sons, and of the many oracles against him, and the rebuilding of the house of God are written in the Commentary on the Book of the Kings. And Amaziah his son reigned in his stead.

ANOTHER CYCLE OF KINGS

Amaziah was twenty-five years old when he began to reign, and he reigned twenty-nine years in Jerusalem. His mother's name was Jehoaddan of Jerusalem. And he did what was right in the eyes of the Lord, yet not with a blameless heart. And as soon as the royal power was firmly in his hand he killed his servants who had slain the king his father. But he did not put their children to death, according to what is written in the law, in the book of Moses, where the Lord commanded, "The father shall not be put to death for the children, or the children be put to death for the fathers; but every man shall die for his own sin."

Then Amaziah assembled the men of Judah, and set them by fathers' houses under commanders of thousands and of hundreds for all Judah and Benjamin. He mustered those twenty years old and upward, and found that they were three hundred thousand picked men, fit for war, able to handle spear and shield. He hired also a hundred thousand mighty men of valor from Israel for a hundred talents of silver. But a man of God came to him and said, "O king, do not let the army of Israel go with you, for the Lord is not with Israel, with all these Ephraimites. But if you suppose that in this way you will be strong for war, God will cast you down before the enemy; for God has power to help or to cast down." And Amaziah said to the man of God, "But what shall we do about the hundred talents which I have given to the army of Israel?" The man of God answered, "The Lord is able to give you much more than this." Then Amaziah discharged the army that had come to him from Ephraim, to go home again. And they became very angry with Judah, and returned home in fierce anger. But Amaziah took courage, and led out his people, and went to the Valley of Salt and smote ten thousand alive, and threw them down from the top of the rock; and they were all dashed to pieces. But the men of the army whom Amaziah sent back, not letting them go with him to battle, fell upon the cities of Judah, from Samaria to Beth-horon, and killed three thousand people in them, and took much spoil.

Then Amaziah king of Judah took counsel and sent to Joash the son of Jehoahaz, son of Jehu, king of Israel, saying, "Come, let us look one another in the face." And Joash the king of Israel sent word to Amaziah king of Judah, "A thistle on Lebanon sent to a cedar on Lebanon, saying, 'Give your daughter to my son for a wife'; and a wild beast of Lebanon passed by and trampled down the thistle. You say, 'See, I have smitten Edom,' and your heart has lifted you up in boastfulness. But now stay at home; why should you provoke trouble so that you fall, you and Judah with you?"

So Joash king of Israel went up; and he and Amaziah king of Judah faced one another in battle at Beth-shemesh, which belongs to Judah. And Judah was defeated by Israel, and every man fled to his home. And Joash king of Israel captured Amaziah king of Judah, the son of Joash, son of Ahaziah, at Beth-shemesh, and brought him to Jerusalem, and broke down the wall of Jerusalem for four hundred cubits, from the Ephraim Gate to the Corner Gate. And he seized all the gold and silver, and all the vessels that were found in the house of God, and Obed-edom with them; he seized also the treasuries of the king's house, and hostages, and he returned to Samaria.

Amaziah the son of Joash king of Judah lived fifteen years after the death of Joash the son of Jehoahaz, king of Israel. Now the rest of the deed of Amaziah, from first to last, are they not written in the Book of the Kings of Judah and Israel? From the time when he turned away from the Lord they made a conspiracy against him in Jerusalem, and he fled to Lachish. But they sent after him to Lachish, and slew him there. And they brought him upon horses; and he was buried with his fathers in the city of David.

And all the people of Judah took Uzziah, who was sixteen years old, and made him king instead of his father Amaziah. He built Eloth and restored it to Judah, after the king slept with his fathers. Uzziah was sixteen years old when he began to reign, and he reigned fifty-two years in Jerusalem. His mother's name was Jecoliah of Jerusalem. And he did what was right in the eyes of the Lord, according to all that his father Amaziah had done.

But when he was strong he grew proud, to his destruction. For he was false to the Lord his God, and entered the temple of the Lord to burn incense on the altar of incense. But Azariah the priest went in after him, with eighty priests of the Lord who were men of valor; and they withstood King Uzziah, and said to him, "It is not for you, Uzziah, to burn incense to the Lord, but for the priests the sons of Aaron, who are consecrated to burn incense. Go out of the sanctuary; for you have done wrong, and it will bring you no honor from the Lord God." Then Uzziah was angry. Now he had a censer in his hand to burn incense, and when he became angry with the priests leprosy broke out on his forehead, in the presence of the priests in the house of the Lord, by the altar of incense. And Azariah the chief priest, and all the priests, looked at him, and behold, he was leprous in his forehead! And they thrust him out quickly, and he himself hastened to go out, because the Lord had smitten him. And King Uzziah was a leper to the day of his death, and being a leper dwelt in a separate house, for he was excluded from the house of the Lord. And Jotham his son was over the king's household, governing the people of the land.

Now the rest of the acts of Uzziah, from first to last, Isaiah the prophet the son of Amoz wrote. And Uzziah slept with his fathers, and they buried him with his fathers in the burial field which belonged to the kings, for they said, "He is a leper." And Jotham his son reigned in his stead.

Jotham was twenty-five years old when he began to reign, and he reigned sixteen years in Jerusalem. His mother's name was Jerushah the daughter of Zadok. And he did what was right in the eyes of the Lord according to all that his father Uzziah had done—only he did not invade the temple of the Lord. But the people still followed corrupt practices. He built the upper gate of the house of the Lord, and did much building on the wall of Ophel. Moreover he built cities in the hill country of Judah, and forts and towers on the wooded hills. He fought with the king of the Ammonites and prevailed against them. And the Ammonites gave him that year a hundred talents of silver, and ten thousand cors of wheat and ten thousand of barley. The Ammonites paid him the same amount in the second and the third years. So Jotham became mighty, because he ordered his ways before the Lord his God. Now the rest of the acts of Jotham, and all his wars, and his ways, behold, they are written in the Book of the Kings of Israel and Judah. He was twenty-five years old when he began to reign, and he reigned sixteen years in Jerusalem. And Jotham slept with his fathers, and they buried him in the city of David; and Ahaz his son reigned in his stead.

CHAPTER SEVENTEEN

The Separated Kingdom of Israel

A MONARCH DEFECTS

And Jeroboam said in his heart, "Now the kingdom will turn back to the house of David; if this people go up to offer sacrifices in the house of the Lord at Jerusalem, then the heart of this people will turn again to their Lord, to Rehoboam king of Judah, and they will kill me and return to Rehoboam king of Judah." So the king took counsel, and made two calves of gold. And he said to the people, "You have gone up to Jerusalem long enough. Behold your gods, O Israel, who brought you up out of the land of Egypt." And he set one in Bethel, and the other he put in Dan. And this thing became a sin, for the people went to the one at Bethel and to the other as far as Dan. He also made houses on high places, and appointed priests from among all the people, who were not of the Levites. And Jeroboam appointed a feast on the fifteenth day of the eighth month like the feast that was in Judah, and he offered sacrifices upon the altar; so he did in Bethel, sacrificing to the calves that he had made. And he placed in Bethel the priests of the high places that he had made. He went up to the altar which he had made in Bethel on the fifteenth day in the eighth month, in the month which he had devised of his own heart; and he ordained a feast for the people of Israel, and went up to the altar to burn incense.

And behold, a man of God came out of Judah by the word of the Lord to Bethel. Jeroboam was standing by the altar to burn incense. And the man cried against the altar by the word of the Lord, and said, "O altar, altar, thus says the Lord: 'Behold, a son shall be born to the house of David, Josiah by name; and he shall sacrifice upon you the priests of the high places who burn incense upon you, and men's bones shall be burned upon you.'" And he gave a sign the same day, saying, "This is the sign that the Lord has spoken: 'Behold, the altar shall be torn down, and the ashes that are upon it shall be poured out.'" And when the king heard the saying of the man of God, which he cried against the altar at Bethel, Jeroboam stretched out his hand from the altar, saying, "Lay hold of him." And his hand, which he stretched out against him, dried up, so that he could not draw it back to himself. The altar also was torn down, and the ashes poured out from the altar, according to the sign which the man of God had given by the word of the Lord. And the king said to the man of God, "Entreat now the favor of the Lord your God, and pray for me, that my hand may be restored to me." And the man of God entreated the Lord; and the king's hand was restored to him, and became as it was before.

After this thing Jeroboam did not turn from his evil way, but made priests for the high places again from among all the people; any who would, he consecrated to be priests of the high places. And this thing became sin to the house of Jeroboam, so as to cut it off and to destroy it from the face of the earth.

THE STORY OF THE FIVE LEADERS

Nadab the son of Jeroboam began to reign over Israel in the second year of Asa king of Judah; and he reigned over Israel two years. He did what was evil in the sight of the Lord, and walked in the way of his father, and in his sin which he made Israel to sin.

Baasha the son of Ahijah, of the house of Issachar, conspired against him; and Baasha struck him down at Gibbethon, which belonged to the Philistines; for Nadab and all Israel were laying siege to Gibbethon. So Baasha killed him in the third year of Asa king of Judah, and reigned in his stead. And as soon as he was king, he killed all the house of Jeroboam; he left to the house of Jeroboam not one that breathed, until he had destroyed it, according to the word of the Lord which he spoke by his servant Ahijah the Shilonite; it was for the sins of Jeroboam which he sinned and which he made Israel to sin, and because of the anger to which he provoked the Lord, the God of Israel.

Now the rest of the acts of Nadab, and all that he did, are they not written in the Book of the Chronicles of the Kings of Israel? And there was war between Asa and Baasha king of Israel all their days.

In the third year of Asa king of Judah, Baasha the son of Ahijah began to reign over all Israel at Tirzah, and reigned twenty-four years. He did what was evil in the sight of the Lord, and walked in the way of Jeroboam and in his sin which he made Israel to sin.

The Separated Kingdom of Israel

In the twenty-sixth year of Asa king of Judah, Elah the son of Baasha began to reign over Israel in Tirzah, and reigned two years. But his servant Zimri, commander of half his chariots, conspired against him. When he was at Tirzah, drinking himself drunk in the house of Arza, who was over the household in Tirzah, Zimri came in and struck him down and killed him, in the twenty-seventh year of Asa king of Judah, and reigned in his stead.

Thus Zimri destroyed all the house of Baasha, according to the word of the Lord, which he spoke against Baasha by Jehu the prophet, for all the sins of Baasha and the sins of Elah his son which they sinned, and which they made Israel to sin, provoking the Lord God of Israel to anger with their idols. Now the rest of the acts of Elah, and all that he did, are they not written in the Book of the Chronicles of the Kings of Israel?

In the twenty-seventh year of Asa king of Judah, Zimri reigned seven days in Tirzah. Now the troops were encamped against Gibbethon, which belonged to the Philistines, and the troops who were encamped heard it said, "Zimri has conspired, and he has killed the king"; therefore all Israel made Omri, the commander of the army, king over Israel that day in the camp. So Omri went up from Gibbethon, and all Israel with him, and they besieged Tirzah. And when Zimri saw that the city was taken, he went into the citadel of the king's house, and burned the king's house over him with fire, and died, because of his sins which he committed, doing evil in the sight of the Lord, walking in the way of Jeroboam, and for his sin which he committed, making Israel to sin.

In the thirty-first year of Asa king of Judah, Omri began to reign over Israel, and reigned for twelve years; six years he reigned in Tirzah. He bought the hill of Samaria from Shemer for two talents of silver; and he fortified the hill, and called the name of the city which he built, Samaria, after the name of Shemer, the owner of the hill.

Omri did what was evil in the sight of the Lord, and did more evil than all who were before him. For he walked in all the way of Jeroboam the son of Nebat, and in the sins which he made Israel to sin, provoking the Lord, the God of Israel, to anger by their idols. Now the rest of the acts of Omri which he did, and the might that he showed, are they not written in the Book of the Chronicles of the Kings of Israel? And Omri slept with his fathers, and was buried in Samaria; and Ahab reigned in his stead.

THE WRATH OF GOD FALLS UPON THE PEOPLE

In the thirty-eighth year of Asa king of Judah, Ahab the son of Omri began to reign over Israel, and Ahab the son of Omri reigned over Israel in Samaria twenty-two years. And Ahab the son of Omri did evil in the sight of the Lord more than all that were before him. And as if it had been a light thing for him to walk in the sins of Jeroboam the son of Nebat, he took for wife Jezebel the daughter of Ethbaal king of the Sidonians, and went and served Baal, and worshiped him. He erected an altar for Baal in the house of Baal, which he built in Samaria. and Ahab made an Asherah. Ahab did more to provoke the Lord, the God of Israel, to anger than all the kings of Israel who were before him. In his days Hiel of Bethel built Jericho; he laid its foundation at the cost of Abiram his first-born, and set up its gates at the cost of his youngest son Segub, according to the word of the Lord, which he spoke by Joshua the son of Nun.

Now Elijah the Tishbite, of Tishbe in Gilead, said to Ahab, "As the Lord God of Israel lives, before whom I stand, there shall be neither dew nor rain these years, except by my word." And the word of the Lord came to him, "Depart from here and turn eastward, and hide yourself by the brook Cherith, that is east of the Jordan. You shall drink from the brook, and I have commanded the ravens to feed you there." So he went and did according to the word of the Lord; he went and dwelt by the brook Cherith that is east of the Jordan. And the ravens brought him bread and meat in the morning, and bread and meat in the evening; and he drank from the brook. And after a while the brook dried up, because there was no rain in the land.

Then the word of the Lord came to him, "Arise, go to Zarephath, which belongs to Sidon, and dwell there. Behold, I have commanded a widow there to feed you." So he arose and went to Zarephath; and when he came to the gate of the city, behold, a widow was there gathering sticks; and he called to her and said, "Bring me a little water in a vessel, that I may drink." And as she was going to bring it, he called to her and said, "Bring me a morsel of bread in your hand." And she said, "As the Lord your God lives, I have nothing baked, only a handful of meal in a jar, and a little oil in a cruse; and now, I am gathering a couple of sticks, that I may go in and prepare it for myself and my son, that we may eat it, and die." And Elijah said to her, "Fear not; go and do as you have said; but first make me a little cake of it and bring it to me, and afterward make for yourself and your son. For thus says the Lord the God of Israel, 'The jar of meal shall not be spent, and the cruse of oil shall not fail, until the day that the Lord sends rain upon the earth.'" And she went and did as Elijah said; and she, and he, and her household ate for many days. The jar of meal was not spent, neither did the cruse of oil fail, according to the word of the Lord which he spoke by Elijah.

After this the son of the woman, the mistress of the house, became ill; and his illness was so severe that there was no breath left in him. And she said to Elijah, "What have you against me, O man of God? You have come to me to bring my sin to remembrance, and to cause the death of my son!" And he said to her, "Give me your son." And he took him from her bosom, and carried him up into the upper chamber, where he lodged, and laid him upon his own bed. And he cried to the Lord, "O Lord my God, hast thou brought calamity even upon the widow with whom I sojourn, by slaying her son?" Then he stretched himself upon the child three times, and cried to the Lord, "O Lord my God, let this child's soul come into him again." And the Lord hearkened to the voice of Elijah; and the soul of the child came into him again, and he revived. And Elijah took the child, and brought him down from the upper chamber into the house, and delivered him to his mother; and Elijah said, "See, your son lives." And the woman said to Elijah, "Now I know that you are a man of God, and that the word of the Lord in your mouth is truth."

A PROPHET COMES TO THE RESCUE

After many days the word of the Lord came to Elijah, in the third year, saying, "Go, show yourself to Ahab; and I will send rain upon the earth." So Elijah went to show himself to Ahab. Now the famine was severe in Samaria. When Ahab saw Elijah, Ahab said to him, "Is it you, you troubler of Israel?" And he answered, "I have not troubled Israel; but you have, and your father's house, because you have forsaken the commandments of the Lord and followed the Baals. Now therefore send and gather all Israel to me at Mount Carmel, and the four hundred and fifty prophets of Baal and the four hundred prophets of Asherah, who eat at Jezebel's table.

So Ahab sent to all the people of Israel, and gathered the prophets together at Mount Carmel. And Elijah came near to all the people, and said, "How long will you go limping with two different opinions? If the Lord is God, follow him; but if Baal, then follow him." And the people did not answer him a word. Then Elijah said to the people, "I, even I only, am left a prophet of the Lord; but Baal's prophets are four hundred and fifty men. Let two bulls be given to us; and let them choose one bull for themselves, and cut it in pieces and lay it on the wood, but put no fire to it; and I will prepare the other bull and lay it on the wood, and put no fire to it. And you call on the name of your god and I will call on the name of the Lord; and the God who answers by fire, he is God." And all the people answered, "It is well spoken." Then Elijah said to the prophets of Baal, "Choose for yourselves one bull and prepare it first, for you are many; and call on the name of your god, but put no fire to it." And they took the bull which was given them, and they prepared it, and called on the name of Baal from morning until noon, saying, "O Baal, answer us!" But there was no voice, and no one answered. And they limped about the altar which they had made. And at noon Elijah mocked them, saying, "Cry aloud, for he is a god; either he is musing, or he has gone aside, or he is on a journey, or perhaps he is asleep and must be awakened." And they cried aloud, and cut themselves after their custom with swords and lances, until the blood gushed out upon them. And as midday passed, they raved on until the time of the offering of the oblation, but there was no voice; no one answered, no one heeded.

Then Elijah said to all the people, "Come near to me"; and all the people came near to him. And he repaired the altar of the Lord that had been thrown down; Elijah took twelve stones, according to the number of the tribes of the sons of Jacob, to whom the word of the Lord came, saying, "Israel shall be your name"; and with the stones he built an altar in the name of the Lord. And he made a trench about the altar, as great as would contain two measures of seed. And he put the wood in order, and cut the bull in pieces and laid it on the wood. And he said, "Fill four jars with water, and pour it on the burnt offering, and on the wood." And he said, "Do it a second time"; and they did it a second time. And he said, "Do it a third time"; and they did it a third time. And the water ran round about the altar, and filled the trench also with water.

And at the time of the offering of the oblation, Elijah the prophet came near and said, "O Lord, God of Abraham, Isaac, and Israel, let it be known this day that thou art God in Israel, and that I am thy servant, and that I have done all these things at thy word. Answer me, O Lord, answer me, that this people may know that thou, O Lord, art

God, and that thou hast turned their hearts back." Then the fire of the Lord fell, and consumed the burnt offering, and the wood, and the stones, and the dust, and licked up the water that was in the trench. And when all the people saw it, they fell on their faces; and they said, "The Lord, he is God; the Lord, he is God." And Elijah said to them, "Seize the prophets of Baal; let not one of them escape." And they seized them; and Elijah brought them down to the brook Kishon, and killed them there.

And Elijah said to Ahab, "Go up, eat and drink; for there is a sound of the rushing rain." So Ahab went up to eat and to drink. And Elijah went up to the top of Carmel; and he bowed himself down upon the earth, and put his face between his knees. And he said to his servant, "Go up now, look toward the sea." And he went up and looked, and said, "There is nothing." And he said, "Go again seven times." And at the seventh time he said, "Behold, a little cloud like a man's hand is rising out of the sea." And he said, "Go up, say to Ahab, 'Prepare your chariot and go down, lest the rain stop you.'" And in a little while the heavens grew black with clouds and wind, and there was a great rain. And Ahab rode and went to Jezreel. And the hand of the Lord was on Elijah; and he girded up his loins and ran before Ahab to the entrance of Jezreel.

Ahab told Jezebel all that Elijah had done, and how he had slain all the prophets with the sword. Then Jezebel sent a messenger to Elijah, saying, "So may the gods do to me, and more also, if I do not make your life as the life of one of them by this time tomorrow." Then he was afraid, and he arose and went for his life, and came to Beersheba, which belongs to Judah, and left his servant there.

But he himself went a day's journey into the wilderness, and came and sat down under a broom tree; and he asked that he might die, saying, "It is enough; now, O Lord, take away my life; for I am no better than my fathers." And he lay down and slept under a broom tree; and behold, an angel touched him, and said to him, "Arise and eat." And he looked, and behold, there was at his head a cake baked on hot stones and a jar of water. And he ate and drank, and lay down again. And the angel of the Lord came again a second time, and touched him, and said, "Arise and eat, else the journey will be too great for you." And he arose, and ate and drank, and went in the strength of that food forty days and forty nights to Horeb the mount of God.

And there he came to a cave, and lodged there; and behold, the word of the Lord came to him, and he said to him, "What are you doing here, Elijah?" He said, "I have been very jealous for the Lord, the God of hosts; for the people of Israel have forsaken thy covenant, thrown down thy altars, and slain thy prophets with the sword; and I, even I only, am left; and they seek my life, to take it away." And he said, "Go forth, and stand upon the mount before the Lord." And behold, the Lord passed by, and a great and strong wind rent the mountains, and broke in pieces the rocks before the Lord, but the Lord was not in the wind; and after the wind an earthquake, but the Lord was not in the earthquake; and after the earthquake a fire, but the Lord was not in the fire; and after the fire a still small voice. And when Elijah heard it, he wrapped his face in his mantle and went out and stood at the entrance of the cave. And behold, there came a voice to him, and said, "What are you doing here, Elijah?" He said, "I have been very jealous for the Lord, the God of hosts; for the people of Israel have forsaken thy covenant, thrown down thy altars, and slain thy prophets with the sword; and I, even I only, am left; and they seek my life, to take it away." And the Lord said to him, "Go, return on your way to the wilderness of Damascus; and when you arrive, you shall anoint Hazael to be king over Syria; and Jehu the son of Nimshi you shall anoint to be king over Israel; and Elisha the son of Shaphat of Abel-meholah you shall anoint to be prophet in your place. And him who escapes from the sword of Hazael shall Jehu slay; and him who escapes from the sword of Jehu shall Elisha slay. Yet I will leave seven thousand in Israel, all the knees that have not bowed to Baal, and every mouth that has not kissed him."

So he departed from there, and found Elisha the son of Shaphat, who was plowing, with twelve yoke of oxen before him, and he was with the twelfth. Elijah passed by him and cast his mantle upon him. And he left the oxen, and ran after Elijah, and said, "Let me kiss my father and my mother, and then I will follow you." And he said to him, "Go back again; for what have I done to you?" And he returned from following him, and took the yoke of oxen, and slew them, and boiled their flesh with the yokes of the oxen, and gave it to the people, and they ate. Then he arose and went after Elijah, and ministered to him.

THE VINEYARD OF NABOTH

Now Naboth the Jezreelite had a vineyard in Jezreel, beside the palace of Ahab king of Samaria. And after this Ahab said to Naboth, "Give me your vineyard, that I may have it for a vegetable garden, because it is near my house; and I will give you a better vineyard for it; or, if it seems good to you, I will give you its value in money." But Naboth said to Ahab, "The Lord forbid that I should give you the inheritance of my fathers."

And Jezebel his wife said to him, "Do you now govern Israel? Arise, and eat bread, and let your heart be cheerful; I will give you the vineyard of Naboth the Jezreelite."

So she wrote letters in Ahab's name and sealed them with his seal, and she sent the letters to the elders and the nobles who dwelt with Naboth in his city. And she wrote in the letters, "Proclaim a fast, and set Naboth on high among the people; and set two base fellows opposite him, and let them bring a charge against him, saying, 'You have cursed God and the king.' Then take him out, and stone him to death." And the men of his city, the elders and the nobles who dwelt in his city, did as Jezebel had sent word to them. As it was written in the letters which she had sent to them, they proclaimed a fast, and set Naboth on high among the people. And the two base fellows came in and sat opposite him; and the base fellows brought a charge against Naboth, in the presence of the people, saying, "Naboth cursed God and the king." So they took him outside the city, and stoned him to death with stones. Then they sent to Jezebel, saying, "Naboth has been stoned; he is dead."

As soon as Jezebel heard that Naboth had been stoned and was dead, Jezebel said to Ahab, "Arise, take possession of the vineyard of Naboth the Jezreelite, which he refused to give you for money; for Naboth is not alive, but dead." And as soon as Ahab heard that Naboth was dead, Ahab arose to go down to the vineyard of Naboth the Jezreelite, to take possession of it.

Then the word of the Lord came to Elijah the Tishbite, saying, "Arise, go down to meet Ahab king of Israel, who is in Samaria; behold, he is in the vineyard of Naboth, where he has gone to take possession. And you shall say to him, 'Thus says the Lord, "Have you killed, and also taken possession?" ' And you shall say to him, 'Thus says the Lord: "In the place where dogs licked up the blood of Naboth shall dogs lick your own blood." ' "

Ahab said to Elijah, "Have you found me, O my enemy?" He answered, "I have found you, because you have sold yourself to do what is evil in the sight of the Lord. And I will make your house like the house of Jeroboam the son of Nebat, and like the house of Baasha the son of Ahijah, for the anger to which you have provoked me, and because you have made Israel to sin. And of Jezebel the Lord also said, 'The dogs shall eat Jezebel within the bounds of Jezreel.' Any one belonging to Ahab who dies in the city the dogs shall eat; and any one of his who dies in the open country the birds of the air shall eat."

(There was none who sold himself to do what was evil in the sight of the Lord like Ahab, whom Jezebel his wife incited. He did very abominably in going after idols, as the Amorites had done, whom the Lord cast out before the people of Israel.)

And when Ahab heard those words, he rent his clothes, and put sackcloth upon his flesh, and fasted and lay in sackcloth, and went about dejectedly. All the word of the Lord came to Elijah the Tishbite, saying, "Have you seen how Ahab has humbled himself before me? Because he has humbled himself before me, I will not bring the evil in his days; but in his son's days I will bring the evil upon his house."

THE DEATH OF A MAN

For three years Syria and Israel continued without war. But in the third year Jehoshaphat the king of Judah came down to the king of Israel. And the king of Israel said to his servants, "Do you know that Ramoth-gilead belongs to us, and we keep quiet and do not take it out of the hand of the king of Syria?" And he said to Jehoshaphat, "Will you go with me to battle at Ramoth-gilead?" And Jehoshaphat said to the king of Israel, "I am as you are, my people as your people, my horses as your horses."

And Jehoshaphat said to the king of Israel, "Inquire first for the word of the Lord." Then the king of Israel gathered the prophets together, about four hundred men, and said to them, "Shall I go to battle against Ramoth-gilead, or shall I forbear?" And they said, "Go up; for the Lord will give it into the hand of the king." But Jehoshaphat said, "Is there not here another prophet of the Lord of whom we may inquire?" And the king of Israel said to Jehoshaphat, "There is yet one man by whom we may inquire of the Lord, Micaiah the son of Imlah; but I hate him, for he never prophesies good concerning me, but evil." And Jehoshaphat said, "Let not the king say so." Then the king of Israel summoned an officer and said, "Bring quickly Micaiah the son of Imlah."

And when he had come to the king, the king said to him, "Micaiah, shall we go to Ramoth-gilead to battle, or shall we forbear?" And he answered him, "Go up and triumph; the Lord will give it into the hand of the king." But the king said to him, "How many times shall I adjure you that you speak to me nothing but the truth in the name of the Lord?" And he said, "I saw all Israel scattered upon the mountains, as sheep that have no shepherd; and the Lord said, 'These have no master; let each return to his home in peace.'"

And the king of Israel said, "Seize Micaiah, and take him back to Amon the governor of the city and to Joash the king's son; and say, 'Thus says the king, "Put this fellow in prison, and feed him with scant fare of bread and water, until I come in peace."'" And Micaiah said, "If you return in peace, the Lord has not spoken by me." And he said, "Hear, all you peoples!"

So the king of Israel and Jehoshaphat the king of Judah went up to Ramoth-gilead. And the king of Israel said to Jehoshaphat, "I will disguise myself and go into battle, but you wear your robes." And the king of Israel disguised himself and went into battle. Now the king of Syria had commanded the thirty-two captains of his chariots, "Fight with neither small nor great, but only with the king of Israel." And when the captains of the chariots saw Jehoshaphat, they said, "It is surely the king of Israel." So they turned to fight against him; and Jehoshaphat cried out. And when the captains of the chariots saw that it was not the king of Israel, they turned back from pursuing him. But a certain man drew his bow at a venture, and struck the king of Israel between the scale armor and the breastplate; therefore he said to the driver of his chariot, "Turn about, and carry me out of the battle, for I am wounded." And the battle grew hot that day, and the king was propped up in his chariot facing the Syrians, until at evening he died; and the blood of the wound flowed into the bottom of the chariot. And about sunset a cry went through the army, "Every man to his city, and every man to his country!"

So the king died, and was brought to Samaria; and they buried the king in Samaria. And they washed the chariot by the pool of Samaria, and the dogs licked up his blood, and the harlots washed themselves in it, according to the word of the Lord which he had spoken. Now the rest of the acts of Ahab, and all that he did, and the ivory house which he built, and all the cities that he built, are they not written in the Book of the Chronicles of the Kings of Israel? So Ahab slept with his fathers; and Ahaziah his son reigned in his stead.

A JOURNEY TO GOD

After the death of Ahab, Moab rebelled against Israel. Now Ahaziah fell through the lattice in his upper chamber in Samaria, and lay sick; so he sent messengers, telling them, "Go, inquire of Baal-zebub, the god of Ekron, whether I shall recover from this sickness." But the angel of the Lord said to Elijah the Tishbite, "Arise, go up to meet the messengers of the king of Samaria, and say to them, 'Is it because there is no God in Israel that you are going to inquire of Baal-zebub, the god of Ekron?' Now therefore thus says the Lord, 'You shall not come down from the bed to which you have gone, but you shall surely die.' " So Elijah went.

The messengers returned to the king, and he said to them, "Why have you returned?" And they said to him, "There came a man to meet us, and said to us, 'Go back to the king who sent you, and say to him, Thus says the Lord, Is it because there is no God in Israel that you are sending to inquire of Baal-zebub, the god of Ekron? Therefore you shall not come down from the bed to which you have gone, but shall surely die.' " He said to them, "What kind of man was he who came to meet you and told you these things?" They answered him, "He wore a garment of haircloth, with a girdle of leather about his loins." And he said, "It is Elijah the Tishbite." So he died according to the word of the Lord which Elijah had spoken. Jehoram, his brother, became king in his stead in the second year of Jehoram the son of Jehoshaphat, king of Judah, because Ahaziah had no son.

Now when the Lord was about to take Elijah up to heaven by a whirlwind, Elijah and Elisha were on their way from Gilgal. And Elijah said to Elisha, "Tarry here, I pray you; for the Lord has sent me as far as Bethel." But Elisha said, "As the Lord lives, and as you yourself live, I will not leave you." So they went down to Bethel. And the sons of the prophets who were in Bethel came out to Elisha, and said to him, "Do you know that today the Lord will take away your master from over you?" And he said, "Yes, I know it; hold your peace."

Elijah said to him, "Elisha, tarry here, I pray you; for the Lord has sent me to Jericho." But he said, "As the Lord lives, and as you yourself live, I will not leave you." So they came to Jericho. The sons of the prophets who were at Jericho drew near to Elisha, and said to him, "Do you know that today the Lord will take away your master from over you?" And he answered, "Yes, I know it; hold your peace."

Then Elijah said to him, "Tarry here, I pray you; for the Lord has sent me to the Jordan." But he said, "As the Lord lives, and as you yourself live, I will not leave you." So the two of them went on. Fifty men of the sons of the prophets also went, and stood at some distance from them, as they both were standing by the Jordan. Then Elijah took his mantle, and rolled it up, and struck the water, and the water was parted to the one side and to the other, till the two of them could go over on dry ground.

When they had crossed, Elijah said to Elisha, "Ask what I shall do for you, before I am taken from you." And Elisha said, "I pray you, let me inherit a double share of your spirit." And he said, "You have asked a hard thing; yet, if you see me as I am being taken from you, it shall be so for you; but if you do not see me, it shall not be so." And as they still went on and talked, behold, a chariot of fire and horses of fire separated the two of them. And Elijah went up by a whirlwind into heaven. And Elisha saw it and cried, "My father, my father! the chariots of Israel and its horsemen!" And he saw him no more.

Then he took hold of his own clothes and rent them in two pieces. And he took up the mantle of Elijah that had fallen from him, and went back and stood on the bank of the Jordan. Then he took the mantle of Elijah that had fallen from him, and struck the water, saying, "Where is the Lord, the God of Elijah?" And when he had struck the water, the water was parted to the one side and to the other; and Elisha went over. Now when the sons of the prophets who were at Jericho saw him over against them, they said, "The spirit of Elijah rests on Elisha." And they came to meet him, and bowed to the ground before him.

AN ARMY GENERAL IS CLEANSED

Naaman, commander of the army of the king of Syria, was a great man with his master and in high favor, because by him the Lord had given victory to Syria. He was a mighty man of valor, but he was a leper. Now the Syrians on one of their raids had carried off a little maid from the land of Israel, and she waited on Naaman's wife. She said to her mistress, "Would that my lord were with the prophet who is in Samaria! He would cure him of his leprosy." So Naaman went in and told his lord, "Thus and so spoke the maiden from the land of Israel." And the king of Syria said, "Go now, and I will send a letter to the king of Israel." So he went, taking with him ten talents of silver, six thousand shekels of gold, and ten festal garments. And he brought the letter to the king of Israel, which read, "When this letter reaches you, know that I have sent to you Naaman my servant, that you may cure him of his leprosy." And when the king of Israel read the letter, he rent his clothes and said, "Am I God, to kill and to make alive, that this man sends word to me to cure a man of his leprosy? Only consider, and see how he is seeking a quarrel with me."

But when Elisha the man of God heard that the king of Israel had rent his clothes, he sent to the king, saying, "Why have you rent your clothes? Let him come now to me, that he may know that there is a prophet in Israel." So Naaman came with his horses and chariots, and halted at the door of Elisha's house. And Elisha sent a messenger to him, saying, "Go and wash in the Jordan seven times, and your flesh shall be restored, and you shall be clean." But Naaman was angry, and went away, saying, "Behold, I thought that he would surely come out to me, and stand, and call on the name of the Lord his God, and wave his hand over the place, and cure the leper. Are not Abana and Pharpar, the rivers of Damascus, better than all the waters of Israel? Could I not wash in them, and be clean?" So he turned and went away in a rage. But his servants came near and said to him, "My father, if the prophet had commanded you to do some great thing, would you not have done it? How much rather, then, when he says to you, 'Wash, and be clean'?" So he went down and dipped himself seven times in the Jordan, according to the word of the man of God; and his flesh was restored like the flesh of a little child, and he was clean.

Then he returned to the man of God, he and all his company, and he came and stood before him; and he said, "Behold, I know that there is no God in all the earth but in Israel; so accept now a present from your servant." But he said, "As the Lord lives, whom I serve, I will receive none." And he urged him to take it, but he refused. Then Naaman said, "If not, I pray you, let there be given to your servant two mules' burden of earth; for henceforth your servant will not offer burnt offering or sacrifice to any god but the Lord. In this matter may the Lord pardon your servant: when my master goes into the house of Rimmon to worship there, leaning on my arm, and I bow myself in the house of Rimmon, when I bow myself in the house of Rimmon, the Lord pardon your servant in this matter." He said to him, "Go in peace."

But when Naaman had gone from him a short distance, Gehazi, the servant of Elisha the man of God, said, "See, my master has spared this Naaman the Syrian, in not accepting from his hand what he brought. As the Lord lives, I will run after him, and get something from him." So Gehazi followed Naaman. And when Naaman saw some one running after him, he alighted from the chariot to meet him, and said, "Is all well?" And he said, "All is well. My master has sent me to say, 'There have just now come to me from the hill country of Ephraim two young men of the sons of the prophets; pray, give them a talent of silver and two festal garments.'" And Naaman said, "Be pleased to accept two talents." And he urged him, and tied up two talents of silver in two bags, with two festal garments, and laid them upon two of his servants; and they carried them before Gehazi. And when he came to the hill, he took them from their hand, and put them in the house; and he sent the men away, and they departed. He went in, and stood before his master, and Elisha said to him, "Where have you been, Gehazi?" And he said, "Your servant went nowhere." But he said to him, "Did I not go with you in spirit when the man turned from his chariot to meet you? Was it a time to accept money and garments, olive orchards and vineyards, sheep and oxen, menservants and maidservants? Therefore the leprosy of Naaman shall cleave to you, and to your descendants for ever." So he went out from his presence a leper, as white as snow.

GREATER WONDERS ARE RECORDED

Now the sons of the prophets said to Elisha, "See, the place where we dwell under your charge is too small for us. Let us go to the Jordan and each of us get there a log, and let us make a place for us to dwell there." And he answered, "Go." Then one of them said, "Be pleased to go with your servants." And he answered, "I will go." So he went with them. And when they came to the Jordan, they cut down trees. But as one was felling a log, his axe head fell into the water; and he cried out, "Alas, my master! It was borrowed." Then the man of God said, "Where did it fall?" When he showed him the place, he cut off a stick, and threw it in there, and made the iron float. And he said, "Take it up." So he reached out his hand and took it.

Once when the king of Syria was warring against Israel, he took counsel with his servants, saying, "At such and such a place shall be my camp." But the man of God sent word to the king of Israel, "Beware that you do not pass this place, for the Syrians are going down there."

And the king of Israel sent to the place of which the man of God told him. Thus he used to warn him, so that he saved himself there more than once or twice.

And the mind of the king of Syria was greatly troubled because of this thing; and he called his servants and said to them, "Will you not show me who of us is for the king of Israel?" And one of the servants said, "None, my lord, O king; but Elisha, the prophet who is in Israel, tells the king of Israel the words that you speak in your bedchamber." And he said, "Go and see where he is, that I may send and seize him." It was told him, "Behold, he is in Dothan." So he sent there horses and chariots and a great army; and they came by night, and surrounded the city.

When the servant of the man of God rose early in the morning and went out, behold, an army with horses and chariots was round about the city. And the servant said, "Alas, my master! What shall we do?" He said, "Fear not, for those who are with us are more than those who are with them." Then Elisha prayed, and said, "O Lord, I pray thee, open his eyes that he may see." So the Lord opened the eyes of the young man, and he saw; and behold, the mountain was full of horses and chariots of fire round about Elisha. And when the Syrians came down against him, Elisha prayed to the Lord, and said, "Strike this people, I pray thee, with blindness." So he struck them with blindness in accordance with the prayer of Elisha. And Elisha said to them, "This is not the way, and this is not the city; follow me, and I will bring you to the man whom you seek." And he led them to Samaria.

As soon as they entered Samaria, Elisha said, "O Lord, open the eyes of these men, that they may see." So the Lord opened their eyes, and they saw; and lo, they were in the midst of Samaria. When the king of Israel saw them he said to Elisha, "My father, shall I slay them? Shall I slay them?" He answered, "You shall not slay them. Would you slay those whom you have taken captive with your sword and with your bow? Set bread and water before them, that they may eat and drink and go to their master." So he prepared for them a great feast; and when they had eaten and drunk, he sent them away, and they went to their master. And the Syrians came no more on raids into the land of Israel.

A KING DEFIES GOD

Then Elisha the prophet called one of the sons of the prophets and said to him, "Gird up your loins, and take this flask of oil in your hand,

and go to Ramoth-gilead. And when you arrive, look there for Jehu the son of Jehoshaphat, son of Nimshi; and go in and bid him rise from among his fellows, and lead him to an inner chamber. Then take the flask of oil, and pour it on his head, and say, 'Thus say the Lord, I anoint you king over Israel.' Then open the door and flee; do not tarry."

So the young man, the prophet, went to Ramoth-gilead. And when he came, behold, the commanders of the army were in council; and he said, "I have an errand to you, O commander." And Jehu said, "To which of us all?" And he said, "To you, O commander." So he arose, and went into the house; and the young man poured the oil on his head, saying to him, "Thus says the Lord the God of Israel, I anoint you king over the people of the Lord, over Israel. And you shall strike down the house of Ahab your master, that I may avenge on Jezebel the blood of all the servants of the Lord. And I will make the house of Ahab like the house of Jeroboam the son of Nebat, and like the house of Baasha the son of Ahijah. And the dogs shall eat Jezebel in the territory of Jezreel, and none shall bury her." Then he opened the door, and fled.

When Jehu came out to the servants of his master, they said to him, "Is all well? Why did this mad fellow come to you?" And he said to them, "You know the fellow and his talk." And they said, "That is not true; tell us now." And he said, "Thus and so he spoke to me, saying, 'Thus says the Lord, I anoint you king over Israel.'" Then in haste every man of them took his garment, and put it under him on the bare steps, and they blew the trumpet, and proclaimed, "Jehu is king."

Thus Jehu the son of Jehoshaphat the son of Nimshi conspired against Joram. (Now Joram with all Israel had been on guard at Ramoth-gilead against Hazael king of Syria; but King Joram had returned to be healed in Jezreel of the wounds which the Syrians had given him, when he fought with Hazael king of Syria.) So Jehu said, "If this is your mind, then let no one slip out of the city to go and tell the news in Jezreel." Then Jehu mounted his chariot, and went to Jezreel, for Joram lay there. And Ahaziah king of Judah had come down to visit Joram.

Now the watchman was standing on the tower in Jezreel, and he spied the company of Jehu as he came, and said, "I see a company." And Joram said, "Take a horseman, and send to meet them, and let him say, 'Is it peace?'" So a man on horseback went to meet him, and said, "Thus says the king, 'Is it peace?'" And Jehu said, "What have you to do with peace? Turn round and ride behind me." And the watchman reported, saying, "The messenger reached them, but he is not coming back." Then he sent out a second horseman, who came to them, and said, "Thus the king has said, 'Is it peace?'" And Jehu answered, "What have you to do with peace? Turn round and ride behind me." Again the watchman reported, "He reached them, but he is not coming back. And the driving is like the driving of Jehu the son of Nimshi; for he drives furiously."

Joram said, "Make ready." And they made ready his chariot. Then Joram king of Israel and Ahaziah king of Judah set out, each in his chariot, and went to meet Jehu, and met him at the property of Naboth the Jezreelite. And when Joram saw Jehu, he said, "Is it peace, Jehu?" He answered, "What peace can there be, so long as the harlotries and the sorceries of your mother Jezebel are so many?" Then Joram reined about and fled, saying to Ahaziah, "Treachery, O Ahaziah!" And Jehu drew his bow with his full strength, and shot Joram between the shoulders, so that the arrow pierced his heart, and he sank in his chariot. Jehu said to Bidkar his aide, "Take him up, and cast him on the plot of ground belonging to Naboth the Jezreelite; for remember, when you and I rode side by side behind Ahab his father, how the Lord uttered this oracle against him: 'As surely as I saw yesterday the blood of Naboth and the blood of his sons—says the Lord—I will requite you on this plot of ground.' Now therefore take him up and cast him on the plot of ground, in accordance with the word of the Lord."

When Ahaziah the king of Judah saw this, he fled in the direction of Beth-haggan. And Jehu pursued him, and said, "Shoot him also"; and they shot him in the chariot at the ascent of Gur, which is by Ibleam. And he fled to Megiddo, and died there. His servants carried him in a chariot to Jerusalem, and buried him in his tomb with his fathers in the city of David.

In the eleventh year of Joram the son of Ahab, Ahaziah began to reign over Judah.

When Jehu came to Jezreel, Jezebel heard of it; and she painted her eyes, and adorned her head, and looked out of the window. And as Jehu entered the gate, she said, "Is it peace, you Zimri, murderer of your master?" And he lifted up his face to the window, and said, "Who is on my side? Who?" Two or three eunuchs looked out at him. He said, "Throw her down." So they threw her down; and some of her blood spattered on the wall and on the horses, and they trampled on her. Then he went in and ate and drank; and he said, "See now to this cursed woman, and bury her; for she is a king's daughter." But when they went to bury her, they found no more of her than the skull and the feet and the palms of her hands. When they came back and told him, he said, "This is the word of the Lord, which he spoke by his servant Elijah the Tishbite, 'In the territory of Jezreel the dogs shall eat the flesh of Jezebel; and the corpse of Jezebel shall be as dung upon the face of the field in the territory of Jezreel, so that no one can say, This is Jezebel.'"

Then Jehu assembled all the people, and said to them, "Ahab served Baal a little; but Jehu will serve him much. Now therefore call to me all the prophets of Baal, all his worshipers and all his priests; let none be missing, for I have a great sacrifice to offer to Baal; whoever is missing shall not live." But Jehu did it with cunning in order to destroy the worshipers of Baal. And Jehu ordered, "Sanctify a solemn assembly for Baal." So they proclaimed it. And Jehu sent throughout all Israel; and all the worshipers of Baal came, so that there was not a man left who did not come. And they entered the house of Baal, and the house of Baal was filled from one end to the other. He said to him who was in charge of the wardrobe, "Bring out the vestments for all the worshipers of Baal." So he brought out the vestments for them. Then Jehu went into the house of Baal with Jehonadab the son of Rechab; and he said to the worshipers of Baal, "Search, and see that there is no servant of the Lord here among you, but only the worshipers of Baal." Then he went in to offer sacrifices and burnt offerings.

Now Jehu had stationed eighty men outside, and said, "The man who allows any of those whom I give into your hands to escape shall forfeit his life." So as soon as he had made an end of offering the burnt offering, Jehu said to the guard and to the officers, "Go in and slay them; let not a man escape." So when they put them to the sword, the guard and the officers cast them out and went into the inner room of the house of Baal and they brought out the pillar that was in the house of Baal, and burned it. And they demolished the pillar of Baal, and demolished the house of Baal, and made it a latrine to this day. Thus Jehu wiped out Baal from Israel. But Jehu did not turn aside from the sins of Jeroboam the son of Nebat, which he made Israel to sin, the golden calves that were in Bethel, and in Dan.

So Jehu slept with his fathers, and they buried him in Samaria. And Jehoahaz his son reigned in his stead. The time that Jehu reigned over Israel in Samaria was twenty-eight years.

THE STORY OF EIGHT KINGDOMS

In the twenty-third year of Joash the son of Ahaziah, king of Judah, Jehoahaz the son of Jehu began to reign over Israel in Samaria, and he reigned seventeen years. He did what was evil in the sight of the Lord, and followed the sins of Jeroboam the son of Nebat, which he made Israel to sin; he did not depart from them. And the anger of the Lord was kindled against Israel, and he gave them continually into the hand of Hazael king of Syria and into the hand of Ben-hadad the son of Hazael. Then Jehoahaz besought the Lord, and the Lord hearkened to him; for he saw the oppression of Israel, how the king of Syria oppressed them. (Therefore the Lord gave Israel a savior, so that they escaped from the hand of the Syrians; and the people of Israel dwelt in their homes as formerly. Nevertheless they did not depart from the sins of the house of Jeroboam, which he made Israel to sin, but walked in them, and the Asherah also remained in Samaria.) For there was not left to Jehoahaz an army of more then fifty horsemen and ten chariots and ten thousand footmen; for the king of Syria had destroyed them and made them like the dust at threshing. Now the rest of the acts of Jehoahaz and all that he did, and his might, are they not written in the Book of the Chronicles of the Kings of Israel? So Jehoahaz slept with his fathers, and they buried him in Samaria; and Joash his son reigned in his stead.

In the thirty-seventh year of Joash king of Judah Jehoash the son of Jehoahaz began to reign over Israel in Samaria, and he reigned sixteen years. He also did what was evil in the sight of the Lord; he did not depart from all the sins of Jeroboam the son of Nebat, which he made Israel to sin, but he walked in them.

Now when Elisha had fallen sick with the illness of which he was to die, Joash king of Israel went down to him, and wept before him, crying, "My father, my father! The chariots of Israel and its horsemen!" And Elisha said to him, "Take a bow and arrows"; so he took a bow and arrows. Then he said to the king of Israel, "Draw the bow"; and he drew it. And Elisha laid his hands upon the king's hands. And he said, "Open the window eastward"; and he opened it. Then Elisha said, "Shoot"; and he shot. And he said, "The Lord's arrow of victory, the arrow of victory over Syria! For you shall fight the Syrians in Aphek until you have made an end of them." And he said, "Take the arrows"; and he took them. And he said to the king of Israel, "Strike the ground with them"; and he struck three times, and stopped. Then the man of

God was angry with him, and said, "You should have struck five or six times; then you would have struck down Syria until you had made an end of it, but now you will strike down Syria only three times."

So Elisha died, and they buried him. Now bands of Moabites used to invade the land in the spring of the year. And as a man was being buried, lo, a marauding band was seen and the man was cast into the grave of Elisha; and as soon as the man touched the bones of Elisha, he revived, and stood on his feet.

Now Hazael king of Syria oppressed Israel all the days of Jehoahaz. But the Lord was gracious to them and had compassion on them, and he turned toward them, because of his covenant with Abraham, Isaac, and Jacob, and would not destroy them; nor has he cast them from his presence until now.

When Hazael king of Syria died, Ben-hadad his son became king in his stead. Then Jehoash the son of Jehoahaz took again from Ben-hadad the son of Hazael the cities which he had taken from Jehoahaz his father in war. Three times Joash defeated him and recovered the cities of Israel.

In the fifteenth year of Amaziah the son of Joash, king of Judah, Jeroboam the son of Joash, king of Israel, began to reign in Samaria, and he reigned forty-one years. And he did what was evil in the sight of the Lord; he did not depart from all the sins of Jeroboam the son of Nebat, which he made Israel to sin. He restored the border of Israel from the entrance of Hamath as far as the Sea of the Arabah, according to the word of the Lord, the God of Israel, which he spoke by his servant Jonah the son of Amittai, the prophet, who was from Gath-hepher. For the Lord saw that the affliction of Israel was very bitter, for there was none left, bond or free, and there was none to help Israel. But the Lord had not said that he would blot out the name of Israel from under heaven, so he saved them by the hand of Jeroboam the son of Joash.

Now the rest of the acts of Jeroboam, and all that he did, and his might, how he fought, and how he recovered for Israel Damascus and Hamath, which had belonged to Judah, are they not written in the Book of the Chronicles of the Kings of Israel? And Jeroboam slept with his fathers, the kings of Israel, and Zechariah his son reigned in his stead.

In the thirty-eighth year of Azariah, king of Judah Zechariah the son of Jeroboam reigned over Israel in Samaria six months. And he did what was evil in the sight of the Lord, as his fathers had done. He did not depart from the sins of Jeroboam the son of Nebat, which he made Israel to sin. Shallum the son of Jabesh conspired against him, and struck him down at Ibleam, and killed him, and reigned in his stead. Shallum the son of Jabesh began to reign in the thirty-ninth year of Uzziah king of Judah, and he reigned one month in Samaria. Then Menahem the son of Gadi came up from Tirzah and came to Samaria, and he struck down Shallum the son of Jabesh in Samaria and slew him, and reigned in his stead.

In the thirty-ninth year of Azariah king of Judah Menahem the son of Gadi began to reign over Israel, and he reigned ten years in Samaria. And he did what was evil in the sight of the Lord; he did not depart all his days from all the sins of Jeroboam the son of Nebat, which he made Israel to sin. Pul the king of Assyria came against the land; and Menahem gave Pul a thousand talents of silver, that he might help him to confirm his hold of the royal power. Menahem exacted the money from Israel, that is, from all the wealthy men, fifty shekels of silver from every man, to give to the king of Assyria. So the king of Assyria turned back, and did not stay there in the land. Now the rest of the deed of Menahem, and all that he did, are they not written in the Book of the Chronicles of the Kings of Israel? And Menahem slept with his fathers, and Pekahiah his son reigned in his stead.

In the fiftieth year of Azariah king of Judah Pekahiah the son of Menahem began to reign over Israel in Samaria, and he reigned two years. And he did what was evil in the sight of the Lord; he did not turn away from the sins of Jeroboam the son of Nebat, which he made Israel to sin. And Pekah the son of Remaliah, his captain, conspired against him with fifty men of the Gileadites, and slew him in Samaria, in the citadel of the king's house; he slew him, and reigned in his stead. Now the rest of the deeds of Pekahiah, and all that he did, behold, they are written in the Book of the Chronicles of the Kings of Israel.

In the fifty-second year of Azariah king of Judah Pekah the son of Remaliah began to reign over Israel in Samaria, and reigned twenty years. And he did what was evil in the sight of the Lord; he did not depart from the sins of Jeroboam the son of Nebat, which he made Israel to sin. In the days of Pekah king of Israel, Tiglath-pileser king of Assyria came and captured Ijon, Abel-beth-maacah, Janoah, Kedesh, Hazor, Gilead, and Galilee, all the land of Naphtali; and he carried the people captive to Assyria. Then Hoshea the son of Elah made a conspiracy against Pekah the son of Remaliah, and struck him down, and slew him, and reigned in his stead, in the twentieth year of Jotham the son of Uzziah.

ISRAEL IN CAPTIVITY

In the twelfth year of Ahaz king of Judah Hoshea the son of Elah began to reign in Samaria over Israel, and he reigned nine years. And he did what was evil in the sight of the Lord, yet not as the kings of Israel who were before him. Against him came up Shalmaneser king of Assyria; and Hoshea became his vassal, and paid him tribute. But the king of Assyria found treachery in Hoshea; for he had sent messengers to So, king of Egypt, and offered no tribute to the king of Assyria, as he had done year by year; therefore the king of Assyria shut him up, and bound him in prison. Then the king of Assyria invaded all the land and came to Samaria, and for three years he besieged it. In the ninth year of Hoshea the king of Assyria captured Samaria, and he carried the Israelites away to Assyria, and placed them in Halah, and on the Habor, the river of Gozan, and in the cities of the Medes. And this was so, because the people of Israel had sinned against the Lord their God, who had brought them up out of the land of Egypt from under the hand of Pharaoh king of Egypt, and had feared other gods.

And the king of Assyria brought people from Babylon, Cuthah, Avva, Hamath, and Sepharvaim, and placed them in the cities of Samaria instead of the people of Israel; and they took possession of Samaria, and dwelt in its cities. And at the beginning of their dwelling there, they did not fear the Lord; therefore the Lord sent lions among them, which killed some of them. So the king of Assyria was told, "The nations which you have carried away and placed in the cities of Samaria do not know the law of the god of the land; therefore he has sent lions among them, and behold, they are killing them, because they do not know the law of the god of the land." Then the king of Assyria commanded, "Send there one of the priests whom you carried away thence; and let him go and dwell there, and teach them the law of the god of the land." So one of the priests whom they had carried away from Samaria came and dwelt in Bethel, and taught them how they should fear the Lord.

But every nation still made gods of its own, and put them in the shrines of the high places which the Samaritans had made, every nation in the cities in which they dwelt; the men of Babylon made Succoth-benoth, the men of Cuth made Nergal, the men of Hamath made Ashima, and the Avvites made Nibhaz and Tartak; and the Sepharvites burned their children in the fire to Adrammelech and Anammelech, the gods of Sepharvaim. They also feared the Lord, and appointed from among themselves all sorts of people as priests of the high places, who sacrificed for them in the shrines of the high places. So they feared the Lord but also served their own gods, after the manner of the nations from among whom they had been carried away. So these nations feared the Lord, and also served their graven images; their children likewise, and their children's children—as their fathers did, so they do to this day.

CHAPTER EIGHTEEN

Significant Prophecies
Uttered About This Time

OSEE'S PROPHECY AGAINST THE KINGDOM OF ISRAEL

The word of the Lord that came to Osee, the son of Beeri, in the days of Ozia, Joatham, Achaz, Ezechia, kings of Juda, and in the days of Jeroboam, son of Joas, king of Israel.

Hear the word of the Lord, O people of Israel, for the Lord has a grievance against the inhabitants of the land: There is no fidelity, no mercy, no knowledge of God in the land. False swearing, lying, murder, stealing, and adultery! In their lawlessness, bloodshed follows bloodshed. Therefore the land mourns, and everything that dwells in it languishes: the beasts of the field, the birds of the air, and even the fish of the sea perish.

But let no one protest, let no one complain; with you is my grievance, O priests! You shall stumble in the day, and the prophets shall stumble with you at night; I will destroy your mother. My people perish for want of knowledge! Since you have rejected knowledge, I will reject you from my priesthood; since you have ignored the law of your God, I will also ignore your sons.

One and all they sin against me, exchanging their glory for shame. They feed on the sin of my people, and are greedy for their guilt. The priests shall fare no better than the people; I will punish them for their ways, and repay them for their deeds.

In their affliction, they shall look for me: "Come, let us return to the Lord, for it is he who has rent, but he will heal us; he has struck us, but he will bind our wounds. He will revive us after two days; on the third day he will raise us up, to live in his presence. Let us know, let us strive to know the Lord; as certain as the dawn is his coming, and his judgment shines forth like the light of day! He will come to us like the rain, like spring rain that waters the earth."

What can I do with you, Ephraim? What can I do with you, Juda? Your piety is like a morning cloud, like the dew that early passes away. For this reason I smote them through the prophets, I slew them by the words of my mouth; for it is love that I desire, not sacrifice, and knowledge of God rather than holocausts.

Because of your utter wickedness: at dawn the king of Israel shall perish.

When Israel was a child I loved him, out of Egypt I called my son. The more I called them, the farther they went from me, sacrificing to the Baals and burning incense to idols. Yet it was I who taught Ephraim to walk, who took them in my arms; I drew them with human cords, with bands of love; I fostered them like one who raises an infant to his cheeks; yet, though I stooped to feed my child, they did not know that I was their healer.

He shall return to the land of Egypt, and Assyria shall be his king; the sword shall begin with his cities and end by consuming his solitudes. Because they refused to repent, their own counsels shall devour them. His people are in suspense about returning to him; and God, though in unison they cry out to him, shall not raise them up.

How could I give you up, O Ephraim, or deliver you up, O Israel? How could I treat you as Adama, or make you like Seboim? My heart is overwhelmed, my pity is stirred. I will not give vent to my blazing anger, I will not destroy Ephraim again; for I am God and not man, the Holy One present among you; I will not let the flames consume you.

They shall follow the Lord, who roars like a lion; when he roars, his sons shall come frightened from the west, out of Egypt they shall come trembling, like sparrows, from the land of Assyria, like doves; and I will resettle them in their homes, says the Lord. Ephraim has surrounded me with lies, the house of Israel, with deceit; Juda is still rebellious against God, against the Holy One, who is faithful.

JOEL PLEADS FOR THE REPENTANCE OF JUDA

The word of the Lord which came to Joel, the son of Phathuel.

Hear this, you elders! Pay attention, all you who dwell in the land! Has the like of this happened in your days, or in the days of your fathers? Tell it to your children, and your children to their children, and their children to the next generation. What the cutter left, the locust swarm has eaten; what the locust swarm left, the grasshopper has eaten; and what the grasshopper left, the devourer has eaten.

Blow the trumpet in Sion, sound the alarm on my holy mountain! Let all who dwell in the land tremble, for the day of the Lord is coming; yes, it is near, a day of darkness and a day of gloom, a day of clouds and somberness!

Like dawn spreading over the mountains, a people numerous and mighty! Their like has not been from of old, nor will it be after them, even to the years of distant generations. Before them a fire devours, and after them a flame enkindles; like the garden of Eden is the land before them, and after them a desert waste; from them there is no escape.

Their appearance is that of horses; like steeds they run. As with the rumble of chariots they leap on the mountaintops; as with the crackling of a fiery flame devouring stubble; like a mighty people arrayed for battle. Before them peoples are in torment, every face blanches.

Like warriors they run, like soldiers they scale the wall; they advance, each in his own lane, without swerving from their paths. No one crowds another, each advances in his own track; though they fall into the ditches, they are not checked.

They assault the city, they run upon the wall, they climb into the houses; in at the windows they come like thieves.

Before them the earth trembles, the heavens shake; the sun and the moon are darkened, and the stars withhold their brightness.

The Lord raises his voice at the head of his army; for immense indeed is his camp, yes, mighty, and it does his bidding. For great is the day of the Lord, and exceedingly terrible; who can bear it? Yet even now, says the Lord, return to me with your whole heart, with fasting, and weeping, and mourning; rend your hearts, not your garments, and return to the Lord, your God. For gracious and merciful is he, slow to anger, rich in kindness, and relenting in punishment. Perhaps he will again relent and leave behind him a blessing, offerings and libations, for the Lord, your God.

Blow the trumpet in Sion! proclaim a fast, call an assembly; gather the people, notify the congregation; assemble the elders, gather the children and the infants at the breast; let the bridegroom quit his room, and the bride her chamber.

Between the porch and the altar let the priests, the ministers of the Lord, weep, and say, "Spare, O Lord, your people, and make not your heritage a reproach, with the nations ruling over them! Why should they say among the peoples, 'Where is their God?' "

Then the Lord was stirred to concern for his land and took pity on his people. The Lord answered and said to his people: See, I will send you grain, and wine, and oil, and you shall be filled with them; no more will I make you a reproach among the nations. No, the northerner I will remove far from you, and drive him out into a land arid and waste, with his van toward the eastern sea, and his rear toward the western sea; and his foulness shall go up, and his stench shall go up.

Fear not, O land! exult and rejoice! for the Lord has done great things. Fear not, beasts of the field! for the pastures of the plain are green; the tree bears its fruit, the fig tree and the vine give their yield.

And do you, O children of Sion, exult and rejoice in the Lord, your God! He has given you the teacher of justice: he has made the rain come down for you, the early and the late rain as before. The threshing floors shall be full of grain and the vats shall overflow with wine and oil.

And I will repay you for the years which the locust has eaten, the grasshopper, the devourer, and the cutter, my great army which I sent among you. You shall eat and be filled, and shall praise the name of the Lord, your God, because he has dealt wondrously with you; my people shall nevermore be put to shame. And you shall know that I am in the midst of Israel; I am the Lord, your God, and there is no other; my people shall nevermore be put to shame.

Then afterward I will pour out my spirit upon all mankind. Your sons and daughters shall prophesy, your old men shall dream dreams, your young men shall see visions; even upon the servants and the handmaids, in those days, I will pour out my spirit.

And I will work wonders in the heavens and on the earth, blood, fire, and columns of smoke; the sun will be turned to darkness, and the moon to blood, at the coming of the Day of the Lord, the great and terrible day. Then everyone shall be rescued who calls on the name of the Lord; for on Mount Sion there shall be a remnant, as the Lord has said, and in Jerusalem survivors whom the Lord shall call.

AMOS PREDICTS THE REJECTION OF ISRAEL

The words of Amos, a shepherd from Thecua, which he received in vision concerning Israel, in the days of Ozia, king of Juda, and in the days of Jeroboam, son of Joas, king of Israel, two years before the earthquake. Hear this word, O men of Israel, that the Lord pronounces over you, over the whole family that I brought up from the land of Egypt: You alone have I favored more than all the families of the earth; therefore I will punish you for all your crimes.

Do two walk together unless they have agreed? Does a lion roar in the forest when it has no prey? Does a young lion cry out from its den unless it has seized something? Is a bird brought to earth by a snare when there is no lure for it? Does a snare spring up from the ground without catching anything? If the trumpet sounds in a city, will the people not be frightened? If evil befalls a city, has not the Lord caused it? Indeed, the Lord God does nothing without revealing his plan to his servants, the prophets.

The lion roars—who will not be afraid! The Lord God speaks—who will not prophesy!

I hate, I spurn your feasts, I take no pleasure in your solemnities; your cereal offerings I will not accept, nor consider your stall-fed peace offerings. Away with your noisy songs! I will not listen to the melodies of your harps. But if you would offer me holocausts, then let justice surge like water, and goodness like an unfailing stream. Did you bring me sacrifices and offerings for forty years in the desert, O house of Israel? You will carry away Sakkuth, your king, and Kaiwan, your star god, the images that you have made for yourselves; for I will exile you beyond Damascus, say I, the Lord, the God of hosts by name.

Are you not like the Ethiopians to me, O men of Israel? says the Lord. Did I not bring the Israelites from the land of Egypt as I brought the Philistines from Caphtor and the Arameans from Kir? The eyes of the Lord God are on this sinful kingdom: I will destroy it from off the face of the earth.

But I will not destroy the house of Jacob completely, says the Lord. For see, I have given the command to sift the house of Israel among all the nations, as one sifts with a sieve, letting no pebble fall to the ground. By the sword shall all sinners among my people die, those who say, "Evil will not reach or overtake us." On that day I will raise up the fallen hut of David; I will wall up its breaches, raise up its ruins, and rebuild it as in the days of old, that they may conquer what is left of Edom and all the nations that shall bear my name, say I, the Lord, who will do this. Yes, days are coming, says the Lord, when the plowman shall overtake the reaper, and the vintager, him who sows the seed; the juice of grapes shall drip down the mountains, and all the hills shall run with it. I will bring about the restoration of my people Israel; they shall rebuild and inhabit their ruined cities, plant vineyards and drink the wine, set out gardens and eat the fruits. I will plant them upon their own ground; never again shall they be plucked from the land I have given them, say I, the Lord, your God.

MICHEA CONSOLES JUDA

The word of the Lord which came to Michea of Moreseth in the days of Joatham, Achaz, and Ezechia, kings of Juda: that is, the vision he received concerning Samaria and Jerusalem.

Hear, O peoples, all of you, give heed, O earth, and all that fills you! Let the Lord God be witness against you, the Lord from his holy temple!

For see, the Lord comes forth from his place, he descends and treads upon the heights of the earth. The mountains melt under him and the valleys split open, like wax before the fire, like water poured down a slope.

For the crime of Jacob all this comes to pass, and for the sins of the house of Israel. What is the crime of Jacob? Is it not Samaria? And what is the sin of the house of Juda? Is it not Jerusalem?

And I said: Hear, you leaders of Jacob, rulers of the house of Israel! Is it not your duty to know what is right, you who hate what is good, and love evil? You who tear their skin from them, and their flesh from their bones! They eat the flesh of my people, and flay their skin from them, and break their bones. They chop them in pieces like flesh in a kettle, and like meat in a caldron. When they cry to the Lord, he shall not answer them; rather shall he hide his face from them at that time, because of the evil they have done.

Thus says the Lord regarding the prophets who lead my people astray; who, when their teeth have something to bite, announce peace, but when one fails to put something in their mouth, proclaim war against him. Therefore you shall have night, not vision, darkness, not divination; the sun shall go down upon the prophets, and the day shall be dark for them.

In days to come the mount of the Lord's house shall be established higher than the mountains; it shall rise high above the hills, and peoples shall stream to it: Many nations shall come, and say, "Come, let us climb the mount of the Lord, to the house of the God of Jacob, that he may instruct us in his ways, that we may walk in his paths." For from Sion shall go forth instruction, and the word of the Lord from Jerusalem. He shall judge between many peoples and impose terms on strong and distant nations; they shall beat their swords into plowshares, and their spears into pruning hooks; one nation shall not raise the sword against another, nor shall they train for war again. Every man shall sit under his own vine or under his own fig tree, undisturbed; for the mouth of the Lord of hosts has spoken. For all the peoples walk each in the name of its god, but we will walk in the name of the Lord, our God, forever and ever.

HABACUC PROPHESIES
THE COMING OF THE CHALDEANS AGAINST JUDA

The oracle which Habacuc the prophet received in vision.

How long, O Lord? I cry for help but you do not listen! I cry out to you, "Violence!" but you do not intervene. Why do you let me see ruin; why must I look at misery? Destruction and violence are before me; there is strife, and clamorous discord. This is why the law is benumbed, and judgment is never rendered: because the wicked circumvent the just; that is why judgment comes forth perverted. Look over the nations and see, and be utterly amazed! For a work is being done in your days that you would not have believed, were it told. For see, I am raising up Chaldea, that bitter and unruly people, that marches the breadth of the land to take dwellings not his own. Terrible and dreadful is he, from himself derive his law and his majesty. Swifter than leopards are his horses, and keener than wolves at evening. His horses prance, his horsemen come from afar: they fly like the eagle hastening to devour.

I will stand at my guard post, and station myself upon the rampart, and keep watch to see what he will say to me, and what answer he will give to my complaint.

Then the Lord answered me and said: Write down the vision clearly upon the tablets, so that one can read it readily. For the vision still has its time, presses on to fulfillment, and will not disappoint; if it delays, wait for it, it will surely come, it will not be late. The rash man has no integrity; but the just man, because of his faith, shall live.

O Lord, I have heard your renown, and feared, O Lord, your work. In the course of the years revive it, in the course of the years make it known; in your wrath remember compassion!

God comes from Theman, the Holy One from Mount Pharan. Covered are the heavens with his glory, and with his praise the earth is filled. His splendor spreads like the light; rays shine forth from beside him, where his power is concealed. Before him goes pestilence, and the plague follows in his steps. He pauses to survey the earth; his look makes the nations tremble. The eternal mountains are shattered, the age-old hills bow low along his ancient ways. I see the tents of Chusan collapse; trembling are the pavilions of the land of Madian.

Is your anger against the streams, O Lord? Is your wrath against the streams, your rage against the sea, that you drive the steeds of your victorious chariot? Bared and ready is your bow, filled with arrows is your quiver. Into streams you split the earth; at sight of you the mountains tremble. A torrent of rain descends; the ocean gives forth its roar. The sun forgets to rise, the moon remains in its shelter, at the light of your flying arrows, at the gleam of your flashing spear.

In wrath you bestride the earth, in fury you trample the nations. You come forth to save your people, to save your anointed one. You crush the heads of the wicked, you lay bare their bases at the neck. You pierce with your shafts the heads of their princes whose boast would be of devouring the wretched in their lair. You tread the sea with your steeds amid the churning of the deep waters.

I hear, and my body trembles; at the sound, my lips quiver. Decay invades my bones, my legs tremble beneath me. I await the day of distress that will come upon the people who attack us. For though the fig tree blossom not nor fruit be on the vines, though the yield of the olive fail and the terraces produce no nourishment, though the flocks disappear from the fold and there be no herd in the stalls, yet will I rejoice in the Lord and exult in my saving God. God, my Lord, is my strength; he makes my feet swift as those of hinds and enables me to go upon the heights.

CHAPTER NINETEEN

Judah Undergoes a Religious Reform

UPHEAVAL DURING THE REIGN OF AHAZ

Ahaz was twenty years old when he began to reign, and he reigned sixteen years in Jerusalem. And he did not do what was right in the eyes of the Lord, like his father David, but walked in the ways of the kings of Israel. He even made molten images for the Baals; and he burned incense in the valley of the son of Hinnom, and burned his sons as an offering, according to the abominable practices of the nations whom the Lord drove out before the people of Israel. And he sacrificed and burned incense on the high places, and on the hills, and under every green tree.

Therefore the Lord his God gave him into the hand of the king of Syria, who defeated him and took captive a great number of his people and brought them to Damascus. He was also given into the hand of the king of Israel, who defeated him with great slaughter. For Pekah the son of Remaliah slew a hundred and twenty thousand in Judah in one day, all of them men of valor, because they had forsaken the Lord, the God of their fathers.

At that time King Ahaz sent to the king of Assyria for help. For the Edomites had again invaded and defeated Judah, and carried away captives. And the Philistines had made raids on the cities in the Shephelah and the Negeb of Judah, and had taken Beth-shemesh, Aijalon, Gederoth, Soco with its villages, Timnah with its villages, and Gimzo with its villages; and they settled there. For the Lord brought Judah low because of Ahaz king of Israel, for he had dealt wantonly in Judah and had been faithless to the Lord. So Tilgath-pilneser king of Assyria came against him, and afflicted him instead of strengthening him. For Ahaz took from the house of the Lord and the house of the king and of the princes, and gave tribute to the king of Assyria; but it did not help him.

In the time of his distress he became yet more faithless to the Lord—this same King Ahaz. For he sacrificed to the gods of Damascus which had defeated him, and said, "Because the gods of the kings of Syria helped them, I will sacrifice to them that they may help me." But they were the ruin of him, and of all Israel. And Ahaz gathered together the vessels of the house of God and cut in pieces the vessels of the house of God, and he shut up the doors of the house of the Lord; and he made himself altars in every corner of Jerusalem. In every city of Judah he made high places to burn incense to other gods, provoking to anger the Lord, the God of his fathers. Now the rest of his acts and all his ways, from first to last, behold, they are written in the Book of the Kings of Judah and Israel. And Ahaz slept with his fathers, and they buried him in the city, in Jerusalem, for they did not bring him into the tombs of the kings of Israel. And Hezekiah his son reigned in his stead.

HEZEKIAH BRINGS ABOUT A CHANGE

Hezekiah began to reign when he was twenty-five years old, and he reigned twenty-nine years in Jerusalem. His mother's name was Abijah the daughter of Zechariah. And he did what was right in the eyes of the Lord, according to all that David his father had done.

In the first year of his reign, in the first month, he opened the doors of the house of the Lord, and repaired them. He brought in the priests and the Levites, and assembled them in the square on the east, and said to them, "Hear me, Levites! Now sanctify yourselves, and sanctify the house of the Lord, the God of your fathers, and carry out the filth from the holy place. For our fathers have been unfaithful and have done what was evil in the sight of the Lord our God; they have forsaken him, and have turned away their faces from the habitation of the Lord, and turned their backs. They also shut the doors of the vestibule and put out the lamps, and have not burned incense or offered burnt offerings in the holy place to the God of Israel."

Then Hezekiah the king rose early and gathered the officials of the city, and went up to the house of the Lord. And they brought seven bulls, seven rams, seven lambs, and seven he-goats for a sin offering for the kingdom and for the sanctuary and for Judah. And he commanded the priests the sons of Aaron to offer them on the altar of the Lord. So they killed the bulls, and the priests received the blood and threw it against the altar; and they killed the rams and their blood was thrown against the altar; and they killed the lambs and their blood was thrown against the altar. Besides the great number of burnt offerings there was the fat of the peace offerings, and there were the libations for the burnt offerings. Thus the service of the house of the Lord was restored. And Hezekiah and all the people rejoiced because of what God had done for the people; for the thing came about suddenly.

Hezekiah sent to all Israel and Judah, and wrote letters also to Ephraim and Manasseh, that they should come to the house of the Lord at Jerusalem, to keep the passover to the Lord the God of Israel. For the king and his princes and all the assembly in Jerusalem had taken counsel to keep the passover in the second month—for they could not keep it in its time because the priests had not sanctified themselves in sufficient number, nor had the people assembled in Jerusalem—and the plan seemed right to the king and all the assembly. So they decreed to make a proclamation throughout all Israel, from Beer-sheba to Dan, that the people should come and keep the passover to the Lord the God of Israel, at Jerusalem; for they had not kept it in great numbers as prescribed.

So couriers went from city to city through the country of Ephraim and Manasseh, and as far as Zebulun; but they laughed them to scorn, and mocked them. Only a few men of Asher, of Manasseh, and of Zebulun humbled themselves and came to Jerusalem. The hand of God was also upon Judah to give them one heart to do what the king and the princes commanded by the word of the Lord. And many people came together in Jerusalem to keep the feast of unleavened bread in the second month, a very great assembly. They set to work and removed the altars that were in Jerusalem, and all the altars for burning incense they took away and threw into the Kidron valley.

AN ARMY IS DESTROYED

In the fourteenth year of King Hezekiah Sennacherib king of Assyria came up against all the fortified cities of Judah and took them. And Hezekiah king of Judah sent to the king of Assyria at Lachish, saying, "I have done wrong; withdraw from me; whatever you impose on me I will bear." And the king of Assyria required of Hezekiah king of Judah three hundred talents of silver and thirty talents of gold. And Hezekiah gave him all the silver that was found in the house of the Lord, and in the treasuries of the king's house. At that time Hezekiah stripped the gold from the doors of the temple of the Lord, and from the door-posts which Hezekiah king of Judah had overlaid and gave it to the king of Assyria. And the king of Assyria sent the Tartan, the Rabsaris, and the Rabshakeh with a great army from Lachish to King Hezekiah at Jerusalem. And they went up and came to Jerusalem. When they arrived, they came and stood by the conduit of the upper pool, which is on the highway to the Fuller's Field. Then Eliakim the son of Hilkiah, who was over the household, and Shebna the secretary, and Joah the son of Asaph, the recorder, came to Hezekiah with their clothes rent, and told him the words of the Rabshakeh.

When King Hezekiah heard it, he rent his clothes, and covered himself with sackcloth, and went into the house of the Lord. And he sent Eliakim, who was over the household, and Shebna the secretary, and the senior priests, covered with sackcloth, to the prophet Isaiah the son of Amoz. They said to him, "Thus says Hezekiah, This day is a day of distress, of rebuke, and of disgrace; children have come to the birth, and there is no strength to bring them forth. It may be that the Lord your God heard all the words of the Rabshakeh, whom his master the king of Assyria has sent to mock the living God, and will rebuke the words which the Lord your God has heard; therefore lift up your prayer for the remnant that is left." When the servants of King Hezekiah came to Isaiah, Isaiah said to them, "Say to your master, 'Thus says the Lord: Do not be afraid because of the words that you have heard, with which the servants of the king of Assyria have reviled me. Behold, I will put a spirit in him, so that he shall hear a rumor and return to his own land; and I will cause him to fall by the sword in his own land.' "

Then Isaiah the son of Amoz sent to Hezekiah, saying, "Thus says the Lord, the God of Israel: Your prayer to me about Sennacherib king of Assyria I have heard. This is the word that the Lord has spoken concerning him: She despises you, she scorns you—the virgin daughter of Zion; she wags her head behind you—the daughter of Jerusalem. Whom have you mocked and reviled? Against whom have you raised your voice and haughtily lifted your eyes? Against the Holy One of Israel!

"Therefore thus says the Lord concerning the king of Assyria. He shall not come into this city or shoot an arrow there, or come before it with a shield or cast up a siege mound against it. By the way that he came, by the same he shall return, and he shall not come into this city, says the Lord. For I will defend this city to save it, for my own sake and for the sake of my servant David."

And that night the angel of the Lord went forth, and slew a hundred and eighty-five thousand in the camp of the Assyrians; and when men arose early in the morning, behold, these were all dead bodies. Then Sennacherib king of Assyria departed, and went home, and dwelt at Nineveh. And as he was worshiping in the house of Nisroch his god, Adrammelech and Sharezer, his sons, slew him with the sword, and escaped into the land of Ararat. And Esarhaddon his son reigned in his stead.

A LEADERSHIP ENDS

In those days Hezekiah became sick and was at the point of death. And Isaiah the prophet the son of Amoz came to him, and said to him, "Thus says the Lord, 'Set your house in order; for you shall die, you shall not recover.'" Then Hezekiah turned his face to the wall, and prayed to the Lord, saying, "Remember now, O Lord, I beseech thee, how I have walked before thee in faithfulness and with a whole heart, and have done what is good in thy sight." And Hezekiah wept bitterly. And before Isaiah had gone out of the middle court, the word of the Lord came to him: "Turn back, and say to Hezekiah the prince of my people, Thus says the Lord, the God of David your father: I have heard your prayer, I have seen your tears; behold, I will heal you; on the third day you shall go up to the house of the Lord."

The song of Hezekiah, king of Judah, after he had been sick and had recovered from his illness: Once I said, "In the noontime of life I must depart! To the gates of the nether world I shall be consigned for the rest of my years." I said, "I shall see the Lord no more in the land of the living. No longer shall I behold my fellow men among those who dwell in the world." My dwelling, like a shepherd's tent, is struck down and borne away from me; You have folded up my life, like a weaver who severs the last thread. Day and night you give me over to torment; I cry out until the dawn. Like a lion he breaks all my bones; [day and night you give me over to torment]. Like a swallow I utter shrill cries; I moan like a dove. My eyes grow weak, gazing heavenward: O Lord, I am in straits; be my surety!

What am I to say or tell him? He has done it! I shall go on through all my years despite the bitterness of my soul. Those live whom the Lord protects; yours . . . the life of my spirit. You have given me health and life; thus is my bitterness transformed into peace. You have preserved my life from the pit of destruction, When you cast behind your back all my sins. For it is not the nether world that gives you thanks, nor death that praises you; Neither do those who go down into the pit await your kindness. The living, the living give you thanks, as I do today. Fathers declare to their sons, O God, your faithfulness. The Lord is our savior; we shall sing to stringed instruments in the house of the Lord all the days of our life.

The rest of the deeds of Hezekiah, and all his might, and how he made the pool and the conduit and brought water into the city, are they not written in the Book of the Chronicles of the Kings of Judah? And Hezekiah slept with his fathers; and Manasseh his son reigned in his stead.

THE WICKED KINGS

Manasseh was twelve years old when he began to reign, and he reigned fifty-five years in Jerusalem. He did what was evil in the sight of the Lord, according to the abominable practices of the nations whom the Lord drove out before the people of Israel. For he rebuilt the high places which his father Hezekiah had broken down, and erected altars to the Baals, and made Asherahs, and worshiped all the host of heaven, and served them. And he built altars in the house of the Lord, of which the Lord had said, "In Jerusalem shall my name be for ever." And he built altars for all the host of heaven in the two courts of the house of the Lord. And he burned his sons as an offering in the valley of the son of Hinnom, and practiced soothsaying and augury and sorcery, and dealt with mediums and with wizards. He did much evil in the sight of the Lord, provoking him to anger. And the image of the idol which he had made he set in the house of God, of which God said to David and Solomon his son, "In this house, and in Jerusalem, which I have chosen out of all the tribes of Israel, I will put my name for ever; and I will no more remove the foot of Israel from the land which I appointed for your fathers, if only they will be careful to do all that I have commanded them, all the law, the statutes, and the ordinances given through Moses." Manasseh seduced Judah and the inhabitants of Jerusalem, so that they did more evil than the nations whom the Lord destroyed before the people of Israel.

The Lord spoke to Manasseh and to his people, but they gave no heed. Therefore the Lord brought upon them the commanders of the army of the king of Assyria, who took Manasseh with hooks and bound him with fetters of bronze and brought him to Babylon. And when he was in distress he entreated the favor of the Lord his God and humbled himself greatly before the God of his fathers. He prayed to him, and God received his entreaty and heard his supplication and brought him again to Jerusalem into his kingdom. Then Manasseh knew that the Lord was God.

Afterwards he built an outer wall for the city of David west of Gihon, in the valley, and for the entrance into the Fish Gate, and carried it round Ophel, and raised it to a very great height; he also put commanders of the army in all the fortified cities of Judah. And he took away the foreign gods and the idol from the house of the Lord, and all the altars that he had built on the mountain of the house of the Lord and in Jerusalem, and he threw them outside of the city. He also restored the altar of the Lord and offered upon it sacrifices of peace offerings and of thanksgiving; and he commanded Judah to serve the Lord the God of Israel. Nevertheless the people still sacrificed at the high places, but only to the Lord their God.

Now the rest of the acts of Manasseh, and his prayer to his God, and the words of the seers who spoke to him in the name of the Lord the God of Israel, behold, they are in the Chronicles of the Kings of Israel. And his prayer, and how God received his entreaty, and the sites on which he built high places and set up the Asherim and the images, before he humbled himself, behold, they are written in the Chronicles of the Seers. So Manasseh slept with his fathers, and they buried him in his house; and Amon his son reigned in his stead.

Amon was twenty-two years old when he began to reign, and he reigned two years in Jerusalem. He did what was evil in the sight of the Lord, as Manasseh his father had done. Amon sacrificed to all the images that Manasseh his father had made, and served them. And he did not humble himself before the Lord, as Manasseh his father had humbled himself, but this Amon incurred guilt more and more. And his servants conspired against him and killed him in his house. But the people of the land slew all those who had conspired against King Amon; and the people of the land made Josiah his son king in his stead.

A KING DESTROYS IDOLATRY

Josiah was eight years old when he began to reign, and he reigned thirty-one years in Jerusalem. He did what was right in the eyes of the Lord, and walked in the ways of David his father; and he did not turn aside to the right or to the left. For in the eighth year of his reign, while he was yet a boy, he began to seek the God of David his father; and in the twelfth year he began to purge Judah and Jerusalem of the high places, the Asherim, and the graven and the molten images. And they broke down the altars of the Baals in his presence; and he hewed down the incense altars which stood above them; and he broke in pieces the Asherim and the graven and the molten images, and he made dust of them and strewed it over the graves of those who had sacrificed to them. He also burned the bones of the priests on their altars, and purged Judah and Jerusalem. And in the cities of Manasseh, Ephraim, and Simeon, and as far as Naphtali, in their ruins round about, he broke down the altars, and beat the Asherim and the images into powder, and hewed down all the incense altars throughout all the land of Israel. Then he returned to Jerusalem. And Josiah took away the abominations from all the territory that belonged to the people of Israel, and made all who were in Israel serve the Lord their God. All his days they did not turn away from following the Lord the God of their fathers.

After all this, when Josiah had prepared the temple, Neco king of Egypt went up to fight at Carchemish on the Euphrates and Josiah went out against him. But he sent envoys to him, saying, "What have we to do with each other, king of Judah? I am not coming against you this day, but against the house with which I am at war; and God has commanded me to make haste. Cease opposing God, who is with me, lest he destroy you." Nevertheless Josiah would not turn away from him, but disguised himself in order to fight with him. He did not listen to the words of Neco from the mouth of God, but joined battle in the plain of Megiddo. And the archers shot King Josiah; and the king said to his servants, "Take me away, for I am badly wounded." So his servants carried him in his second chariot and brought him to Jerusalem. And he died, and was buried in the tombs of his fathers. All Judah and Jerusalem mourned for Josiah. Jeremiah also uttered a lament for Josiah; and all the singing men and singing women have spoken of Josiah in their laments to this day. They made these an ordinance in Israel; behold, they are written in the Laments.

CHAPTER TWENTY

The Prophecy of Isaia*

THE SINFULNESS OF ISRAEL

The vision which Isaia, son of Amos, had concerning Juda and Jerusalem in the days of Ozia, Joatham, Achaz and Ezechia, kings of Juda.

Hear, O heavens, and listen, O earth, for the Lord speaks: Sons have I raised and reared, but they have disowned me! An ox knows its owner, and an ass, its master's manger; but Israel does not know, my people has not understood. Ah! sinful nation, people laden with wickedness, evil race, corrupt children! They have forsaken the Lord, spurned the Holy One of Israel, apostatized. Where would you yet be struck, you that rebel again and again? The whole head is sick, the whole heart faint. From the sole of the foot to the head there is no sound spot: wound and welt and gaping gash, not drained, or bandaged, or eased with salve. Your country is waste, your cities burnt with fire; your land before your eyes strangers devour [a waste, like Sodom overthrown]—And daughter Sion is left like a hut in a vineyard, like a shed in a melon patch, like a city blockaded.

Unless the Lord of hosts had left us a scanty remnant, we had become as Sodom, we should be like Gomorra.

This is what Isaia, son of Amos, saw concerning Juda and Jerusalem.

In days to come, the mountain of the Lord's house shall be established as the highest mountain and raised above the hills. All nations shall stream toward it; many people shall come and say: "Come, let us climb the Lord's mountain, to the house of the God of Jacob, that he may instruct us in his ways, and we may walk in his paths." For from Sion shall go forth instruction, and the word of the Lord from Jerusalem. He shall judge between the nations, and impose terms on many peoples. They shall beat their swords into plowshares and their spears into

* It should be noted here that the prophet Isaia's prophecies were spoken during the reigns mentioned in the preceding chapter.

pruning hooks; one nation shall not raise the sword against another, nor shall they train for war again.

O house of Jacob, come, let us walk in the light of the Lord!

Let me now sing of my friend, my friend's song concerning his vineyard. My friend had a vineyard on a fertile hillside; he spaded it, cleared it of stones, and planted the choicest vines; within it he built a watchtower, and hewed out a wine press. Then he looked for the crop of grapes, but what it yielded was wild grapes.

Now, inhabitants of Jerusalem and men of Juda, judge between me and my vineyard: what more was there to do for my vineyard that I had not done? Why, when I looked for the crop of grapes, did it bring forth wild grapes? Now, I will let you know what I mean to do to my vineyard: take away its hedge, give it to grazing, break through its wall, let it be trampled! Yes, I will make it a ruin; it shall not be pruned or hoed, but overgrown with thorns and briers; I will command the clouds not to send rain upon it. The vineyard of the Lord of hosts is the house of Israel, and the men of Juda are his cherished plant; he looked for judgment, but see, bloodshed! for justice, but hark, the outcry!

In the year King Ozia died, I saw the Lord seated on a high and lofty throne, with the train of his garment filling the temple. Seraphim were stationed above; each of them had six wings: with two they veiled their faces, with two they veiled their feet, and with two they hovered aloft.

"Holy, holy, holy is the Lord of hosts!" they cried one to the other. "All the earth is filled with his glory!" At the sound of that cry, the frame of the door shook and the house was filled with smoke.

Then I said, "Woe is me, I am doomed! For I am a man of unclean lips, living among a people of unclean lips; yet my eyes have seen the King, the Lord of hosts!" Then one of the seraphim flew to me, holding an ember which he had taken with tongs from the altar.

He touched my mouth with it. "See," he said, "now that this has touched your lips, your wickedness is removed, your sin purged."

Then I heard the voice of the Lord saying, "Whom shall I send? Who will go for us?" "Here I am," I said; "send me!" And he replied: Go and say to this people: Listen carefully, but you shall not understand! Look intently, but you shall know nothing! You are to make the heart of this people sluggish, to dull their ears and close their eyes; else their eyes will see, their ears hear, their heart understand, and they will turn and be healed.

"How long, O Lord?" I asked. And he replied: Until the cities are desolate, without inhabitants, houses, without a man, and the earth is a desolate waste.

CHRIST AND HIS KINGDOM IS FORESEEN

In the days of Achaz, king of Juda, son of Joatham, son of Ozia, Rasin, king of Aram, and Phacee, king of Israel, son of Romelia, went up to attack Jerusalem, but they were not able to conquer it.

Again the Lord spoke to Achaz: Ask for a sign from the Lord, your God; let it be deep as the nether world, or high as the sky! But Achaz answered, "I will not ask! I will not tempt the Lord!"

Then he said: Listen, O house of David! Is it not enough for you to weary men, must you also weary my God? Therefore the Lord himself will give you this sign: the virgin shall be with child, and bear a son, and shall name him Emmanuel. He shall be living on curds and honey by the time he learns to reject the bad and choose the good. For before the child learns to reject the bad and choose the good, the land of those two kings whom you dread shall be deserted.

And the Lord said to me: With the Lord of hosts make your alliance—for him be your fear and your awe. Yet he shall be a snare, an obstacle and a stumbling stone to both the houses of Israel, a trap and a snare to those who dwell in Jerusalem; and many among them shall stumble and fall, broken, snared, and captured."

First he degraded the land of Zabulon and the land of Nephthali; but in the end he has glorified the seaward road, the land west of the Jordan, the District of the Gentiles. Anguish has taken wing, dispelled is darkness: for there is no gloom where but now there was distress.

The people who walked in darkness have seen a great light; upon those who dwelt in the land of gloom a light has shone. You have brought them abundant joy and great rejoicing, as they rejoice before you as at the harvest, as men make merry when dividing spoils. For the yoke that burdened them, the pole on their shoulder, and the rod of their taskmaster you have smashed, as on the day of Madian. For every boot that tramped in battle, every cloak rolled in blood, will be burned as fuel for flames.

For a child is born to us, a son is given us; upon his shoulder dominion rests. They name him Wonder-Counselor, God-Hero, Father-Forever, Prince of Peace. His dominion is vast and forever peaceful, from David's throne, and over his kingdom, which he confirms and sustains by judgment and justice, both now and forever. The zeal of the Lord of hosts will do this!

But a shoot shall sprout from the stump of Jesse, and from his roots a bud shall blossom. The spirit of the Lord shall rest upon him: a spirit of wisdom and of understanding, a spirit of counsel and of strength, a spirit of knowledge and of fear of the Lord, and his delight shall be the fear of the Lord. Not by appearance shall he judge, nor by hearsay shall he decide, but he shall judge the poor with justice, and decide aright for the land's afflicted. He shall strike the ruthless with the rod of his mouth, and with the breath of his lips he shall slay the wicked. Justice shall be the band around his waist, and faithfulness a belt upon his hips.

Then the wolf shall be a guest of the lamb, and the leopard shall lie down with the kid; the calf and the young lion shall browse together, with a little child to guide them. The cow and the bear shall be neighbors, together their young shall rest; the lion shall eat hay like the ox. The baby shall play by the cobra's den, and the child lay his hand on the adder's lair. There shall be no harm or ruin on all my holy mountain; for the earth shall be filled with knowledge of the Lord, as water covers the sea.

On that day, you will say: I give you thanks, O Lord; though you have been angry with me, your anger has abated, and you have consoled me. God indeed is my savior; I am confident and unafraid. My strength and my courage is the Lord, and he has been my savior.

With joy you will draw water at the fountain of salvation, and say on that day: Give thanks to the Lord, acclaim his name; among the nations make known his deeds, proclaim how exalted is his name. Sing praise to the Lord for his glorious achievement; let this be known throughout all the earth. Shout with exultation, O city of Sion, for great in your midst is the Holy One of Israel!

THE RESETTLEMENT OF JUDA PREDICTED

The desert and the parched land will exult; the steppe will rejoice and bloom. They will bloom with abundant flowers, and rejoice with joyful song. The glory of Lebanon will be given to them, the splendor of Carmel and Saron; they will see the glory of the Lord, the splendor of our God.

Strengthen the hands that are feeble, make firm the knees that are weak, say to those whose hearts are frightened: Be strong, fear not! Here is your God, he comes with vindication; with divine recompense he comes to save you. Then will the eyes of the blind be opened, the ears of the deaf be cleared; then will the lame leap like a stag, then the tongue of the dumb will sing.

Streams will burst forth in the desert, and rivers in the steppe. The burning sands will become pools, and the thirsty ground, springs of water; the abode where jackals lurk will be a marsh for the reed and papyrus. A highway will be there, called the holy way; no one unclean may pass over it, nor fools go astray on it. No lion will be there, nor beast of prey go up to be met upon it. It is for those with a journey to make, and on it the redeemed will walk. Those whom the Lord has ransomed will return and enter Sion singing, crowned with everlasting joy; they will meet with joy and gladness, sorrow and mourning will flee.

Comfort, give comfort to my people, says your God. Speak tenderly to Jerusalem, and proclaim to her that her service is at an end, her guilt is expiated; indeed, she has received from the hand of the Lord double for all her sins.

A voice cries out: In the desert prepare the way of the Lord! Make straight in the wasteland a highway for our God! Every valley shall be filled in, every mountain and hill shall be made low; the rugged land shall be made a plain, the rough country, a broad valley. Then the glory of the Lord shall be revealed, and all mankind shall see it together; for the mouth of the Lord has spoken.

A voice says, "Cry out!" I answer, "What shall I cry out?" "All mankind is grass, and all their glory like the flower of the field. The grass withers, the flower wilts, when the breath of the Lord blows upon it. [So then, the people is the grass.] Though the grass withers and the flower wilts, the word of our God stands forever."

Go up onto a high mountain, Sion, herald of glad tidings; cry out at the top of your voice, Jerusalem, herald of good news! Fear not to cry out and say to the cities of Juda: Here is your God! Here comes with power the Lord God, who rules by his strong arm; here is his reward with him, his recompense before him. Like a shepherd he feeds his flock; in his arms he gathers the lambs, carrying them in his bosom, and leading the ewes with care.

Here is my servant whom I uphold, my chosen one with whom I am pleased, upon whom I have put my spirit; he shall bring forth justice to the nations, not crying out, not shouting, not making his voice heard in the street. A bruised reed he shall not break, and a smoldering wick he shall not quench, until he establishes justice on the earth; the coastlands will wait for his teaching.

Thus says God, the Lord, who created the heavens and stretched them out, who spreads out the earth with its crops, who gives breath to its people and spirit to those who walk on it: I, the Lord, have called you for the victory of justice, I have grasped you by the hand; I formed you, and set you as a covenant of the people, a light for the nations, to open the eyes of the blind, to bring out prisoners from confinement, and from the dungeon, those who live in darkness. Let justice descend, O heavens, like dew from above, like gentle rain let the skies drop it down. Let the earth open and salvation bud forth; let justice also spring up! I, the Lord, have created this.

Thus says the Lord: The earnings of Egypt, the gain of Ethiopia, and the Sabeans, tall of stature, shall come over to you and belong to you; they shall follow you, coming in chains. Before you they shall fall prostrate, saying in prayer: "With you only is God, and nowhere else; the gods are nought. Truly with you God is hidden, the God of Israel, the savior! Those are put to shame and disgrace who vent their anger against him; those go in disgrace who carve images. Israel, you are saved by the Lord, saved forever! You shall never be put to shame or disgrace in future ages." For thus says the Lord, the creator of the heavens, who is God, the designer and maker of the earth who established it, not creating it to be a waste, but designing it to be lived in: I am the Lord, and there is no other. I have not spoken from hiding nor from some dark place of the earth, and I have not said to the descendants of Jacob, "Look for me in an empty waste." I, the Lord, promise justice, I foretell what is right.

Come and assemble, gather together, you fugitives from among the gentiles! They are without knowledge who bear wooden idols and pray to gods that cannot save. Come here and declare in counsel together: Who announced this from the beginning and foretold it from of old? Was it not I, the Lord, besides whom there is no other God? There is no just and saving God but me. Turn to me and be safe, all you ends of the earth, for I am God; there is no other!

By myself I swear, uttering my just decree and my unalterable word: To me every knee shall bend; by me every tongue shall swear, saying, "Only in the Lord are just deeds and power. Before him in shame shall come all who vent their anger against him. In the Lord shall be the vindication and the glory of all the descendants of Israel."

ANOTHER PREDICTION OF THE COMING
OF CHRIST AND HIS PASSION

Awake, awake! Put on your strength, O Sion; put on your glorious garments, O Jerusalem, holy city. No longer shall the uncircumcised or the unclean enter you. Shake off the dust, ascend to the throne, Jerusalem; loose the bonds from your neck, O captive daughter of Sion! For thus says the Lord: You were sold for nothing, and without money you shall be redeemed.

Thus says the Lord God: To Egypt in the beginning my people went down, to sojourn there; Assyria, too, oppressed them for nought. But now, what am I to do here? says the Lord. My people have been taken away without redress; their rulers make a boast of it, says the Lord; all the day my name is constantly reviled. Therefore on that day my people shall know my renown, that it is I who have foretold it. Here I am! How beautiful upon the mountains are the feet of him who brings glad tidings, announcing peace, bearing good news, announcing salvation, and saying to Sion, "Your God is King!"

Hark! Your watchmen raise a cry, together they shout for joy, for they see directly, before their eyes, the Lord restoring Sion. Break out together in song, O ruins of Jerusalem! For the Lord comforts his people, he redeems Jerusalem. The Lord has bared his holy arm in the sight of all the nations; all the ends of the earth will behold the salvation of our God.

Depart, depart, come forth from there, touch nothing unclean! Out from there! Purify yourselves, you who carry the vessels of the Lord. Yet not in fearful haste will you come out, nor leave in headlong flight, for the Lord comes before you, and your rear guard is the God of Israel.

See, my servant shall prosper, he shall be raised high and greatly exalted. Even as many were amazed at him—so marred was his look beyond that of man, and his appearance beyond that of mortals—so shall he startle many nations, because of him kings shall stand speechless; for those who have not been told shall see, those who have not heard shall ponder it.

Who would believe what we have heard? To whom has the arm of the Lord been revealed? He grew up like a sapling before him, like a shoot from the parched earth; there was in him no stately bearing to make us look at him, nor appearance that would attract us to him. He was spurned and avoided by men, a man of suffering, accustomed to infirmity, one of those from whom men hide their faces, spurned, and we held him in no esteem.

Yet it was our infirmities that he bore, our sufferings that he endured, while we thought of him as stricken, as one smitten by God and afflicted. But he was pierced for our offenses, crushed for our sins; upon him was the chastisement that makes us whole, by his stripes we were healed. We had all gone astray like sheep, each following his own way; but the Lord laid upon him the guilt of us all.

Though he was harshly treated, he submitted and opened not his mouth; like a lamb led to the slaughter or a sheep before the shearers, he was silent and opened not his mouth. Oppressed and condemned, he was taken away, and who would have thought any more of his destiny? When he was cut off from the land of the living, and smitten for the sin of his people, a grave was assigned him among the wicked and a burial place with evildoers, though he had done no wrong nor spoken any falsehood. [But the Lord was pleased to crush him in infirmity.]

If he gives his life as an offering for sin, he shall see his descendants in a long life, and the will of the Lord shall be accomplished through him. Because of his affliction he shall see the light in fullness of days; through his suffering, my servant shall justify many, and their guilt he shall bear. Therefore I will give him his portion among the great, and he shall divide the spoils with the mighty, because he surrendered himself to death and was counted among the wicked; and he shall take away the sins of many, and win pardon for their offenses.

THE MERCY OF GOD IS CERTAIN

All you who are thirsty, come to the water! You who have no money, come, receive grain and eat; come, without paying and without cost, drink wine and milk! Why spend your money for what is not bread; your wages for what fails to satisfy? Heed me, and you shall eat well, you shall delight in rich fare. Come to me heedfully, listen, that you may have life. I will renew with you the everlasting covenant, the benefits assured to David. As I made him a witness to the peoples, a leader and commander of nations, so shall you summon a nation you knew not, and nations that knew you not shall run to you, because of the Lord, your God, the Holy One of Israel, who has glorified you.

Seek the Lord while he may be found, call him while he is near. Let the scoundrel forsake his way, and the wicked man his thoughts; let him turn to the Lord for mercy; to our God, who is generous in forgiving. For my thoughts are not your thoughts, nor are your ways my ways, says the Lord. As high as the heavens are above the earth, so high are my ways above your ways and my thoughts above your thoughts.

For just as from the heavens the rain and snow come down and do not return there till they have watered the earth, making it fertile and fruitful, giving seed to him who sows and bread to him who eats, so shall my word be that goes forth from my mouth; it shall not return to me void, but shall do my will, achieving the end for which I sent it.

Yes, in joy you shall depart, in peace you shall be brought back; mountains and hills shall break out in song before you, and all the trees of the countryside shall clap their hands. In place of the thornbush, the cypress shall grow, instead of nettles, the myrtle. This shall be to the Lord's renown, an everlasting imperishable sign.

THE GENTILES ARE CONVERTED

Rise up in splendor! Your light has come, the glory of the Lord shines upon you. See, darkness covers the earth, and thick clouds cover the peoples; but upon you the Lord shines, and over you appears his glory. Nations shall walk by your light, and kings by your shining radiance. Raise your eyes and look about; they all gather and come to you: your sons come from afar, and your daughters in the arms of their nurses.

Then you shall be radiant at what you see, your heart shall throb and overflow, for the riches of the sea shall be emptied out before you, the wealth of nations shall be brought to you. Caravans of camels shall fill you, dromedaries from Madian and Epha; all from Saba shall come bearing gold and frankincense, and proclaiming the praises of the Lord.

The spirit of the Lord God is upon me, because the Lord has anointed me; he has sent me to bring glad tidings to the lowly, to heal the brokenhearted, to proclaim liberty to the captives and release to the prisoners, to announce a year of favor from the Lord and a day of vindication by our God, to comfort all who mourn; to place on those who mourn in Sion a diadem instead of ashes, to give them oil of gladness in place of mourning, a glorious mantle instead of a listless spirit. They will be called oaks of justice, planted by the Lord to show his glory.

They shall rebuild the ancient ruins, the former wastes they shall raise up and restore the ruined cities, desolate now for generations.

Their descendants shall be renowned among the nations, and their offspring among the peoples; all who see them shall acknowledge them as a race the Lord has blessed.

I rejoice heartily in the Lord, in my God is the joy of my soul; for he has clothed me with a robe of salvation, and wrapped me in a mantle of justice, like a bridegroom adorned with a diadem, like a bride bedecked with her jewels. As the earth brings forth its plants, and a garden makes its growth spring up, so will the Lord God make justice and praise spring up before all the nations.

For Sion's sake I will not be silent, for Jerusalem's sake I will not be quiet, until her vindication shines forth like the dawn and her victory like a burning torch.

Nations shall behold your vindication, and all kings your glory; you shall be called by a new name pronounced by the mouth of the Lord. You shall be a glorious crown in the hand of the Lord, a royal diadem held by your God. No more shall men call you "Forsaken," or your land "Desolate," but you shall be called "My Delight," and your land "Espoused." For the Lord delights in you, and makes your land his spouse.

THE PASSION OF CHRIST AND HIS WISDOM

Who is this that comes from Edom, in crimsoned garments, from Bosra—this one arrayed in majesty, marching in the greatness of his strength? "It is I, I who announce vindication, I who am mighty to save." Why is your apparel red, and your garments like those of the wine presser?

"The wine press I have trodden alone, and of my people there was no one with me. I trod them in my anger, and trampled them down in my wrath; their blood spurted on my garments; all my apparel I stained. For the day of vengeance was in my heart, my year for redeeming was at hand. I looked about, but there was no one to help, I was appalled that there was no one to lend support; so my own arm brought about the victory and my own wrath lent me its support. I trampled down the peoples in my anger, I crushed them in my wrath, and I let their blood run out upon the ground."

The favors of the Lord I will recall, the glorious deeds of the Lord, because of all he has done for us; for he is good to the house of Israel, he has favored us according to his mercy and his great kindness.

He said: They are indeed my people, children who are not disloyal; so he became their savior in their every affliction. It was not a messenger or an angel, but he himself who saved them. Because of his love and pity he redeemed them himself, lifting them and carrying them all the days of old. But they rebelled, and grieved his holy spirit; so he turned on them like an enemy, and fought against them.

Look down from heaven and regard us from your holy and glorious palace! Where is your zealous care and your might, your surge of pity and your mercy? O Lord, hold not back, for you are our father. Were Abraham not to know us, nor Israel to acknowledge us, you, Lord, are our father, our redeemer you are named forever. Why do you let us wander, O Lord, from your ways, and harden our hearts so that we fear you not? Return for the sake of your servants, the tribes of your heritage. Why have the wicked invaded your holy place, why have our enemies trampled your sanctuary? Too long have we been like those you do not rule, who do not bear your name.

CHAPTER TWENTY-ONE

The Fall of the Holy City;
The Prophecy of Jeremia

THE CHALDEANS ENTER JERUSALEM

Jehoahaz was twenty-three years old when he began to reign, and he reigned three months in Jerusalem. His mother's name was Hamutal the daughter of Jeremiah of Libnah. And he did what was evil in the sight of the Lord, according to all that his fathers had done. And Pharaoh Neco put him in bonds at Riblah in the land of Hamath, that he might not reign in Jerusalem, and laid upon the land a tribute of a hundred talents of silver and a talent of gold. And Pharaoh Neco made Eliakim the son of Josiah king in the place of Josiah his father, and changed his name to Jehoiakim. But he took Jehoahaz away, and he came to Egypt, and died there. And Jehoiakim gave the silver and the gold of the people of the land, from every one according to his assessment, to give it to Pharaoh Neco.

Jehoiakim was twenty-five years old when he began to reign, and he reigned eleven years in Jerusalem. His mother's name was Zebidah the daughter of Pedaiah of Rumah. 'And he did what was evil in the sight of the Lord, according to all that his fathers had done.

In his days Nebuchadnezzar king of Babylon came up, and Jehoiakim became his servant three years; then he turned and rebelled against him. And the Lord sent against him bands of the Chaldeans, and bands of the Syrians, and bands of the Moabites, and bands of the Ammonites, and sent them against Judah to destroy it, according to the word of the Lord which he spoke by his servants the prophets. Surely this came upon Judah at the command of the Lord, to remove them out of his sight, for the sins of Manasseh, according to all that he had done, and also for the innocent blood that he had shed; for he filled Jerusalem with innocent blood, and the Lord would not pardon. Now the rest of the deeds of Jehoiakim, and all that he did, are they not written in the Book of the Chronicles of the Kings of Judah? So Jehoiakim slept with his fathers, and Jehoiachin his son reigned in his stead. And the king of Egypt did not come again out of his land, for the king of Babylon had taken all that belonged to the king of Egypt from the Brook of Egypt to the river Euphrates.

Jehoiachin was eighteen years old when he became king, and he reigned three months in Jerusalem. His mother's name was Nehushta the daughter of Elnathan of Jerusalem. And he did what was evil in the sight of the Lord, according to all that his fathers had done.

At that time the servants of Nebuchadnezzar king of Babylon came up to Jerusalem, and the city was besieged. And Nebuchadnezzar king of Babylon came to the city, while his servants were besieging it; and Jehoiachin the king of Judah gave himself up to the king of Babylon, himself, and his mother, and his servants, and his princes, and his palace officials. The king of Babylon took him prisoner in the eighth year of his reign, and carried off all the treasures of the king's house, and cut in pieces all the vessels of gold in the temple of the Lord, which Solomon king of Israel had made, as the Lord had foretold. He carried away all Jerusalem, and all the princes, and all the mighty men of valor, ten thousand captives, and all the craftsmen and the smiths; none remained, except the poorest people of the land. And he carried away Jehoiachin to Babylon; the king's mother, the king's wives, his officials, and the chief men of the land, he took into captivity from Jerusalem to Babylon. And the king of Babylon brought captive to Babylon all the men of valor, seven thousand, and the craftsmen and the smiths, one thousand, all of them strong and fit for war. And the king of Babylon made Mattaniah, Jehoiachin's uncle, king in his stead, and changed his name to Zedekiah.

Zedekiah was twenty-one years old when he became king, and he reigned eleven years in Jerusalem. His mother's name was Hamutal the daughter of Jeremiah of Libnah. And he did what was evil in the sight of the Lord, according to all that Jehoiakim had done. For because of the anger of the Lord it came to the point in Jerusalem and Judah that he cast them out from his presence. And Zedekiah rebelled against the king of Babylon.

THE DESTRUCTION OF JERUSALEM

And in the ninth year of his reign, in the tenth month, on the tenth day of the month, Nebuchadnezzar king of Babylon came with all his army against Jerusalem, and laid siege to it; and they built siegeworks against it round about. So the city was besieged till the eleventh year of King Zedekiah. On the ninth day of the fourth month the famine was so severe in the city that there was no food for the people of the land. Then a breach was made in the city; the king with all the men of war fled by night by the way of the gate between the two walls, by the king's garden, though the Chaldeans were around the city. And they went in the direction of the Arabah. But the army of the Chaldeans pursued the king, and overtook him in the plains of Jericho; and all his army was scattered from him. Then they captured the king, and brought him up to the king of Babylon at Riblah, who passed sentence upon him. They slew the sons of Zedekiah before his eyes, and put out the eyes of Zedekiah, and bound him in fetters, and took him to Babylon.

In the fifth month, on the seventh day of the month—which was the nineteenth year of King Nebuchadnezzar, king of Babylon—Nebuzar-adan, the captain of the bodyguard, a servant of the king of Babylon, came to Jerusalem. And he burned the house of the Lord, and the king's house and all the houses of Jerusalem; every great house he burned down. And all the army of the Chaldeans, who were with the captain of the guard, broke down the walls around Jerusalem. And the rest of the people who were left in the city and the deserters who had deserted to the king of Babylon, together with the rest of the multitude, Nebuzaradan the captain of the guard carried into exile. But the captain of the guard left some of the poorest of the land to be vinedressers and plowmen.

And the pillars of bronze that were in the house of the Lord, and the stands and the bronze sea that were in the house of the Lord, the Chaldeans broke in pieces, and carried the bronze to Babylon. And they took away the pots, and the shovels, and the snuffers, and the dishes for incense and all the vessels of bronze used in the temple service, the fire-pans also, and the bowls. What was of gold the captain of the guard took away as gold, and what was of silver, as silver. As for the two pillars, the one sea, and the stands, which Solomon had made for the house of the Lord, the bronze of all these vessels was beyond weight. The height of the one pillar was eighteen cubits, and upon it was a capital of bronze; the height of the capital was three cubits; a network and pomegranates, all of bronze, were upon the capital round about. And the second pillar had the like, with the network.

And the captain of the guard took Seraiah the chief priest, and Zephaniah the second priest, and the three keepers of the threshold;

and from the city he took an officer who had been in command of the men of war, and five men of the king's council who were found in the city; and the secretary of the commander of the army who mustered the people of the land; and sixty men of the people of the land who were found in the city. And Nebuzaradan the captain of the guard took them, and brought them to the king of Babylon at Riblah in the land of Hamath, so Judah was taken into exile out of its land.

JEREMIA IS CALLED AND PREDICTS THE FALL OF JERUSALEM

The words of Jeremia, son of Helcia, of a priestly family in Anathoth, in the land of Benjamin. The word of the Lord first came to him in the days of Josia, son of Amon, king of Juda, in the thirteenth year of his reign, and continued through the reign of Joakim, son of Josia, king of Juda, and until the downfall and exile of Jerusalem in the fifth month of the eleventh year of Sedecia, son of Josia, king of Juda.

The word of the Lord came to me thus: Before I formed you in the womb I knew you, before you were born I dedicated you, a prophet to the nations I appointed you.

"Ah, Lord God!" I said, "I know not how to speak; I am too young."

But the Lord answered me, Say not, "I am too young." To whomever I send you, you shall go; whatever I command you, you shall speak. Have no fear before them, because I am with you to deliver you, says the Lord.

Then the Lord extended his hand and touched my mouth, saying, See, I place my words in your mouth! This day I set you over nations and over kingdoms, to root up and to tear down, to destroy and to demolish, to build and to plant.

For it is I this day who have made you a fortified city, a pillar of iron, a wall of brass, against the whole land: against Juda's kings and princes, against its priests and people. They will fight against you, but not prevail over you, for I am with you to deliver you, says the Lord.

The following message came to Jeremia from the Lord: Stand at the gate of the house of the Lord, and there proclaim this message: Hear the word of the Lord, all you of Juda who enter these gates to worship the Lord!

Cut off your dedicated hair and throw it away! on the heights intone an elegy; for the Lord has rejected and cast off the generation that draws down his wrath.

The corpses of this people will be food for the birds of the sky and for the beasts of the field, which no one will drive away. In the cities of Juda and in the streets of Jerusalem I will silence the cry of joy, the cry of gladness, the voice of the bridegroom and the voice of the bride; for the land will be turned to rubble.

Would that I had in the desert a travelers' lodge! That I might leave my people and depart from them. They are all adulterers, a faithless band. They ready their tongues like a drawn bow, with lying, and not with truth, they hold forth in the land. They go from evil to evil, but me they know not, says the Lord. Be on your guard, everyone against his neighbor; put no trust in any brother. Every brother apes Jacob, the supplanter, every friend is guilty of slander. Each one deceives the other, no one speaks the truth. They have accustomed their tongues to lying, and are perverse, and cannot repent. Violence upon violence, deceit upon deceit; they refuse to recognize me, says the Lord.

Therefore, thus says the Lord of hosts: I will smelt them and test them; how else should I deal with their wickedness?

JEREMIA MEETS THE ENEMY

A conspiracy has been found, the Lord said to me, among the men of Juda and the citizens of Jerusalem. They have returned to the crimes of their forefathers who refused to obey my words. They also have followed and served strange gods; the covenant which I had made with their fathers, the house of Israel and the house of Juda have broken. Therefore, thus says the Lord: See, I bring upon them misfortune which they cannot escape. Though they cry out to me, I will not listen to them. Then the cities of Juda and the citizens of Jerusalem will go and cry out to the gods to which they have been offering incense. But these gods will give them no help whatever when misfortune strikes.

For as numerous as your cities are your gods, O Juda! And as many as the streets of Jerusalem are the altars for offering sacrifice to Baal. Do not intercede on behalf of this people, nor utter a plea for them. I will not listen when they call to me at the time of their misfortune.

I knew it because the Lord informed me; at that time you, O Lord, showed me their doings. Yet I, like a trusting lamb led to slaughter, had not realized that they were hatching plots against me: "Let us destroy the tree in its vigor; let us cut him off from the land of the living, so that his name will be spoken no more."

But, you, O Lord of hosts, O just Judge, searcher of mind and heart, let me witness the vengeance you take on them, for to you I have entrusted my cause!

Therefore, thus says the Lord concerning the men of Anathoth who seek your life, saying, "Do not prophesy in the name of the Lord; else you shall die by our hand." Therefore, thus says the Lord of hosts: I am going to punish them. The young men shall die by the sword; their sons and daughters shall die by famine. None shall be spared among them, for I will bring misfortune upon the men of Anathoth, the year of their punishment.

"Come," they said, "let us contrive a plot against Jeremia. It will not mean the loss of instruction from the priests, nor of counsel from the wise, nor of messages from the prophets. And so, let us destroy him by his own tongue; let us carefully note his every word."

Heed me, O Lord, and listen to what my adversaries say. Must good be repaid with evil that they should dig a pit to take my life? Remember that I stood before you to speak in their behalf, to turn away your wrath from them. So now, deliver their children to famine, do away with them by the sword. Let their wives be made childless and widows; let their men die of pestilence, their young men be slain by the sword in battle. May cries be heard from their homes, when suddenly you send plunderers against them. For they have dug a pit to capture me, they have hid snares for my feet; but you, O Lord, know all their plans to slay me. Forgive not their crime, blot not out their sin in your sight! Let them go down before you, proceed against them in the time of your anger.

JEREMIA FORESEES FREEDOM FOR ISRAEL

Woe to the shepherds who mislead and scatter the flock of my pasture, says the Lord. Therefore, thus says the Lord, the God of Israel, against the shepherds who shepherd my people: You have scattered my sheep and driven them away. You have not cared for them, but I will take care to punish your evil deeds. I myself will gather the remnant of my flock from all the lands to which I have driven them and bring them back to their meadow; there they shall increase and multiply. I will appoint shepherds for them who will shepherd them so that they need no longer fear and tremble; and none shall be missing, says the Lord.

Behold, the days are coming, says the Lord, when I will raise up a righteous shoot to David; as king he shall reign and govern wisely, he shall do what is just and right in the land. In his days Juda shall be saved, Israel shall dwell in security. This is the name they give him: "The Lord our justice."

Therefore, the days will come, says the Lord, when they shall no longer say, "As the Lord lives, who brought the Israelites out of the land of Egypt"; but rather, "As the Lord lives, who brought the descendants of the house of Israel up from the land of the north"—and from all the lands to which I banished them; they shall again live on their own land.

The word that came to Jeremia concerning all the people of Juda, in the fourth year of Joakim, son of Josia, king of Juda (the first year of Nabuchodonosor, king of Babylon). This word the prophet Jeremia spoke to all the people of Juda and all the citizens of Jerusalem: Since the thirteenth year of Josia, son of Amon, king of Juda, to this day—these three and twenty years—the word of the Lord has come to me and I spoke to you untiringly, but you would not listen. Though you refused to listen or pay heed, the Lord has sent you without fail all his servants the prophets with this message: Turn back, each of you, from your evil way and from your evil deeds; then you shall remain in the land which the Lord gave you and your fathers, from of old and forever. Do not follow strange gods to serve and adore them, lest you provoke me with your handiwork, and I bring evil upon you. But you would not listen to me, says the Lord, and so you provoked me with your handiwork to your own harm. Hence, thus says the Lord of hosts: Since you would not listen to my words, lo! I will send for and fetch all the tribes of the north, says the Lord (and I will send to Nabuchodonosor, king of Babylon, my servant); I will bring them against this land, against its inhabitants, and against all these neighboring nations. I will doom them, making them an object of horror, of ridicule, of everlasting reproach. Among them I will bring to an end the song of joy and the song of gladness, the voice of the bridegroom and the voice of the bride, the sound of the millstone and the light of the lamp. This whole land shall be a ruin and a desert. Seventy years these nations shall be enslaved to the king of Babylon; but when the seventy years have elapsed, I will punish the king of Babylon and the nation and the land of the Chaldeans for their guilt, says the Lord. Their land I will turn into an everlasting desert.

At that time, says the Lord, I will be the God of all the tribes of Israel, and they shall be my people. Thus says the Lord: The people that escaped the sword have found favor in the desert. As Israel comes forward to be given his rest, the Lord appears to him from afar: With age-old love I have loved you; so I have kept my mercy toward you. Again I will restore you, and you shall be rebuilt, O virgin Israel; carrying your festive tambourines, you shall go forth dancing with the merrymakers. Again you shall plant vineyards on the mountains of Samaria; those who plant them shall enjoy the fruits.

Hear the word of the Lord, O nations, proclaim it on distant coasts, and say: He who scattered Israel, now gathers them together, he guards them as a shepherd his flock. The Lord shall ransom Jacob, he shall redeem him from the hand of his conqueror. Shouting, they shall mount the heights of Sion, they shall come streaming to the Lord's blessings: the grain, the wine, and the oil, the sheep and the oxen; they themselves shall be like watered gardens, never again shall they languish. Then the virgins shall make merry and dance, and young men and old as well. I will turn their mourning into joy, I will console and gladden them after their sorrows. I will lavish choice portions upon the priests, and my people shall be filled with my blessings, says the Lord.

But this is the covenant which I will make with the house of Israel after those days, says the Lord. I will place my law within them, and write it upon their hearts; I will be their God, and they shall be my people. No longer will they have need to teach their friends and kinsmen how to know the Lord. All, from least to greatest, shall know me, says the Lord, for I will forgive their evildoing and remember their sin no more.

THE LAMENTS OF JEREMIA AND THE MERCY OF GOD

How lonely she is now, the once crowded city! Widowed is she who was mistress over nations; the princess among the provinces has been made a toiling slave.

Bitterly she weeps at night, tears upon her cheeks, with not one to console her of all her dear ones; her friends have all betrayed her and become her enemies.

Juda has fled into exile from oppression and cruel slavery; yet where she lives among the nations she finds no place to rest: all her persecutors come upon her where she is narrowly confined.

The roads to Sion mourn for lack of pilgrims going to her feasts; all her gateways are deserted, her priests groan, her virgins sigh; she is in bitter grief.

Her foes are uppermost, her enemies are at ease; the Lord has punished her for her many sins. Her little ones have gone away, captive before the foe.

Gone from daughter Sion is all her glory: her princes, like rams that find no pasture, have gone off without strength before their captors.

Jerusalem is mindful of the days of her wretched homelessness, when her people fell into enemy hands, and she had no one to help her; when her foes gloated over her, laughed at her ruin.

Through the sin of which she is guilty, Jerusalem is defiled; all who esteemed her think her vile now that they see her nakedness; she herself groans and turns away.

Her filth is on her skirt; she gave no thought how she would end. Astounding is her downfall, with no one to console her. Look, O Lord, upon her misery, for the enemy has triumphed!

The foe stretched out his hand to all her treasures; she has seen those nations enter her sanctuary whom you forbade to come into your assembly.

All her people groan, searching for bread; they give their treasures for food, to retain the breath of life. "Look, O Lord, and see how worthless I have become!

"Come, all you who pass by the way, look and see whether there is any suffering like my suffering, which has been dealt me when the Lord afflicted me on the day of his blazing wrath.

"From on high he sent fire down into my very frame; he spread a net for my feet, and overthrew me. He left me desolate, in pain all the day.

"He has kept watch over my sins; by his hand they have been plaited: they have settled about my neck, he has brought my strength to its knees; the Lord has delivered me into their grip, I am unable to rise."

The Lord marked for destruction the wall of daughter Sion: he stretched out the measuring line; his hand brought ruin; yet he did not relent—he brought grief on wall and rampart till both succumbed.

Sunk into the ground are her gates; he has removed and broken her bars. Her king and her princes are among the pagans; priestly instruction is wanting, and her prophets have not received any vision from the Lord.

On the ground in silence sit the old men of daughter Sion; they strew dust on their heads and gird themselves with sackcloth; the maidens of Jerusalem bow their heads to the ground.

Worn out from weeping are my eyes, within me all is in ferment; my gall is poured out on the ground because of the downfall of the daughter of my people, as child and infant faint away in the open spaces of the town.

They ask their mothers, "Where is the cereal?"—in vain, as they faint away like the wounded in the streets of the city, and breathe their last in their mothers' arms.

To what can I liken or compare you, O daughter Jerusalem? What example can I show you for your comfort, virgin daughter Sion? For great as the sea is your downfall; who can heal you?

Your prophets had for you false and specious visions; they did not lay bare your guilt, to avert your fate; they beheld for you in vision false and misleading portents.

All who pass by clap their hands at you; they hiss and wag their heads over daughter Jerusalem: "Is this the all-beautiful city, the joy of the whole earth?"

I am a man who knows affliction from the rod of his anger, one whom he has led and forced to walk in darkness, not in the light; against me alone he brings back his hand again and again all the day.

He has worn away my flesh and my skin, he has broken my bones; he has beset me round about with poverty and weariness; he has left me to dwell in the dark like those long dead.

He has hemmed me in with no escape and weighed me down with chains; even when I cry out for help, he stops my prayer; he has blocked my ways with fitted stones, and turned my paths aside.

The favors of the Lord are not exhausted, his mercies are not spent; they are renewed each morning, so great is his faithfulness. My portion is the Lord, says my soul; therefore will I hope in him.

Good is the Lord to one who waits for him, to the soul that seeks him; it is good to hope in silence for the saving help of the Lord. It is good for a man to bear the yoke from his youth.

Let him sit alone and in silence, when it is laid upon him. Let him put his mouth to the dust; there may yet be hope. Let him offer his cheek to be struck, let him be filled with disgrace.

How tarnished is the gold, how changed the noble metal; how the sacred stones lie strewn at every street corner!

Sion's precious sons, fine gold their counterpart, now worth no more than earthen jars made by the hands of a potter!

Even the jackals bare their breasts and suckle their young; the daughter of my people has become as cruel as the ostrich in the desert.

The tongue of the suckling cleaves to the roof of its mouth in thirst; the babes cry for food, but there is no one to give it to them.

Those accustomed to dainty food perish in the streets; those brought up in purple now cling to the ash heaps.

The punishment of the daughter of my people is greater than the penalty of Sodom, which was overthrown in an instant without the turning of a hand.

Brighter than snow were her princes, whiter than milk, more ruddy than coral, more precious than sapphire.

Now their appearance is blacker than soot, they are unrecognized on the streets; their skin shrinks on their bones, as dry as wood.

Remember, O Lord, what has befallen us, look, and see our disgrace: our inherited lands have been turned over to strangers, our homes to foreigners. We have become orphans, fatherless; widowed are our mothers. The water we drink we must buy, for our own wood we must pay. On our necks is the yoke of those who drive us; we are worn out, but allowed no rest.

To Egypt we submitted, and to Assyria, to fill our need of bread. Our fathers, who sinned, are no more; but we bear their guilt. Slaves rule over us; there is no one to rescue us from their hands. At the peril of our lives we bring in our sustenance, in the face of the desert heat; our skin is shriveled up, as though by a furnace, with the searing blasts of famine.

The wives in Sion were ravished by the enemy, the maidens in the cities of Juda.

You, O Lord, are enthroned forever; your throne stands from age to age. Why, then, should you forget us, abandon us so long a time? Lead us back to you, O Lord, that we may be restored: give us anew such days as we had of old. For now you have indeed rejected us, and in full measure turned your wrath against us.

CHAPTER TWENTY-TWO

A History of Morals

THE SUFFERING OF JOB*

In the land of Us there was a blameless and upright man named Job, who feared God and avoided evil. Seven sons and three daughters were born to him; and he had seven thousand sheep, three thousand camels, five hundred yoke of oxen, five hundred she-asses, and a great number of work animals, so that he was greater than any of the men of the East. His sons used to take turns giving feasts, sending invitations to their three sisters to eat and drink with them. And when each feast had run its course, Job would send for them and sanctify them, rising early and offering holocausts for every one of them. For Job said, "It may be that my sons have sinned and blasphemed God in their hearts." This Job did habitually.

One day, when the sons of God came to present themselves before the Lord, Satan also came among them. And the Lord said to Satan, "Whence do you come?" Then Satan answered the Lord and said, "From roaming the earth and patrolling it." And the Lord said to Satan, "Have you noticed my servant Job, and that there is no one on earth like him, blameless and upright, fearing God and avoiding evil?" But Satan answered the Lord and said, "Is it for nothing that Job is God-fearing? Have you not surrounded him and his family and all that he has with your protection? You have blessed the work of his hands, and his livestock are spread over the land. But now put forth your hand and touch anything that he has, and surely he will blaspheme you to your face." And the Lord said to Satan, "Behold, all that he has is in your power; only do not lay a hand upon his person." So Satan went forth from the presence of the Lord.

And so one day, while his sons and his daughters were eating and drinking wine in the house of their eldest brother, a messenger came to Job and said, "The oxen were plowing and the asses grazing beside them,

* It is not known when the Book of Job was composed or to what period it refers.

and the Sabeans carried them off in a raid. They put the herdsmen to the sword, and I alone have escaped to tell you." While he was yet speaking, another came and said, "Lightning has fallen from heaven and struck the sheep and their shepherds and consumed them; and I alone have escaped to tell you." While he was yet speaking, another came and said, "The Chaldeans formed three columns, seized the camels, carried them off, and put those tending them to the sword, and I alone have escaped to tell you." While he was yet speaking, another came and said, "Your sons and daughters were eating and drinking wine in the house of their eldest brother, when suddenly a great wind came across the desert and smote the four corners of the house. It fell upon the young people and they are dead; and I alone have escaped to tell you." Then Job began to tear his cloak and cut off his hair. He cast himself prostrate upon the ground, and said, "Naked I came forth from my mother's womb, and naked shall I go back again. The Lord gave and the Lord has taken away; blessed be the name of the Lord!" In all this Job did not sin, nor did he say anything disrespectful of God.

Once again the sons of God came to present themselves before the Lord, and Satan also came with them. And the Lord said to Satan, "Whence do you come?" And Satan answered the Lord and said, "From roaming the earth and patrolling it." And the Lord said to Satan, "Have you noticed my servant Job, and that there is no one on earth like him, faultless and upright, fearing God and avoiding evil? He still holds fast to his innocence although you incited me against him to ruin him without cause." And Satan answered the Lord and said, "Skin for skin! All that a man has will he give for his life. But now put forth your hand and touch his bone and his flesh, and surely he will blaspheme you to your face." And the Lord said to Satan, "He is in your power; only spare his life." So Satan went forth from the presence of the Lord and smote Job with severe boils from the soles of his feet to the crown of his head. And he took a potsherd to scrape himself, as he sat among the ashes. Then his wife said to him, "Are you still holding to your innocence? Curse God and die." But he said to her, "Are even you going to speak as senseless women do? We accept good things from God; and should we not accept evil?" Through all this, Job said nothing sinful.

JOB REPLIES TO ELIPHAZ

Now when three of Job's friends heard of all the misfortune that had come upon him, they set out each one from his own place: Eliphaz from

Theman, Baldad from Sue, and Sophar from Naama. They met and journeyed together to give him sympathy and comfort. But when, at a distance, they lifted up their eyes and did not recognize him, they began to weep aloud; they tore their cloaks and threw dust upon their heads. Then they sat down upon the ground with him seven days and seven nights, but none of them spoke a word to him; for they saw how great was his suffering.

After this, Job opened his mouth and cursed his day. Job spoke out and said: Perish the day on which I was born, the night when they said, "The child is a boy!" May that day be darkness: let not God above call for it, nor light shine upon it! May darkness and gloom claim it, clouds settle upon it, the blackness of night affright it! May obscurity seize that day; let it not occur among the days of the year, nor enter into the count of the months! May that night be barren; let no joyful outcry greet it! Let them curse it who curse the sea, the appointed disturbers of Leviathan! May the stars of its twilight be darkened; may it look for daylight, but have none, nor gaze on the eyes of the dawn, because it kept not shut the doors of the womb to shield my eyes from trouble!

Why did I not perish at birth, come forth from the womb and expire? Or why was I not buried away like an untimely birth, like babes that have never seen the light? Wherefore did the knees receive me? or why did I suck at the breasts?

For then I should have lain down and been tranquil; had I slept, I should then have been at rest with kings and counselors of the earth who built where now there are ruins, or with princes who had gold and filled their houses with silver; there the wicked cease from troubling, there the weary are at rest.

Then spoke Eliphaz the Themanite, who said: If someone attempts a word with you, will you mind? For how can anyone refrain from speaking? Behold, you have instructed many, and have made firm their feeble hands. Your words have upheld the stumbler; you have strengthened his faltering knees. But now that it comes to you, you are impatient; when it touches yourself, you are dismayed. Is not your piety a source of confidence, and your integrity of life your hope?

Reflect now, what innocent person perishes? Since when are the upright destroyed?

For a word was stealthily brought to me, and my ear caught a whisper of it. In my thoughts during visions of the night, when deep sleep falls on men, fear came upon me, and shuddering, that terrified me to the bones. Then a spirit passed before me, and the hair of my flesh stood up. It paused, but its likeness I could not discern; a figure was before my eyes, and I heard a still voice: "Can a man be righteous as against God? Can a mortal be blameless against his Maker? Lo, he puts no trust in his servants, and with his angels he can find fault. How much more with those that dwell in houses of clay, whose foundation is in the dust, who are crushed more easily than the moth!"

Then Job answered and said: Ah, could my anguish but be measured and my calamity laid with it in the scales, they would now outweigh the sands of the sea! Because of this I speak without restraint. For the arrows of the Almighty pierce me, and my spirit drinks in their poison; the terrors of God are arrayed against me.

Is not man's life on earth a drudgery? Are not his days those of a hireling? He is a slave who longs for the shade, a hireling who waits for his wages. So I have been assigned months of misery, and troubled nights have been told off for me.

If in bed I say, "When shall I arise?" Then the night drags on; I am filled with restlessness until the dawn. My flesh is clothed with worms and scabs; my skin cracks and festers; my days are swifter than a weaver's shuttle; they come to an end without hope. Remember that my life is like the wind; I shall not see happiness again.

What is man, that you make much of him, or pay him any heed? You observe him with each new day and try him at every moment! How long will it be before you look away from me, and let me alone long enough to swallow my spittle? Though I have sinned, what can I do to you, O watcher of men? Why have you set me up as an object of attack; or why should I be a burden to you? Why do you not pardon my offense, or take away my guilt? For soon I shall lie down in the dust; and should you seek me I shall then be gone.

JOB REPLIES TO BALDAD

Baldad the Sueite spoke out and said: How long will you utter such things? The words from your mouth are like a mighty wind! Does God pervert judgment, and does the Almighty distort justice? If your children have sinned against him and he has left them in the grip of their guilt, still, if you yourself have recourse to God and make supplication to the Almighty, should you be blameless and upright, surely now he will awake for you and restore your rightful domain; your former state will be of little moment, for in time to come you will flourish indeed.

Then Job answered and said: I know well that it is so; but how can a man be justified before God? Should one wish to contend with him, he could not answer him once in a thousand times. God is wise in heart and mighty in strength; who has withstood him and remained unscathed?

He removes the mountains before they know it; he overturns them in his anger. He shakes the earth out of its place, and the pillars beneath it tremble. He commands the sun, and it rises not; he seals up the stars.

He alone stretches out the heavens and treads upon the crests of the sea. He made the Bear and Orion, the Pleiades and the constellations of the south; he does great things past finding out, marvelous things beyond reckoning.

Why then did you bring me forth from the womb? I should have died and no eye have seen me. I should be as though I had never lived; I should have been taken from the womb to the grave. Are not the days of my life few? Let me alone, that I may recover a little before I go whence I shall not return, to the land of darkness and of gloom, the black, disordered land where darkness is the only light.

Man, born of woman, is short-lived and full of trouble. Like a flower that springs up and fades, swift as a shadow that does not abide, even so he wastes away like a rotten thing; like a garment that the moth has consumed. Upon such a one will you cast your eyes so as to bring me into judgment before you? Can a man be found who is clean of defilement? There is none, however short his days. You know the number of his months; you have fixed the limit which he cannot pass. Look away from him and let him be, while, like a hireling, he completes his day.

For a tree there is hope, if it be cut down, that it will sprout again and that its tender shoots will not cease. Even though its root grow old in the earth, and its stump die in the dust, yet at the first whiff of water it may flourish again and put forth branches like a young plant. But when a man dies, all vigor leaves him; when man expires, where then is he? As when the waters of a lake fail, or a stream grows dry and parches, so men lie down and rise not again. Till the heavens are no more, they shall not awake, nor be roused out of their sleep.

Oh, that you would hide me in the nether world and keep me sheltered till your wrath is past; would fix a time for me, and then remember me! When a man has died, were he to live again, all the days of my drudgery I would wait, until my relief should come.

AGAIN JOB REPLIES TO ELIPHAZ

Then Eliphaz the Themanite spoke and said: Why do your notions carry you away, and why do your eyes blink, so that you turn your anger against

God and let such words escape your mouth! What is a man that he should be blameless, one born of woman that he should be righteous? If in his holy ones God places no confidence, and if the heavens are not clean in his sight, how much less so is the abominable, the corrupt: man, who drinks in iniquity like water!

Then Job answered and said: How long will you vex my soul, grind me down with words? These ten times you have reviled me, have assailed me without shame! Be it indeed that I am at fault and that my fault remains with me, even so, if you would vaunt yourselves against me and cast up to me my reproach, know then that God has dealt unfairly with me, and compassed me round with his net.

If I cry out "Injustice!" I am not heard. I cry for help, but there is no redress. He has barred my way and I cannot pass; he has veiled my path in darkness; he has stripped me of my glory, and taken the diadem from my brow. He breaks me down on every side, and I am gone; my hope he has uprooted like a tree. His wrath he has kindled against me; he counts me among his enemies. His troops advance as one man; they build up their road to attack me, and they encamp around my tent.

My brethren have withdrawn from me, and my friends are wholly estranged. My kinsfolk and companions neglect me, and my guests have forgotten me. Even my handmaids treat me as a stranger; I am an alien in their sight. I call my servant, but he gives no answer, though in my speech I plead with him. My breath is abhorred by my wife; I am loathsome to the men of my family.

The young children, too, despise me; when I appear, they speak against me. All my intimate friends hold me in horror; those whom I loved have turned against me! My bones cleave to my skin, and I have escaped with my flesh between my teeth. Pity me, pity me, O you my friends, for the hand of God has struck me! Why do you hound me as though you were divine, and insatiably prey upon me?

Oh, would that my words were written down! Would that they were inscribed in a record: That with an iron chisel and with lead they were cut in the rock forever! But as for me, I know that my Vindicator lives, and that he will at last stand forth upon the dust whom I myself shall see, and not another—and from my flesh I shall see God; my inmost being is consumed with longing.

But what is man's lot from God above, his inheritance from the Almighty on high? Is it not calamity for the unrighteous, and woe for evildoers? Does he not see my ways, and number all my steps? Let God weigh me in the scales of justice; thus will he know my innocence.

If I have walked in falsehood and my foot has hastened to deceit; if my steps have turned out of the way, and my heart has followed my eyes, or any stain clings to my hands, then may I sow, but another eat of it, or may my planting be rooted up!

THE WORD AND MERCY OF GOD COMES TO JOB

Then the Lord addressed Job out of the storm and said: Who is this that obscures divine plans with words of ignorance? Gird up your loins now, like a man; I will question you, and you tell me the answers! Where were you when I founded the earth? Tell me, if you have understanding. Who determined its size; do you know? Who stretched out the measuring line for it? Into what were its pedestals sunk, and who laid the cornerstone, while the morning stars sang in chorus and all the sons of God shouted for joy?

Do you know the ordinances of the heavens; can you put into effect their plan on the earth? Can you raise your voice among the clouds, or veil yourself in the waters of the storm? Can you send forth the lightnings on their way, or will they say to you, "Here we are"?

Then Job answered the Lord and said: I know that you can do all things, and that no purpose of yours can be hindered. I have dealt with great things that I do not understand; things too wonderful for me, which I cannot know. I had heard of you by word of mouth, but now my eye has seen you. Therefore I disown what I have said, and repent in dust and ashes.

And it came to pass after the Lord had spoken these words to Job, that the Lord said to Eliphaz the Themanite, "I am angry with you and with your two friends, for you have not spoken rightly concerning me, as has my servant Job. Now, therefore, take seven bullocks and seven rams, and go to my servant Job, and offer up a holocaust for yourselves; and let my servant Job pray for you; for his prayer I will accept, not to punish you severely. For you have not spoken rightly concerning me, as has my servant Job." Then Eliphaz the Themanite, and Baldad the Sueite, and Sophar the Naamaite, went and did as the Lord had commanded them. And the Lord accepted the intercession of Job.

Also, the Lord restored the prosperity of Job, after he had prayed for his friends; the Lord even gave to Job twice as much as he had before. Then all his brethren and his sisters came to him, and all his former acquaintances, and they dined with him in his house. They condoled with him and comforted him for all the evil which the Lord had brought upon him; and each one gave him a piece of money and a gold ring.

Thus the Lord blessed the latter days of Job more than his earlier ones. For he had fourteen thousand sheep, six thousand camels, a thousand yoke of oxen, and a thousand she-asses. And he had seven sons and three daughters, of whom he called the first Jemima, the second Cassia, and the third Ceren-happuch. In all the land no other women were as beautiful as the daughters of Job; and their father gave them an inheritance among their brethren. After this, Job lived a hundred and forty years; and he saw his children, his grandchildren, and even his great-grandchildren. Then Job died, old and full of years.

THE STORY OF JONA

This is the word of the Lord that came to Jona, son of Amathi: "Set out for the great city of Ninive, and preach against it; their wickedness has come up before me." But Jona made ready to flee to Tharsis away from the Lord. He went down to Joppe, found a ship going to Tharsis, paid the fare, and went aboard to journey with them to Tharsis, away from the Lord.

The Lord, however, hurled a violent wind upon the sea, and in the furious tempest that arose the ship was on the point of breaking up. Then the mariners became frightened and each one cried to his god. To lighten the ship for themselves, they threw its cargo into the sea. Meanwhile, Jona had gone down into the hold of the ship, and lay there fast asleep. The captain came to him and said, "What are you doing asleep? Rise up, call upon your God! Perhaps God will be mindful of us so that we may not perish."

Then they said to one another, "Come, let us cast lots to find out on whose account we have met with this misfortune." So they cast lots, and thus singled out Jona. "Tell us," they said, "what is your business? Where do you come from? What is your country, and to what people do you belong?" "I am a Hebrew," Jona answered them; "I worship the Lord, the God of heaven, who made the sea and the dry land."

Now the men were seized with great fear and said to him, "How could you do such a thing!"—They knew that he was fleeing from the Lord, because he had told them.—"What shall we do with you," they asked, "that the sea may quiet down for us?" For the sea was growing more and more turbulent. Jona said to them, "Pick me up and throw me into the sea, that it may quiet down for you; since I know it is because of me that this violent storm has come upon you."

Still the men rowed hard to regain the land, but they could not, for the sea grew ever more turbulent. Then they took Jona and threw him into the sea, and the sea's raging abated. Struck with great fear of the Lord, the men offered sacrifice and made vows to him.

But the Lord sent a large fish, that swallowed Jona; and he remained in the belly of the fish three days and three nights. From the belly of the fish Jona said this prayer to the Lord, his God:

Out of my distress I called to the Lord, and he answered me; from the midst of the nether world I cried for help; and you heard my voice. For you cast me into the deep, into the heart of the sea; and the flood enveloped me; all your breakers and your billows passed over me. Then I said, "I am banished from your sight! yet would I again look upon your holy temple." The waters swirled about me, threatening my life; the abyss enveloped me; seaweed clung about my head. Down I went to the roots of the mountains; the bars of the nether world were closing behind me forever, but you brought up my life from the pit, O Lord, my God. When my soul fainted within me, I remembered the Lord; my prayer reached you in your holy temple. Those who worship vain idols forsake their source of mercy. But I, with resounding praise, will sacrifice to you; what I have vowed I will pay: deliverance is from the Lord.

Then the Lord commanded the fish to spew Jona upon the shore.

The word of the Lord came to Jona a second time: "Set out for the great city of Ninive, and announce to it the message that I will tell you." So Jona made ready and went to Ninive, according to the Lord's bidding. Now Ninive was an enormously large city; it took three days to go through it. Jona began his journey through the city, and had gone but a single day's walk announcing, "Forty days more and Ninive shall be destroyed." And the men of Ninive believed in God: and they proclaimed a fast and all of them, great and small, put on sackcloth.

When the news reached the king of Ninive, he rose from his throne, laid aside his robe, covered himself with sackcloth, and sat in the ashes. Then he had this proclaimed throughout Ninive, by decree of the king and his nobles: "Neither man nor beast, neither cattle nor sheep, shall taste anything; they shall not eat, nor shall they drink water. Man and beast shall be covered with sackcloth and call loudly to God; every man shall turn from his evil way and from the violence he has in hand. Who knows, God may relent and forgive, and withhold his blazing wrath, so that we shall not perish." When God saw by their actions how they turned from their evil way, he repented of the veil that he had threatened to do to them; he did not carry it out.

But this was greatly displeasing to Jona, and he became angry. "I beseech you, Lord," he prayed, "is not this what I said while I was still in my own country? This is why I fled at first to Tharsis. I knew that you are a gracious and merciful God, slow to anger, rich in clemency, loathe to punish. And now, Lord, please take my life from me; for it is better for me to die than to live." But the Lord asked, "Have you reason to be angry?"

Jona then left the city for a place to the east of it, where he built himself a hut and waited under it in the shade, to see what would happen to the city. And when the Lord God provided a gourd plant, that grew up over Jona's head, giving shade that relieved him of any discomfort, Jona was very happy over the plant. But the next morning at dawn God sent a worm which attacked the plant, so that it withered. And when the sun arose, God sent a burning east wind; and the sun beat upon Jona's head till he became faint. Then he asked for death, saying, "I would be better off dead than alive."

But God said to Jona, "Have you reason to be angry over the plant?" "I have reason to be angry," Jona answered, "angry enough to die." Then the Lord said, "You are concerned over the plant which cost you no labor and which you did not raise; it came up in one night and in one night it perished. And should I not be concerned over Ninive, the great city, in which there are more than a hundred and twenty thousand persons who cannot distinguish their right hand from their left, not to mention the many cattle?"

DANIEL AND HIS COMPANIONS

In the third year of the reign of Joakim, king of Juda, King Nabuchodonosor of Babylon came and laid siege to Jerusalem. The Lord handed over to him Joakim, king of Juda, and some of the vessels of the temple of God, which he carried off to the land of Senaar, and placed in the temple treasury of his god.

The king told Asphenaz, his chief chamberlain, to bring in some of the Israelites of royal blood and of the nobility, young men without any defect, handsome, intelligent and wise, quick to learn, and prudent in judgment, such as could take their place in the king's palace; they were to be taught the language and literature of the Chaldeans: after three years' training they were to enter the king's service. The king allotted them a daily portion of food and wine from the royal table. Among these were men of Juda: Daniel, Anania, Misael, and Azaria. The chief chamberlain changed their names: Daniel to Baltassar, Anania to Sidrach, Misael to Misach, and Azaria to Abdenago.

When the king had spoken with all of them, none was found equal to Daniel, Anania, Misael, and Azaria; and so they entered the king's service. In any question of wisdom or prudence which the king put to them, he found them ten times better than all the magicians and enchanters in his kingdom. Daniel remained there until the first year of King Cyrus.

THE FIERY FURNACE

King Nabuchodonosor had a golden statue made, sixty cubits high and six cubits wide, which he set up in the plain of Dura in the province of Babylon. He then ordered the satraps, prefects, and governors, the counselors, treasurers, judges, magistrates and all the officials of the provinces to be summoned to the dedication of the statue which he had set up. The satraps, prefects, and governors, the counselors, treasurers, judges, and magistrates and all the officials of the provinces, all these came together for the dedication and stood before the statue which King Nabuchodonosor had set up. A herald cried out: "Nations and peoples of every language, when you hear the sound of the trumpet, flute, lyre, harp, psaltery, bagpipe, and all the other musical instruments, you are ordered to fall down and worship the golden statue which King Nabuchodonosor has set up. Whoever does not fall down and worship shall be instantly cast into a white-hot furnace." Therefore, as soon as they heard the sound of the trumpet, flute, lyre, harp, psaltery, bagpipe, and all the other musical instruments, the nations and peoples of every language all fell down and worshiped the golden statue which King Nabuchodonosor had set up.

At that point, some of the Chaldeans came and accused the Jews to King Nabuchodonosor: "O king, live forever! O king, you issued a decree that everyone who heard the sound of the trumpet, flute, lyre, harp, psaltery, bagpipe, and all the other musical instruments should fall down and worship the golden statue; whoever did not was to be cast into a white-hot furnace. There are certain Jews whom you have made administrators of the province of Babylon: Sidrach, Misach, Abdenago; these men, O king, have paid no attention to you; they will not serve your god or worship the golden statue which you set up."

Nabuchodonosor flew into a rage and sent for Sidrach, Misach, and Abdenago, who were promptly brought before the king. King Nabuchodonosor questioned them: "Is it true, Sidrach, Misach, and Abdenago, that you will not serve my god, or worship the golden statue that I set up? Be ready now to fall down and worship the statue I had made, whenever you hear the sound of the trumpet, flute, lyre, harp, psaltery, bagpipe, and all the other musical instruments; otherwise, you shall be instantly cast into the white-hot furnace; and who is the God that can deliver you out of my hands?" Sidrach, Misach, and Abdenago answered King Nabuchodonosor, "There is no need for us to defend ourselves before you in this matter. If our God, whom we serve, can save us from the white-hot furnace and from your hands, O king, may he save us! But even if he will not, know, O king, that we will not serve your god or worship the golden statue which you set up."

Nabuchodonosor's face became livid with utter rage against Sidrach, Misach, and Abdenago. He ordered the furnace to be heated seven times more than usual and had some of the strongest men in his army bind Sidrach, Misach, and Abdenago and cast them into the white-hot furnace. They were bound and cast into the white-hot furnace with their coats, hats, shoes and other garments, for the king's order was urgent. So huge a fire was kindled in the furnace that the flames devoured the men who threw Sidrach, Misach, and Abdenago into it. But these three fell, bound, into the midst of the white-hot furnace. They walked about in the flames, singing to God and blessing the Lord.

Now the king's men who had thrown them in continued to stoke the furnace with brimstone, pitch, tow, and faggots. The flames rose forty-nine cubits above the furnace, and spread out, burning the Chaldeans nearby. But the angel of the Lord went down into the furnace with Azaria and his companions, drove the fiery flames out of the furnace, and made the inside of the furnace as though a dew-laden breeze were blowing through it. The fire in no way touched them or caused them pain or harm. Then these three in the furnace with one voice sang, glorifying and blessing God: "Blessed are you, O Lord, the God of our fathers, praiseworthy and exalted above all forever; and blessed is your holy and glorious name, praiseworthy and exalted above all for all ages. Blessed are you in the temple of your holy glory, praiseworthy and glorious above all forever. Blessed are you on the throne of your kingdom, praiseworthy and exalted above all forever. Blessed are you who look into the depths from your throne upon the cherubim, praiseworthy and exalted above all forever. Blessed are you in the firmament of heaven, praiseworthy and glorious forever.

"Bless the Lord, all you works of the Lord, praise and exalt him above all forever. Angels of the Lord, bless the Lord, praise and exalt him above all forever. You heavens, bless the Lord, praise and exalt him above all forever. All you waters above the heavens, bless the Lord, praise and exalt him above all forever. All you hosts of the Lord, bless the Lord; praise and exalt him above all forever. Sun and moon, bless the Lord; praise and exalt him above all forever. Stars of heaven, bless the Lord; praise and exalt him above all forever. Every shower and dew, bless the Lord; praise and exalt him above all forever. All you winds, bless the Lord; praise and exalt him above all forever. Fire and heat, bless the Lord; praise and exalt him above all forever. [Cold and chill, bless the Lord; praise and exalt him above all forever. Dew and rain, bless the Lord; praise and exalt him above all forever.] Frost and chill, bless the Lord; praise and exalt him above all forever. Ice and snow, bless the Lord; praise and exalt him above all forever. Nights and days, bless the Lord; praise and exalt him above all forever. Light and darkness, bless the Lord; praise and exalt him above all forever. Lightnings and clouds, bless the Lord; praise and exalt him above all forever.

"Let the earth bless the Lord, praise and exalt him above all forever. Mountains and hills, bless the Lord; praise and exalt him above all forever. Everything growing from the earth, bless the Lord; praise and exalt him above all forever. You springs, bless the Lord; praise and exalt him above all forever. Seas and rivers, bless the Lord; praise and exalt him above all forever. You dolphins and all water creatures, bless the Lord; praise and exalt him above all forever. All you birds of the air, bless the Lord; praise and exalt him above all forever. All you beasts, wild and tame, bless the Lord; praise and exalt him above all forever. You sons of men, bless the Lord; praise and exalt him above all forever. O Israel, bless the Lord; praise and exalt him above all forever. Priests of the Lord, bless the Lord; praise and exalt him above all forever. Servants of the Lord, bless the Lord; praise and exalt him above all forever. Spirits and souls of the just, bless the Lord; praise and exalt him above all forever. Holy men of humble heart, bless the Lord; praise and exalt him above all forever. Anania, Azaria, Misael, bless the Lord; praise and exalt him above all forever. For he has delivered us from the nether world, and saved us from the power of death; he has freed us from the raging flame and delivered us from the fire. Give thanks to the Lord, for he is good, for his mercy endures forever. Bless the God of gods, all you who fear the Lord; praise him and give him thanks, because his mercy endures forever."

Hearing them sing, and astonished at seeing them alive, King Nabuchodonosor rose in haste and asked his nobles, "Did we not cast three men bound into the fire?" "Assuredly, O king," they answered. "But," he replied, "I see four men unfettered and unhurt, walking in the fire, and the fourth looks like a son of God." Then Nabuchodonosor came to the opening of the white-hot furnace and called to Sidrach, Misach, and Abdenago: "Servants of the most high God, come out." Thereupon Sidrach, Misach, and Abdenago came out of the fire. When the satraps, prefects, governors, and nobles of the king came together, they saw that the fire had had no power over the bodies of these men; not a hair of their heads had been singed, nor were their garments altered; there was not even a smell of fire about them. Nabuchodonosor exclaimed, "Blessed be the God of Sidrach, Misach, and Abdenago, who sent his angel to deliver the servants that trusted in him; they disobeyed the royal command and yielded their bodies rather than serve or worship any god except their own God. Therefore I decree for nations and peoples of every language that whoever blasphemes the God of Sidrach, Misach, and Abdenago shall be cut to pieces and his house destroyed. For there is no other God who can rescue like this." Then the king promoted Sidrach, Misach, and Abdenago in the province of Babylon.

THE WRITING ON THE WALL

King Belsassar gave a great banquet for a thousand of his lords, with whom he drank. Under the influence of the wine, he ordered the gold and silver vessels which Nabuchodonosor, his father, had taken from the temple in Jerusalem, to be brought in so that the king, his lords, his wives and his entertainers might drink from them. When the gold and silver vessels taken from the house of God in Jerusalem had been brought in, and while the king, his lords, his wives and his entertainers were drinking wine from them, they praised their gods of gold and silver, bronze and iron, wood and stone.

Suddenly, opposite the lampstand, the fingers of a human hand appeared, writing on the plaster of the wall in the king's palace. When the king saw the wrist, and hand that wrote, his face blanched; his thoughts terrified him, his hip joints shook, and his knees knocked. The king shouted for the enchanters, Chaldeans, and astrologers to be brought in. "Whoever reads this writing and tells me what it means," he said to the wise men of Babylon, "shall be clothed in purple, wear a golden collar about his neck, and be third in the government of the kingdom." But though all the king's wise men came in, none of them could either read the writing or tell the king what it meant. Then King Belsassar was greatly terrified; his face went ashen, and his lords were thrown into confusion.

Then Daniel was brought into the presence of the king. The king asked him, "Are you the Daniel, the Jewish exile, whom my father, the king, brought from Juda? I have heard that the spirit of God is in you, that you possess brilliant knowledge and extraordinary wisdom. Now, the wise men and enchanters were brought in to me to read this writing and tell me its meaning, but they could not say what the words meant. But I have heard that you can interpret dreams and solve difficulties; if you are able to read the writing and tell me what it means, you shall be clothed in purple, wear a gold collar about your neck, and be third in the government of the kingdom."

Daniel answered the king: "You may keep your gifts, or give your presents to someone else; but the writing I will read for you, O king, and tell you what it means. The Most High God gave your father Nabuchodonosor a great kingdom and glorious majesty. You, his son, Belsassar, have not humbled your heart, though you knew all this; you have rebelled against the Lord of heaven. You had the vessels of his temple brought before you, so that you and your nobles, your wives and your entertainers, might drink wine from them; and you praised the gods of silver and gold, bronze and iron, wood and stone, that neither see nor hear nor have intelligence. But the God in whose hand is your life breath and the whole course of your life, you did not glorify. By him were the wrist and hand sent, and the writing set down.

"This is the writing that was inscribed: MENE, TEKEL, and PERES. These words mean: MENE, God has numbered your kingdom and put an end to it; TEKEL, you have been weighed on the scales and found wanting; PERES, your kingdom has been divided and given to the Medes and Persians."

Then by order of Belsassar they clothed Daniel in purple, with a gold collar about his neck, and proclaimed him third in the government of the kingdom. The same night Belsassar, the Chaldean king, was slain. And Darius the Mede succeeded to the kingdom at the age of sixty-two.

THE LIONS' DEN

Darius decided to appoint over his entire kingdom one hundred and twenty satraps, to safeguard his interests; these were accountable to three supervisors, one of whom was Daniel. Daniel outshone all the supervisors and satraps because an extraordinary spirit was in him, and the king thought of giving him authority over the entire kingdom. Therefore the supervisors and satraps tried to find grounds for accusation against Daniel as regards the administration. But they could accuse him of no wrongdoing; because he was trustworthy, no fault of neglect or misconduct was to be found in him. Then these men said to themselves, "We shall find no grounds for accusation against this Daniel unless by way of the law of his God." So these supervisors and satraps went thronging to the king and said to him, "King Darius, live forever! All the supervisors of the kingdom, the prefects, satraps, nobles, and governors are agreed that the following prohibition ought to be put in force by royal decree: no one is to address any petition to god or man for thirty days, except to you, O king; otherwise he shall be cast into a den of lions. Now, O king, issue the prohibition over your signature, immutable and irrevocable under Mede and Persian law." So King Darius signed the prohibition and made it law.

Even after Daniel heard that this law had been signed, he continued his custom of going home to kneel in prayer and give thanks to his God in the upper chamber three times a day, with the windows open toward Jerusalem. So these men rushed in and found Daniel praying and pleading before his God. Then they went to remind the king about the prohibition: "Did you not decree, O king, that no one is to address a petition to god or man for thirty days, except to you, O king; otherwise he shall be cast into a den of lions?" The king answered them, "The decree is absolute, irrevocable under the Mede and Persian law." To this they replied, "Daniel, the Jewish exile, has paid no attention to you, O king, or to the decree you issued; three times a day he offers his prayer." The king was deeply grieved at this news and he made up his mind to save Daniel; he worked till sunset to rescue him. But these men insisted. "Keep in mind, O king," they said, "that under the Mede and Persian law every royal prohibition or decree is irrevocable." So the king ordered Daniel to be brought and cast into the lions' den. To Daniel he said, "May your God, whom you serve so constantly, save you." To forestall any tampering, the king sealed with his own ring and the rings of the

334

lords the stone that had been brought to block the opening of the den.

Then the king returned to his palace for the night; he refused to eat and he dismissed the entertainers. Since sleep was impossible for him, the king rose very early the next morning and hastened to the lions' den. As he drew near, he cried out to Daniel sorrowfully, "O Daniel, servant of the living God, has the God whom you serve so constantly been able to save you from the lions?" Danied answered the king: "O king, live forever! My God has sent his angel and closed the lions' mouths so that they have not hurt me. For I have been found innocent before him; neither to you have I done any harm, O king!" This gave the king great joy. At his order Daniel was removed from the den, unhurt because he trusted in his God. The king then ordered the men who had accused Daniel, along with their children and their wives, to be cast into the lions' den. Before they reached the bottom of the den, the lions overpowered them and crushed all their bones.

Then King Darius wrote to the nations and peoples of every language, wherever they dwell on the earth: "All peace to you! I decree that throughout my royal domain the God of Daniel is to be reverenced and feared: For he is the living God, enduring forever; his kingdom shall not be destroyed, and his dominion shall be without end. He is a deliverer and savior, working signs and wonders in heaven and on earth, and he delivered Daniel from the lions' power."

So Daniel fared well during the reign of Darius and the reign of Cyrus the Persian.

TOBIAS BEGINS HIS DIFFICULT JOURNEY *

The book of the acts of Tobit the son of Tobiel, son of Ananiel, son of Aduel, son of Gabael, of the descendants of Asiel and the tribe of Naphtali, who in the days of Shalmaneser, king of the Assyrians, was taken into captivity from Thisbe, which is to the south of Kedesh Naphtali in Galilee above Asher.

I, Tobit, walked in the ways of truth and righteousness all the days of my life, and I performed many acts of charity to my brethren and countrymen who went with me into the land of the Assyrians, to Nineveh. Now when I was in my own country, in the land of Israel, while I was still a young man, the whole tribe of Naphtali my forefather deserted

---

* The story of Tobias refers to the time when the ten tribes were led into captivity, but the date of its composition is not known nor the events that prompted its unique style of writing.

the house of Jerusalem. This was the place which had been chosen from among all the tribes of Israel, where all the tribes should sacrifice and where the temple of the dwelling of the Most High was consecrated and established for all generations for ever.

All the tribes that joined in apostasy used to sacrifice to the calf Baal, and so did the house of Naphtali my forefather. But I alone went often to Jerusalem for the feasts, as it is ordained for all Israel by an everlasting decree. Taking the first fruits and the tithes of my produce and the first shearings, I would give these to the priests, the sons of Aaron, at the altar. Of all my produce I would give a tenth to the sons of Levi who ministered at Jerusalem; a second tenth I would sell, and I would go and spend the proceeds each year at Jerusalem; the third tenth I would give to those to whom it was my duty, as Deborah my father's mother had commanded me, for I was left an orphan by my father. When I became a man I married Anna, a member of our family, and by her I became the father of Tobias.

Now when I was carried away captive to Nineveh, all my brethren and my relatives ate the food of the Gentiles; but I kept myself from eating it, because I remembered God with all my heart. Then the Most High gave me favor and good appearance in the sight of Shalmaneser, and I was his buyer of provisions. So I used to go into Media, and once at Rages in Media I left ten talents of silver in trust with Gabael, the brother of Gabrias. But when Shalmaneser died, Sennacherib his son reigned in his place; and under him the highways were unsafe, so that I could no longer go into Media.

In the days of Shalmaneser I performed many acts of charity to my brethren. I would give my bread to the hungry and my clothing to the naked; and if I saw one of my people dead and thrown out behind the wall of Nineveh, I would bury him. And if Sennacherib the king put to death any who came fleeing from Judea, I buried them secretly. For in his anger he put many to death. When the bodies were sought by the king, they were not found.

On the same night I returned from burying, and because I was defiled I slept by the wall of the courtyard, and my face was uncovered. I did not know that there were sparrows on the wall and their fresh droppings fell into my open eyes and white films formed on my eyes.

Then in my grief I wept, and I prayed in anguish, saying, "Righteous art thou, O Lord; all thy deeds and all thy ways are mercy and truth, and thou dost render true and righteous judgment for ever. Remember me and look favorably upon me; do not punish me for my sins and for my unwitting offenses and those which my fathers committed before thee. For they disobeyed thy commandments, and thou gavest us over to plunder, captivity, and death; thou madest us a byword of reproach in all the nations among which we have been dispersed. And now thy many judgments are true in exacting penalty from me for my sins and those of my fathers, because we did not keep thy commandments. For we did not walk in truth before thee. And now deal with me according to thy pleasure; command my spirit to be taken up, that I may depart and become dust. For it is better for me to die than to live, because I have heard false reproaches, and great is the sorrow within me. Command that I now be released from my distress to go to the eternal abode; do not turn thy face away from me."

On the same day, at Ecbatana in Media, it also happened that Sarah, the daughter of Raguel, was reproached by her father's maids, because she had been given to seven husbands, and the evil demon Asmodeus had slain each of them before he had been with her as his wife.

When she heard these things she was deeply grieved, even to the thought of hanging herself. But she prayed by her window and the prayer of both was heard in the presence of the glory of the great God. And Raphael was sent to heal the two of them.

On that day Tobit remembered the money which he had left in trust with Gabael at Rages in Media, and he said to himself: "I have asked for death. Why do I not call my son Tobias so that I may explain to him about the money before I die?" So he called him and said, "My son, when I die, bury me, and do not neglect your mother. Honor her all the days of your life; do what is pleasing to her, and do not grieve her. Remember, my son, that she faced many dangers for you while you were yet unborn. When she dies, bury her beside me in the same grave.

"Remember the Lord our God all your days, my son, and refuse to sin or to transgress his commandments. Live uprightly all the days of your life, and do not walk in the ways of wrongdoing. For if you do what is true, your ways will prosper through your deeds. Give alms from your possessions to all who live uprightly, and do not let your eye begrudge the gift when you make it. Do not turn your face away from any poor man, and the face of God will not be turned away from you. If you have many possessions, make your gift from them in proportion; if few, do not be afraid to give according to the little you have. So you will be laying up a good treasure for yourself against the day of necessity. And now let me explain to you about the ten talents of silver which I left in trust with Gabael the son of Gabrias at Rages in Media. Do not be afraid, my son, because we have become poor. You have great wealth if you fear God and refrain from every sin and do what is pleasing in his sight."

Then Tobias answered him, "Father, I will do everything that you have commanded me; but how can I obtain the money when I do not know the man?" Then Tobit gave him the receipt, and said to him, "Find a man to go with you and I will pay him wages as long as I live; and go and get the money." So he went to look for a man; and he found Raphael, who was an angel, but Tobias did not know it. Tobias said to him, "Can you go with me to Rages in Media? Are you acquainted with that region?" The angel replied, "I will go with you; I am familiar with the way, and I have stayed with our brother Gabael." Then Tobias said to him, "Wait for me, and I shall tell my father." And he said to him, "Go, and do not delay." So he went in and said to his father, "I have found some one to go with me." He said, "Call him to me, so that I may learn to what tribe he belongs, and whether he is a reliable man to go with you."

Then he said to Tobias, "Get ready for the journey, and good success to you both." So his son made the preparations for the journey. And his father said to him, "Go with this man; God who dwells in heaven will prosper your way, and may his angel attend you." So they both went out and departed, and the young man's dog was with them.

Now as they proceeded on their way they came at evening to the Tigris river and camped there. Then the young man went down to wash himself. A fish leaped up from the river and would have swallowed the young man; and the angel said to him, "Catch the fish." So the young man seized the fish and threw it up on the land. Then the angel said to him, "Cut open the fish and take the heart and liver and gall and put them away safely." So the young man did as the angel told him; and they roasted and ate the fish.

And they both continued on their way until they came near to Ecbatana. Then the young man said to the angel, "Brother Azarias, of what use is the liver and heart and gall of the fish?" He replied, "As for the heart and liver, if a demon or evil spirit gives trouble to any one, you make a smoke from these before the man or woman, and that person will never be troubled again. And as for the gall, anoint with it a man who has white films in his eyes, and he will be cured."

When they approached Ecbatana, the angel said to the young man, "Brother, today we shall stay with Raguel. He is your relative, and he has an only daughter named Sarah. I will suggest that she be given to you in marriage, because you are entitled to her and to her inheritance, for you are her only eligible kinsman. The girl is also beautiful and sensible. Now listen to my plan. I will speak to her father, and as soon as we return from Rages we will celebrate the marriage. For I know that Raguel, according to the law of Moses, cannot give her to another man without incurring the penalty of death, because you rather than any other man are entitled to the inheritance."

Then the young man said to the angel, "Brother Azarias, I have heard that the girl has been given to seven husbands and that each died in the bridal chamber. Now I am the only son my father has, and I am afraid that if I go in I will die as those before me did, for a demon is in love with her, and he harms no one except those who approach her. So now I fear that I may die and bring the lives of my father and mother to the grave in sorrow on my account. And they have no other son to bury them."

But the angel said to him, "Do you not remember the words with which your father commanded you to take a wife from among your own people? Now listen to me, brother, for she will become your wife; and do not worry about the demon, for this very night she will be given to you in marriage. When you enter the bridal chamber, you shall take live ashes of incense and lay upon them some of the heart and liver of the fish so as to make a smoke. Then the demon will smell it and flee away, and will never again return.

"Heed me well," said the angel, "and you shall hear why the demon has power to hurt some and not others. The demon has power over such as go about their mating with all thought of God shut out of their hearts and minds, wholly intent on their lust, as if they were horse or mule, brutes without reason. Not such be thy mating, when thou hast won thy bride. For three days deny thyself her favors, and let all thy dalliance be to join with her in prayer.

"On the second night," the angel said, "union you shall have, but with the company of the holy patriarchs. The third night, your prayer shall win you a blessing, of children safely born to thee and to her. Then, when the third night is past, take the maid to thyself with the fear of the Lord upon thee, moved rather by the hope of begetting children than by any lust of thine. So, in the true line of Abraham, you shall have joy of thy fatherhood."

The angel said to the young man, "Do not be afraid, for she was destined for you from eternity. You will save her, and she will go with you." When Tobias heard these things, he fell in love with her and yearned deeply for her.

When they reached Ecbatana and arrived at the house of Raguel, Sarah met them and greeted them. They returned her greeting, and she brought them into the house. Then Raguel said to his wife Edna, "How much the young man resembles my cousin Tobit!" And Raguel asked them, "Where are you from, brethren?" They answered him, "We belong to the sons of Naphtali, who are captives in Nineveh." So he said to them, "Do you know our brother Tobit?" And they said, "Yes, we do." And he asked them, "Is he in good health?" They replied, "He is alive and in good health." And Tobias said, "He is my father." Then Raguel sprang up and kissed him and wept. And he blessed him and exclaimed, "Son of that good and noble man!" When he heard that Tobit had lost his sight, he was stricken with grief and wept. And his wife Edna and his daughter Sarah wept. They received them very warmly; and they killed a ram from the flock and set large servings of food before them.

Then Tobias said to Raphael, "Brother Azarias, speak of those things which you talked about on the journey, and let the matter be settled." So he communicated the proposal to Raguel. And Raguel said to Tobias, "Eat, drink, and be merry; for it is your right to take my child. But let me explain the true situation to you. I have given my daughter to seven husbands, and when each came to her he died in the night. But for the present be merry." And Tobias said, "I will eat nothing here until you make a binding agreement with me."

Upon hearing this, Raguel was much taken aback; and the fear assailed him, "What if this one fares no better?" But while he hummed and hawed over his answer, the angel said, "Do not be afraid to give him your daughter's hand; for his pious care she was destined, that is why those other wooers could not gain their suit." "Why then," answered Raguel, "all those prayers and sighs of mine were not wasted; God has granted them audience, and I doubt not his design in bringing you here to have my daughter matched with one of her own kin, as the law of Moses bade."

Then he said to Tobias, "Have no fear, she is yours." And so, taking his daughter by the right hand and putting it into the right hand of Tobias, he gave them his blessing: "May the God of Abraham, Isaac and Jacob be with you, and himself join you in one, and fulfil his merciful purpose in you."

So they took paper, and signed a contract of marriage; then they sat down to their feasting, and gave thanks to God.

And Raguel called his wife Edna and said to her, "Sister, make up the other room, and take her into it." So she did as he said, and took her there; and the girl began to weep. But the mother comforted her daughter in her tears, and said to her, "Be brave, my child; the Lord of heaven and earth grant you joy in place of this sorrow of yours. Be brave, my daughter."

Then Tobias called Raphael and said to him, "Brother Azarias, take a servant and two camels with you and go to Gabael at Rages in Media and get the money for me; and bring him to the wedding feast." So Raphael made the journey and stayed overnight with Gabael. He gave him the receipt, and Gabael brought out the money bags with their seals intact and gave them to him. In the morning they both got up early and came to the wedding feast. And Gabael blessed Tobias and his wife.

THE TRIUMPHANT RETURN OF TOBIAS

After this Tobias went on his way, praising God because he had made his journey a success. And he blessed Raguel and his wife Edna.

So he continued on his way until they came near to Nineveh. Then Raphael said to Tobias, "Are you not aware, brother, of how you left your father? Let us run ahead of your wife and prepare the house. And take the gall of the fish with you." So they went their way, and the dog went along behind them.

Now Anna sat looking intently down the road for her son. And she caught sight of him coming, and said to his father, "Behold, your son is coming, and so is the man who went with him!"

Yet he was not to reach the house first. The dog that had accompanied him on his travels ran on before him, heralding the good news with the caress of his wagging tail.

Raphael said, "I know, Tobias, that your father will open his eyes. You therefore must anoint his eyes with the gall; and when they smart he will rub them, and will cause the white films to fall away, and he will see you."

Then Anna ran to meet them, and embraced her son, and said to him, "I have seen you, my child; now I am ready to die." And they both wept. Tobit started toward the door, and stumbled. But his son ran to him and took hold of his father, and he sprinkled the gall upon his father's eyes, saying, "Be of good cheer, father." And when his eyes began to smart he rubbed them, and the white films scaled off from the corners of his eyes. Then he saw his son and embraced him, and he wept and said, "Blessed art thou, O God, and blessed is thy name for ever, and blessed are all thy holy angels. For thou hast afflicted me, but thou hast had mercy upon me; here I see my son Tobias!" And his son went in rejoicing, and he reported to his father the great things that had happened to him in Media.

Then Tobit went out to meet his daughter-in-law at the gate of Nineveh, rejoicing and praising God. Those who saw him as he went were amazed because he could see. And Tobit gave thanks before them that God had been merciful to him. When Tobit came near to Sarah his daughter-in-law, he blessed her, saying, "Welcome, daughter! Blessed is God who has brought you to us, and blessed are your father and your mother." So there was rejoicing among all his brethren in Nineveh. Ahikar and his nephew Nadab came, and Tobias' marriage was celebrated for seven days with great festivity.

Tobit then called his son Tobias and said to him, "My son, see to the wages of the man who went with you; and he must also be given more." He replied, "Father, it would do me no harm to give him half of what I have brought back. For he has led me back to you safely, he cured my wife, he obtained the money for me, and he also healed you." The old man said, "He deserves it." So he called the angel and said to him, "Take half of all that you two have brought back."

Then the angel called the two of them privately and said to them: "Praise God and give thanks to him; exalt him and give thanks to him in the presence of all the living for what he has done for you. It is good to praise God and to exalt his name, worthily declaring the works of God. Do not be slow to give him thanks. It is good to guard the secret of a king, but gloriously to reveal the works of God. Do good, and evil will not overtake you. Prayer is good when accompanied by fasting, almsgiving, and righteousness. A little with righteousness is better than much with wrongdoing. It is better to give alms than to treasure up gold. For almsgiving delivers from death, and it will purge away every sin. Those who perform deeds of charity and of righteousness will have fulness of life; but those who commit sin are the enemies of their own lives.

"I will not conceal anything from you. I have said, 'It is good to guard the secret of a king, but gloriously to reveal the works of God.' And so, when you and your daughter-in-law Sarah prayed, I brought a reminder of your prayer before the Holy One; and when you buried the dead, I was likewise present with you. When you did not hesitate to rise and leave your dinner in order to go and lay out the dead, your good deed was not hidden from me, but I was with you. So now God sent me to heal you and your daughter-in-law Sarah. I am Raphael, one of the seven holy angels who present the prayers of the saints and enter into the presence of the glory of the Holy One."

They were both alarmed; and they fell upon their faces, for they were afraid. But he said to them, "Do not be afraid; you will be safe. But praise God for ever. For I did not come as a favor on my part, but by the will of our God. Therefore praise him for ever. All these days I merely appeared to you and did not eat or drink, but you were seeing a vision. And now give thanks to God, for I am ascending to him who sent me. Write in a book everything that has happened." Then they stood up; but they saw him no more. So they confessed the great and wonderful works of God, and acknowledged that the angel of the Lord had appeared to them.

Then Tobit wrote a prayer of rejoicing and said: "Blessed is God who lives for ever, and blessed is his kingdom. For he afflicts, and he shows mercy; he leads down to Hades, and brings up again, and there is no one who can escape his hand. Acknowledge him before the nations, O sons of Israel; for he has scattered us among them. Make his greatness known there, and exalt him in the presence of all the living; because he is our Lord and God, he is our Father for ever. He will afflict us for our iniquities; and again he will show mercy, and will gather us from all the nations among whom you have been scattered. If you turn to him with all your heart and with all your soul, to do what is true before him, then he will turn to you and will not hide his face from you. But see what he will do with you; give thanks to him with your full voice. Praise the Lord of righteousness, and exalt the King of the ages. I give him thanks in the land of my captivity, and I show his power and majesty to a nation of sinners. Turn back, you sinners, and do right before him; who knows if he will accept you and have mercy on you? I exalt my God; my soul exalts the King of heaven, and will rejoice in his majesty. Let all men speak, and give him thanks in Jerusalem. O Jerusalem, the holy city, he will afflict you for the deeds of your sons, but again he will show mercy to the sons of the righteous. Give thanks worthily to the Lord, and praise the King of the ages, that his tent may be raised for you again with joy. May he cheer those within you who are captives, and love those within you who are distressed, to all generations for ever."

AN EVIL KING PREPARES FOR WAR

In the eighteenth year, on the twenty-second day of the first month, there was talk in the palace of Nebuchadnezzar king of the Assyrians about carrying out his revenge on the whole region, just as he had said. He called together all his officers and all his nobles and set forth to them his secret plan and recounted fully, with his own lips, all the wickedness of the region; and it was decided that every one who had not obeyed his command should be destroyed. When he had finished setting forth his plan, Nebuchadnezzar king of the Assyrians called Holofernes, the chief general of his army, second only to himself, and said to him:

"Thus says the Great King, the lord of the whole earth: When you leave my presence, take with you men confident in their strength, to the number of one hundred and twenty thousand foot soldiers and twelve thousand cavalry. Go and attack the whole west country, because they disobeyed my orders. Tell them to prepare earth and water, for I am coming against them in my anger, and will cover the whole face of the earth with the feet of my armies, and will hand them over to be plundered by my troops, till their wounded shall fill their valleys, and every brook and river shall be filled with their dead, and overflow; and I will lead them away captive to the ends of the whole earth. You shall go and seize all their territory for me in advance. They will yield themselves to you, and you shall hold them for me till the day of their punishment."

By this time the people of Israel living in Judea heard of everything that Holofernes, the general of Nebuchadnezzar the king of the Assyrians, had done to the nations, and how he had plundered and destroyed all their temples; they were therefore very greatly terrified at his approach, and were alarmed both for Jerusalem and for the temple of the Lord their God. For they had only recently returned from the captivity, and all the people of Judea were newly gathered together, and the sacred vessels and the altar and the temple had been consecrated after their profanation. So they sent to every district of Samaria, and to Kona and Beth-horon and Belmain and Jericho and to Choba and Aesora and the valley of Salem, and immediately seized all the high hilltops and fortified the villages on them and stored up food in preparation for war—since their fields had recently been harvested.

The next day Holofernes ordered his whole army, and all the allies who had joined him, to break camp and move against Bethulia, and to seize the passes up into the hill country and make war on the Israelites.

On the second day Holofernes led out all his cavalry in full view of the Israelites in Bethulia, and examined the approaches to the city, and visited the springs that supplied their water, and seized them and set guards of soldiers over them, and then returned to his army.

Then all the people, the young men, the women, and the children, gathered about Uzziah and the rulers of the city and cried out with a loud voice, and said before all the elders, "God be judge between you and us! For you have done us a great injury in not making peace with the Assyrians. For now we have no one to help us; God has sold us into their hands, to strew us on the ground before them with thirst and utter destruction. Now call them in and surrender the whole city to the army of Holofernes and to all his forces, to be plundered. For it would be better for us to be captured by them; for we will be slaves, but our lives will be spared, and we shall not witness the death of our babes before our eyes, or see our wives and children draw their last breath. We call to witness against you heaven and earth and our God, the Lord of our fathers, who punishes us according to our sins and the sins of our fathers. Let him not do this day the things which we have described!"

Then great and general lamentation arose throughout the assembly, and they cried out to the Lord with a loud voice. And Uzziah said to them, "Have courage, my brothers! Let us hold out for five more days; by that time the Lord our God will restore to us his mercy. But if these days pass by, and no help comes for us, I will do what you say."

JUDITH SLAYS HOLOFERNES
AND LIBERATES HER PEOPLE

At that time Judith heard about these things: she was the daughter of Merari the son of Ox, son of Joseph, son of Oziel, son of Elkiah, son of Ananias, son of Ahitub, son of Elijah, son of Hilkiah, son of Eliab, son of Nathana-el, son of Israel. Judith had lived at home as a widow for three years and four months. She was beautiful in appearance, and had a very lovely face; and her husband Manasseh had left her gold and silver, and men and women slaves, and cattle, and fields; and she maintained this estate. No one spoke ill of her, for she feared God with great devotion.

When Judith heard the wicked words spoken by the people against the ruler, because they were faint for lack of water, and when she heard all that Uzziah said to them, and how he promised them under oath to surrender the city to the Assyrians after five days, she sent her maid, who was in charge of all she possessed, to summon Chabris and Charmis, the elders of her city. They came to her, and she said to them, "Listen to me, rulers of the people of Bethulia! What you have said to the people today is not right; you have even sworn and pronounced this oath between God and you, promising to surrender the city to our enemies unless the Lord turns and helps us within so many days. Who are you, that have put God to the test this day, and are setting yourselves up in the place of God among the sons of men? You are putting the Lord Almighty to the test— but you will never know anything! You cannot plumb the depths of the human heart, nor find out what a man is thinking; how do you expect to search out God, who made all these things, and find out his mind or comprehend his thought? No, my brethren, do not provoke the Lord our God to anger."

Judith said to them, "Listen to me. I am about to do a thing which will go down through all generations of our descendants. Stand at the city gate tonight, and I will go out with my maid; and within the days after which you have promised to surrender the city to our enemies, the Lord will deliver Israel by my hand. Only, do not try to find out what I plan; for I will not tell you until I have finished what I am about to do."

Uzziah and the elders said to her, "Go in peace, and may the Lord God go before you, to take revenge upon our enemies." So they returned from the tent and went to their posts.

Then Judith fell upon her face, and put ashes on her head, and uncovered the sackcloth she was wearing; and at the very time when that evening's incense was being offered in the house of God in Jerusalem, Judith cried out to the Lord with a loud voice, and said, "Hear, O hear me, God of my father, God of the inheritance of Israel, Lord of heaven and earth, Creator of the waters, King of all thy creation, hear my prayer! Make my deceitful words to be their wound and stripe, for they have planned cruel things against thy covenant, and against thy consecrated house, and against the top of Zion, and against the house possessed by thy children. And cause thy whole nation and every tribe to know and understand that thou art God, the God of all power and might, and that there is no other who protects the people of Israel but thou alone!"

When Judith had ceased crying out to the God of Israel, and had ended all these words, she rose from where she lay prostrate and called her maid and went down into the house where she lived on sabbaths and on her feast days; and she removed the sackcloth which she had been wearing, and took off her widow's garments, and bathed her body with water, and anointed herself with precious ointment, and combed her hair and put on a tiara, and arrayed herself in her gayest apparel, which she used to wear while her husband Manasseh was living. And she put on her anklets and bracelets and rings, and her earrings and all her ornaments, and made herself very beautiful, to entice the eyes of all men who might see her.

Then Judith went out, she and her maid with her; and the men of the city watched her until she had gone down the mountain and passed through the valley and they could no longer see her. The women went straight on through the valley; and an Assyrian patrol met her and took her into custody, and asked her, "To what people do you belong, and where are you coming from, and where are you going?" She replied, "I am a daughter of the Hebrews, but I am fleeing from them, for they are about to be handed over to you to be devoured." And they chose from their number a hundred men to accompany her and her maid, and they brought them to the tent of Holofernes.

Then he commanded them to bring her in where his silver dishes were kept, and ordered them to set a table for her with some of his own food and to serve her with his own wine. Then the servants of Holofernes brought her into the tent, and she slept until midnight. Along toward the morning watch she arose and sent to Holofernes and said, "Let my lord now command that your servant be permitted to go out and pray." So Holofernes commanded his guards not to hinder her. And she remained in the camp for three days, and went out each night to the valley of Bethulia, and bathed at the spring in the camp. When she came up from the spring she prayed the Lord God of Israel to direct her way for the raising up of her people. So she returned clean and stayed in the tent until she ate her food toward evening.

When evening came, his slaves quickly withdrew, and Bagoas closed the tent from outside and shut out the attendants from his master's presence; and they went to bed, for they all were weary because the banquet had lasted long. So Judith was left alone in the tent, with Holofernes stretched out on his bed, for he was overcome with wine.

Now Judith had told her maid to stand outside the bedchamber and to wait for her to come out, as she did every day; for she said she would be going out for her prayers. And she had said the same thing to Bagoas. So every one went out, and no one, either small or great, was left in the bedchamber. Then Judith, standing beside his bed, said in her heart, "O Lord God of all might, look in this hour upon the work of my hands for the exaltation of Jerusalem. For now is the time to help thy inheritance, and to carry out my undertaking for the destruction of the enemies who have risen up against us."

She went up to the post at the end of the bed, above Holofernes' head, and took down his sword that hung there. She came close to his bed and took hold of the hair of his head, and said, "Give me strength this day, O Lord God of Israel!" And she struck his neck twice with all her might, and severed his head from his body. Then she tumbled his body off the bed and pulled down the canopy from the posts; after a moment she went out, and gave Holofernes' head to her maid, who placed it in her food bag.

Then the two of them went out together, as they were accustomed to go for prayer; and they passed through the camp and circled around the valley and went up the mountain to Bethulia and came to its gates. Judith called out from afar to the watchmen at the gates, "Open, open the gate! God, our God, is still with us, to show his power in Israel, and his strength against our enemies, even as he has done this day!"

When the men of her city heard her voice, they hurried down to the city gate and called together the elders of the city. They all ran together, both small and great, for it was unbelievable that she had returned; they opened the gate and admitted them, and they kindled a fire for light, and gathered around them. Then she said to them with a loud voice, "Praise God, O praise him! Praise God, who has not withdrawn his mercy from the house of Israel, but had destroyed our enemies by my hand this very night!"

Then she took the head out of the bag and showed it to them, and said, "See, here is the head of Holofernes, the commander of the Assyrian army, and here is the canopy beneath which he lay in his drunken stupor. The Lord has struck him down by the hand of a woman. As the Lord lives, who has protected me in the way I went, it was my face that tricked him to his destruction, and yet he committed no act of sin with me, to defile and shame me."

All the people were greatly astonished, and, bowed down and worshiped God, and said with one accord, "Blessed art thou, our God, who hast brought into contempt this day the enemies of the people."

And Uzziah said to her, "O daughter, you are blessed by the Most High God above all women on earth; and blessed be the Lord God, who created the heavens and the earth, who has guided you to strike the head of the leader of our enemies. Your hope will never depart from the hearts of men, as they remember the power of God. May God grant this to be a perpetual honor to you, and may he visit you with blessings, because you did not spare your own life when our nation was brought low, but

have avenged our ruin, walking in the straight path before our God."
And all the people said, "So be it, so be it!"

When the men in the tents heard it, they were amazed at what
had happened. Fear and trembling came over them, so that they did not
wait for one another, but with one impulse all rushed out and fled by
every path across the plain and through the hill country. Those who had
camped in the hills around Bethulia also took to flight. Then the men of
Israel, every one that was a soldier rushed out upon them.

Then Joakim the high priest, and the senate of the people of Israel
who lived at Jerusalem, came to witness the good things which the Lord
had done for Israel, and to see Judith and to greet her. And when they
met her they all blessed her with one accord and said to her, "You are
the exaltation of Jerusalem, you are the great glory of Israel, you are the
great pride of our nation! You have done all this singlehanded; you
have done great good to Israel, and God is well pleased with it. May the
Almighty Lord bless you for ever!" And all the people said, "So be it!"

Then Judith began this thanksgiving before all Israel, and all the
people loudly sang this song of praise. And Judith said, "Begin a song to
my God with tambourines, sing to my Lord with cymbals. Raise to him
a new psalm; exalt him, and call upon his name. I will sing to my God
a new song: O Lord, thou art great and glorious, wonderful in strength,
invincible. Let all thy creatures serve thee, for thou didst speak, and they
were made. Thou didst send forth thy Spirit, and it formed them; there
is none that can resist thy voice. For the mountains shall be shaken to
their foundations with the waters; at thy presence the rocks shall melt like
wax, but to those who fear thee thou wilt continue to show mercy. For
every sacrifice as a fragrant offering is a small thing, and all fat for burnt
offerings to thee is a very little thing, but he who fears the Lord shall be
great for ever. Woe to the nations that rise up against my people! The
Lord Almighty will take vengeance on them in the day of judgment; fire
and worms he will give to their flesh; they shall weep in pain for ever."

THE LIFE OF A KING IS SAVED

In the days of Ahasu-erus, the Ahasu-erus who reigned from India to
Ethiopia over one hundred and twenty-seven provinces, in those days
when King Ahasu-erus sat on his royal throne in Susa the capital. Then
the king's servants who attended him said, "Let beautiful young virgins
be sought out for the king. And let the king appoint officers in all the

provinces of his kingdom to gather all the beautiful young virgins to the harem in Susa the capital, under custody of Hegai the king's eunuch who is in charge of the women; let their ointments be given them."

Now there was a Jew in Susa the capital whose name was Mordecai, the son of Jair, son of Shime-i, son of Kish, a Benjaminite, who had been carried away with Jeconiah king of Judah, whom Nebuchadnezzar king of Babylon had carried away. He had brought up Hadassah, that is Esther, the daughter of his uncle, for she had neither father nor mother; the maiden was beautiful and lovely, and when her father and her mother died, Mordecai adopted her as his own daughter. So when the king's order and his edict were proclaimed, and when many maidens were gathered in Susa the capital in custody of Hegai, Esther also was taken into the king's palace and put in custody of Hegai who had charge of the women.

The king loved Esther more than all the women, and she found grace and favor in his sight more than all the virgins, so that he set the royal crown on her head and made her queen. When the virgins were gathered together the second time, Mordecai was sitting at the king's gate. Now Esther had not made known her kindred or her people, as Mordecai had charged her; for Esther obeyed Mordecai just as when she was brought up by him. And in those days, as Mordecai was sitting at the king's gate, Bigthan and Teresh, two of the king's eunuchs, who guarded the threshold, became angry and sought to lay hands on King Ahasu-erus. And this came to the knowledge of Mordecai, and he told it to Queen Esther, and Esther told the king in the name of Mordecai. When the affair was investigated and found to be so, the men were both hanged on the gallows. And it was recorded in the Book of the Chronicles in the presence of the king.

A VICIOUS PLOT IS UNFOLDED

After these things King Ahasu-erus promoted Haman the Agagite, the son of Hammedatha, and advanced him and set his seat above all the princes who were with him. And all the king's servants who were at the king's gate bowed down and did obeisance to Haman; for the king had so commanded concerning him. But Mordecai did not bow down or do obeisance. Then the king's servants who were at the king's gate said to Mordecai, "Why do you transgress the king's command?" And when they spoke to him day after day and he would not listen to them, they told Haman, in order to see whether Mordecai's words would avail; for he had told them that he was a Jew. And when Haman saw that Mordecai did not bow down or do obeisance to him, Haman was filled with fury. But he disdained to lay hands on Mordecai alone. So, as they had made known to him the people of Mordecai, Haman sought to destroy all the Jews, the people of Mordecai, throughout the whole kingdom of Ahasu-erus.

In the first month, which is the month of Nisan, in the twelfth year of King Ahasu-erus, they cast Pur, that is the lot, before Haman day after day; and they cast it month after month till the twelfth month, which is the month of Adar. Then Haman said to King Ahasu-erus, "There is a certain people scattered abroad and dispersed among the peoples in all the provinces of your kingdom; their laws are different from those of every other people, and they do not keep the king's laws, so that it is not for the king's profit to tolerate them. If it please the king, let it be decreed that they be destroyed, and I will pay ten thousand talents of silver into the hands of those who have charge of the king's business, that they may put it into the king's treasuries." So the king took his signet ring from his hand and gave it to Haman the Agagite, the son of Hammedatha, the enemy of the Jews. And the king said to Haman, "The money is given to you, the people also, to do with them as it seems good to you."

Then the king's secretaries were summoned on the thirteenth day of the first month, and an edict, according to all that Haman commanded, was written to the king's satraps and to the governors over all the provinces and to the princes of all the peoples, to every province in its own script and every people in its own language; it was written in the name of King Ahasu-erus and sealed with the king's ring. Letters were sent by couriers to all the king's provinces, to destroy, to slay, and to annihilate all Jews, young and old, women and children, in one day, the thirteenth day of the twelfth month, which is the month of Adar, and to plunder their goods. A copy of the document was to be issued as a decree in every province by proclamation to all the peoples to be ready for that day. The couriers went in haste by order of the king, and the decree was issued in Susa the capital. And the king and Haman sat down to drink; but the city of Susa was perplexed.

THE TRIUMPH OF ESTHER AND MORDECAI

When Mordecai learned all that had been done, Mordecai rent his clothes and put on sackcloth and ashes, and went out into the midst of the city,

351

wailing with a loud and bitter cry; he went up to the entrance of the king's gate, for no one might enter the king's gate clothed with sackcloth. And in every province, wherever the king's command and his decree came, there was great mourning among the Jews, with fasting and weeping and lamenting, and most of them lay in sackcloth and ashes.

When Esther's maids and her eunuchs came and told her, the queen was deeply distressed; she sent garments to clothe Mordecai, so that he might take off his sackcloth, but he would not accept them. Then Esther called for Hathach, one of the king's eunuchs, who had been appointed to attend her, and ordered him to go to Mordecai to learn what this was and why it was. Hathach went out to Mordecai in the open square of the city in front of the king's gate, and Mordecai told him all that had happened to him, and the exact sum of money that Haman had promised to pay into the king's treasuries for the destruction of the Jews. Mordecai also gave him a copy of the written decree issued in Susa for their destruction, that he might show it to Esther and explain it to her and charge her to go to the king to make supplication to him and entreat him for her people. And Hathach went and told Esther what Mordecai had said. Then Esther spoke to Hathach and gave him a message for Mordecai, saying, "All the king's servants and the people of the king's provinces know that if any man or woman goes to the king inside the inner court without being called, there is but one law; all alike are to be put to death, except the one to whom the king holds out the golden scepter that he may live. And I have not been called to come in to the king these thirty days." And they told Mordecai what Esther had said. Then Mordecai told them to return answer to Esther, "Think not that in the king's palace you will escape any more than all the other Jews. For if you keep silence at such a time as this, relief and deliverance will rise for the Jews from another quarter, but you and your father's house will perish. And who knows whether you have not come to the kingdom for such a time as this?" Then Esther told them to reply to Mordecai, "Go; gather all the Jews to be found in Susa, and hold a fast on my behalf, and neither eat nor drink for three days, night or day. I and my maids will also fast as you do. Then I will go to the king, though it is against the law; and if I perish, I perish." Mordecai then went away and did everything as Esther had ordered him.

On the third day Esther put on her royal robes and stood in the inner court of the king's palace, opposite the king's hall. The king was sitting on his royal throne inside the palace opposite the entrance to the palace; and when the king saw Queen Esther standing in the court, she found favor in his sight and he held out to Esther the golden scepter that was in his hand. Then Esther approached and touched the top of the scepter. And the king said to her, "What is it, Queen Esther? What is your request? It shall be given you, even to the half of my kingdom."

But Esther said, "My petition and my request is: If I have found favor in the sight of the king, and if it please the king to grant my petition and fulfil my request, let the king and Haman come tomorrow to the dinner which I will prepare for them, and tomorrow I will do as the king has said."

And Haman went out that day joyful and glad of heart. But when Haman saw Mordecai in the king's gate, that he neither rose nor trembled before him, he was filled with wrath against Mordecai. Nevertheless Haman restrained himself, and went home; and he sent and fetched his friends and his wife Zeresh. And Haman recounted to them the splendor of his riches, the number of his sons, all the promotions with which the king had honored him, and how he had advanced him above the princes and the servants of the king. And Haman added, "Even Queen Esther let no one come with the king to the banquet she prepared but myself. And tomorrow also I am invited by her together with the king. Yet all this does me no good, so long as I see Mordecai the Jew sitting at the king's gate." Then his wife Zeresh and all his friends said to him, "Let a gallows fifty cubits high be made, and in the morning tell the king to have Mordecai hanged upon it; then go merrily with the king to the dinner." This counsel pleased Haman, and he had the gallows made.

On that night the king could not sleep; and he gave orders to bring the book of memorable deeds, the chronicles, and they were read before the king. And it was found written how Mordecai had told about Bigthan and Teresh, two of the king's eunuchs, who guarded the threshold, and who had sought to lay hands upon King Ahasu-erus. And the king said, "What honor or dignity has been bestowed on Mordecai for this?" The king's servants who attended him said, "Nothing has been done for him." And the king said, "Who is in the court?" Now Haman had just entered the outer court of the king's palace to speak to the king about having Mordecai hanged on the gallows that he had prepared for him. So the king's servants told him, "Haman is there, standing in the court." And the king said, "Let him come in." So Haman came in, and the king said to him, "What shall be done to the man whom the king delights to honor?" And Haman said to himself, "Whom would the king delight to honor more than me?" And Haman said to the king, "For the man whom the king delights to honor, let royal robes be brought, which the king has worn, and the horse which the king has ridden, and on whose head a royal crown is set; and let the robes and the horse be handed over to one of the king's most noble princes; let him array the man whom the king delights to honor, and let him conduct the man on horseback through the open square of the city, proclaiming before him: 'Thus shall it be done to the man whom the king delights to honor.' " Then the king said to Haman, "Make haste, take the robes and the horse, as you have said, and do so to Mordecai the Jew who sits at the king's gate. Leave out nothing that you have mentioned." So Haman took the robes and the horse, and he arrayed Mordecai and made him ride through the open square of the city, proclaiming, "Thus shall it be done to the man whom the king delights to honor."

Then Mordecai returned to the king's gate. But Haman hurried to his house, mourning and with his head covered. And Haman told his wife Zeresh and all his friends everything that had befallen him. Then his wise men and his wife Zeresh said to him, "If Mordecai, before whom you have begun to fall, is of the Jewish people, you will not prevail against him but will surely fall before him."

While they were yet talking with him, the king's eunuchs arrived and brought Haman in haste to the banquet that Esther had prepared.

So the king and Haman went in to the feast with Queen Esther. And on the second day, as they were drinking wine, the king again said to Esther, "What is your petition, Queen Esther? It shall be granted you. And what is your request? Even to the half of my kingdom, it shall be fulfilled." Then Queen Esther answered, "If I have found favor in your sight, O king, and if it please the king, let my life be given me at my petition, and my people at my request. For we are sold, I and my people, to be destroyed, to be slain, and to be annihilated. If we had been sold merely as slaves, men and women, I would have held my peace; for our affliction is not to be compared with the loss to the king." Then King Ahasu-erus said to Queen Esther, "Who is he, and where is he, that would presume to do this?" And Esther said, "A foe and enemy! This wicked Haman!" Then Haman was in terror before the king and the queen. And the king rose from the feast in wrath and went into the palace garden; but Haman stayed to beg his life from Queen Esther, for he saw that evil was determined against him by the king. And the king returned from the palace garden to the place where they were drinking wine, as Haman was falling on the couch where Esther was; and the king said, "Will he even assault the queen in my presence, in my own house?" As the words left the mouth of the king, they covered Haman's face. Then said Harbona, one of the eunuchs in attendance on the king, "Moreover, the gallows which Haman has prepared for Mordecai, whose word saved the king, is standing in Haman's house, fifty cubits high." And the king said, "Hang him on that." So they hanged Haman on the gallows which he had prepared for Mordecai. Then the anger of the king abated.

On that day King Ahasu-erus gave to Queen Esther the house of Haman, the enemy of the Jews. And Mordecai came before the king, for Esther had told what he was to her; and the king took off his signet ring, which he had taken from Haman, and gave it to Mordecai. And Esther set Mordecai over the house of Haman.

The Jews had light and gladness and joy and honor. And in every province and in every city, wherever the king's command and his edict came, there was gladness and joy among the Jews, a feast and a holiday. And many from the peoples of the country declared themselves Jews, for the fear of the Jews had fallen upon them.

So the Jews smote all their enemies with the sword, slaughtering, and destroying them, and did as they pleased to those who hated them.

CHAPTER TWENTY-THREE

Prophecies Uttered During the Captivity

EZECHIEL IS SUMMONED *

In the thirtieth year, on the fifth day of the fourth month, while I was among the exiles by the river Chobar, the heavens opened, and I saw divine visions.—On the fifth day of the month, the fifth year, that is, of King Joachin's exile, the word of the Lord came to the priest Ezechiel, the son of Buzi, in the land of the Chaldeans by the river Chobar.—There the hand of the Lord came upon me.

As I looked, a stormwind came from the North, a huge cloud with flashing fire [enveloped in brightness], from the midst of which [the midst of the fire] something gleamed like electrum. Within it were figures resembling four living creatures that looked like this: their form was human, but each had four faces and four wings, and their legs went straight down; the soles of their feet were round. They sparkled with a gleam like burnished bronze. Human hands were under their wings, and the wings of one touched those of another. Their faces [and their wings] looked out on all their four sides; they did not turn when they moved, but each went straight forward. Their faces were like this: each of the four had the face of a man, but on the right side was the face of a lion, and on the left side the face of an ox, and finally each had the face of an eagle. Each had two wings spread out above so that they touched one another's, while the other two wings of each covered his body. [Each went straight forward; wherever the spirit wished to go, there they went; they did not turn when they moved.]

Above the firmament over their heads something like a throne could be seen, looking like sapphire. Upon it was seated, up above, one who had the appearance of a man. Upward from what resembled

* The prophet Ezechiel uttered his prophecies in the earlier years of the Jewish captivity.

his waist I saw what gleamed like electrum; downward from what resembled his waist I saw what looked like fire; he was surrounded with splendor. Like the bow which appears in the clouds on a rainy day was the splendor that surrounded him. Such was the vision of the likeness of the glory of the Lord.

At the end of seven days, the word of the Lord came to me: Son of man, I have appointed you a watchman for the house of Israel. When you hear a word from my mouth, you shall warn them for me.

If I say to the wicked man, You shall surely die; and you do not warn him or speak out to dissuade him from his wicked conduct so that he may live: that wicked man shall die for his sin, but I will hold you responsible for his death. If, on the other hand, you have warned the wicked man, yet he has not turned away from his evil nor from his wicked conduct, then he shall die for his sin, but you shall save your life.

If a virtuous man turns away from virtue and does wrong when I place a stumbling block before him, he shall die. He shall die for his sin, and his virtuous deeds shall not be remembered; but I will hold you responsible for his death if you did not warn him. When, on the other hand, you have warned a virtuous man not to sin, and he has in fact not sinned, he shall surely live because of the warning, and you shall save your own life.

THE SAVIOR'S WRATH AGAINST JERUSALEM

On the fifth day of the sixth month, in the sixth year, as I was sitting in my house, and the elders of Juda sat before me, the hand of the Lord God fell upon me there. I looked up and saw a form that looked like a man. Downward from what seemed to be his waist, there was fire; from his waist upward there seemed to be a brightness like the sheen of electrum. He stretched out what appeared to be a hand and seized me by the hair of my head [and the] spirit lifted me up in the air and brought me in divine visions to Jerusalem, to the entrance of the north gate, where stood the statue of jealousy which stirs up jealousy. I saw there the glory of the God of Israel, like the vision I had seen in the plain.

Thus the word of the Lord came to me: Son of man, prophesy against the prophets of Israel, prophesy! Say to those who prophesy their own thought: Hear the word of the Lord: Thus says the Lord God: Woe to those prophets who are fools, who follow their own spirit and have seen no vision. Like foxes among ruins are your prophets, O Israel! You did not step into the breach, nor did you build a wall about the house of Israel that would stand firm against attack on the day of the Lord. Their visions are false and their divination lying. They say, "Thus says the Lord!" though the Lord did not send them; then they wait for him to fulfill their words! Therefore thus says the Lord God: Because you have spoken falsehood and have seen lying visions, therefore see! I am coming at you, says the Lord God. But I will stretch out my hand against the prophets who have false visions and who foretell lies. They shall not belong to the community of my people, nor be recorded in the register of the house of Israel, nor enter the land of Israel; thus you shall know that I am the Lord.

For the very reason that they led my people astray, saying, "Peace!" when there was no peace, and that, as one built a wall, they would cover it with whitewash, say then to the whitewashers: I will bring down a flooding rain; hailstones shall fall, and a stormwind shall break out. And when the wall has fallen, will you not be asked: Where is the whitewash you spread on?

Therefore thus says the Lord God: In my fury I will let loose storm-winds; because of my anger there shall be a flooding rain, and hailstones shall fall with destructive wrath. I will tear down the wall that you have whitewashed and level it to the ground, laying bare its foundations. When it falls, you shall be crushed beneath it; thus you shall know that I am the Lord. When I have spent my fury on the wall and its whitewashers, I tell you there shall be no wall, nor shall there be whitewashers—those prophets of Israel who prophesied to Jerusalem and saw for it visions of peace when there was no peace, says the Lord God.

THE NEW TEMPLE IS SEEN BY EZECHIEL

On the tenth day of the month beginning the twenty-fifth year of our exile, fourteen years after the city was taken, that very day the hand of the Lord came upon me and brought me in divine visions to the land of Israel, where he set me down on a very high mountain. On it there seemed to be a city being built before me. When he had brought me there, all at once I saw a man whose appearance was that of bronze; he was standing in the gate, holding a linen cord and a measuring rod. The man said to me, "Son of man, look carefully and listen intently, and pay strict attention to all that I will show you, for you have been brought here so that I might show it to you. Tell the house of Israel all that you see." [Then I saw an outer wall that completely surrounded the temple. The man was holding a measuring rod six cubits long, each cubit being a cubit and a handbreadth; he measured the width and the height of the structure, each of which were found to be one rod.]

Then he measured the court, which was a hundred cubits long and a hundred cubits wide, a perfect square. The altar stood in front of the temple.

Then he brought me into the vestibule of the temple and measured the pilasters on each side, which were five cubits. The width of the doorway was fourteen cubits, and the side walls on either side of the door measured three cubits. The vestibule was twenty cubits wide and twelve cubits deep; ten steps led up to it, and there were columns by the pilasters, one on either side.

Then he brought me back to the outer gate of the sanctuary, facing the east; but it was closed. He said to me: This gate is to remain closed; it is not to be opened for anyone to enter by it; since the Lord, the God of Israel, has entered by it, it shall remain closed. Only the prince may sit down in it to eat his meal in the presence of the Lord. He must enter by way of the vestibule of the gate, and leave by the same way.

Then he brought me back to the entrance of the temple, and I saw water flowing out from beneath the threshold of the temple toward the east, for the façade of the temple was toward the east; the water flowed down from the southern side of the temple, south of the altar. He led me outside by the north gate, and around to the outer gate facing the east, where I saw water trickling from the southern side. Then when he had walked off to the east with a measuring cord in his hand, he measured off a thousand cubits and had me wade through the water, which was ankle-deep. He measured off another thousand and once more had me wade through the water, which was now knee-deep. Again he measured off a thousand and had me wade; the water was up to my waist. Once more he measured off a thousand, but there was now a river through which I could not wade; for the water had risen so high it had become a river that could not be crossed except by swimming. He asked me, "Have you seen this, son of man?" Then he brought me to the bank of the river, where he had me sit. Along the bank of the river I saw very many trees on both sides. He said to me, "This water flows into the eastern district down upon the Araba, and empties into the sea, the salt waters, which it makes fresh. Wherever the river flows, every sort of living creature that can multiply shall live, and there shall be abundant fish, for wherever this water comes the sea shall be made fresh. Fishermen shall be standing along it from En-gaddi to En-gallim, spreading their nets there. Its kinds of fish shall be those of the Great Sea, very numerous. Only its marshes and swamps shall not be made fresh; they shall be left for salt. Along both banks of the river, fruit trees of every kind shall grow; their leaves shall not fade, nor their fruit fail. Every month they shall bear fresh fruit, for they shall be watered by the flow from the sanctuary. Their fruit shall serve for food, and their leaves for medicine."

Thus says the Lord God: These are the boundaries within which you shall apportion the land among the twelve tribes of Israel [Joseph having two portions]. All of you shall have a like portion in this land which I swore to give to your fathers, that it might fall to you as your inheritance. This is the boundary of the land on the north side: from the Great Sea in the direction of Hethalon, past Labo of Hamath, to Sedada, Berotha, and Sabarim, along the frontiers of Hamath and Damascus, to Hasar-Enon which is on the border of the Hauran. Thus the border shall extend from the sea to Hasar-Enon, with the frontier of Hamath and Damascus to the north. This is the northern boundary. The eastern boundary: between the Hauran—toward Damascus—and Galaad on the one side, and the land of Israel on the other side, the Jordan shall form the boundary down to the eastern sea as far as Thamar. This is the eastern boundary. The southern boundary: from Thamar to the waters of Meribath-Cades, thence to the Wadi of Egypt, and on to the Great Sea. This is the southern boundary. The western boundary: the Great Sea forms the boundary up to a point parallel to Labo of Hamath. This is the western boundary.

You shall distribute this land among yourselves according to the tribes of Israel. You shall allot it as inheritances for yourselves and for the aliens resident in your midst who have bred children among you. The latter shall be to you like native Israelites; along with you they shall receive inheritances among the tribes of Israel. In whatever tribe the alien may be resident, there you shall assign him his inheritance, says the Lord God.

VISION OF THE FOUR BEASTS *

In the first year of King Belsassar of Babylon, Daniel had a dream as he lay in bed, and was terrified by the visions of his mind. Then he wrote down the dream; the account began: In the vision I saw during the night, suddenly the four winds of heaven stirred up the great sea, from which emerged four immense beasts, each different from the others. The first was like a lion, but with eagle's wings. While I watched, the wings were plucked; it was raised from the ground to stand on two feet like a man, and given a human mind. The second was like a bear; it was raised up on one side, and among the teeth in its mouth were three tusks. It was given the order, "Up, devour much flesh." After this I looked and saw another beast, like a leopard; on its back were four wings like those of a bird, and it had four heads. To this beast dominion was given. After this, in the visions of the night I saw the fourth beast, different from all the others, terrifying, horrible, and of extraordinary strength; it had great iron teeth with which it devoured and crushed, and what was left it trampled with its feet. I was considering the ten horns it had, when suddenly another, a little horn, sprang out of their midst, and three of the previous horns were torn away to make room for it. This horn had eyes like a man, and a mouth that spoke arrogantly. As I watched, thrones were set up and the Ancient One took his throne. His clothing was snow bright, the hair on his head as white as wool; his throne was flames of fire, with wheels of burning fire. A surging stream of fire flowed out from where he sat; thousands upon thousands were ministering to him, and myriads upon myriads attended him.

The court was convened, and the books were opened. I watched, then, from the first of the arrogant words which the horn spoke, until the beast was slain and its body thrown into the fire to be burnt up. The other beasts, which also lost their dominion, were granted a prolongation of life for a time and a season. As the visions during the night continued, I saw one like a son of man coming, on the clouds of heaven; when he reached the Ancient One and was presented before him, he received dominion, glory, and kingship; nations and peoples of every language serve him. His dominion is an everlasting

* The prophet Daniel lived during the captivity, but his prophecies dealt primarily with the kingdoms that came later, up to the time of Christ.

dominion that shall not be taken away, his kingship shall not be destroyed.

VISION OF THE RAM AND HE-GOAT

After this first vision, I, Daniel, had another, in the third year of the reign of King Belsassar. In my vision I saw myself in the fortress of Susa in the province of Elam; I was beside the river Ulai. I looked up and saw standing by the river a ram with two great horns, the one larger and newer than the other. I saw the ram butting toward the west, north, and south. No beast could withstand it or be rescued from its power; it did what it pleased and became very powerful.

As I was reflecting, a he-goat with a prominent horn on its forehead suddenly came from the west across the whole earth without touching the ground. It approached the two-horned ram I had seen standing by the river, and rushed toward it with savage force. I saw it attack the ram with furious blows when they met, and break both its horns. It threw the ram, which had not the force to withstand it, to the ground, and trampled upon it; and no one could rescue it from its power.

The he-goat became very powerful, but at the height of its power the great horn was shattered, and in its place came up four others, facing the four winds of heaven. Out of one of them came a little horn which kept growing toward the south, the east, and the glorious country. Its power extended to the host of heaven, so that it cast down to earth some of the host and some of the stars and trampled on them. It boasted even against the prince of the host, from whom it removed the daily sacrifice, and whose sanctuary it cast down, as well as the host, while sin replaced the daily sacrifice. It cast truth to the ground and was succeeding in its undertaking.

I heard a holy one speaking, and another said to whichever one it was that spoke, "How long shall the events of this vision last concerning the daily sacrifice, the desolating sin which is placed there, the sanctuary, and the trampled host?" He answered him, "For two thousand three hundred evenings and mornings; then the sanctuary shall be purified."

While I, Daniel, sought the meaning of the vision I had seen, a manlike figure stood before me, and on the Ulai I heard a human voice that cried out, "Gabriel, explain the vision to this man." When he came near where I was standing, I fell prostrate in terror. But he said to me, "Understand, son of man, that the vision refers to the end time." As he spoke to me, I fell forward in a faint; he touched me and made me stand up. "I will show you," he said, "what is to happen later in the period of wrath; for at the appointed time, there will be an end.

"The two-horned ram you saw represents the kings of the Medes and Persians. The he-goat is the king of the Greeks, and the great horn on its forehead is the first king. The four that rose in its place when it was broken are four kingdoms that will issue from his nation, but without his strength.

"After their reign, when sinners have reached their measure, there shall arise a king, impudent and skilled in intrigue. He shall be strong and powerful, bring about fearful ruin, and succeed in his undertaking. He shall destroy powerful peoples; his cunning shall be against the holy ones, his treacherous conduct shall succeed. He shall be proud of heart and destroy many by stealth. But when he rises against the prince of princes, he shall be broken without a hand being raised. The vision of the evenings and the mornings is true, as spoken; do you, however, keep this vision undisclosed, because the days are to be many."

I, Daniel, was weak and ill for some days; then I arose and took care of the king's affairs. But I was appalled at the vision, which I could not understand.

GABRIEL AND THE SEVENTY WEEKS

It was the first year that Darius, son of Xerxes, of the race of the Medes, reigned over the kingdom of the Chaldeans; in the first year of his reign I, Daniel, tried to understand in the Scriptures the counting of the years of which the Lord spoke to the prophet Jeremia: that for the ruins of Jerusalem seventy years must be fulfilled.

I turned to the Lord God, pleading in earnest prayer, with fasting, sackcloth, and ashes. I prayed to the Lord, my God, and confessed, "Ah, Lord, great and awesome God, you who keep your merciful covenant toward those who love you and observe your commandments! We have sinned, been wicked and done evil; we have rebelled and departed from your commandments and your laws. We have not obeyed your servants the prophets, who spoke in your name to our kings, our princes, our fathers, and all the people of the land."

I was still occupied with my prayer, confessing my sin and the sin of my people Israel, presenting my petition to the Lord, my God, on behalf of his holy mountain—I was still occupied with his prayer, when Gabriel, the one whom I had seen before in vision, came to me in rapid flight at the time of the evening sacrifice. He instructed me in these words: "Daniel, I have now come to give you understanding. When you began your petition, an answer was given which I have come to announce, because you are beloved. Therefore, mark the answer and understand the vision.

"Seventy weeks are decreed for your people and for your holy city: then transgression will stop and sin will end, guilt will be expiated, everlasting justice will be introduced, vision and prophecy ratified, and a most holy will be anointed. Know and understand this: from the utterance of the word that Jerusalem was to be rebuilt until one who is anointed and a leader, there shall be seven weeks. During sixty-two weeks it shall be rebuilt, with streets and trenches, in time of affliction. After the sixty-two weeks an anointed shall be cut down when he does not possess the city; and the people of a leader who will come shall destroy the sanctuary. Then the end shall come like a torrent; until the end there shall be war, the desolation that is decreed. For one week he shall make a firm compact with the many; half the week he shall abolish sacrifice and oblation; on the temple wing shall be the horrible abomination until the ruin that is decreed is poured out upon the horror."

VISION OF THE HELLENISTIC WARS

In the third year of Cyrus, king of Persia, a revelation was given to Daniel, who had been named Baltassar. The revelation was certain: a great war; he understood it from the vision. In those days, I, Daniel, mourned three full weeks. I ate no savory food, I took no meat or wine, and I did not anoint myself at all until the end of the three weeks.

On the twenty-fourth day of the first month I was on the bank of the great river, the Tigris. As I looked up, I saw a man dressed in linen with a belt of fine gold around his waist. His body was like chrysolite, his face shone like lightning, his eyes were like fiery torches, his arms and feet looked like burnished bronze, and his voice sounded like the roar of a multitude. I alone, Daniel, saw the vision; but great fear seized the men who were with me; they fled and hid themselves, although they did not see the vision. So I was left alone, seeing this great vision. No strength remained in me; I turned the color of death and was powerless. When I heard the sound of his voice, I fell face forward in a faint.

But then a hand touched me, raising me to my hands and knees. "Daniel, beloved," he said to me, "understand the words which I am speaking to you; stand up, for my mission now is to you." When he said this to me, I stood up trembling. "Fear not, Daniel," he continued; "from the first day you made up your mind to acquire understanding and humble yourself before God, your prayer was heard. Because of it I started out, but the prince of the kingdom of Persia stood in my way for twenty-one days, until finally Michael, one of the chief princes, came to help me. I left him there with the prince of the kings of Persia, and came to make you understand what shall happen to your people in the days to come; for there is yet a vision concerning those days."

While he was speaking thus to me, I fell forward and kept silent. Then something like a man's hand touched my lips; I opened my mouth and said to the one facing me, "My Lord, I was seized with pangs at the vision and I was powerless. How can my lord's servant speak with you, my lord? For now no strength or even breath is left in me." The one who looked like a man touched me again and strengthened me, saying, "Fear not, beloved, you are safe; take courage and be strong." When he spoke to me, I grew strong and said, "Speak, my lord, for you have strengthened me." "Do you know," he asked, "why I have come to you? Soon I must fight the prince of Persia again. When I leave, the prince of Greece will come; but I shall tell you what is written in the truthful book. No one supports me against all these except Michael, your prince, standing as a reinforcement and a bulwark for me. Now I shall tell you the truth.

"Three kings of Persia are yet to come; and a fourth shall acquire the greatest riches of all. Strengthened by his riches, he shall rouse all the kingdom of Greece. But a powerful king shall appear and rule with great might, doing as he pleases. No sooner shall he appear than his kingdom shall be broken and divided in the four directions under heaven; but not among his descendants or in keeping with his mighty rule, for his kingdom shall be torn to pieces and belong to others than they.

"At that time there shall arise Michael, the great prince, guardian of your people; it shall be a time unsurpassed in distress since nations began until that time. At that time your people shall escape, everyone who is found written in the book.

"Many of those who sleep in the dust of the earth shall awake; some shall live forever, others shall be an everlasting horror and disgrace. But the wise shall shine brightly like the splendor of the firmament, and those who lead the many to justice shall be like the stars forever.

"As for you, Daniel, keep secret the message and seal the book until the end time; many shall fall away and evil shall increase."

CHAPTER TWENTY-FOUR

The Return from Captivity

THE RENEWAL OF WORSHIP AT JERUSALEM

In the first year of Cyrus king of Persia, that the word of the Lord by the mouth of Jeremiah might be accomplished, the Lord stirred up the spirit of Cyrus king of Persia so that he made a proclamation throughout all his kingdom and also put it in writing: "Thus says Cyrus king of Persia: The Lord, the God of heaven, has given me all the kingdoms of the earth, and he has charged me to build him a house at Jerusalem, which is in Judah. Whoever is among you of all his people, may his God be with him, and let him go up to Jerusalem, which is in Judah, and rebuild the house of the Lord, the God of Israel—he is the God who is in Jerusalem; and let each survivor, in whatever place he sojourns, be assisted by the men of his place with silver and gold, with goods and with beasts, besides freewill offerings for the house of God which is in Jerusalem."

Then rose up the heads of the fathers' houses of Judah and Benjamin, and the priests and the Levites, every one whose spirit God had stirred to go up to rebuild the house of the Lord which is in Jerusalem; and all who were about them aided them with vessels of silver, with gold, with goods, with beasts, and with costly wares, besides all that was freely offered. Cyrus the king also brought out the vessels of the house of the Lord which Nebuchadnezzar had carried away from Jerusalem and placed in the house of his gods.

When the seventh month came, and the sons of Israel were in the towns, the people gathered as one man to Jerusalem. Then arose Jeshua the son of Jozadak, with his fellow priests, and Zerubbabel the son of She-alti-el with his kinsmen, and they built the altar of the God of Israel, to offer burnt offerings upon it, as it is written in the law of Moses the man of God. They set the altar in its place, for fear was upon them because of the peoples of the lands, and they offered burnt offerings upon it to the Lord, burnt offerings morning and evening. And they kept the feast of booths, as it is written, and offered the daily burnt offerings by number according to the ordinance, as each day required, and after that the continual burnt offerings, the offerings at the new moon and at all the appointed feasts of the Lord, and the offerings of every one who made a freewill offering to the Lord. From the first day of the seventh month they began to offer burnt offerings to the Lord. But the foundation of the temple of the Lord was not yet laid. So they gave money to the masons and the carpenters, and food, drink, and oil to the Sidonians and the Tyrians to bring cedar trees from Lebanon to the sea, to Joppa, according to the grant which they had from Cyrus king of Persia.

Now in the second year of their coming to the house of God at Jerusalem, in the second month, Zerubbabel the son of She-alti-el and Jeshua the son of Jozadak made a beginning, together with the rest of their brethren, the priests and the Levites and all who had come to Jerusalem from the captivity. They appointed the Levites, from twenty years old and upward, to have the oversight of the work of the house of the Lord. And Jeshua with his sons and his kinsmen, and Kadmi-el and his sons, the sons of Judah, together took the oversight of the workmen in the house of God, along with the sons of Henadad and the Levites, their sons and kinsmen.

And when the builders laid the foundation of the temple of the Lord, the priests in their vestments came forward with trumpets, and the Levites, the sons of Asaph, with cymbals, to praise the Lord, according to the directions of David king of Israel; and they sang responsively, praising and giving thanks to the Lord, "For he is good, for his steadfast love endures for ever toward Israel." And all the people shouted with a great shout, when they praised the Lord, because the foundation of the house of the Lord was laid. But many of the priests and the Levites and heads of fathers' houses, old men who had seen the first house, wept with a loud voice when they saw the foundation of this house being laid, though many shouted aloud for joy; so that the people could not distinguish the sound of the joyful shout from the sound of the people's weeping, for the people shouted with a great shout, and the sound was heard afar.

AN EXHORTATION TO REBUILD THE TEMPLE OF THE LORD

On the first day of the sixth month in the second year of King Darius, the word of the Lord came through the prophet Aggai to the governor of Juda, Zorobabel, son of Salathiel, and to the high priest Josue, son of Josedec: Thus says the Lord of hosts: This people says: "Not now has the time come to rebuild the house of the Lord." (Then this word of the Lord came through Aggai, the prophet:) Is it time for you to dwell in your own paneled houses, while this house lies in ruins? Now thus says the Lord of hosts: Consider your ways: You have sown much, but have brought in little; you have eaten, but have not been satisfied; you have drunk, but have not been exhilarated; have clothed yourselves, but not been warmed; and he who earned wages earned them for a bag with holes in it.

Thus says the Lord of hosts: Consider your ways! Go up into the hill country; bring timber, and build the house that I may take pleasure in it and receive my glory, says the Lord. You expected much, but it came to little; and what you brought home, I blew away. For what cause? says the Lord of hosts. Because my house lies in ruins, while each of you hurries to his own house. Therefore the heavens withheld from you their dew, and the earth her crops. And I called for a drought upon the land and upon the mountains; upon the grain, and upon the wine, and upon the oil, and upon all that the ground brings forth; upon men and upon beasts, and upon all that is produced by hand.

Then Zorobabel, son of Salathiel, and the high priest Josue, son of Josedec, and all the remnant of the people listened to the voice of the Lord, their God, and to the words of the prophet Aggai, because of the Lord, their God, had sent him, and the people feared because of the Lord. And the Lord's messenger, Aggai, proclaimed to the people as the message of the Lord: I am with you, says the Lord.

Then the Lord stirred up the spirit of the governor of Juda, Zorobabel, son of Salathiel, and the spirit of the high priest Josue, son of Josedec, and the spirit of all the remnant of the people, so that they came and set to work on the house of the Lord of hosts, their God, on the twenty-fourth day of the sixth month.

In the second year of King Darius, on the twenty-first day of the seventh month, the word of the Lord came through the prophet Aggai: Tell this to the governor of Juda, Zorobabel, son of Salathiel, and to the high priest Josue, son of Josedec, and to the remnant of the people: Who is left among you that saw this house in its former glory? And how do you see it now? Does it not seem like nothing in your eyes? But now take courage, Zorobabel, says the Lord, and take courage, Josue, high priest, son of Josedec, and take courage, all you people of the land, says the Lord, and work! For I am with you, says the Lord of hosts. This is the pact that I made with you when you came out of Egypt, and my spirit continues in your midst; do not fear!

For thus says the Lord of hosts: One moment yet, a little while, and I will shake the heavens and the earth, the sea and the dry land. I will shake all the nations, and the treasures of all the nations will come in, and I will fill this house with glory, says the Lord of hosts. Mine is the silver and mine the gold, says the Lord of hosts. Greater will be the future glory of this house than the former, says the Lord of hosts; and in this place I will give peace, says the Lord of hosts!

"LO, A DAY SHALL COME . . ."

In the second year of Darius, in the eighth month, the word of the Lord came to the prophet Zacharia, son of Barachia, son of Addo: The Lord was indeed angry with your fathers. . . . and say to them: Thus says the Lord of hosts: Return to me, says the Lord of hosts, and I will return to you, says the Lord of hosts.

Sing and rejoice, O daughter Sion! See, I am coming to dwell among you, says the Lord. Many nations shall join themselves to the Lord on that day, and they shall be his people, and he will dwell among you, and you shall know that the Lord of hosts has sent me to you. The Lord will possess Juda as his portion in the holy land, and he will again choose Jerusalem. Silence, all mankind, in the presence of the Lord! for he stirs forth from his holy dwelling.

Then he showed me Josue the high priest standing before the angel of the Lord, while Satan stood at his right hand to accuse him. And the angel of the Lord said to Satan, "May the Lord rebuke you, Satan; may the Lord who has chosen Jerusalem rebuke you! Is not this man a brand snatched from the fire?" Now Josue was standing before the angel clad in filthy garments. He spoke and said to those who were standing before him, "Take off his filthy garments, and clothe him in festal garments." He also said, "Put on a clean miter on his head." And they put a clean miter on his head and clothed him with the garments. Then the angel of the Lord, standing, said, "See, I have taken away your guilt."

The angel of the Lord then gave Josue this assurance: "Thus says the Lord of hosts: If you walk in my ways and heed my charge, you shall judge my house and keep my courts, and I will give you access among these standing here. Listen, O Josue, high priest! You and your associates who sit before you are men of good omen. Yes, I will bring my servant the Shoot. Look at the stone that I have placed before Josue, one stone with seven facets. I will engrave its inscription, says the Lord of hosts, and I will take away the guilt of the land in one day. On that day, says the Lord of hosts, you will invite one another under your vines and fig trees."

Rejoice heartily, O daughter Sion, shout for joy, O daughter Jerusalem! See, your king shall come to you; a just savior is he, meek, and riding on an ass, on a colt, the foal of an ass. He shall banish the chariot from Ephraim, and the horse from Jerusalem; the warrior's bow shall be banished, and he shall proclaim peace to the nations. His dominion shall be from sea to sea, and from the River to the ends of the earth. And the Lord, their God, shall save them on that day, his people, like a flock. For they are the jewels in a crown raised aloft over his land. For what wealth is theirs, and what beauty! grain that makes the youths flourish, and new wine, the maidens!

Lo, a day shall come for the Lord when the spoils shall be divided in your midst. And I will gather all the nations against Jerusalem for battle: the city shall be taken, houses plundered, women ravished; half of the city shall go into exile, but the rest of the people shall not be removed from the city. Then the Lord shall go forth and fight against those nations, fighting as on a day of battle. That day his feet shall rest upon the Mount of Olives, which is opposite Jerusalem to the east. The Mount of Olives shall be cleft in two from east to west by a very deep valley, and half of the mountain shall move to the north and half of it to the south. And the valley of the Lord's mountain shall be filled up when the valley of those two mountains reaches its edge; it shall be filled up as it was filled up by the earthquake in the days of King Ozia of Juda. Then the Lord, my God, shall come, and all his holy ones with him.

On that day there shall no longer be cold or frost. There shall be one continuous day, known to the Lord, not day and night, for in the evening time there shall be light. On that day, living waters shall flow from Jerusalem, half to the eastern sea, and half to the western sea, and it shall be so in summer and in winter. The Lord shall become king over the whole earth; on that day the Lord shall be the only one, and his name the only one.

THE TEMPLE REBUILT AND DEDICATED

Now the prophets, Haggai and Zechariah the son of Iddo, prophesied to the Jews who were in Judah and Jerusalem, in the name of the God of Israel who was over them. Then Zerubbabel the son of She-alti-el and Jeshua the son of Jozadak arose and began to rebuild the house of God which is in Jerusalem; and with them were the prophets of God, helping them.

At the same time Tattenai the governor of the province Beyond the River and Shethar-bozenai and their associates came to them and spoke to them thus, "Who gave you a decree to build this house and to finish this structure?" They also asked them this, "What are the names of the men who are building this building?" But the eye of their God was upon the elders of the Jews, and they did not stop them till a report should reach Darius and then answer be returned by letter concerning it.

The copy of the letter which Tattenai the governor of the province Beyond the River and Shethar-bozenai and his associates the governors who were in the province Beyond the River sent to Darius the king; they sent him a report, in which was written as follows: "To Darius the king, all peace. Be it known to the king that we went to the province of Judah, to the house of the great God. It is being built with huge stones, and timber is laid in the walls; this work goes on diligently and prospers in their hands. Then we asked those elders and spoke to them thus, 'Who gave you a decree to build this house and to finish this structure?' We also asked them their names for your information, that we might write down the names of the men at their head."

Then Darius the king made a decree, and search was made in Babylonia, in the house of the archives where the documents were stored. And in Ecbatana, the capital which is in the province of Media, a scroll was found on which this was written: "A record. In the first year of Cyrus the king, Cyrus the king issued a decree: Concerning the house of God at Jerusalem, let the house be rebuilt, the place where sacrifices are offered and burnt offerings are brought; its height shall be sixty cubits and its breadth sixty cubits, with three courses of great stones and one course of timber; let the cost be paid from the royal treasury. And also let the gold and silver vessels of the house of God, which Nebuchadnezzar took out of the temple that is in Jerusalem and brought to Babylon, be restored and brought back to the temple which is in Jerusalem, each to its place; you shall put them in the house of God."

Then, according to the word sent by Darius the king, Tattenai, the governor of the province Beyond the River, Shethar-bozenai, and their associates did with all diligence what Darius the king had ordered. And the elders of the Jews built and prospered, through the prophesying of

Haggai the prophet and Zechariah the son of Iddo. They finished their building by command of the God of Israel and by decree of Cyrus and Darius and Ar-ta-xerxes king of Persia; and this house was finished on the third day of the month of Adar, in the sixth year of the reign of Darius the king. And the people of Israel, the priests and the Levites, and the rest of the returned exiles, celebrated the dedication of this house of God with joy. They offered at the dedication of this house of God one hundred bulls, two hundred rams, four hundred lambs, and as a sin offering for all Israel twelve he-goats, according to the number of the tribes of Israel. And they set the priests in their divisions and the Levites in their courses, for the service of God at Jerusalem, as it is written in the book of Moses.

On the fourteenth day of the first month the returned exiles kept the passover. For the priests and the Levites had purified themselves together; all of them were clean. So they killed the passover lamb for all the returned exiles, for their fellow priests, and for themselves; it was eaten by the people of Israel who had returned from exile, and also by every one who had joined them and separated himself from the pollutions of the peoples of the land to worship the Lord, the God of Israel. And they kept the feast of unleavened bread seven days with joy; for the Lord had made them joyful, and had turned the heart of the king of Assyria to them, so that he aided them in the work of the house of God, the God of Israel.

THE EXPULSION OF FOREIGN WIVES

After these things had been done, the officials approached me and said, "The people of Israel and the priests and the Levites have not separated themselves from the peoples of the lands with their abominations, from the Canaanites, the Hittites, the Perizzites, the Jebusites, the Ammonites, the Moabites, the Egyptians, and the Amorites. For they have taken some of their daughters to be wives for themselves and for their sons; so that the holy race has mixed itself with the peoples of the lands. And in this faithlessness the hand of the officials and chief men has been foremost." When I heard this, I rent my garments and my mantle, and pulled hair from my head and beard, and sat appalled. Then all who trembled at the words of the God of Israel, because of the faithlessness of the returned exiles, gathered round me while I sat appalled until the evening sacrifice. And at the evening sacrifice I rose from my fasting, with my garments and my mantle rent, and fell upon my knees and spread out my hands to the Lord my God, saying, "O my God, I am ashamed and blush to lift my face to thee, my God, for our iniquities have risen higher than our heads, and our guilt has mounted up to the heavens. From the days of our fathers to this day we have been in great guilt; and for our iniquities we, our kings, and our priests have been given into the hand of the kings of the lands, to the sword, to captivity, to plundering, and to utter shame, as at this day. But now for a brief moment favor has been shown by the Lord our God, to leave us a remnant, and to give us a secure hold within his holy place, that our God may brighten our eyes and grant us a little reviving in our bondage. For we are bondmen; yet our God has not forsaken us in our bondage, but has extended to us his steadfast love before the kings of Persia, to grant us some reviving to set up the house of our God, to repair its ruins, and to give protection in Judea and Jerusalem.

"And now, O our God, what shall we say after this? For we have forsaken thy commandments, which thou didst command by thy servants the prophets, saying, 'The land which you are entering, to take possession of it, is a land unclean with the pollutions of the peoples of the lands, with their abominations which have filled it from end to end with their uncleanness. Therefore give not your daughters to their sons, neither take their daughters for your sons, and never seek their peace or prosperity, that you may be strong, and eat the good of the land, and leave it for an inheritance to your children for ever.' And after all that has come upon us for our evil deeds and our great guilt, seeing that thou, our God, hast punished us less than our iniquities deserved and hast given us such a remnant as this, shall we break thy commandments again and intermarry with the peoples who practice these abominations? Wouldst thou not be angry with us till thou wouldst consume us, so that there should be no remnant, nor any to escape? O Lord the God of Israel, thou art just, for we are left a remnant that has escaped, as at this day. Behold, we are before thee in our guilt, for none can stand before thee because of this."

While Ezra prayed and made confession, weeping and casting himself down before the house of God, a very great assembly of men, women, and children, gathered to him out of Israel; for the people wept bitterly. And Shecaniah the son of Jehiel, of the sons of Elam, addressed Ezra: "We have broken faith with our God and have married foreign women from the peoples of the land, but even now there is hope for Israel in spite of this. Therefore let us make a covenant with our God to put away all these wives and their children, according to the counsel of my lord and of those who tremble at the commandment of our God; and let it be done according to the law. Arise, for it is your task, and we are with you; be strong and do it." Then Ezra arose and made the leading priests and Levites and all Israel take oath that they would do as had been said. So they took the oath.

Then Ezra withdrew from before the house of God, and went to the chamber of Jeho-hanan the son of Eliashib, where he spent the night, neither eating bread nor drinking water; for he was mourning over the faithlessness of the exiles. And a proclamation was made throughout Judah and Jerusalem to all the returned exiles that they should assemble at Jerusalem, and that if any one did not come within three days, by order of the officials and the elders all his property should be forfeited, and he himself banned from the congregation of the exiles.

Then all the men of Judah and Benjamin assembled at Jerusalem within the three days; it was the ninth month, on the twentieth day of the month. And all the people sat in the open square before the house of God, trembling because of this matter and because of the heavy rain. And Ezra the priest stood up and said to them, "You have trespassed and married foreign women, and so increased the guilt of Israel. Now then make confession to the Lord the God of your fathers, and do his will; separate yourselves from the peoples of the land and from the foreign wives." Then all the assembly answered with a loud voice, "It is so; we must do as you have said. But the people are many, and it is a time of heavy rain; we cannot stand in the open. Nor is this a work for one day or for two; for we have greatly transgressed in this matter. Let our officials stand for the whole assembly; let all in our cities who have taken foreign wives come at appointed times, and with them the elders and judges of every city, till the fierce wrath of our God over this matter be averted from us." Only Jonathan the son of Asahel and Jahzeiah the son of Tikvah opposed this, and Meshullam and Shabbethai the Levite supported them. Then the returned exiles did so. Ezra the priest selected men, heads of fathers' houses, each of them designated by name. On the first day of the tenth month they sat down to examine the matter; and by the first day of the first month they had come to the end of all the men who had married foreign women.

NEHEMIAH BEGINS REBUILDING JERUSALEM

The words of Nehemiah the son of Hacaliah. Now it happened in the month of Chislev, in the twentieth year, as I was in Susa the capital, that Hanani, one of my brethren, came with certain men out of Judah; and I asked them concerning the Jews that survived, who had escaped exile, and concerning Jerusalem. And they said to me, "The survivors there in the province who escaped exile are in great trouble and shame; the wall of Jerusalem is broken down, and its gates are destroyed by fire."

When I heard these words I sat down and wept, and mourned for days; and I continued fasting and praying before the God of heaven.

In the month of Nisan, in the twentieth year of King Ar-ta-xerxes, when wine was before him, I took up the wine and gave it to the king. Now I had not been sad in his presence. And the king said to me, "Why is your face sad, seeing you are not sick? This is nothing else but sadness of the heart." Then I was very much afraid. I said to the king, "Let the king live for ever! Why should not my face be sad, when the city, the place of my fathers' sepulchres, lies waste, and its gates have been destroyed by fire?" Then the king said to me, "For what do you make request?" So I prayed to the God of heaven. And I said to the king, "If it pleases the king, and if your servant has found favor in your sight, that you send me to Judah, to the city of my fathers' sepulchres, that I may rebuild it." And the king said to me (the queen sitting beside him), "How long will you be gone, and when will you return?" So it pleased the king to send me; and I set him a time. And I said to the king, "If it pleases the king, let letters be given me to the governors of the province Beyond the River, that they may let me pass through until I come to Judah; and a letter to Asaph, the keeper of the king's forest, that he may give me timber to make beams for the gates of the fortress of the temple, and for the wall of the city, and for the house which I shall occupy." And the king granted me what I asked, for the good hand of my God was upon me.

Then I came to the governors of the province Beyond the River, and gave them the king's letters. Now the king had sent with me officers of the army and horsemen. But when Sanballat the Horonite and Tobiah the servant, the Ammonite, heard this, it displeased them greatly that some one had come to seek the welfare of the children of Israel.

So I came to Jerusalem and was there three days. Then I arose in the night, I and a few men with me; and I told no one what my God had put into my heart to do for Jerusalem. There was no beast with me but the beast on which I rode. I went out by night by the Valley Gate to the Jackal's Well and to the Dung Gate, and I inspected the walls of Jerusalem which were broken down and its gates which had been destroyed by fire. Then I went on to the Fountain Gate and to the King's Pool; but there was no place for the beast that was under me to pass. Then I went up in the night by the valley and inspected the wall; and I turned back and entered by the Valley Gate, and so returned. And the officials did not know where I had gone or what I was doing; and I had not yet told the Jews, the priests, the nobles, the officials, and the rest that were to do the work. Then I said to them, "You see the trouble we are in, how Jerusalem lies in ruins with its gates burned. Come, let us build the wall of Jerusalem, that we may no longer suffer disgrace." And I told them of the hand of my God which had been upon me for good, and also of the words which the king had spoken to me. And they said, "Let us rise up and build." So they strengthened their hands for the good work. But when Sanballat the Horonite and Tobiah the servant, the Ammonite, and Geshem the Arab heard of it, they derided us and despised us and said, "What is this thing that you are doing? Are you rebelling against the king?" Then I replied to them, "The God of heaven will make us prosper, and we his servants will arise and build; but you have no portion or right or memorial in Jerusalem."

Now when Sanballat heard that we were building the wall, he was angry and greatly enraged, and he ridiculed the Jews. And he said in the presence of his brethren and of the army of Samaria, "What are these feeble Jews doing? Will they restore things? Will they sacrifice? Will they finish up in a day? Will they revive the stones out of the heaps of rubbish, and burned ones at that?" Tobiah the Ammonite was by him, and he said, "Yes, what they are building—if a fox goes up on it he will break down their stone wall!" Hear, O our God, for we are despised; turn back their taunt upon their own heads, and give them up to be plundered in a land where they are captives. Do not cover their guilt, and let not their sin be blotted out from thy sight; for they have provoked thee to anger before the builders.

So we built the wall; and all the wall was joined together to half its height. For the people had a mind to work.

But when Sanballat and Tobiah and the Arabs and the Ammonites and the Ashdodites heard that the repairing of the walls of Jerusalem was going forward and that the breaches were beginning to be closed, they were very angry; and they all plotted together to come and fight against Jerusalem and to cause confusion in it. And we prayed to our God, and set a guard as a protection against them day and night.

But Judah said, "The strength of the burden-bearers is failing, and there is much rubbish; we are not able to work on the wall." And our enemies said, "They will not know or see till we come into the midst of them and kill them and stop the work." When the Jews who lived by them came they said to us ten times, "From all the places where they live they will come up against us." So in the lowest parts of the space behind the wall, in open places, I stationed the people according to their families, with their swords, their spears, and their bows. And I looked, and arose, and said to the nobles and to the officials and to the rest of the people, "Do not be afraid of them. Remember the Lord, who is great and terrible, and fight for your brethren, your sons, your daughters, your wives, and your homes."

When our enemies heard that it was known to us and that God had frustrated their plan, we all returned to the wall, each to his work. From that day on, half of my servants worked on construction, and half held the spears, shields, bows, and coats of mail; and the leaders stood behind all the house of Judah, who were building on the wall. Those who carried burdens were laden in such a way that each with one hand labored on the work and with the other held his weapon. And each of the builders had his sword girded at his side while he built. The man who sounded the trumpet was beside me. And I said to the nobles and to the officials and to the rest of the people, "The work is great and widely spread; and we are separated on the wall, far from one another. In the place where you hear the sound of the trumpet, rally to us there. Our God will fight for us."

So we labored at the work, and half of them held the spears from the break of dawn till the stars came out. I also said to the people at that time, "Let every man and his servant pass the night within Jerusalem, that they may be a guard for us by night and may labor by day." So neither I nor my brethren nor my servants nor the men of the guard who followed me, none of us took off our clothes; each kept his weapon in his hand.

NEHEMIAH REBUKES THE PROFITEERS AND COMPLETES THE WALL

Now there arose a great outcry of the people and of their wives against their Jewish brethren. For there were those who said, "With our sons and our daughters, we are many; let us get grain, that we may eat and keep alive." There were also those who said, "We are mortgaging our fields, our vineyards, and our houses to get grain because of the famine."

And there were those who said, "We have borrowed money for the king's tax upon our fields and our vineyards. Now our flesh is as the flesh of our brethren, our children are as their children; yet we are forcing our sons and our daughters to be slaves, and some of our daughters have already been enslaved; but it is not in our power to help it, for other men have our fields and our vineyards."

I was very angry when I heard their outcry and these words. I took counsel with myself, and I brought charges against the nobles and the officials. I said to them, "You are exacting interest, each from his brother." And I held a great assembly against them, and said to them, "We, as far as we are able, have bought back our Jewish brethren who have been sold to the nations; but you even sell your brethren that they may be sold to us!" They were silent, and could not find a word to say. So I said, "The thing that you are doing is not good. Ought you not to walk in the fear of our God to prevent the taunts of the nations our enemies? Moreover I and my brethren and my servants are lending them money and grain. Let us leave off this interest. Return to them this very day their fields, their vineyards, their olive orchards, and their houses, and the hundredth of money, grain, wine, and oil which you have been exacting of them." Then they said, "We will restore these and require nothing from them. We will do as you say." And I called the priests, and took an oath of them to do as they had promised. I also shook out my lap and said, "So may God shake out every man from his house and from his labor who does not perform this promise. So may he be shaken out and emptied." And all the assembly said "Amen" and praised the Lord. And the people did as they had promised. Moreover from the time that I was appointed to be their governor in the land of Judah, from the twentieth year to the thirty-second year of Ar-ta-xerxes the king, twelve years, neither I nor my brethren ate the food allowance of the governor. The former governors who were before me laid heavy burdens upon the people, and took from them food and wine, besides forty shekels of silver. Even their servants lorded it over the people. But I did not do so, because of the fear of God.

I also held to the work on this wall, and acquired no land; and all my servants were gathered there for the work. Moreover there were at my table a hundred and fifty men, Jews and officials, besides those who came to us from the nations which were about us. Now that which was prepared for one day was one ox and six choice sheep; fowls likewise were prepared for me, and every ten days skins of wine in abundance; yet with all this I did not demand the food allowance of the governor, because the servitude was heavy upon this people. Remember for my good, O my God, all that I have done for this people.

Now when it was reported to Sanballat and Tobiah and to Geshem the Arab and to the rest of our enemies that I had built the wall and that there was no breach left in it (although up to that time I had not set up the doors in the gates), Sanballat and Geshem sent to me, saying, "Come and let us meet together in one of the villages in the plain of Ono." But they intended to do me harm. And I sent messengers to them, saying, "I am doing a great work and I cannot come down. Why should the work stop while I leave it and come down to you?" And they sent to me four times in this way and I answered them in the same manner. In the same way Sanballat for the fifth time sent his servant to me with an open letter in his hand. In it was written, "It is reported among the nations, and Geshem also says it, that you and the Jews intend to rebel; that is why you are building the wall; and you wish to become their king, according to this report. And you have also set up prophets to proclaim concerning you in Jerusalem, 'There is a king in Judah.' And now it will be reported to the king according to these words. So now come, and let us take counsel together." Then I sent to him, saying, "No such things as you say have been done, for you are inventing them out of your own mind." For they all wanted to frighten us, thinking, "Their hands will drop from the work, and it will not be done." But now, O God, strengthen thou my hands.

Now when I went into the house of Shemaiah the son of Delaiah, son of Mehetabel, who was shut up, he said, "Let us meet together in the house of God, within the temple, and let us close the doors of the temple; for they are coming to kill you, at night they are coming to kill you." But I said, "Should such a man as I flee? And what man such as I could go into the temple and live? I will not go in." And I understood, and saw that God had not sent him, but he had pronounced the prophecy against me because Tobiah and Sanballat had hired him. For this purpose he was hired, that I should be afraid and act in this way and sin, and so they could give me an evil name, in order to taunt me. Remember Tobiah and Sanballat, O my God, according to these things that they did, and also the prophetess No-adiah and the rest of the prophets who wanted to make me afraid.

So the wall was finished on the twenty-fifth day of the month Elul, in fifty-two days. And when all our enemies heard of it, all the nations round about us were afraid and fell greatly in their own esteem; for they perceived that this work had been accomplished with the help of our God.

THE JEWS BIND THEMSELVES
TO THE OBSERVANCE OF THE LAW

And when the seventh month had come, the children of Israel were in their towns. And all the people gathered as one man into the square before the Water Gate; and they told Ezra the scribe to bring the book of the law of Moses which the Lord had given to Israel. And Ezra the priest brought the law before the assembly, both men and women and all who could hear with understanding, on the first day of the seventh month. And he read from it facing the square before the Water Gate from early morning until midday, in the presence of the men and the women and those who could understand; and the ears of all the people were attentive to the book of the law.

And Nehemiah, who was the governor, and Ezra the priest and scribe, and the Levites who taught the people said to all the people, "This day is holy to the Lord your God; do not mourn or weep." For all the people wept when they heard the words of the law. Then he said to them, "Go your way, eat the fat and drink sweet wine and send portions to him for whom nothing is prepared; for this day is holy to our Lord; and do not be grieved, for the joy of the Lord is your strength." So the Levites stilled all the people, saying, "Be quiet, for this day is holy; do not be grieved." And all the people went their way to eat and drink and to send portions and to make great rejoicing, because they had understood the words that were declared to them.

On the second day the heads of fathers' houses of all the people, with the priests and the Levites, came together to Ezra the scribe in order to study the words of the law. And they found it written in the law that the Lord had commanded by Moses that the people of Israel should dwell in booths during the feast of the seventh month, and that they should publish and proclaim in all their towns and in Jerusalem, "Go out to the hills and bring branches of olive, wild olive, myrtle, palm, and other leafy trees to make booths, as it is written." So the people went out and brought them and made booths for themselves, each on his roof, and in their courts and in the courts of the house of God, and in the square at the Water Gate and in the square at the Gate of Ephraim. And all the assembly of those who had returned from the captivity made booths and dwelt in the booths; for from the days of Jeshua the son of Nun to that day the people of Israel had not done so. And there was very great rejoicing. And day by day, from the first day to the last day, he read from the book of the law of God. They kept the feast seven days; and on the eighth day there was a solemn assembly, according to the ordinance.

Now on the twenty-fourth day of this month the people of Israel were assembled with fasting and in sackcloth, and with earth upon their heads. And the Israelites separated themselves from all foreigners, and stood and confessed their sins and the iniquities of their fathers. And they stood up in their place and read from the book of the law of the Lord their God for a fourth of the day; for another fourth of it they made confession and worshiped the Lord their God.

Then the Levites, Jeshua, Kadmi-el, Bani, Hashabneiah, Sherebiah, Hodiah, Shebaniah, and Pethahiah, said, "Stand up and bless the Lord your God from everlasting to everlasting. Blessed be thy glorious name which is exalted above all blessing and praise."

And Ezra said: "Thou art the Lord, thou alone; thou hast made heaven, the heaven of heavens, with all their host, the earth and all that is on it, the seas and all that is in them; and the host of heaven worships thee. Our kings, our princes, our priests, and our fathers have not kept thy law or heeded thy commandments and thy warnings which thou didst give them. They did not serve thee in their kingdom, and in thy great goodness which thou gavest them, and in the large and rich land which thou didst set before them; and they did not turn from their wicked works. Behold, we are slaves this day; in the land that thou gavest to our fathers to enjoy its fruits and its good gifts, behold, we are slaves. And its rich yield goes to the kings whom thou hast set over us because of our sins; they have power also over our bodies and over our cattle at their pleasure; and we are in great distress."

Because of all this we make a firm covenant and write it, and our princes, our Levites, and our priests set their seal to it, and join with their brethren, their nobles, and enter into a curse and an oath to walk in God's law which was given by Moses the servant of God, and to observe and do all the commandments of the Lord our Lord and his ordinances and his statutes. We will not give our daughters to the peoples of the land or take their daughters for our sons; and if the peoples of the land bring in wares or any grain on the sabbath day to sell, we will not buy from them on the sabbath or on a holy day; and we will forego the crops of the seventh year and the exaction of every debt. We also lay upon ourselves the obligation to charge ourselves yearly with the third part of a shekel for the service of the house of our God; for the show-bread, the continual cereal offering, the continual burnt offering, the sabbaths, the new moons, the appointed feasts, the holy things, and the sin offerings to make atonement for Israel, and for all the work of the house of our God. We have likewise cast lots, the priests, the Levites, and the people, for the wood offering, to bring it into the house of our God, according to our fathers' houses, at times appointed, year by year, to burn upon the altar of the Lord our God, as it is written in the law. We obligate ourselves to bring the first fruits of our ground and the first fruits of all fruit of every tree, year by year, to the house of the Lord; also to bring to the house of our God, to the priests who minister in the house of our God, the first-born of our sons and of our cattle, as it is written in the law, and the firstlings of our herds and of our flocks; and to bring the first of our coarse meal, and our contributions, the fruit of every tree, the wine and the oil, to the priests, to the chambers of the house of our God; and to bring to the Levites the tithes from our ground, for it is the Levites who collect the tithes in all our rural towns. And the priest, the son of Aaron, shall be with the Levites when the Levites receive the tithes; and the Levites shall bring up the tithe of the tithes to the house of our God, to the chambers, to the storehouse. For the people of Israel and the sons of Levi shall bring the contribution of grain, wine, and oil to the chambers, and the priests that minister, and the gatekeepers and the singers. We will not neglect the house of our God.

On that day they read from the book of Moses in the hearing of the people; and in it was found written that no Ammonite or Moabite should ever enter the assembly of God; for they did not meet the children of Israel with bread and water, but hired Balaam against them to curse them—yet our God turned the curse into a blessing. When the people heard the law, they separated from Israel all those of foreign descent.

Now before this, Eliashib the priest, who was appointed over the chambers of the house of our God, and who was connected with Tobiah, prepared for Tobiah a large chamber where they had previously put the cereal offering, the frankincense, the vessels, and the tithes of grain, wine, and oil, which were given by commandment to the Levites, singers, and gatekeepers, and the contributions for the priests. While this was taking place I was not in Jerusalem, for in the thirty-second year of Ar-ta-xerxes king of Babylon I went to the king. And after some time I asked leave of the king and came to Jerusalem, and I then discovered the evil that Eliashib had done for Tobiah, preparing for him a chamber in the courts of the house of God. And I was very angry, and I threw all the household furniture of Tobiah out of the chamber. Then I gave orders and they cleansed the chambers; and I brought back thither the vessels of the house of God, with the cereal offering and the frankincense.

I also found out that the portions of the Levites had not been given to them; so that the Levites and the singers, who did the work, had fled each to his field. So I remonstrated with the officials and said, "Why is the house of God forsaken?" And I gathered them together and set them in their stations. Then all Judah brought the tithe of the grain, wine, and oil in the storehouses. And I appointed Shelemiah the priest, Zadok the scribe, and Pedaiah of the Levites, and as their assistant Hanan the son of Zaccur, son of Mattaniah, for they were counted faithful; and their duty was to distribute to their brethren. Remember me, O my God, concerning this, and wipe not out my good deeds that I have done for the house of my God and for his service.

In those days I saw in Judah men treading wine presses on the sabbath, and bringing in heaps of grain and loading them on asses; and also wine, grapes, figs, and all kinds of burdens, which they brought into Jerusalem on the sabbath day; and I warned them on the day when they sold food. Men of Tyre also, who lived in the city, brought in fish and all kinds of wares and sold them on the sabbath to the people of Judah, and in Jerusalem. Then I remonstrated with the nobles of Judah and said to them, "What is this evil thing which you are doing, profaning the sabbath day? Did not your fathers act in this way, and did not our God bring all this evil on us and on this city? Yet you bring more wrath upon Israel by profaning the sabbath."

When it began to be dark at the gates of Jerusalem before the sabbath, I commanded that the doors should be shut and gave orders that they should not be opened until after the sabbath. And I set some of my servants over the gates, that no burden might be brought in on the sabbath day. Then the merchants and sellers of all kinds of wares lodged outside Jerusalem once or twice. But I warned them and said to them, "Why do you lodge before the wall? If you do so again I will lay hands on you." From that time on they did not come on the sabbath. And I commanded the Levites that they should purify themselves and come and guard the gates, to keep the sabbath day holy. Remember this also in my favor, O my God, and spare me according to the greatness of thy steadfast love.

In those days also I saw the Jews who had married women of Ashdod, Ammon, and Moab; and half of their children spoke the language of Ashdod, and they could not speak the language of Judah, but the language of each people. And I contended with them and cursed them and beat some of them and pulled out their hair; and I made them take oath in the name of God, saying, "You shall not give your daughters to their sons, or take their daughters for your sons or for yourselves. Did not Solomon king of Israel sin on account of such women? Among the many nations there was no king like him, and he was beloved by his God, and God made him king over all Israel; nevertheless foreign women made even him to sin. Shall we then listen to you and do all this great evil and act treacherously against our God by marrying foreign women?" And one of the sons of Jehoiada, the son of Eliashib the high priest, was the son-in-law of Sanballat the Horonite; therefore I chased him from me. Remember them, O my God, because they have defiled the priesthood and the covenant of the priesthood and the Levites.

Thus I cleansed them from everything foreign, and I established the duties of the priests and Levites, each in his work; and I provided for the wood offering, at appointed times, and for the first fruits. Remember me, O my God, for good.

A WORD OF WARNING

An oracle. The word of the Lord to Israel through Malachi. I have loved you, says the Lord; but you say, "How have you loved us?" Was not Esau Jacob's brother? says the Lord: yet I loved Jacob, but hated Esau; I made his mountains a waste, his heritage a desert for jackals. If Edom says, "We have been crushed but we will rebuild the ruins," thus says the Lord of hosts: They indeed may build, but I will tear down, and they shall be called the land of guilt, the people with whom the Lord is angry forever. Your own eyes shall see it, and you will say, "Great is the Lord, even beyond the land of Israel."

A son honors his father, and a servant fears his master; if then I am a father, where is the honor due to me? And if I am a master, where is the reverence due to me?—So says the Lord of hosts to you, O priests, who despise his name. But you ask, "How have we despised your name?" By offering polluted food on my altar! Then you ask, "How have we polluted it?" By saying the table of the Lord may be slighted! When you offer a blind animal for sacrifice, is this not evil? When you offer the lame or the sick, is it not evil? Present it to your governor; see if he will accept it, or welcome you, says the Lord of hosts. So now if you implore God for mercy on us, when you have done the like will he welcome any of you? says the Lord of hosts.

Oh, that one among you would shut the temple gates to keep you from kindling fire on my altar in vain! I have no pleasure in you, says the Lord of hosts; neither will I accept any sacrifice from your hands, for from the rising of the sun, even to its setting, my name is great among the nations; and everywhere they bring sacrifice to my name, and a pure offering; for great is my name among the nations, says the Lord of hosts.

And now, O priests, this commandment is for you: If you do not listen, and if you do not lay it to heart, to give glory to my name, says the Lord of hosts, I will send a curse upon you and of your blessing I will make a curse. Yes, I have already cursed it, because you do not lay it to heart. Lo, I will deprive you of the shoulder and I will strew dung in your faces, the dung of your feasts, and you will be carried off with it. Then you will know that I sent you this commandment because I have a covenant with Levi, says the Lord of hosts. My covenant with him was one of life and peace; fear I put in him, and he feared me, and stood in awe of my name. True doctrine was in his mouth, and no dishonesty was found upon his lips; he walked with me in integrity and uprightness, and turned many away from evil. For the lips of the priest are to keep knowledge, and instruction is to be sought from his mouth, because he is the messenger of the Lord of hosts. But you have turned aside from the way, and have caused many to falter by your instruction; you have made void the covenant of Levi, says the Lord of hosts. I, therefore, have made you contemptible and base before all the people, since you do not keep my ways, but show partiality in your decisions. Have we not all the one Father? Has not the one God created us? Why then do we break faith with each other, violating the covenant of our fathers?

Lo, I am sending my messenger to prepare the way before me; and suddenly there will come to the temple the Lord whom you seek, and the messenger of the covenant whom you desire. Yes, he is coming, says the Lord of hosts. But who will endure the day of his coming? And who can stand when he appears? For he is like the refiner's fire, or like the fuller's lye. He will sit refining and purifying [silver], and he will purify the sons of Levi, refining them like gold or like silver that they may offer due sacrifice to the Lord. Then the sacrifice of Juda and Jerusalem will please the Lord, as in years gone by. I will draw near to you for judgment, and I will be swift to bear witness against the sorcerers, adulterers, and perjurers, those who defraud the hired man of his wages, against those who defraud widows and orphans; those who turn aside the stranger, and those who do not fear me, says the Lord of hosts.

Surely I, the Lord, do not change, nor do you cease to be sons of Jacob. Since the days of your fathers you have turned aside from my statutes, and have not kept them. Return to me, and I will return to you, says the Lord of hosts. Yet you say, "How must we return?" Dare a man rob God? Yet you are robbing me! And you say, "How do we rob you?" In tithes and in offerings! You are indeed accursed, for you, the whole nation, rob me. Bring the whole tithe into the storehouse, that there may be food in my house, and try me in this, says the Lord of hosts: shall I not open for you the floodgates of heaven, to pour down blessing upon you without measure? For your sake I will forbid the locust to destroy your crops; and the vine in the field will not be barren, says the Lord of hosts. Then all nations will call you blessed, for you will be a delightful land, says the Lord of hosts.

For lo, the day is coming, blazing like an oven, when all the proud and all evildoers will be stubble, and the day that is coming will set them on fire, leaving them neither root nor branch, says the Lord of hosts. But for you who fear my name, there will arise the sun of justice with its healing rays; and you will gambol like calves out of the stall and tread down the wicked; they will become ashes under the soles of your feet, on the day I take action, says the Lord of hosts. Remember the law of Moses my servant, which I enjoined upon him on Horeb, the statutes and ordinances for all Israel.

Lo, I will send you Elia, the prophet, before the day of the Lord comes, the great and terrible day, to turn the hearts of the fathers to their children, and the hearts of the children to their fathers, lest I come and strike the land with doom.

Lo, I will send you Elia, the prophet, before the day of the Lord comes, the great and terrible day.

387

CHAPTER TWENTY-FIVE

The Saga of Judas Maccabeus

THE OVERTHROW OF HELIODORUS

After Alexander son of Philip, the Macedonian, who came from the land of Kittim, had defeated Darius, king of the Persians and the Medes, he succeeded him as king. (He had previously become king of Greece.) He fought many battles, conquered strongholds, and put to death the kings of the earth. He advanced to the ends of the earth, and plundered many nations. When the earth became quiet before him, he was exalted, and his heart was lifted up. He gathered a very strong army and ruled over countries, nations, and princes, and they became tributary to him.

After this he fell sick and perceived that he was dying. So he summoned his most honored officers, who had been brought up with him from youth, and divided his kingdom among them while he was still alive. And after Alexander had reigned twelve years, he died. Then his officers began to rule, each in his own place. They all put on crowns after his death, and so did their sons after them for many years; and they caused many evils on the earth.

While the holy city was inhabited in unbroken peace and the laws were very well observed because of the piety of the high priest Onias and his hatred of wickedness, it came about that the kings themselves honored the place and glorified the temple with the finest presents, so that even Seleucus, the king of Asia, defrayed from his own revenues all the expenses connected with the service of the sacrifices. But a man named Simon, of the tribe of Benjamin, who had been made captain of the temple, had a disagreement with the high priest about the administration of the city market; and when he could prevail over Onias he went to Apollonius of Tarsus, who at that time was governor of Coele-syria and Phoenicia. He reported to him that the treasury in Jerusalem was full of untold sums of money, so that the amount of the funds could not be reckoned, and that they did not belong to the account of the sacrifices, but that it was possible for them to fall under the control of the king. When Apollonius met the king, he told him of the money about which he had been informed. The king chose Heliodorus, who was in charge of his affairs, and sent him with commands to effect the removal of the aforesaid money. Heliodorus at once set out on his journey, ostensibly to make a tour of inspection of the cities of Coele-syria and Phoenicia, but in fact to carry out the king's purpose.

When he had arrived at Jerusalem and had been kindly welcomed by the high priest of the city, he told about the disclosure that had been made and stated why he had come, and he inquired whether this really was the situation. The high priest explained that there were some deposits belonging to widows and orphans, and also some money of Hyrcanus, son of Tobias, a man of very prominent position, and that it totaled in all four hundred talents of silver and two hundred of gold. To such an extent the impious Simon had misrepresented the facts. And he said that it was utterly impossible that wrong should be done to those people who had trusted in the holiness of the place and in the sanctity and inviolability of the temple which is honored throughout the whole world. But Heliodorus, because of the king's commands which he had, said that this money must in any case be confiscated for the king's treasury. So he set a day and went in to direct the inspection of these funds.

There was no little distress throughout the whole city. The priests prostrated themselves before the altar in their priestly garments and called toward heaven upon him who had given the law about deposits, that he should keep them safe for those who had deposited them. To see the appearance of the high priest was to be wounded at heart, for his face and the change in his color disclosed the anguish of his soul. For terror and bodily trembling had come over the man, which plainly showed to those who looked at him the pain lodged in his heart. People also hurried out of their houses in crowds to make a general supplication because the holy place was about to be brought into contempt. Women, girded with sackcloth under their breasts, thronged the streets. Some of the maidens who were kept indoors ran together to the gates, and some to the walls, while others peered out of the windows. And holding up their hands to heaven, they all made entreaty. There was something pitiable in the prostration of the whole populace and the anxiety of the high priest in his great anguish.

While they were calling upon the Almighty Lord that he would keep what had been entrusted safe and secure for those who had entrusted it, Heliodorus went on with what had been decided. But when he arrived at the treasury with his bodyguard, then and there the Sovereign of spirits and of all authority caused so great a manifestation that all who had been so bold as to accompany him were astounded by the power of God, and became faint with terror. For there appeared to them a magnificently caparisoned horse, with a rider of frightening mien, and it rushed furiously at Heliodorus and struck at him with its front hoofs. Its rider was seen to have armor and weapons of gold. Two young men also appeared to him, remarkably strong, gloriously beautiful and splendidly dressed, who stood on each side of him and scourged him continuously, inflicting many blows on him. When he suddenly fell to the ground and deep darkness came over him, his men took him up and put him on a stretcher and carried him away, this man who had just entered the aforesaid treasury with a great retinue and all his bodyguard but was now unable to help himself; and they recognized clearly the sovereign power of God. While he lay prostrate, speechless because of the divine intervention and deprived of any hope of recovery, they praised the Lord who had acted marvelously for his own place. And the temple, which a little while before was full of fear and disturbance, was filled with joy and gladness, now that the Almighty Lord had appeared.

Quickly some of Heliodorus' friends asked Onias to call upon the Most High and to grant life to one who was lying quite at his last breath. And the high priest, fearing that the king might get the notion that some foul play had been perpetrated by the Jews with regard to Heliodorus, offered sacrifice for the man's recovery. While the high priest was making the offering of atonement, the same young men appeared again to Heliodorus, dressed in the same clothing, and they stood and said, "Be very grateful to Onias the high priest, since for his sake the Lord has granted you your life. And see that you, who have been scourged by heaven, report to all men the majestic power of God." Having said this they vanished.

Then Heliodorus offered sacrifice to the Lord and made very great vows to the Savior of his life, and having bidden Onias farewell, he marched off with his forces to the king. And he bore testimony to all men of the deeds of the supreme God, which he had seen with his own eyes. When the king asked Heliodorus what sort of person would be suitable to send on another mission to Jerusalem, he replied, "If you have any enemy or plotter against your government, send him there, for you will get him back thoroughly scourged, if he escapes at all, for there certainly is about the place some power of God. For he who has his dwelling in heaven watches over that place himself and brings it aid, and he strikes and destroys those who come to do it injury." This was the outcome of the episode of Heliodorus and the protection of the treasury.

THE STORY OF GOD'S PEOPLE AND THE
JEWISH MARTYRS

When Seleucus died and Antiochus who was called Epiphanes succeeded to the kingdom, Jason the brother of Onias obtained the high priesthood by corruption, promising the king at an interview three hundred and sixty talents of silver and, from another source of revenue, eighty talents. In addition to this he promised to pay one hundred and fifty more if permission were given to establish by his authority a gymnasium and a body of youth for it, and to enroll the men of Jerusalem as citizens of Antioch. When the king assented and Jason came to office, he at once shifted his countrymen over to the Greek way of life. He set aside the existing royal concessions to the Jews, secured through John the father of Eupolemus, who went on the mission to establish friendship and alliance with the Romans; and he destroyed the lawful ways of living and introduced new customs contrary to the law.

In those days lawless men came forth from Israel, and misled many, saying, "Let us go and make a covenant with the Gentiles round about us, for since we separated from them many evils have come upon us." This proposal pleased them, and some of the people eagerly went to the king. He authorized them to observe the ordinances of the Gentiles. So they built a gymnasium in Jerusalem, according to Gentile custom, and removed the marks of circumcision, and abandoned the holy covenant. They joined with the Gentiles and sold themselves to do evil.

There was such an extreme of Hellenization and increase in the adoption of foreign ways because of the surpassing wickedness of Jason, who was ungodly and no high priest, that the priests were no longer intent upon their service at the altar. Despising the sanctuary and neglecting the sacrifices, they hastened to take part in the unlawful proceedings in the wrestling arena after the call to the discus, disdaining the honors prized by their fathers and putting the highest value upon Greek forms of prestige. For this reason heavy disaster overtook them, and those whose ways of living they admired and wished to imitate completely became their enemies and punished them. For it is no light thing to show irreverence to the divine laws—a fact which later events will make clear.

When Antiochus saw that his kingdom was established, he determined to become king of the land of Egypt, that he might reign over both kingdoms. So he invaded Egypt with a strong force, with chariots and elephants and cavalry and with a large fleet. He engaged Ptolemy king of Egypt in battle, and Ptolemy turned and fled before him, and many were wounded and fell. And they captured the fortified cities in the land of Egypt, and he plundered the land of Egypt.

After subduing Egypt, Antiochus returned in the one hundred and forty-third year. He went up against Israel and came to Jerusalem with a strong force. He arrogantly entered the sanctuary and took the golden altar, the lampstand for the light, and all its utensils. He took also the table for the bread of the Presence, the cups for drink offerings, the bowls, the golden censers, the curtain, the crowns, and the gold decoration on the front of the temple; he stripped it all off. He took the silver and the gold, and the costly vessels; he took also the hidden treasures which he found. Taking them all, he departed to his own land. He committed deeds of murder, and spoke with great arrogance.

Two years later the king sent to the cities of Judah a chief collector of tribute, and he came to Jerusalem with a large force. Deceitfully he spoke peaceable words to them, and they believed him; but he suddenly fell upon the city, dealt it a severe blow, and destroyed many people of Israel. He plundered the city, burned it with fire, and tore down its houses and its surrounding walls. And they took captive the women and children, and seized the cattle. Then they fortified the city of David with a great strong wall and strong towers, and it became their citadel. And they stationed there a sinful people, lawless men. These strengthened their position; they stored up arms and food, and collecting the spoils of Jerusalem they stored them there, and became a great snare. It became an ambush against the sanctuary, an evil adversary of Israel continually. On every side of the sanctuary they shed innocent blood; they even defiled the sanctuary.

Now on the fifteenth day of Chislev, in the one hundred and forty-fifth year, they erected a desolating sacrilege upon the altar of burnt offering. They also built altars in the surrounding cities of Judah, and burned incense at the doors of the houses and in the streets. The books of the law which they found they tore to pieces and burned with fire. Where the book of the covenant was found in the possession of any one, or if any one adhered to the law, the decree of the king condemned him to death. They kept using violence against Israel, against those found month after month in the cities. And on the twenty-fifth day of the month they offered sacrifice on the altar which was upon the altar of burnt offering. According to the decree, they put to death the women who had their children circumcised, and their families and those who circumcised them; and they hung the infants from their mothers' necks. But many in Israel stood firm and were resolved in their hearts not to eat unclean food. They chose to die rather than to be defiled by food or to profane the holy covenant; and they did die. And very great wrath came upon Israel.

Eleazar, one of the scribes in high position, a man now advanced in age and of noble presence, was being forced to open his mouth to eat swine's flesh. But he, welcoming death with honor rather than life with pollution, went up to the rack of his own accord, spitting out the flesh, as men ought to go who have the courage to refuse things that it is not right to taste, even for the natural love of life.

Those who were in charge of that unlawful sacrifice took the man aside, because of their long acquaintance with him, and privately urged him to bring meat of his own providing, proper for him to use, and pretend that he was eating the flesh of the sacrificial meal which had been commanded by the king, so that by doing this he might be saved from death, and be treated kindly on account of his old friendship with them. But making a high resolve, worthy of his years and the dignity of his old age and the gray hairs which he had reached with distinction and his excellent life even from childhood, and moreover according to the holy God-given law, he declared himself quickly, telling them to send him to Hades.

"Such pretense is not worthy of our time of life," he said, "lest many of the young should suppose that Eleazar in his ninetieth year has gone over to an alien religion, and through my pretense, for the sake of living a brief moment longer, they should be led astray because of me, while I defile and disgrace my old age."

So in this way he died, leaving in his death an example of nobility and a memorial of courage, not only to the young but to the great body of his nation.

It happened also that seven brothers and their mother were arrested and were being compelled by the king, under torture with whips and cords, to partake of unlawful swine's flesh. One of them, acting as their spokesman, said, "What do you intend to ask and learn from us? For we are ready to die rather than transgress the laws of our fathers."

The king fell into a rage, and gave orders that pans and caldrons be heated. These were heated immediately, and he commanded that the tongue of their spokesman be cut out and that they scalp him and cut off his hands and feet, while the rest of the brothers and the mother looked on. When he was utterly helpless, the king ordered them to take him to the fire, still breathing, and to fry him in a pan. The smoke from the pan spread widely, but the brothers and their mother encouraged one another to die nobly, saying, "The Lord God is watching over us, as Moses declared in his song which bore witness against the people to their faces, when he said, 'And he will have compassion on his servants.'"

After the first brother had died in this way, they brought the second for their sport. They tore off the skin of his head with the hair, and asked him, "Will you eat rather than have your body punished limb by limb?" He replied in the language of his fathers, and said to them, "No." Therefore he in turn underwent tortures as the first brother had done. And when he was at his last breath, he said, "You accursed wretch, you dismiss us from this present life, but the King of the universe will raise us up to an everlasting renewal of life, because we have died for his laws."

After him, the third was the victim of their sport. When it was demanded, he quickly put out his tongue and courageously stretched forth his hands, and said nobly, "I got these from Heaven, and because of his laws I disdain them, and from him I hope to get them back again." As a result the king himself and those with him were astonished at the young man's spirit, for he regarded his sufferings as nothing.

When he too had died, they maltreated and tortured the fourth in the same way. And when he was near death, he said, "One cannot but choose to die at the hands of men and to cherish the hope that God gives of being raised again by him. But for you there will be no resurrection to life!"

Next they brought forward the fifth and maltreated him. But he looked at the king, and said, "Because you have authority among men, mortal though you are, you do what you please. But do not think that God has forsaken our people. Keep on, and see how his mighty power will torture you and your descendants!"

After him they brought forward the sixth. And when he was about to die, he said, "Do not deceive yourself in vain. For we are suffering these things on our own account, because of our sins against our own God. Therefore astounding things have happened. But do not think that you go unpunished for having tried to fight against God!"

The youngest brother being still alive, Antiochus not only appealed to him in words, but promised with oaths that he would make him rich and enviable if he would turn from the ways of his fathers, and that he would take him for his friend and entrust him with public affairs. Since the young man would not listen to him at all, the king called the mother to him and urged her to advise the youth to save himself. After much urging on his part, she undertook to persuade her son. But, leaning close to him, she spoke in their native tongue as follows, deriding the cruel tyrant: "My son, have pity on me. I carried you nine months in my womb, and nursed you for three years, and have reared you and brought you up to this point in your life, and have taken care of you. I beseech you, my child, to look at the heaven and the earth and see everything that is in them, and recognize that God did not make them out of things that existed. Thus also mankind comes into being. Do not fear this butcher, but prove worthy of your brothers. Accept death, so that in God's mercy I may get you back again with your brothers."

While she was still speaking, the young man said, "What are you waiting for? I will not obey the king's command, but I obey the command of the law that was given to our fathers through Moses. I, like my brothers, give up body and life for the laws of our fathers, appealing to God to show mercy soon to our nation and by afflictions and plagues to make you confess that he alone is God, and through me and my brothers to bring to an end the wrath of the Almighty which has justly fallen on our whole nation."

The king fell into a rage, and handled him worse than the others, being exasperated at his scorn. So he died in his integrity, putting his whole trust in the Lord. Last of all, the mother died, after her sons.

Let this be enough, then, about the eating of sacrifices and the extreme tortures.

AN UPRIGHT MAN DEFENDS ISRAEL

In those days Mattathias the son of John, son of Simeon, a priest of the sons of Joarib, moved from Jerusalem and settled in Modein. He had five sons, John surnamed Gaddi, Simon called Thassi, Judas called Maccabeus, Eleazar called Avaran, and Jonathan called Apphus. He saw the blasphemies being committed in Judah and Jerusalem.

And Mattathias and his sons rent their clothes, put on sackcloth and mourned greatly. Then the king's officers came to the city of Modein to make them offer sacrifice. But Mattathias answered and said in a loud voice: "Even if all the nations that live under the rule of the king obey him, and have chosen to do his commandments, departing each one from the religion of his fathers, yet I and my sons and my brothers will live by the covenant of our fathers. Far be it from us to desert the law and the ordinances. We will not obey the king's words by turning aside from our religion to the right hand or to the left."

When he had finished speaking these words, a Jew came forward in the sight of all to offer sacrifice upon the altar in Modein, according to the king's command. When Mattathias saw it, he burned with zeal and his heart was stirred. He gave vent to righteous anger; he ran and killed him upon the altar. At the same time he killed the king's officer who was forcing them to sacrifice, and he tore down the altar. Thus he burned with zeal for the law, as Phinehas did against Zimri the son of Salu.

Then Mattathias cried out in the city with a loud voice, saying: "Let every one who is zealous for the law and supports the covenant come out with me!" And he and his sons fled to the hills and left all that they had in the city.

Then many who were seeking righteousness and justice went down to the wilderness to dwell there, they, their sons, their wives, and their cattle, because evils pressed heavily upon them. And it was reported to the king's officers, and to the troops in Jerusalem the city of David, that men who had rejected the king's command had gone down to the hiding places in the wilderness. Many pursued them, and overtook them; they encamped opposite them and prepared for battle against them on the sabbath day. And they said to them, "Enough of this! Come out and do what the king commands, and you will live." But they said, "We will not come out, nor will we do what the king commands and so profane the sabbath day." Then the enemy hastened to attack them. But they did not answer them or hurl a stone at them or block up their hiding places, for they said, "Let us all die in our innocence; heaven and earth testify for us that you are killing us unjustly." So they attacked them on the sabbath, and they died with their wives and children and cattle, to the number of a thousand persons.

When Mattathias and his friends learned of it, they mourned for them deeply. And each said to his neighbor: "If we all do as our brethren have done and refuse to fight with the Gentiles for our lives and our ordinances, they will quickly destroy us from the earth." So they made this decision that day: "Let us fight against every man who comes to attack us on the sabbath day; let us not all die as our brethren died in their hiding places."

Then there united with them a company of Hasideans, mighty warriors of Israel, every one who offered himself willingly for the law. And all who became fugitives to escape their troubles joined them and reinforced them. They organized an army, and struck down sinners in their anger and lawless men in their wrath; the survivors fled to the Gentiles for safety. And Mattathias and his friends went about and tore down the altars; they forcibly circumcised all the uncircumcised boys that they found within the borders of Israel. They hunted down the arrogant men, and the work prospered in their hands. They rescued the law out of the hands of the Gentiles and kings, and they never let the sinner gain the upper hand.

Now the days drew near for Mattathias to die, and he said to his sons: "Arrogance and reproach have now become strong; it is a time of ruin and furious anger. Now, my children, show zeal for the law, and give your lives for the covenant of our fathers."

Then he blessed them, and was gathered to his fathers. He died in the one hundred and forty-sixth year and was buried in the tomb of his fathers at Modein. And all Israel mourned for him with great lamentation.

THE RISE OF JUDAS MACCABEUS

Then Judas his son, who was called Maccabeus, took command in his place. All his brothers and all who had joined his father helped him; they gladly fought for Israel. But Apollonius gathered together Gentiles and a large force from Samaria to fight against Israel. When Judas learned of it, he went out to meet him, and he defeated and killed him. Many were wounded and fell, and the rest fled. Then they seized their spoils; and Judas took the sword of Apollonius, and used it in battle the rest of his life. Now when Seron, the commander of the Syrian army, heard that Judas had gathered a large company, including a body of faithful men who stayed with him and went out to battle, he said, "I will make a name for myself and win honor in the kingdom. I will make war on Judas and his companions, who scorn the king's command."

When King Antiochus heard these reports, he was greatly angered;

and he sent and gathered all the forces of his kingdom, a very strong army. He left Lysias, a distinguished man of royal lineage, in charge of the king's affairs from the river Euphrates to the borders of Egypt. Lysias was also to take care of Antiochus his son until he returned. And he turned over to Lysias half of his troops and the elephants, and gave him orders about all that he wanted done. As for the residents of Judea and Jerusalem, Lysias was to send a force against them to wipe out and destroy the strength of Israel and the remnant of Jerusalem; he was to banish the memory of them from the place.

Lysias chose Ptolemy the son of Dorymenes, and Nicanor and Gorgias, mighty men among the friends of the king, and sent with them forty thousand infantry and seven thousand cavalry to go into the land of Judah and destroy it, as the king had commanded. So they departed with their entire force, and when they arrived they encamped near Emmaus in the plain. When the traders of the region heard what was said of them, they took silver and gold in immense amount, and fetters, and went to the camp to get the sons of Israel for slaves. And forces from Syria and the land of the Philistines joined with them.

Now Gorgias took five thousand infantry and a thousand picked cavalry, and this division moved out by night to fall upon the camp of the Jews and attack them suddenly. Men from the citadel were his guides. But Judas heard of it, and he and his mighty men moved out to attack the king's force in Emmaus while the division was still absent from the camp. Then the men with Judas blew their trumpets and engaged in battle. The Gentiles were crushed and fled into the plain, and all those in the rear fell by the sword. They pursued them to Gazara, and to the plains of Idumea, and to Azotus and Jamnia; and three thousand of them fell. Thus Israel had a great deliverance that day. Those of the foreigners who escaped went and reported to Lysias all that had happened. When he heard it, he was perplexed and discouraged, for things had not happened to Israel as he had intended, nor had they turned out as the king had commanded him. But the next year he mustered sixty thousand picked infantrymen and five thousand cavalry to subdue them. They came into Idumea and encamped at Beth-zur, and Judas met them with ten thousand men.

Then both sides attacked, and there fell of the army of Lysias five thousand men; they fell in action. And when Lysias saw the rout of his troops and observed the boldness which inspired those of Judas, and how ready they were either to live or to die nobly, he departed to

Antioch and enlisted mercenaries to invade Judea again with an even larger army.

Then said Judas and his brothers, "Behold, our enemies are crushed; let us go up to cleanse the sanctuary and dedicate it." So all the army assembled and they went up to Mount Zion. And they saw the sanctuary desolate, the altar profaned, and the gates burned. In the courts they saw bushes sprung up as in a thicket, or as on one of the mountains. They saw also the chambers of the priests in ruins. Then they rent their clothes, and mourned with great lamentation, and sprinkled themselves with ashes. They fell face down on the ground, and sounded the signal on the trumpets, and cried out to Heaven. Then Judas detailed men to fight against those in the citadel until he had cleansed the sanctuary. He chose blameless priests devoted to the law, and they cleansed the sanctuary and removed the defiled stones to an unclean place.

Early in the morning on the twenty-fifth day of the ninth month, which is the month of Chislev, in the one hundred and forty-eighth year, they rose and offered sacrifice, as the law directs, on the new altar of burnt offering which they had built. At the very season and on the very day that the Gentiles had profaned it, it was dedicated with songs and harps and lutes and cymbals. All the people fell on their faces and worshiped and blessed Heaven, who had prospered them. So they celebrated the dedication of the altar for eight days, and offered burnt offerings with gladness; they offered a sacrifice of deliverance and praise.

FURTHER VICTORIES OF THE "HAMMER"

King Antiochus was going through the upper provinces when he heard that Elymais in Persia was a city famed for its wealth in silver and gold. Then some one came to him and reported that the armies which had gone into the land of Judah had been routed. When the king heard this news, he was astounded and badly shaken. He took to his bed and became sick from grief, because things had not turned out for him as he had planned. He lay there for many days, because deep grief continually gripped him, and he concluded that he was dying. So he called all his friends and said to them, "Sleep departs from my eyes and I am downhearted with worry."

Then he called for Philip, one of his friends, and made him ruler over all his kingdom. He gave him the crown and his robe and the signet, that he might guide Antiochus his son and bring him up to be king. Thus Antiochus the king died there in the one hundred and forty-ninth year. And when Lysias learned that the king was dead, he set up Antiochus the king's son to reign. Lysias had brought him up as a boy, and he named him Eupator.

And the Jews went about their farming. But some of the governors in various places, Timothy and Apollonius the son of Gennaeus, as well as Hieronymus and Demophon, and in addition to these Nicanor the governor of Cyprus, would not let them live quietly and in peace. And some men of Joppa did so ungodly a deed as this: they invited the Jews who lived among them to embark, with their wives and children, on boats which they had provided, as though there were no ill will to the Jews; and this was done by public vote of the city. And when they accepted, because they wished to live peaceably and suspected nothing, the men of Joppa took them out to sea and drowned them, not less than two hundred. When Judas heard of the cruelty visited on his countrymen, he gave orders to his men and, calling upon God the righteous Judge, attacked the murderers of his brethren. He set fire to the harbor by night, and burned the boats, and massacred those who had taken refuge there. But learning that the men in Jamnia meant in the same way to wipe out the Jews who were living among them, he attacked the people of Jamnia by night and set fire to the harbor and the fleet, so that the glow of the light was seen in Jerusalem, thirty miles distant.

When they had gone more than a mile from there, on their march against Timothy, not less than five thousand Arabs with five hundred horsemen attacked them. After a hard fight Judas and his men won the victory, by the help of God. The defeated nomads besought Judas to grant them pledges of friendship, promising to give him cattle and to help his people in all other ways. Judas, thinking that they might really be useful in many ways, agreed to make peace with them; and after receiving his pledges they departed to their tents.

He also attacked a certain city which was strongly fortified with earthworks and walls, and inhabited by all sorts of Gentiles. Its name was Caspin. They took the city by the will of God, and slaughtered untold numbers, so that the adjoining lake, a quarter of a mile wide, appeared to be running over with blood.

When they had gone ninety-five miles from there, they came to Charax, to the Jews who are called Toubiani. They did not find Timothy in that region, for he had by then departed from the region without accomplishing anything, though in one place he had left a very strong garrison. Dositheus and Sosipater, who were captains under Maccabeus, marched out and destroyed those whom Timothy had left in the stronghold, more than ten thousand men. But Maccabeus arranged his army in divisions, and hastened after Timothy, who had with him a hundred and twenty thousand infantry and two thousand five hundred cavalry. When Timothy learned of the approach of Judas, he sent off the women and the children and also the baggage to a place called Carnaim; for that place was hard to besiege and difficult of access because of the narrowness of all the approaches. But when Judas' first division appeared, terror and fear came over the enemy at the manifestation to them of him who sees all things; and they rushed off in flight and were swept on, this way and that, so that often they were injured by their own men and pierced by the points of their swords. And Judas pressed the pursuit with the utmost vigor, putting the sinners to the sword, and destroyed as many as thirty thousand men.

After the feast called Pentecost, they hastened against Gorgias, the governor of Idumea. And he came out with three thousand infantry and four hundred cavalry. When they joined battle, Judas called upon the Lord to show himself their ally and leader in the battle. In the language of their fathers he raised the battle cry, with hymns; then he charged against Gorgias' men when they were not expecting it, and put them to flight.

Then Judas assembled his army and went to the city of Adullam. As the seventh day was coming on, they purified themselves according to the custom, and they kept the sabbath there. On the next day, as by that time it had become necessary, Judas and his men went to take up the bodies of the fallen and to bring them back to lie with their kinsmen in the sepulchres of their fathers. Then under the tunic of every one of the dead they found sacred tokens of the idols of Jamnia, which the law forbids the Jews to wear. And it became clear to all that this was why these men had fallen. So they all blessed the ways of the Lord, the righteous Judge, who reveals the things that are hidden; and they turned to prayer, beseeching that the sin which had been committed might be wholly blotted out. And the noble Judas exhorted the people to keep themselves free from sin, for they had seen with their own eyes what had happened because of the sin of those who had fallen. He also took up a collection, man by man, to the amount of two thousand drachmas of silver, and sent it to Jerusalem to provide for a sin offering. In doing this he acted very well and honorably, taking account of the resurrection. For if he were not expecting that those who had fallen would rise again, it would have been superfluous and foolish to pray for the dead. But if he was looking to the splendid reward that is laid up for those who fall asleep in godliness, it was a holy and pious thought. Therefore he made atonement for the dead, that they might be delivered from their sin.

AN ALLIANCE WITH THE ROMANS

Now the men in the citadel kept hemming Israel in around the sanctuary. They were trying in every way to harm them and strengthen the Gentiles. So Judas decided to destroy them, and assembled all the people to besiege them. They gathered together and besieged the citadel in the one hundred and fiftieth year; and he built siege towers and other engines of war.

The king was enraged when he heard this. He assembled all his friends, the commanders of his forces and those in authority. And mercenary forces came to him from other kingdoms and from islands of the seas. The number of his forces was a hundred thousand foot soldiers, twenty thousand horsemen, and thirty-two elephants accustomed to war. They came through Idumea and encamped against Beth-zur, and for many days they fought and built engines of war; but the Jews sallied out and burned these with fire, and fought manfully. Then Judas marched away from the citadel and encamped at Beth-zechariah, opposite the camp of the king. And when the Jews saw the royal might and the fierce attack of the forces, they turned away in flight.

The soldiers of the king's army went up to Jerusalem against them, and the king encamped in Judea and at Mount Zion. He made peace with the men of Beth-zur, and they evacuated the city, because they had no provisions there to withstand a siege, since it was a sabbatical year for the land. So the king took Beth-zur and stationed a guard there to hold it. Then he encamped before the sanctuary for many days. He set up siege towers, engines of war to throw fire and stones, machines to shoot arrows, and catapults. The Jews also made engines of war to match theirs, and fought for many days. But they had no food in storage, because it was the seventh year; those who found safety in Judea from the Gentiles had consumed the last of the stores. Few men were left in the sanctuary, because famine had prevailed over the rest and they had been scattered, each to his own place.

Then Lysias heard that Philip, whom King Antiochus while still living had appointed to bring up Antiochus his son to be king, had returned from Persia and Media with the forces that had gone with the king, and that he was trying to seize control of the government. So he quickly gave orders to depart, and said to the king, to the commanders of the forces, and to the men. "We daily grow weaker, our food supply is scant, the place against which we are fighting is strong, and the affairs of the kingdom press urgently upon us. Now then let us come to terms with these men, and make peace with them and with all their nation, and agree to let them live by their laws as they did before; for it was on account of their laws which we abolished that they became angry and did all these things."

The speech pleased the king and the commanders, and he sent to the Jews an offer of peace, and they accepted it. So the king and the commanders gave them their oath. On these conditions the Jews evacuated the stronghold. But when the king entered Mount Zion and saw what a strong fortress the place was, he broke the oath he had sworn and gave orders to tear down the wall all around. Then he departed with haste and returned to Antioch. He found Philip in control of the city, but he fought against him, and took the city by force.

In the one hundred and fifty-first year Demetrius the son of Seleucus set forth from Rome, sailed with a few men to a city by the sea, and there began to reign. As he was entering the royal palace of his fathers, the army seized Antiochus and Lysias to bring them to him. But when this act became known to him, he said, "Do not let me see their faces!" So the army killed them, and Demetrius took his seat upon the throne of his kingdom.

Then there came to him all the lawless and ungodly men of Israel; they were led by Alcimus, who wanted to be high priest. And they brought to the king this accusation against the people: "Judas and his brothers have destroyed all your friends, and have driven us out of our land. Now then send a man whom you trust; let him go and see all the ruin which Judas has brought upon us and upon the land of the king, and let him punish them and all who help them."

So the king chose Bacchides, one of the king's friends, governor of the province Beyond the River; he was a great man in the kingdom and was faithful to the king. And he sent him, and with him the ungodly Alcimus, whom he made high priest; and he commanded him to take vengeance on the sons of Israel. So they marched away and came with a large force into the land of Judah; and he sent messengers to Judas and his brothers with peaceable but treacherous words. But they paid no attention to their words, for they saw that they had come with a large force.

Then a group of scribes appeared in a body before Alcimus and Bacchides to ask for just terms. The Hasideans were the first among the sons of Israel to seek peace from them, for they said, "A priest of the line of Aaron has come with the army, and he will not harm us." And he spoke peaceable words to them and swore this oath to them, "We will not seek to injure you or your friends." So they trusted him; but he seized sixty of them and killed them in one day, in accordance with the word which was written, "The flesh of thy saints and their blood they poured out round about Jerusalem, and there was none to bury them." Then the fear and dread of them fell upon all the people, for they said, "There is no truth or justice in them, for they have violated the agreement and the oath which they swore."

Then Bacchides departed from Jerusalem and encamped in Bethzaith. And he sent and seized many of the men who had deserted to him, and some of the people, and killed them and threw them into the great pit. He placed Alcimus in charge of the country and left with him a force to help him; then Bacchides went back to the king.

Alcimus strove for the high priesthood, and all who were troubling their people joined him. They gained control of the land of Judah and did great damage in Israel. And Judas saw all the evil that Alcimus and those with him had done among the sons of Israel; it was more than the Gentiles had done. So Judas went out into all the surrounding parts of Judea, and took vengeance on the men who had deserted, and he prevented those in the city from going out into the country. When Alcimus saw that Judas and those with him had grown strong, and realized that he could not withstand them, he returned to the king and brought wicked charges against them.

Then the king sent Nicanor, one of his honored princes, who hated and detested Israel, and he commanded him to destroy the people. So Nicanor came to Jerusalem with a large force, and treacherously sent to Judas and his brothers this peaceable message, "Let there be no fighting between me and you; I shall come with a few men to see you face to face in peace." So he came to Judas, and they greeted one another peaceably. But the enemy were ready to seize Judas. It became known to Judas that Nicanor had come to him with treacherous intent, and he was afraid of him and would not meet him again. When Nicanor learned that his plan had been disclosed, he went out to meet Judas in battle near Capharsalama. About five hundred men of the army of Nicanor fell, and the rest fled into the city of David.

After these events Nicanor went up to Mount Zion. Some of the priests came out of the sanctuary, and some of the elders of the people, to greet him peaceably and to show him the burnt offering that was being offered for the king. But he mocked them and derided them and defiled them and spoke arrogantly, and in anger he swore this oath, "Unless Judas and his army are delivered into my hands this time, then if I return safely I will burn up this house." And he went out in great anger. Then the priests went in and stood before the altar and the temple, and they wept and said, "Thou didst choose this house to be called by thy name, and to be for thy people a house of prayer and supplication. Take vengeance on this man and on his army, and let them fall by the sword; remember their blasphemies, and let them live no longer."

Now Nicanor went out from Jerusalem and encamped in Beth-horon, and the Syrian army joined him. And Judas encamped in Adasa with three thousand men. Then Judas prayed and said, "When the messengers from the king spoke blasphemy, thy angel went forth and struck down one hundred and eighty-five thousand of the Assyrians. So also crush this army before us today; let the rest learn that Nicanor has spoken wickedly against thy sanctuary, and judge him according to this wickedness." So the armies met in battle on the thirteenth day of the month of Adar. The army of Nicanor was crushed, and he himself was the first to fall in the battle. When his army saw that Nicanor had fallen, they threw down their arms and fled. The Jews pursued them a day's journey, from Adasa as far as Gazara, and as they followed kept sounding the battle call on the trumpets. And men came out of all the villages of Judea round about, and they outflanked the enemy and drove them back to their pursuers, so that they all fell by the sword; not even one of them was left. Then the Jews seized the spoils and the plunder, and they cut off Nicanor's head and the right hand which he had so arrogantly stretched out, and brought them and displayed them just outside of Jerusalem. The people rejoiced greatly and celebrated that day as a day of great gladness. And they decreed that this day should be celebrated each year on the thirteenth day of Adar. So the land of Judah had rest for a few days.

Now Judas heard of the fame of the Romans, that they were very strong and were well-disposed toward all who made an alliance with them, that they pledged friendship to those who came to them, and that they were very strong. So Judas chose Eupolemus the son of John, son of Accos, and Jason the son of Eleazar, and sent them to Rome to establish friendship and alliance, and to free themselves from the yoke; for they saw that the kingdom of the Greeks was completely enslaving Israel. They went to Rome, a very long journey; and they entered the senate chamber and spoke as follows: "Judas, who is also called Maccabeus, and his brothers and the people of the Jews have sent us to you to establish alliance and peace with you, that we may be enrolled as your allies and friends." The proposal pleased them, and this is a copy of the letter which they wrote in reply, on bronze tablets, and sent to Jerusalem to remain with them there as a memorial of peace and alliance: "May all go well with the Romans and with the nation of the Jews at sea and on land for ever, and may sword and enemy be far from them. If war comes first to Rome or to any of their allies in all their dominion, the nation of the Jews shall act as their allies wholeheartedly, as the occasion may indicate to them. And to the enemy who makes war they shall not give or supply grain, arms, money, or ships, as Rome has decided; and they shall keep their obligations without receiving any return. In the same way, if war comes first to the nation of the Jews, the Romans shall willingly act as their allies, as the occasion may indicate to them. And to the enemy allies shall be given no grain, arms, money, or ships, as Rome has decided; and they shall keep these obligations and do so without deceit. Thus on these terms the Romans make a treaty with the Jewish people. If after these terms are in effect both parties shall determine to add or delete anything, they shall do so at their discretion, and any addition or deletion that they may make shall be valid.

"And concerning the wrongs which King Demetrius is doing to them we have written to him as follows, 'Why have you made your yoke heavy upon our friends and allies the Jews? If now they appeal again for help against you, we will defend their rights and fight you on sea and on land.' "

THE DEATH OF THE LIBERATOR OF ISRAEL

When Demetrius heard that Nicanor and his army had fallen in battle, he sent Bacchides and Alcimus into the land of Judah a second time, and with them the right wing of the army. They went by the road which leads to Gilgal and encamped against Mesaloth in Arbela, and they took it and killed many people. In the first month of the one hundred and fifty-second year they encamped against Jerusalem; then they marched off and went to Berea with twenty thousand foot soldiers and two thousand cavalry.

Now Judas was encamped in Elasa, and with him were three thousand picked men. When they saw the huge number of the enemy forces, they were greatly frightened, and many slipped away from the camp, until no more than eight hundred of them were left.

When Judas saw that his army had slipped away and the battle was imminent, he was crushed in spirit, for he had no time to assemble them. He became faint, but he said to those who were left, "Let us rise and go up against our enemies. We may be able to fight them." But they tried to dissuade him, saying, "We are not able. Let us rather save our own lives now, and let us come back with our brethren and fight them; we are too few." But Judas said, "Far be it from us to do such a thing as to flee from them. If our time has come, let us die bravely for our brethren, and leave no cause to question our honor."

Then the army of Bacchides marched out from the camp and took its stand for the encounter. The cavalry was divided into two companies, and the slingers and the archers went ahead of the army, as did all the chief warriors. Bacchides was on the right wing. Flanked by the two companies, the phalanx advanced to the sound of the trumpets; and the men with Judas also blew their trumpets. The earth was shaken by the noise of the armies, and the battle raged from morning till evening.

Judas saw that Bacchides and the strength of his army were on the right; then all the stouthearted men went with him, and they crushed the right wing, and he pursued them as far as Mount Azotus. When those on the left wing saw that the right wing was crushed, they turned and followed close behind Judas and his men. The battle became desperate, and many on both sides were wounded and fell. Judas also fell, and the rest fled.

Then Jonathan and Simon took Judas their brother and buried him in the tomb of their fathers at Modein, and wept for him. And all Israel made great lamentation for him; they mourned many days and said, "How is the mighty fallen, the savior of Israel!"

Then Jonathan with his men, and Simon, withdrew to Beth-basi in the wilderness; he rebuilt the parts of it that had been demolished, and they fortified it. When Bacchides learned of this, he assembled all his forces, and sent orders to the men of Judea. Then he came and encamped against Beth-basi; he fought against it for many days and made machines of war.

But Jonathan left Simon his brother in the city, while he went out into the country; and he went with only a few men. He struck down Odomera and his brothers and the sons of Phasiron in their tents. Then he began to attack and went into battle with his forces; and Simon and his men sallied out from the city and set fire to the machines of war. They fought with Bacchides, and he was crushed by them. They distressed him greatly, for his plan and his expedition had been in vain. So he was greatly enraged at the lawless men who had counseled him to come into the country, and he killed many of them. Then he decided to depart to his own land.

When Jonathan learned of this, he sent ambassadors to him to make peace with him and obtain release of the captives. He agreed, and did as he said; and he swore to Jonathan that he would not try to harm him as long as he lived. He restored to him the captives whom he had formerly taken from the land of Judah; then he turned and departed to his own land, and came no more into their territory. Thus the sword ceased from Israel. And Jonathan dwelt in Michmash. And Jonathan began to judge the people, and he destroyed the ungodly out of Israel.

In the one hundred and sixtieth year Alexander Epiphanes, the son of Antiochus, landed and occupied Ptolemais. They welcomed him, and there he began to reign. In the one hundred and sixty-fifth year Demetrius the son of Demetrius came from Crete to the land of his fathers. When Alexander the king heard of it, he was greatly grieved and returned to Antioch.

So King Ptolemy gained control of the coastal cities as far as Seleucia by the sea, and he kept devising evil designs against Alexander. He sent envoys to Demetrius the king, saying, "Come, let us make a covenant with each other, and I will give you in marriage my daughter who was Alexander's wife, and you shall reign over your father's kingdom. For I now regret that I gave him my daughter, for he has tried to kill me." He threw blame on Alexander because he coveted his kingdom. So he took his daughter away from him and gave her to Demetrius. He was estranged from Alexander, and their enmity became manifest. Then Ptolemy entered Antioch and put on the crown of Asia. Thus he put two crowns upon his head, the crown of Egypt and that of Asia.

Now Alexander the king was in Cilicia at that time, because the people of that region were in revolt. And Alexander heard of it and came against him in battle. Ptolemy marched out and met him with a strong force, and put him to flight. So Alexander fled into Arabia to find protection there, and King Ptolemy was exalted. And Zabdiel the Arab cut off the head of Alexander and sent it to Ptolemy. But King Ptolemy died three days later, and his troops in the strongholds were killed by the inhabitants of the strongholds. So Demetrius became king in the one hundred and sixty-seventh year.

Now when Demetrius the king saw that the land was quiet before him and that there was no opposition to him, he dismissed all his troops, each man to his own place, except the foreign troops which he had recruited from the islands of the nations. So all the troops who had served his fathers hated him. Now Trypho had formerly been one of Alexander's supporters. He saw that all the troops were murmuring against Demetrius. So he went to Imalkue the Arab, who was bringing up Antiochus, the young son of Alexander, and insistently urged him to hand Antiochus over to him, to become king in place of his father. He also reported to Imalkue what Demetrius had done and told of the hatred which the troops of Demetrius had for him; and he stayed there many days.

Now Jonathan sent to Demetrius the king the request that he remove the troops of the citadel from Jerusalem, and the troops in the strongholds; for they kept fighting against Israel. And Demetrius sent this message to Jonathan, "Not only will I do these things for you and your nation, but I will confer great honor on you and your nation, if I find an opportunity. Now then you will do well to send me men who will help me, for all my troops have revolted." So Jonathan sent three thousand stalwart men to him at Antioch, and when they came to the king, the king rejoiced at their arrival.

Then the men of the city assembled within the city, to the number of a hundred and twenty thousand, and they wanted to kill the king. But the king fled into the palace. Then the men of the city seized the main streets of the city and began to fight. So the king called the Jews to his aid, and they all rallied about him and then spread out through the city; and they killed on that day as many as a hundred thousand men. They set fire to the city and seized much spoil on that day, and they saved the king. When the men of the city saw that the Jews had gained control of the city as they pleased, their courage failed and they cried out to the king with this entreaty, "Grant us peace, and make the Jews stop fighting against us and our city." And they threw down their arms and made peace. So the Jews gained glory in the eyes of the king and of all the people in his kingdom, and they returned to Jerusalem with much spoil.

THE BOOK OF ISRAEL COMES TO AN END

Then Trypho attempted to become king of Asia and put on the crown, and to raise his hand against Antiochus the king. He feared that Jonathan might not permit him to do so, but might make war on him, so he kept seeking to seize and kill him, and he marched forth and came to Beth-shan. Jonathan went out to meet him with forty thousand picked fighting men, and he came to Beth-shan. When Trypho saw that he had come with a large army, he was afraid to raise his hand against him. So he received him with honor and commended him to all his friends, and he gave him gifts and commanded his friends and his troops to obey him as they would himself. Then he said to Jonathan, "Why have you wearied all these people when we are not at war? Dismiss them now to their homes and choose for yourself a few men to stay with you, and come with me to Ptolemais. I will hand it over to you as well as the other strongholds and the remaining troops and all the officials, and will turn around and go home. For that is why I am here."

Jonathan trusted him and did as he said; he sent away the troops, and they returned to the land of Judah. He kept with himself three thousand men, two thousand of whom he left in Galilee, while a thousand accompanied him. But when Jonathan entered Ptolemais, the men of Ptolemais closed the gates and seized him, and all who had entered with him they killed with the sword.

Simon heard that Trypho had assembled a large army to invade the land of Judah and destroy it, so he assembled all the warriors and hastened to complete the walls of Jerusalem, and he fortified it on every side. He sent Jonathan the son of Absalom to Joppa, and with him a considerable army; he drove out its occupants and remained there.

Then Trypho departed from Ptolemais with a large army to invade the land of Judah, and Jonathan was with him under guard. And Simon encamped in Adida, facing the plain. Trypho learned that Simon had risen up in place of Jonathan his brother, and that he was about to join battle with him, so he sent envoys to him and said, "It is for the money that Jonathan your brother owed the royal treasury, in connection with the offices he held, that we are detaining him. Send now a hundred talents of silver and two of his sons as hostages, so that when released he will not revolt against us, and we will release him."

Simon knew that they were speaking deceitfully to him, but he sent to get the money and the sons, lest he arouse great hostility among the people, who might say, "Because Simon did not send him the money and the sons, he perished." So he sent the sons and the hundred talents, but Trypho broke his word and did not release Jonathan.

After this Trypho came to invade the country and destroy it, and he circled around by the way to Adora. But Simon and his army kept marching along opposite him to every place he went. Now the men in the citadel kept sending envoys to Trypho urging him to come to them by way of the wilderness and to send them food. So Trypho got all his cavalry ready to go, but that night a very heavy snow fell, and he did not go because of the snow. He marched off and went into the land of Gilead. When he approached Baskama, he killed Jonathan, and he was buried there. Then Trypho turned back and departed to his own land.

The land had rest all the days of Simon. He sought the good of his nation; his rule was pleasing to them, as was the honor shown him, all his days.

Antiochus, the son of Demetrius the king, sent a letter from the islands of the sea to Simon, the priest and ethnarch of the Jews, and to all the nation; its contents were as follows: "King Antiochus to Simon the high priest and ethnarch and to the nation of the Jews, greeting. Whereas certain pestilent men have gained control of the kingdom of our fathers, and I intend to lay claim to the kingdom so that I may restore it as it formerly was, and have recruited a host of mercenary troops and have equipped warships, and intend to make a landing in the country so that I may proceed against those who have destroyed our country and those who have devastated many cities in my kingdom, now therefore I confirm to you all the tax remissions that the kings before me have granted you, and release from all the other payments from which they have released you. I permit you to mint your own coinage as money for your country, and I grant freedom to Jerusalem and the sanctuary. All the weapons which you have prepared and the strongholds which you have built and now hold shall remain yours. Every debt you owe to the royal treasury and any such future debts shall be canceled for you from henceforth and for all time. When we gain control of our kingdom, we will bestow great honor upon you and your nation and the temple, so that your glory will become manifest in all the earth."

In the one hundred and seventy-fourth year Antiochus set out and invaded the land of his fathers. All the troops rallied to him, so that there were few with Trypho. Antiochus pursued him, and he came in his flight to Dor, which is by the sea; for he knew that troubles had converged upon him. So Antiochus encamped against Dor, and with him were a hundred and twenty thousand warriors and eight thousand cavalry. He surrounded the city, and the ships joined battle from the sea; he pressed the city hard from land and sea, and permitted no one to leave or enter it. And Simon sent to Antiochus two thousand picked men, to fight for him, and silver and gold and much military equipment.

But he refused to receive them, and he broke all the agreements he formerly had made with Simon, and became estranged from him. He sent to him Athenobius, one of his friends, to confer with him, saying, "You hold control of Joppa and Gazara and the citadel in Jerusalem; they are cities of my kingdom. You have devastated their territory, you have done great damage in the land, and you have taken possession of many places in my kingdom. Now then, hand over the cities which you have seized and the tribute money of the places which you have conquered outside the borders of Judea; or else give me for them five hundred talents of silver, and for the destruction that you have caused and the tribute money of the cities, five hundred talents more. Otherwise we will come and conquer you."

So Athenobius the friend of the king came to Jerusalem, and when he saw the splendor of Simon, and the sideboard with its gold and silver plate, and his great magnificence, he was amazed. He reported to him the words of the king, but Simon gave him this reply: "We have neither taken foreign land nor seized foreign property, but only the inheritance of our fathers, which at one time had been unjustly taken by our enemies. Now that we have the opportunity, we are firmly holding the inheritance of our fathers. As for Joppa and Gazara, which you demand, they were causing great damage among the people and to our land; for them we will give a hundred talents." Athenobius did not answer him a word, but returned in wrath to the king and reported to him these words and the splendor of Simon and all that he had seen. And the king was greatly angered.

Now Trypho embarked on a ship and escaped to Orthosia. Then the king made Cendebeus commander-in-chief of the coastal country, and gave him troops of infantry and cavalry. He commanded him to encamp against Judea and commanded him to build up Kedron and fortify its gates, and to make war on the people; but the king pursued Trypho. So Cendebeus came to Jamnia and began to provoke the people and invade Judea and take the people captive and kill them. He built up Kedron and stationed there horsemen and troops, so that they might go out and make raids along the highways of Judea, as the king had ordered him.

John went up from Gazara and reported to Simon his father what Cendebeus had done. And Simon called in his two older sons Judas and John, and said to them: "I and my brothers and the house of my father have fought the wars of Israel from our youth until this day, and things have prospered in our hands so that we have delivered Israel many times. But now I have grown old, and you by His mercy are mature in years. Take my place and my brother's, and go out and fight for our nation, and may the help which comes from Heaven be with you." So John chose out of the country twenty thousand warriors and horsemen, and they marched against Cendebeus and encamped for the night in Modein. Early in the morning they arose and marched into the plain, and behold, a large force of infantry and horsemen was coming to meet them. Then he and his army lined up against them. And he saw that the soldiers were afraid to cross the stream, so he crossed over first; and when his men saw him, they crossed over after him. Then he divided the army and placed the horsemen in the midst of the infantry, for the cavalry of the enemy were very numerous. And they sounded the trumpets, and Cendebeus and his army were put to flight, and many of them were wounded and fell; the rest fled into the stronghold. At that time Judas the brother of John was wounded, but John pursued them until Cendebeus reached Kedron, which he had built. They also fled into the towers that were in the fields of Azotus, and John burned it with fire, and about two thousand of them fell. And he returned to Judea safely.

Now Ptolemy the son of Abubus had been appointed governor over the plain of Jericho, and he had much silver and gold, for he was son-in-law of the high priest. His heart was lifted up; he determined to get control of the country, and made treacherous plans against Simon and his sons, to do away with them. Now Simon was visiting the cities of the country and attending to their needs, and he went down to Jericho with Mattathias and Judas his sons, in the one hundred and seventy-seventh year, in the eleventh month, which is the month of Shebat. The son of Abubus received them treacherously in the little stronghold called Dok, which he had built; he gave them a great banquet, and hid men there. When Simon and his sons were drunk, Ptolemy and his men rose up, took their weapons, and rushed in against Simon in the banquet hall, and they killed him and his two sons and some of his servants. So he committed an act of great treachery and returned evil for good.

Then Ptolemy wrote a report about these things and sent it to the king, asking him to send troops to aid him and to turn over to him the cities and the country. He sent other men to Gazara to do away with

John; he sent letters to the captains asking them to come to him so that he might give them silver and gold and gifts; and he sent other men to take possession of Jerusalem and the temple hill. But some one ran ahead and reported to John at Gazara that his father and brothers had perished, and that "he has sent men to kill you also." When he heard this, he was greatly shocked; and he seized the men who came to destroy him and killed them, for he had found out that they were seeking to destroy him.

The rest of the acts of John and his wars and the brave deeds which he did, and the building of the walls which he built, and his achievements, behold, they are written in the chronicles of his priesthood, from the time that he became high priest after his father.

This, then, is how matters turned out. So I too will here end my story. If it is well told and to the point, that is what I myself desired; if it is poorly done and mediocre, that was the best I could do. For just as it is harmful to drink wine alone, or again, to drink water alone, while wine mixed with water is sweet and delicious and enhances one's enjoyment, so also the style of the story delights the ears of those who read the work. And here will be the end.

SCRIPTURAL REFERENCES

CHAPTER II:

The Chosen People: Their Struggle and Triumph

Scriptural References

The Passover of the Lord, Exodus 12:1–14, 21–28

The First-born Are Killed, Exodus 12:29–30

Pharao Relents, Exodus 12:31–36

The Jews Leave Egypt, Exodus 12:37–42; 13:17–22; 14:1–9

The Crossing of the Red Sea, Exodus 14:10–17, 19–22

The Destruction of the Egyptians, Exodus 14:23–31

Song of the Hebrews, Exodus 15:1–21

The Jews Become Impatient, Exodus 15:22–27; 16:1–8, 13–16, 19–30; 17:1–2, 4–7

Mount Sinai and the Ten Commandments, Exodus 19:1–25; 20:1–21; 24:12–18

God's Tent in the Desert, Exodus 25:1–2, 8–11, 17–24, 30–31, 37; 26:1, 7, 14–16, 31–35; 27:1–2, 9–10, 20–21; 28:1–5; 30:1–8, 25–33

The Jews Worship an Idol, Exodus 32:1–6, 15–20, 26–28

The Ten Commandments Are Renewed, Exodus 34:1–11, 27–28

God's Craftsmen Build His Desert Dwelling, Exodus 35:30–35; 36:1–7; 40:16–33; Numbers 9:15–18

CHAPTER III:

Laws and Rituals

God Instills Fear, Exodus 20:22–23; Leviticus 19:4; Exodus 22:19; 20:24–26; Leviticus 19:5–8

Bodily Harm, Exodus 21:12–16, 18–21, 26–27, 22–25

Personal Integrity, Exodus 22:6–8, 24–26, 21–23; 23:1–3, 6–8; Leviticus 19:15–16

Various Rules of Conduct, Leviticus 19:1–3, 26, 31, 27–29; Exodus 22:15–16, 18; Leviticus 19:35–36, 13; Exodus 23:4–5; Leviticus 19:14, 32, 37, 30

The Sanctity of Sex, Leviticus 18:1–3, 6–7; 20:11–21; 18:24–26, 28–30; Numbers 5:12–31; Deuteronomy 22:13–21; Leviticus 10:10–11

Scriptural References

The Crossing of the Jordan, Josue 3:1–17

The Fall of Jericho, Josue 6:1–27

The Defeat of Hai and the Capture of Hai, Josue 7:1–26; 8:1–35

The Day the Sun Stood Still; Defeat of the Five Kings, Josue 10:1–27

Other Battles in Chanaan, Josue 10:28–43

Josue's Final Plea, Josue 23:1–16

A Pertinent Reminder, Josue 24:1–28

The Death of Josue, Josue 24:29–33

CHAPTER VII:

God's People and Their Ungodly Neighbors

The Jews Turn from God, Judges 2:10–19; 3:5–15, 31; 4:1–3

Debora and Barac, Judges 4:4–24; 5:32

The Call of Gedeon, Defender of Israel, Judges 6:1, 11–16, 33–40; 7:2–8, 16–23

Jephte, Another Protector, Judges 10:6–7; 11:1–12, 28–40

The Story of Samson, Judges 13:1–5, 24–25; 14:1–4; 15:1–20; 16:4–6, 16–31; 21:23–25

CHAPTER VIII:

A Beautiful Example of Filial Piety

Ruth and Noemi, Ruth 1:1–10, 14–18

Ruth and Booz, Ruth 2:1–9, 14–20; 3:3–18

The Marriage of Ruth, Ruth 4:1–17

CHAPTER IX:

The Chosen People Plead for a King

The Birth of Samuel; His Vocation, 1 Samuel 1:1–5, 11, 20, 24–25, 27–28

Anna Sings for Joy, 1 Samuel 2:1–12, 22–26

CHAPTER X:

The History of Saul's Reign

CHAPTER XI:

The Kingdom of David

The Ark Is Recovered, 2 Samuel 6:1–2, 13–23; 7:1–9, 12–17

Peace Comes to David, 2 Samuel 8:1–6; 9:1–10, 12–13

The Transgression of David, 2 Samuel 11:1–27; 12:1–24

David's Flight Before His Son Absalom, 2 Samuel 14:25–26; 15:2–18, 30–37; 16:5–14

Absalom Reaches His End, 2 Samuel 16:15–23; 17:1–14, 23–29; 18:1, 5–33; 19:15–23

The Tragedies of King David's Reign, 2 Samuel 21:1–14; 24:1–25

David's Final Moments, 1 Chronicles 28:1–10; 29:1–28

CHAPTER XII:

The Psalms of King David

(As Numbered in the Text)

CHAPTER XIII:

The Kingdom of Solomon

The Wisdom of Solomon, 1 Kings 3:1–28; 4:21–34

Plans for the Temple and the Palace, 1 Kings 5:1–18

The Fulfillment of a Dream, 1 Kings 6:1–23; 7:1–2, 48–51

The Dedication of the Temple, 1 Kings 8:1–66; 9:1–9, 26–28

The Riches of Solomon's Court; His Death, 1 Kings 10:1–15, 23–27; 11:1–14, 26–43

CHAPTER XIV:

The Literature of King Solomon

A Lesson in Wisdom and Reason, Proverbs 1:1–9; 3:1–17; 8:1–36; 9:1–11

The Wisdom of Prudence, Proverbs 25:2–7, 21–22; 31:10–31

All Is Vanity, Ecclesiastes 1:1–11; 2:1–2, 8–16; 4:1–4; 11:1–3; 12:13–14

Scriptural References

CHAPTER XIX:

Judah Undergoes a Religious Reform

Upheaval During the Reign of Ahaz, 2 Chronicles 28:1–6, 16–27

Hezekiah Brings About a Change, 2 Chronicles 29:1–7, 20–22, 35–36; 30:1–5, 10–14

An Army Is Destroyed, 2 Kings 18:13–17, 37; 19:1–7, 20–22, 32–37

A Leadership Ends, 2 Kings 20:1–5; Isaia 38:9–20; 2 Kings 20:20–21

The Wicked Kings, 2 Chronicles 33:1–25

A King Destroys Idolatry, 2 Chronicles 34:1–7, 33; 35:20–25

CHAPTER XX:

The Prophecy of Isaia

The Sinfulness of Israel, Isaia 1:1–9; 2:1–5; 5:1–7; 6:1–11

Christ and His Kingdom Is Foreseen, Isaia 7:1, 10–16; 8:13–15, 23; 9:1–6; 11:1–9; 12:1–6

The Resettlement of Juda Predicted, Isaia 35:1–10; 40:1–11; 42:1–7; 45:8, 14–25

Another Prediction of the Coming of Christ and His Passion, Isaia 52:1–15; 53:1–12

The Mercy of God Is Certain, Isaia 55:1–13

The Gentiles Are Converted, Isaia 60:1–6; 61:1–4, 9–11; 62:1–4

The Passion of Christ and His Wisdom, Isaia 63:1–10, 15–19

CHAPTER XXI:

The Fall of the Holy City; The Prophecy of Jeremia

The Chaldeans Enter Jerusalem, 2 Kings 23:31–37; 24:1–20

The Destruction of Jerusalem, 2 Kings 25:1–21

Jeremia Is Called and Predicts the Fall of Jerusalem, Jeremia 1:1–10, 18–19; 7:1–2, 29, 33–34; 9:1–6

Jeremia Meets the Enemy, Jeremia 11:9–14, 18; 12:19–23; 18:18–23

Jeremia Foresees Freedom for Israel, Jeremia 23:1–8; 25:1–12; 31:1–5, 10–14, 33–34

The Laments of Jeremia and the Mercy of God, Lamentations 1:1–14; 2:8–15; 3:1–9, 22–30; 4:1–8; 5:1–11, 19–22

CHAPTER XXII:

A History of Morals

The Suffering of Job, Job 1:1–22; 2:1–10

Job Replies to Eliphaz, Job 2:11–13; 3:1–17; 4:1–7, 12–19; 6:1–4; 7:1–7, 17–21

Job Replies to Baldad, Job 8:1–7; 9:1–10; 10:18–22; 14:1–14

Again Job Replies to Eliphaz, Job 15:1, 12–16; 19:1–27; 31:2–8

The Word and Mercy of God Comes to Job, Job 38:1–7, 33-35; 42:1–17

The Story of Jona, Jona 1:1–16; 2:1–11; 3:1–10; 4:1–11

Daniel and His Companions, 1:1–7, 19–21

The Fiery Furnace, Daniel 3:1–24, 46–97

The Writing on the Wall, Daniel 5:1–9, 13–18, 22–30; 6:1

The Lions' Den, Daniel 6:2–29

Tobias Begins His Difficult Journey, Tobit 1:1–18; 2:9–10; 3:1–8, 10–11, 16–17; 4:1–9, 20–21; 5:1–8, 16; 6:1–22; 7:1–20; 9:1–2, 5–6

The Triumphant Return of Tobias, Tobit 11:1–19; 12:1–22; 13:1–10

An Evil King Prepares for War, Judith 2:1–10; 4:1–5; 7:1, 6–7, 23–31

Judith Slays Holofernes and Liberates Her People, Judith 8:1, 4, 7–14, 32–35; 9:1, 12–14; 10:1–4, 10–12, 17; 12:1, 5–9; 13:1–20; 15:1–3, 8–10; 16:1–2, 13–17

The Life of a King Is Saved, Esther 1:1–2; 2:2–3, 5–8, 17, 19–23

A Vicious Plot Is Unfolded, Esther 3:1–15

The Triumph of Esther and Mordecai, Esther 4:1–17; 5:1–3, 7–14; 6:1–14; 7:1–10; 8:1–2, 16–17; 9:5

CHAPTER XXV

The Saga of Judas Maccabeus

The Overthrow of Heliodorus, 1 Maccabees 1:1–9; 2 Maccabees 3:1–40

The Story of God's People and the Jewish Martyrs, 2 Maccabees 4:7–11; 1 Maccabees 1:11–15; 2 Maccabees 4:13–17; 1 Maccabees 1:16–24, 29–37, 54–64; 2 Maccabees 6:18–25, 31; 7:1–19, 24–30, 37–42

An Upright Man Defends Israel, 1 Maccabees 2:1–6, 14–15, 19–50, 69–70

The Rise of Judas Maccabeus, 1 Maccabees 3:1–2, 10–14, 27, 32–35, 38–41; 4:1–4, 13–15, 25–29, 34–43, 52–56

Further Victories of the "Hammer," 1 Maccabees 6:1, 5, 8–10, 14–17; 2 Maccabees 12:1–6, 8–13, 16–23, 32–34, 38–45

An Alliance with the Romans, 1 Maccabees 6:18–20, 28–32, 47–63; 7:1–50; 8:1–2, 17–32

The Death of the Liberator of Israel, 1 Maccabees 9:1–21, 62–73; 10:1, 67–68; 11:8–19, 38–51

The Book of Israel Comes to an End, 1 Maccabees 12:39–48; 13:1, 10–24; 14:4; 15:1–14, 26–41; 16:1–24; 2 Maccabees 15:37–40